Items should be returned to the library from which
they were borrowed on or before the date stamped
above, unless a renewal has been granted.

SWINDON
BOROUGH COUNCIL

THE WORK OF
WILLIAM
MORRIS

PAUL THOMPSON

Oxford   New York
OXFORD UNIVERSITY PRESS
1991

Oxford University Press, Walton Street, Oxford OX2 6DP
Oxford New York Toronto
Delhi Bombay Calcutta Madras Karachi
Petaling Jaya Singapore Hong Kong Tokyo
Nairobi Dar es Salaam Cape Town
Melbourne Auckland

and associated companies in
Berlin Ibadan

Oxford is a trade mark of Oxford University Press

First edition published 1967
Second edition published 1977
Third edition published 1991

British Library Cataloguing in Publication Data
Thompson, Paul, 1935 –
The work of William Morris — 3rd ed.
1. English visual arts. Morris, William, 1834–1896
I. Title
709.2
ISBN 0–19–212279–7

Library of Congress Cataloging in Publication Data
Thompson, Paul Richard, 1935 –
The work of William Morris/Paul Thompson. — 3rd ed.
p. cm.
Includes bibliographical references.
1. Morris, William, 1834–1896. 2. Socialism — Great Britain — History — 19th century.
3. Decorative arts — Great Britain — History — 19th century. 4. Authors, English — 19th
century — Biography. 5. Socialists — Great Britain — Biography. 6. Designers—Great
Britain—Biography. I. Title.
821.8—dc20   PR5084.T46   1991   90–34792
ISBN 0–19–212279–7

Typeset by Pentacor PLC
Printed in Hong Kong

TO THEA

PREFACE

I had two aims in writing this book. The first was that, while notable biographies of Morris exist by J. W. Mackail and by E. P. Thompson, both are very long, and none of the shorter biographies is satisfactory. There is no brief introduction to his work and ideas which takes account of all the important revaluations of recent years. This book is an attempt to meet that need.

The second purpose was to reconsider the relation of Morris as an artist to the Victorian period. The interpretation of Morris as a pioneer, which goes back to Mackail but has been most notably expressed in Nikolaus Pevsner's *Pioneers of Modern Design,* must always seem difficult to reconcile with his designs which, even if they do not look like the common image of Victorian work, certainly do not look modern. Yet why was he so admired by the first modern architects and designers? I tried to answer this problem.

Twenty-five years later, both purposes still stand. Nevertheless, I have felt a need to make quite a few changes to this book. Some are to take account of recent research. I have been influenced in particular by the new perspectives brought by feminist scholarship; and also by the closer understanding of the history of socialist thought, which has brought out the originality of Morris's combination of Marxism, humanism, and theories of art in his own time, and also as a precursor of modern socialism. But other changes I have made for deeper reasons. Morris has been part of my own life since I wrote about him, and as I have myself been altered by personal experience, so my feeling for him has deepened. The essential unity of his life and its importance as a practical example becomes increasingly impressive. So does the relevance of his ideas today.

The question which has concerned so many Morris biographers until recently—whether Morris was a romantic, an anarchist, a Marxist, or even a crypto-Fabian—now seems to miss the essential point. Morris was an *original* socialist thinker. At a time when orthodox Marxism took a narrowly constricted form and most of the early writings of Marx remained unpublished, Morris was able to create a socialist world view of extraordinary richness. He took from Marx his economic and class interpretation of history. But Morris's understanding of the fundamental importance to mankind of fulfilment in work—of alienation—was an independent insight, parallel to that of Marx himself. It allowed

Morris to fuse with his Marxism the moral power of the radical romantic tradition. But Morris went much further than this. Although no successful socialist revolution had yet taken place, he was able to leap forward into an imaginative portrayal of the kind of society which could be created in the future. And unlike so many political idealists, Morris remained always strongly aware of the need in such a future to distinguish means from ends: to place at the forefront the realization, in a world freed of material inequality, asceticism, and alienation, of a new consciousness of desire and fulfilment in mankind.

This is the heart of the continuing relevance of Morris's ideas. Again and again, his concerns echo those of the present: the destruction by the international economy, not just of ancient cultures, but of the natural resources and ecology of the earth itself, the crippling of local independence by spreading centralization and bureaucracy; the stifling of the natural creativity and zest for learning of children by institutionalized schooling; the cramming of working people into mean and minimal housing, and the need for an architecture built to give pleasure to those who use it, rather than to express status, or purely mechanical 'functionalism'—let alone for mere profit. But Morris was more than a forerunner of environmentalists and Greens, an anticipation of child-centred education, who foresaw the need for socialist societies to foster creative individualism. His ideas hang together as a whole. If we have lost our sense of the way forward today, we are the more in need to return to them.

Behind this lies a special reason for his importance: Morris's remarkable anticipation of the problems of socialism within a consumer society. Socialism was originally the product of the age of the factory, and it bears that mark in its primary focus upon work. This is a major reason why socialism has always had a more direct appeal to men than to women, and equally why, with the growth of leisure and a home-centred way of life, its significance to ordinary life has become less and less obvious. But Morris stands alone among major socialist thinkers in being as consistently concerned with housework and the home as with work in the factory. 'To him, the man lived in the house almost as the soul lived in the body.' The transformation of both factory and home was equally necessary for the future fulfilment of men and women. Morris wanted everyday life as a whole to become the basic form of creativity, of art: 'For a socialist, a house, a knife, a cup, a steam engine, must be either a work of art, or a denial of art.' There is no split between Morris the socialist and the Morris of the wallpaper and textile patterns, the champion of 'The Lesser Arts' who would '*Have nothing in your houses that you do not know to be useful or believe to be beautiful'*. On the contrary, his true greatness and his continuing importance lies in the vision which saw the common root of his own life concerns.

Morris, in short, claims us as a whole: as an artist and craftsman who has left us far-scattered sources of pleasure in the beauty which he created; as an active political campaigner; and through his mind. He was a serious, highly coherent, and imaginative thinker. 'A man must have time for serious individual thought, for imagination, for dreaming even, or the race of men will inevitably worsen.'[1] A dreamer indeed, whom we neglect to our own peril.

ACKNOWLEDGEMENTS

THE diversity of William Morris's activities makes a biographer especially reliant on the help of experts. For the original edition I owe a particular debt to the advice of A. C. Sewter on stained glass and for the list of Morris windows which he gave me; to the assistance of Barbara Morris at the Victoria and Albert Museum and to her comments on Chapters 4 and 5; to the advice of Jonathan Alexander on calligraphy and illumination; to the comments of Elizabeth Aslin on Chapter 3 and of Christopher Salvesen on Chapters 8 to 10; and to the attempts of Natalie Rothstein to teach me the technicalities of weaving and dyeing. Shirley Bury, the Master of Peterhouse, John Brandon-Jones, Malcolm Cormack, and Michael Archer generously showed me material; and Lionel Lambourne and Richard Ormond kindly spent days showing me the collections at Walthamstow and Birmingham. Thea Thompson carried out some of the research for Chapter 11 and criticized the text throughout.

I am indebted to all the sources acknowledged in the list of illustrations and in the footnotes and also to Colin Ward and John Gorman for their help in elucidating illustration 40. The Society of Antiquaries of London and Keeper of Manuscripts of the British Museum kindly permitted the quotation on pages 232–3.

The revisions which I have made in two subsequent editions both draw on newly published documentation and criticism, and also, equally importantly, reflect the changing standpoint from which we see Morris. I have been especially helped in this by encouragement and comments from Natasha Burchardt, and by discussions with Leonore Davidoff, Florence Boos, Don Green, Jacquie Sarsby, Michael Saler, and Linda Richardson. Lastly, my special thanks also to Bee and Alex Hill, for welcoming me in the summer of 1989 to share their own Culm valley earthly paradise for the rewriting.

CONTENTS

LIST OF ILLUSTRATIONS

Illustrations in the Text

Black and White Plates

Colour Plates

The author and publishers have made every effort to trace copyright holders of illustrations. They would be pleased to hear from anyone who has not been acknowledged and will put this right in future editions.

THE WORK OF
WILLIAM MORRIS

THE LIFE OF WILLIAM MORRIS

WALTHAMSTOW when William Morris was born was a big village pleasantly scattered between the southern ride of Epping Forest and the wide marshes and meadows of the Lea valley. In the 1870s, when the railways provided cheap workmen's trains to London, it was to become a suburb of dingy, densely packed, brown-brick terraces for commuting artisans. In 1834 it attracted prosperous business men.

The Morris family had come from the Welsh border to business in Worcester. William Morris senior moved from Worcester to London in the 1820s to join a firm of city stockbrokers, and after his marriage to Emma Skelton, who came from a distinguished professional Worcester family, he and his wife at first continued to live above the firm's premises in Lombard Street. By 1833, when their first two daughters had been born, increasing prosperity and probably the generally growing awareness of London's unhealthiness induced them to move out to Elm House at Walthamstow, an unpretentious roomy villa with a pretty veranda and fine views from its well-planted garden. William Morris, their eldest son, was born there on 24 March 1834.

The family expanded, until eventually William Morris had four younger brothers and two younger sisters. They moved to a much larger house in 1840, Woodford Hall, an impressive Palladian brick mansion with a pedimented central block flanked by lower wings, and a double flight of steps to the door. It was one of several prosperous Georgian houses around Woodford church and green, and it had a 50-acre park and a 100-acre farm stretching down to the Roding valley and the edge of Epping Forest. The family lived there in some style, with their own brewery, bakery, and buttery, the governesses and staff observing ancient feasts and festivals with elaborate ceremony. William Morris senior secured a coat of arms in 1843. Then in 1844 he happened to acquire 272 £1 shares in a new Devonshire copper-mining company, and this investment converted a very respectable prosperity into real affluence. The mine turned out to be far richer than was expected, and within six months the shares were worth £200,000. Although the company later went into a slow decline, this fortune was sufficient to give his son the independence of a private income when he came of age.

As a child William Morris was delicate, taking after his father rather than the long-lived Skeltons. He was kept alive by calves-foot jelly and beef tea. Hence he learnt to read young, and is said to have been reading Scott's novels at the age of 4. By the time of the move to Woodford he was stronger, and was soon exploring the countryside, fishing, shooting rabbits, and starting to look at churches. His governesses, and the nearby school which he attended after 1843, made slow progress with his formal teaching in writing and spelling, but he was educating himself, and these early impressions remained important. Epping Forest he knew 'yard by yard', remembering as an old man the romantic effect of the clustered long poles of pollarded hornbeams seen against the mass of black wood behind.[1] 'I was always a lover of the sad lowland country', of the river meadows with their brown marshes and lush marigolds, 'the wide green sea of Essex marshland, with the great domed line of the sky, and the sun shining down in one flood of peaceful light over the long distance'.[2] His first enthusiasm for tapestry came from 'a room hung with faded greenery' at Queen Elizabeth's Lodge in the forest, and the power of architecture burst on him when he was taken by his father into Canterbury Cathedral at the age of 8 'thinking that the gates of heaven had been opened to me'.[3]

William Morris senior died in 1847 when he was just 50. This ended the opulence of Woodford Hall, and the family moved back to Walthamstow. Until 1856 they lived in Water House, a solid bow-windowed Georgian house in Forest Road which is now the William Morris Museum. But there was enough money to support Emma Morris in her long retirement at The Lordship at Much Hadham, a beautiful early eighteenth-century house, where she died in 1894 at the age of 90, and to set up the second son Stanley as a Hampshire gentleman farmer, as well as to provide an inheritance for William. Of the younger brothers, Rendall and Arthur went into the army, while Edgar was an unsuccessful businessman. Henrietta, the second sister, stayed at home as a companion to her widowed mother, but the other three married, Emma the eldest to a clergyman, working for over thirty years among the Derbyshire miners, Alice to a banker, and Isabella to a naval captain, in later life becoming a nursing deaconess in south London.

His father's early death left the young William head of his family. Years later he rescued the bankrupt Edgar, who ended working as a dyer for the Morris firm; and he also gave houseroom and work to his wife's sister Bessie, until she was launched as a professional embroideress. His later letters to his ageing but always vigorous mother—who walked daily in almost all weathers, and read and talked incessantly—

are tender and caring, and the grandchildren were regular visitors to her. But as a boy it was his elder sisters Emma and Henrietta to whom he was closest. Emma had looked after him as a child, and it was with them that he began to read and explore the countryside and old buildings. Perhaps this early experience of sisterly companionship underlay his much later attitudes to women as friends. Certainly it was to Emma that he poured out his news in his letters from school.

It had already been arranged that William Morris should go to Marlborough College and he was sent there at the beginning of 1848. As it happened this did not much affect his method of learning. The college had been set up in 1843 in the imposing Castle Inn at the end of the broad street of the old coaching town. It owed its growth to the insatiable educational enthusiasm of the early Victorian middle classes rather than to any educational merits. Partly in order to keep down costs to parents, the school had taken the new step of boarding all the boys within the school itself, rather than in houses out in the town. But under a weak headmaster there was little organization, no uniform, no prefects, no organized games, the whole lower school was taught in one big room, and above all, there was no public school ethos. The boys spent much of their time rambling and bird's-nesting, bringing frequent complaints from locals of damage to crops and animals. Between lessons they amused themselves in the school playground by smoking and stone-throwing. It was 'a new and very rough school. As far as my school instruction went, I think I may fairly say I learned next to nothing there, for indeed next to nothing was taught.'[4] The only direct influence of the school on Morris was religious. The Morris family were evangelical, but the school atmosphere was Tractarian, and in the new Gothic chapel the school choir sang newly rediscovered Elizabethan church music. Morris left Marlborough intending to become a High Church clergyman.

For the rest, he continued to teach himself. In the school library he found a good collection of books on archaeology and Gothic architecture. He spent his ample free time on long walks, muttering romantic stories of knights and magic to himself, in the beautiful surrounding countryside. The long beech avenues and thickets of Savernake Forest lay east of the town, while westwards up the Kennet valley was Avebury, with its fallen stone circles and the huge circular mound of Silbury Hill. North and south chalk grassland rose with burial mounds on the ridges and grey glacial stones scattered in its folds. The high bank of the Wansdyke ran for miles along the southern range of hills which flank the Vale of Pewsey like the limbs of great shorn green panthers.

Nowhere in southern England are history and landscape more power-fully mingled.

In the autumn of 1851 disorder in the school culminated in an organized rebellion. It was the last of the major public school riots which had earlier also convulsed Eton and Winchester. Although Morris played no prominent part, the experience left its mark. He was taken away from the school by his parents at the end of 1851, and prepared for Oxford by a private classical tutor. He came up to Exeter College at the beginning of 1853. Visually Oxford was all that he had expected. The railway had come, building was just starting in north Oxford, and the old city was already fringed by workmen's brick suburbs, but they seemed small blemishes on the ancient university, the 'vision of grey-roofed houses and a long winding street, and the sound of many bells'.[5] The medieval colleges were unspoilt by restoration, the Georgian buildings of soft Headington stone were weathered but not yet blistered, the High Street and Broad Street were pink cobbled cambered ridges between old grey buildings, disturbed only by leisurely farm carts and discoursing dons. Less fortunately for Morris, educa-tional reform, like architectural change, had barely begun. At Exeter the college was overfull, so that Morris had to eat out during the day and sleep in the third room of an older man's set at night. The rector was non-resident, and the college tutors seemed bored and indifferent. Teaching was not by individual tutorial, but lecture classes conducted like formal school teaching. Morris was bitterly disappointed.

He was not, however, thrown back this time entirely on his own resources. Within a week he had made a close friend in Edward Burne-Jones, a tall, thin, pale boy with straight, colourless hair, light grey eyes, and a smooth-domed forehead, a gilder's son, who had come from Birmingham Grammar School intending, like Morris, to become an Anglo-Catholic clergyman. They were soon walking together, angrily discussing their disappointment, thinking of setting up a brotherhood, a new monastic order for a 'crusade and Holy Warfare against the age, "the heartless coldness of the times"',[6] and predictably within a few months considering seceding to Roman Catholicism. In spite of the dramatic changes in viewpoint which both were to undergo, this was the beginning of a close lifelong friendship.

Apart from Fulford Adams, a schoolfriend from Marlborough who eventually became an Oxfordshire vicar and neighbour, Morris found few other friends at Exeter, but through Burne-Jones he was introduced to a circle of Birmingham friends at Pembroke. This group was concerned not only with religion, but with modern secular writing, poetry, and social problems, Factory Acts, and sanitation. They were more interested in Christian Socialism than in Anglo-Catholicism. The group met in the rooms of Charles Faulkner, who was to become an Oxford mathematics fellow, and one of Morris's closest friends. Here, between violent arguments and practical jokes, they held readings of Shakespeare, Tennyson, Carlyle, Ruskin, and other favourite authors.

Morris was able to convey his enthusiasm for the visual arts to the group. He was constantly sketching architectural details in his note-books and taking friends to look at Merton Chapel or New College cloisters. He took the principal architectural weekly, the *Builder*, decorated his walls with brass rubbings, studied the illuminated manuscripts in the Bodleian, and began to examine the design of furniture and carpets. It was Morris who discovered Ruskin, whom he liked to chant in a great singing voice. He came back from his first journey abroad with his sister Henrietta in the summer of 1854 to tell of the architectural wonders of Amiens, Beauvais, and Chartres, and the new excitement he had found in Flemish painting. He was the artistic aristocrat of the group, wealthy, elegantly dressed with purple trousers and a swaggering bow tie, his dark curly hair framing a sensitive, finely shaped white face. In spite of his explosive temper and violent rages, he no doubt excelled in the group's attempt to model their manners on the medieval chivalry of *The Heir of Redclyffe*. He sailed and fenced with zest, and spoke with a husky shout.

Equally Morris learnt from the group. Their interest in social and political questions helped him to see that a monastic life would be pure escapism. Among these friends he fully grasped the importance of Carlyle's essay on a monastic community in *Past and Present* and Ruskin's chapter, 'The Nature of Gothic', in *The Stones of Venice*. The Middle Ages had been more than feudal chivalry and Gothic art: they had been a coherent way of life with a sound understanding of social and communal duties, and their art was the expression of the free and happy life of their craftsmen.

At the same time he probably acquired his enthusiasm for Dickens. More important, he shared the group's admiration for Shelley, Keats, and Tennyson, and began to take seriously his own poetry-writing, which had been until then a private whim. One day in 1854 he read a poem to his friends, who thought it the first that he had written. It was called 'The Willow and the Red Cliff'. It had the strange images and awkwardness of his first published poems, and its odd originality immediately impressed his audience.[7] 'Well, if this is poetry, it is very easy to write,' he commented prophetically. From now on he regularly read new poems to his friends.

Morris came of age in March 1855, inheriting an income of £900 a year. Encouraged by his financial resources, the group began to plan the publication of a literary magazine. Some Cambridge friends of the Birmingham men were drawn in to help. It was decided that it should consist of poetry, romantic tales, and social articles, but politics were to be almost eschewed. Morris was to be proprietor and editor, and he hoped that it would not cost him more than £300 a year. During the summer he started writing a series of short prose romances for publication in the magazine.

He went abroad again in August, this time with Burne-Jones and Fulford, the eldest of the Birmingham set. It was intended to be a walking holiday in Picardy and Normandy, visiting Amiens, Beauvais, Chartres and Rouen, with a sketchbook and a volume of Keats. As it happened Morris went lame, so that they were forced to travel by 'a nasty, brimstone, noisy, shrieking railway train . . . verily railways are ABOMINATIONS'. Burne-Jones insisted on a visit to Paris to see the Louvre paintings, where by chance they saw an exhibition of English pre-Raphaelite paintings. Once again Morris was enchanted by the countryside, the poplar meadows and cornfields, the 'blue cornflowers, and red poppies, growing together with the corn round the roots of the fruit trees, in their shadows, and sweeping up to the brows of the long low hills till they reached the sky, changing sometimes into long fields of vines, or delicate, lush green forage'.[8] Once again he was overwhelmed by the glory of the early French Gothic cathedrals. Burne-Jones, who had already been trying his hand at book illustrations and sketching around Oxford and had been deeply impressed by a painting by Rossetti he had seen in Oxford, was equally inspired by the wonders of the Louvre. On the last night of their holiday, pacing the quays at Le Havre, Morris and Burne-Jones decided that it was art, and not the Church, to which they must dedicate their lives. They would finish with Oxford as quickly as possible, Morris to become an architect, Burne-Jones a painter.

For their family circles, such a change seemed bewildering, even shocking. And it momentarily betrayed a deeper crisis in religious faith of which neither spoke much. A long letter from Burne-Jones to his cousin Maria in October 1855 reveals how reading French and German philosophy had shattered ('shivered') the belief of Morris and 'palsied' his own, broken up their plan for a 'little brotherhood in the heart of London', and left him 'doubting, doubting, doubting . . . friendly sympathy growing colder as the void broadens and deepens'; and he could not any more even hope to 'grace my friends now by holding that highly *respectable* position of a clergyman, a sore point that . . . '9.

Morris too returned to break the news to his mother that he intended to enter a new and distinctly less respectable profession. He chose to be a pupil of George Edmund Street, whose office was then in Beaumont Street, Oxford. Street was a High Churchman, one of the most original and most successful of the younger Gothic revivalists, an expert on Italian and Spanish Gothic, who shared Morris's enthusiasm for Flemish painting and church music. After taking a pass degree, Morris started as a pupil at the beginning of 1856. Immediately he made a new friend in the senior clerk, Philip Webb. Webb was told to help him, 'and this was done pleasantly and easily, as we understood each other at once'. When a difficult point arose, or a compass stuck on the drawing board, Morris 'would beat his head with his fists till I thought it would stun him . . . He was out of place in an office.'10

The decision to become an architect was in fact rapidly overtaken by Morris's development in other fields. His evenings were still spent with his old friends at Pembroke. The first number of the *Oxford and Cambridge Magazine* was published in January, and although he decided to employ Fulford as salaried editor, tales and poetry for publication took up much time during the year. In all, twelve monthly numbers were published. Meanwhile Morris was seeing himself more and more as an artist. He grew a moustache and long hair, and took up wood engraving, clay modelling, carving, and illuminating. At the weekends he went to London to see Burne-Jones, who had gone there to become a pupil of Rossetti.

The son of a revolutionary refugee, Dante Gabriel Rossetti in 1856 was a brilliant figure, at the height of his powers as a pre-Raphaelite poet and painter, a daring conversationalist, a handsome young Italian with long dark hair and a short neat Shakespearian beard. Soon Morris too was falling under his influence, accepting his insistence on the supreme importance of painting. He decided to buy Arthur Hughes's 'April Love', a delicate, wistful portrait of a young woman standing by a wall of ivy leaves, which is now in the Tate Gallery. In July he decided to divide his day between painting and his architectural work. 'Rossetti says I ought to paint, he says I shall be able; now as he is a very great man, and speaks with authority and not as the scribes, I *must* try.'11 A month later Street moved his office to London, and Morris took rooms in Bloomsbury, so that contact with Rossetti became more frequent. In the autumn, after completing their competition drawings for the new cathedral at Lille, Street and Morris visited the Low Countries together, and once again the intense medieval realism and colour of Van Eyck's painting inspired him. At the end of the year, to his mother's dismay, he suddenly announced a second change of profession; he was to be a painter.

At the same time he moved into a house at 17 Red Lion Square, with Burne-Jones. It was a Georgian terrace house with a window which had been heightened to let in more light, making an excellent studio. The walls were again hung with brass rubbings, and since no suitable Gothic furniture could be bought in the sale rooms, Morris made some rough drawings for tables, chairs, and a settle which were made by a local carpenter. They were extremely primitive, made of thick criss-crossed planks, fixed together by rudimentary protruding pins. This was probably the only furniture which Morris himself ever designed. The settle had a high back and coved canopy, and on its panels and the chairbacks Rossetti painted stories of Dante and of Sir Galahad. A huge plain wardrobe followed, which Burne-Jones painted with scenes from Chaucer's 'Prioress's Tale'.

Red Lion Square remained Morris's London home until 1859. He was now hard at work studying for painting, beginning his first complete picture of a subject taken from Tennyson's 'Morte d'Arthur', Sir Tristram after his illness in the garden of King Mark's palace, recognized by the dog he had given to Iseult. It was closely studied from nature. There is no doubt that he found the work difficult, and his strained nerves were increasingly relieved by violent shouts and fits of temper. The studio was littered with piles of clothes, candlegrease, and even the droppings of a pet owl, so that the boisterous young painters were lucky to find a housekeeper who could enjoy their odd humour. The legendary Red Lion Mary had to tolerate Morris throwing his plum pudding down from the landing because the portion was too small. Yet he even persuaded her to execute his experiments in embroidery designing.

Later in the year Morris found himself suddenly thrown into a public commission. In July 1857 Morris and Rossetti went up to Oxford to see Rossetti's friend Benjamin Woodward, the Dublin architect who had been chosen to design the University Museum and the Union debating hall, which is now the Union library. Woodward was an imaginative architect, fusing a variety of Italian and other Gothic motifs into a style of his own, with big heavy shapes, thick towers, and subtly coloured materials. The Museum is built of brown and greenish stone, with blue and green slates on its steep roof, and inside is an extraordinary hall

1. Rossetti and Ruskin, with William Bell Scott, c.1863

roofed in Gothic iron and glass. Woodward brought with him from Dublin his own talented sculptors, the O'Shea brothers, who covered the building with cats, rabbits, birds, and foliage, before they were dismissed for carving parrots in mortar boards. In his enthusiasm with the new buildings, Rossetti offered to cover the apsed upper walls and high raftered roof of the Union debating hall with frescos. The Union building committee accepted the impetuous free offer, agreeing to supply materials and pay the artists' expenses.

9

Morris and Burne-Jones, as pupils of Rossetti, were each allotted a space to paint. Rossetti persuaded other pre-Raphaelite friends to help: Arthur Hughes, Spencer Stanhope, Val Prinsep and Hungerford Pollen. Rossetti's master and friend Ford Madox Brown refused. There were to be ten scenes from 'Morte d'Arthur', one in each bay. It was an unsuitable position for paintings, since each bay was pierced by large foliated round windows, so that the composition was broken up and the frescos could only be seen against the light. Moreover, Rossetti had only a very vague knowledge of the technique of fresco painting, with the result that the work was done in distemper on the bare brick with only a ground of whitewash before the mortar had been allowed to dry out. Consequently the paintings had hardly been finished a few months before they began to rub off. The whole effect of brightly coloured illuminations was completely lost. They have been restored several times since, but have never remained visible for long. Altogether it was to be a sad waste of effort. As Ruskin wrote in December, 'The roof *is* and is *not* satisfactory—clever but not right. You know the fact is they're all the least bit crazy.'[12]

For Morris the return to Oxford was important in several ways. To begin with, the fresco was too ambitious a task for so inexperienced a painter. The subject was 'How Sir Palomydes loved La Belle Iseult with exceeding great love out of measure and how she loved him not again but rather Sir Tristram', the theme of the unsuccessful lover to which he was often to return. He started seriously, designing a helmet, chain mail, and splendid sword for his model which were made by a local blacksmith. Burne-Jones one afternoon 'heard a strange bellowing in the building, and turning round to find the cause, saw an unwonted sight. The basinet was being tried on, but the visor, for some reason, would not lift, and I saw Morris embedded in iron, dancing with rage and roaring inside.'[13] But in spite of his efforts, the picture proved a failure, the figures absurdly proportioned and nearly lost in a mass of huge sunflowers. Rossetti's laughter was all too justified. Being the first to finish, Morris then began on the roof, and although here too the decorations have disappeared, he seems to have been far more successful with this purely decorative work. The experience was to help him to find his real talent.

At the same time, the constant company of friends helped keep away despondency. In addition to the other painters who were naturally drawn into the circle, Morris now met Swinburne, a restless, boneless, whitefaced youth with vague green eyes and a mass of red hair, who became one of the most fervent admirers of Morris's early poetry.

Swinburne adopted Rossetti's Dantesque romanticism in its most exaggerated form. Visiting dons who came to see the progress of the frescos were shocked to hear loud disputes over the nature of kisses in paradise and the vision of heaven as 'a rose-garden full of stunners'.[14] In the evening at dinner Arthurian jokes would be interspersed with talk of 'stunners', as beautiful women were invariably called. Rossetti would then stretch himself languidly on a sofa and call on Morris to 'read us one of your grinds'. Val Prinsep remembered on his first evening Morris producing a large clasped book, 'which he deposited on the table. He read in a kind of melodious growl with a considerable sing-song, resting his head on one hand, while with the other he ceaselessly twisted his watch-chain. Two stanzas from two different poems still remain in my memory . . .

> Gold on her head, and gold on her feet,
> And gold where the hems of her kirtle meet,
> And a golden girdle around my sweet.
> Ah! qu'elle est belle la Marguerite . . .

> "They have hammered out my basnet point
> Into a round salade", he said;
> "The basnet being quite out of joint,
> Natheless the salade rasps my head".'[15]

More important still was the discovery of Jane Burden. She was spotted by Rossetti one evening at the theatre, and persuaded to sit as a model for the frescos. Jane's background could hardly have differed more sharply. Most likely herself a young servant, her father was a stablehand, her mother an illiterate domestic servant, both from village farm-labouring families. They lived in cramped courts close to the Holywell Street stables where gentlemen's horses were boarded and hired. Jane kept her childhood to herself in later years, but there are hints of sadness: an older sister's death, and parental conflict. But Morris was immediately attracted to her strange, reticent beauty: tall, white-necked, thin pursed lips and a long hard chin, dark dreamy eyes, and a great mane of dark crisp undulating hair. He courted her with readings from Dickens and by February 1858 he had persuaded her to marry him. She could, indeed, have scarcely refused his offer. Swinburne was horrified that romance should thus descend to sordid reality. Morris should have been content to have 'that wonderful and most perfect stunner of his to—look at or speak to. The idea of his marrying her is insane. To kiss her feet is the utmost man should think of doing.'[16] One may suspect that his caution was based on sound intuition. They can have scarcely known each other. Nor did their months of engagement offer much more opportunity. Jane it seems prepared herself for her new role by learning the piano, and it may be that she found her zest for reading, so apparent in later letters, at the same time; but Morris was too often away, working in London, travelling in France, to have shared much in her discoveries.

For the moment, marriage seemed a solution to his search for a vocation. He was now certain that he could never become a great painter. Instead, he was dreaming of a new paradise, a 'Palace of Art' peopled by his wife and children. In fact, had Morris given himself time,

2. Red House, Bexley Heath, Kent, 1859, by Webb, built for Morris on his marriage, and his home until 1865: the garden front

his achievement as a painter might have been considerable. His pen drawings of 1862 for the St George's cabinet show real promise: the bare-shouldered princess, head down, chained to a pole, her brilliantly careful hair, the close, regular, cropped grass, a stream and tall slender wood behind, and a rough black indication of the dragon; or the beautifully studied return, two men carrying the dragon slumped on a pole, the cobbles and old houses behind, the tired heroes, the rich dresses, and the crowd of feathered hats. These are drawings of real imaginative beauty. His earlier awkwardness and stiffness with figures had been largely overcome. At the same time he undoubtedly had an unusual sense of colour. Four panels at the Victoria and Albert Museum, which were probably painted for furniture in about 1860, are of women, rather formally conceived, admiring or smelling flowers, with patterns behind; but the colour of one of these, with long flaxen hair, wearing a deep blue dress with sleeves embroidered red, a background of orange pink diaper, and green leaves against a blue and white sky, is as sensuous as impressionism. Had he the patience Morris might have become an important painter, but patience was rare in him.

Once again he seems to have made up his mind in France, this time on a holiday with Philip Webb, rowing down the Seine from Paris in August 1858. Encouraged by Morris, Webb decided to set up his own practice 'to build me a house very medieval in spirit'.[17] The first rough drawings were made in their French Bradshaw. In the autumn Morris was in France again collecting old ironwork, armour, enamel, and manuscripts for the new house.

Meanwhile he had suffered another disappointment. In March a selection of his early poems was published, *The Defence of Guenevere*. Browning thought the poems admirable, 'the only new poems to my mind since there's no telling when'.[18] But the volume was generally ignored by the reviewers, and most of the few notices were unfavourable. The *Spectator* thought his poetic style 'as bad as bad can be. Mr Morris imitates little save faults. He combines the mawkish simplicity of the Cockney school with the prosaic baldness of the worst passages of Tennyson, and the occasional obscurity and affectation of plainness that characterize Browning and his followers.'[19] If Morris came later to scorn reviewers, there is no doubt that he was shaken by this hostile reception. He had been producing poetry fast in the previous months. Now he was abruptly checked, and for the next five years wrote little, until eventually he found a new confidence in a second style.

A site was found for the new house in a Kentish orchard at Bexley Heath, then three miles from the nearest station, but close enough to London not to be isolated. The designs were complete by April 1859, but the building was not ready for occupation before the end of the summer of 1860. Morris therefore started married life in furnished rooms in Great Ormond Street. The wedding was in Oxford, conducted by his friend Dixon in St Michael's church, recently restored by Street, with Faulkner as best man. Jane's family, of whom she would now see very little, were there; but of his whom she now joined, none.

Red House is often mistakenly regarded as a turning point in architectural history. In fact it is a happy example of the secular brick Gothic style evolved for village schools and parsonages by Butterfield and Street in the early 1850s. Webb's notebooks from this period

3. Benfleet Hall, Cobham, by Webb, for the painter Spencer Stanhope – Webb's second thoughts after Red House

contain several sketches of buildings by Butterfield. The characteristic features of Red House, the ample-hipped red tiled roof, the sash windows, the tall battered chimney-breasts, are all derived from these two masters. Brick was chosen because it was the local material; on another site stone might have been used. The circular landing windows, which give a very secular effect, were meant to be seen as unfoliated tracery circles, and one of them is grouped in this way above a pair of sash windows. Certainly Morris regarded the design of the house as in 'the style of the thirteenth century'.[20] It received no publicity in the contemporary press and it was only towards the end of the century that it was rediscovered as a pioneer of the arts and crafts architectural movement.

It is equally wrong to think of the interior as a reaction from High Victorian gloom and clutter. The principal rooms are rather dark, and they were elaborately furnished to create the atmosphere of a miniature medieval palace. The walls were either to be painted with scenes from the Trojan War and the romance of Sir Degrevaunt, or hung with embroideries of Chaucer's red and flaxen-haired women, and bright flowers on a rough blue-serge ground. These paintings and embroideries were never more than partly completed. The ceilings were pricked out with patterns executed in distemper, the main drawing room upstairs with a roof rising like a tent painted with wide stripes and bands of foliage. The fireplaces were in rubbed red brick, inscribed with mottoes, 'Our content is our best having' and 'Ars Longa Vita Brevis', the largest in the drawing room rising to a simplified Gothic hood. On the floors were rich Persian carpets. The great oak staircase had tall pointed posts and Burne-Jones designed allegorical stained glass for the windows. The painted settle and Chaucer wardrobe were moved in from Red Lion Square, and Webb built in the settle at the end of the drawing room with a miniature minstrel gallery on top. The new furniture was all designed by Webb in a plain heavy Gothic style, a great oak table, dressers for the Dutch china, beds and chairs, brass candlesticks, grates and fire-irons, simple table glass, and even a Gothic waggonette for country drives. Outside creepers were planted against the walls and the garden divided up with rose wattle hedges and planted with lilies and sunflowers. In the angle of the house was a circular wooden well-house with a tall conical tiled roof. It was indeed a dream house, 'more a poem than a house' as Rossetti put it:[21] but rich and elaborate, the very reverse of modern light and clarity.

The furnishing of Red House took several years and once again showed the impossibility of buying anything modern in the right style. Secular stained glass and embroideries were unobtainable, and good Gothic furniture had to be made to architects' designs. Webb was again designing complete sets of furniture, wardrobes, washstands, pianos, tables of all shapes, for the houses he was now building for Spencer Stanhope and Major Gillum. At the recommendation of Rossetti, Burne-Jones had started stained glass designs for James Powell of Whitefriars in 1857, and his first important windows for Woodward at Oxford cathedral and for William Burges at Waltham Abbey were executed in 1859–61. Ford Madox Brown, who through Rossetti had become a friend, was also designing furniture and stained glass. It was these activities which prompted Brown's suggestion, perhaps not originally serious, that they should combine to form an art decorator's firm. If their fierce ambition to improve public taste and reshape the market was rare, there was in itself nothing very new in artists providing designs for commercial production. The group of men around Henry Cole who had organized the Great Exhibition and the Government Schools of Design had been encouraging this since the 1840s, and in some fields, such as wallpapers, where their critical theories had been supported by the designs of Pugin and Owen Jones, they had already considerably influenced English taste. The important innovation proposed by Brown was that the artists should take part in the production and sale of their designs. Cole and his friends had believed that commercial production could be improved by simply raising the standards of design. Through Ruskin the Gothic revivalists had learnt that work produced under modern factory conditions would be inevitably mechanical and shoddy.

Ruskin had taught them that the gargoyles and goblins of medieval architecture were signs, not of primitive ignorance, but of 'the life and liberty of every workman who struck the stone; a freedom of thought, and rank in scale of being, such as no laws, no charters, no charities can secure; but which it must be the first aim of all Europe at this day to regain for her children'. He had attacked the division of manual and intellectual labour which produced a society 'of morbid thinkers, and miserable workers . . . It would be well if all of us were good handicraftsmen in some kind, and the dishonour of manual labour done away with altogether.'[22] A firm of artists and friends producing their own designs in a co-operative effort would be an answer to Ruskin's call.

Morris, Marshall, Faulkner and Company, soon generally known as Morris and Company, was formed in April 1861. The partners, Morris, Burne-Jones, Webb, Faulkner, Rossetti, Madox Brown, and Marshall (a surveyor friend of Brown), each put up only £1 so that the main capital was £100 lent by Emma Morris. Morris himself was made manager, with an annual salary of £150, but the firm's annual deficits could only be met by his own loans. Premises were taken at 8 Red Lion Square, above a jeweller's workshop. A kiln for firing stained glass and tiles was set up in the basement, and other workrooms, an office and showroom in the upper floors. A prospectus was issued emphasizing the need for artistic supervision and detailed co-operation in the execution of decorative work, and offering to produce wall paintings and decoration, stained glass, metalwork and jewellery, sculpture, embroidery, and furniture of all kinds for either houses or churches 'at the smallest possible expense'. In practice the firm's work was far from cheap and it relied on generous commissions from Webb to furnish houses and from High Church architects for stained glass, and wall and roof decorations. Among their most important early patrons were Street, his friend

William White, and G. F. Bodley, who had probably been drawn into contact with the group through the Hogarth Club, an association of artists, poets, and architects founded by Rossetti in 1858.

For the stained glass work, George Campfield, a glass painter discovered by Morris at the Working Men's College, was engaged as foreman, and boys were employed from a Boys' Home in the Euston Road. Embroidery and painted tiles were executed by women from family and friends. The furniture was at first made by a local cabinet-maker, jewellery by the jeweller on the ground floor, and table glass by Powell's of Whitefriars. All the partners except for Faulkner were at first supplying designs, and other artists, including Albert Moore and Simeon Solomon, helped with the stained glass. A year after its formation the firm had sufficient stock to make up two stalls at the 1862 International Exhibition. One stall was entirely of stained glass, the other of embroideries and brightly painted Gothic furniture. The plain oak furniture already being made to designs by Madox Brown and Webb was not exhibited and the first wallpapers were not designed until later in the year. It was as extreme medievalists that Morris and Company made their first public impact, indeed so much so that some hostile stained glass firms attempted to disqualify their glass as being merely old work touched up.

In these first years of marriage Morris seems to have been unusually contented. The Oxford group had now broken up, some to join the Church, others to go abroad, but Swinburne had come to London and a new circle had grown up with the firm. Burne-Jones and Rossetti had both married in 1860. Georgiana Burne-Jones, who drew quickly close to Morris, was the small gay daughter of a Methodist minister; her sisters were to be mothers of Rudyard Kipling and Stanley Baldwin. Rossetti's marriage was to the tall, delicate, silent, coppery-haired Elizabeth Siddal, whom he had known and loved intensely between frequent quarrels for ten years, the Beatrice of his early water-colours. She was already ill when they married, probably neurotic with jealousy, and she committed suicide in 1862. But for the moment this tragedy was an exceptional discord. Red House became a jovial meeting place for Burne-Jones, Madox Brown, Arthur Hughes and their wives, Faulkner and his sisters, Webb and Swinburne, the progress of decoration broken off for summer bowls in the garden and the ample stock of wine in the cellar. There were constant practical jokes, books falling from the door-tops, illegible orders and empty parcels sent to the firm, Morris sent to Coventry or persuaded that there was no food, explosions of anger followed by laughter and games. Georgiana and Janey would embroider and take country drives together. Before long both were pregnant. The two Morris children were both born here, Jenny in January 1861 and May in March 1862. A nanny was recommended by Janey's mother-in-law, with whom she now got on well. In his work for the firm Morris was at last finding fulfilment for his talents. It was symbolic of his settled state that with other patriotic friends he joined the volunteer militia in 1859–62.

Unfortunately for Morris this pleasant Kentish life came to an end in 1865. At a moment when he needed all his income to meet the annual deficits of Morris and Company the yield of his copper shares was declining. For a while he hoped to find a solution in moving the firm's workshops to Red House, building a half-timbered wing for Burne-Jones to form a courtyard round the well, and so making the house into a community. The scheme failed because Burne-Jones, already prone to illness and worried by his health, thought Red House too cold. Bitterly disappointed—'I cried, but I have got over it now'—[23] Morris was forced to choose between the firm and Red House. He decided to move back to London to live above new and larger premises for the firm at 26 Queen Square, in the same district fringing on Bloomsbury a little to the north of Red Lion Square. He never returned to Red House, which passed beyond his circle of friends. It has had many owners, including at one time the editor of the arts and crafts magazine, the *Studio*. After being used by the National Assistance Board in the 1940s and threatened with demolition, it is now appropriately occupied by a group of architects.

By 1865 the early co-operation of the firm's partners had given place to the dominant direction of Morris. Faulkner had returned to Oxford and Marshall to surveying, while Rossetti was mourning in Chelsea, his work confined to painting. Madox Brown, Burne-Jones and Webb, with Morris himself, continued to supply designs, but the production was wholly supervised by Morris, and he tended to rely on his two close friends rather than Brown for designs. Until 1864 Faulkner had been business manager. In 1865 he was succeeded by Warington Taylor, a friend of Swinburne from Eton, a lean, unkempt, hook-nosed, rather wild-spoken man who had sunk through a chequered career to ticket collecting at the opera. Although soon after he began his health collapsed and much of his direction of the firm was through letters to Webb from south coast resorts, Taylor's excitable energy and business sense helped to lay a new basis for the future of the firm before his death from consumption in 1870. His letters were a series of orders with the insistent refrain, '*see to it*'. He instituted a regular pricing policy based on

4. Morris photographed by Frederick Hollyer at the age of 41

costs. Again and again he complained, 'You may be certain that you will charge £9 for that which costs you £10. I *know* your ways of calculating profits.' 'You don't care do you. Last quarter disgraceful, worked out on last winter's estimate—Bodley's—one of his, you know him— decoration talk—Bodley X Morris immense—turn 5.30 p.m., Bodley speaks, Give me an estimate—tother does it—And—don't.' Taylor also tried to regularize the erratic production of the firm and create a regular workflow. Morris tended to undertake too much work and then to finish nothing. 'Morris is very nervous about work; and he consequently suddenly takes men off work and puts them on another. There is in this great loss of time. When I was there, I was able in some way to counteract this: I used to quiet him.' At the same time he was bombarding Morris with warnings of bankruptcy, advising him to use cheaper candles, 'not to keep too many fires burning, reduce kitchen fire, and not use the front room too much, that fire consumes enormously . . . you ought really to have only *one* servant with occasional help', and no more than one dinner a day; 'drink beer instead

19

of wine . . . If you have soup for dinner you must have nothing else save the meat.' With his falling inherited income, Taylor calculated that Morris was drawing £200 a year from his remaining capital, which at his rate of spending would be exhausted by 1869 or 1870. Then he would 'be on to his old game of drawing small cheques from the firm and at end of quarter express surprise at amount overdrawn'. And indeed, although by 1870 Morris was earning some £200 a year from his new books, his share income had fallen from £682 in 1865 to £396 in 1869 and a mere £187 in 1870. That year, finally driven 'through necessity, William Morris became a committed man of business': his own salary from the firm was raised to £200 a year, with a 10 per cent bonus on profits.[24] Taylor's realism as manager helped to prepare Morris for this. But he had been little help in finding commissions or developing a new market strategy. The real upswing of the firm, which together with the new success of his poetry was to save his financial situation, was to come only after 1870 when Morris himself took a much more active control.

By the later 1860s stained glass had come to dominate the firm's work, although even these commissions were shrinking. In the early years there had been several houses to furnish and decorate for Webb, and most of the partners bought furniture for themselves. Morris especially spent a lot of money on Red House and then at Queen Square. Then in 1866–7 the firm secured its first two important public commissions, for the Armoury and Tapestry Rooms at St James's Palace and the Green Dining Room at the Victoria and Albert Museum. After this there was no important secular work until 1870. The chief commissions for general church decoration, all from Bodley, also consisted of two early schemes at St Michael's, Brighton, and St Martin's, Scarborough, both in 1862, and two others in 1866–7 for Jesus College Chapel and All Saints' Church, Cambridge. Yet in 1867, which was thus a particularly busy year, stained glass accounted for £2,300 out of a total of £3,000. Except for glass and these few special commissions the firm's work must have been very limited. Morris had designed a small number of charmingly naïve naturalistic wallpapers in 1862–6, which were produced by an outside firm, but they appear to have attracted no public notice. Taylor advised that, 'considering the few interested in decoration and limited sale of our papers', new designs would not be profitable,[25] and consequently Morris designed no more papers until 1872. The firm produced no textiles apart from embroideries in this period. After the first years there was little demand for ambitious and expensive handpainted tiles and most of Webb's furniture was in plain unpainted wood. Two types of chair adapted from old country patterns, the black, turned-wood, rush–bottomed Sussex chairs and settees, and the 'Morris' adjustable upholstered armchair, probably did not become fashionable before the 1870s, even though neither design was as unconventional as is often thought. Thus in these years Morris was able to concentrate much of his artistic energy on stained-glass work. There are very few undistinguished Morris windows from the 1860s, and a high proportion of the very best.

While at Red House, Morris had tried a little poetry, but his scheme for a cycle of poems on the Trojan War was left unfinished. The fragments which he wrote still have the bite of his early work, combined with a much clearer narrative. Hesitation after the failure of *Guenevere* combined with the demands of family and the new firm to prevent their completion. With the move back to London and Taylor's appointment as business manager, Morris was able to find more time for writing and he began a more ambitious cycle of narrative poems which had been talked of at Red House, *The Earthly Paradise*. He settled on a smoother, melodious style which made his stories very much easier reading, but at the cost of most of the sharp images and confrontations of his early poetry. The tales were chosen from both classical and medieval sources and written rapidly. In his fluent enthusiasm Morris found the length of some stories beyond control and decided to publish one of the first, *The Life and Death of Jason*, as an independent poem. His publisher, Bell and Daldy, refused to risk another loss, so *Jason* was issued in June 1867 at Morris's own expense. It proved an extraordinary success not only with the reviewers but still more with the public. The tired or neurotic middle-class businessman or lady of the house found the soothing story an ideal form of literature. For these,

when we light the lamp and draw the curtains after a hard day's work on some autumn evening, comes the turn of the poet who is willing and able to amuse us. It is then that we seek for verse which can soothe the wearied mind with images of beauty, which can be enjoyed without effort, and which condescends to be entertaining.[26]

Morris was applauded for his avoidance of self-consciousness and 'morbid introversion'. 'The reader walks in a Southern garden which fronts the sea. We have the pungent air, the moving sapphire of the waters, and the fresh verdure of the trees; but the forms that glance through the last are marble, not flesh.'[27]

To modern readers for whom poetry is an intense and generally rare form of literature, the lack of personal emotional drama in the poem almost destroys its undoubted narrative mastery. The Victorian audience was equally aware of this quality, but they liked it. A second edition was issued immediately, and within five years the poem was into its seventh edition with over 3,000 copies sold. Greatly encouraged, Morris went on rapidly with *The Earthly Paradise*. A new publisher, F. S. Ellis, undertook the book and the first volume (Parts I and II) was published in April 1868. The third and last volume, making up a total of 42,000 lines, came out in December 1870. Some of the critics were by now finding Morris monotonous. 'The natural langour of Mr Morris's style makes his verse at once diffuse and tedious.'[28] Even the loyal Burne-Jones complained of the 'drowsy sleepy parts'.[29] But the poem was again a complete public success, 'a choice reading for the long dark of London winter evenings'.[30] His 'excessively delicate manner' in handling 'the numerous *amours* of the gods, so coarsely and barely set forth in the orthodox prose versions' was especially welcomed.[31] *The Earthly Paradise* was perfectly 'adapted for conveying to our wives and daughters a refined, though not diluted, version of those wonderful creations of Greek fancy which the rougher sex alone is permitted to imbibe at first hand'.[32] Five editions of Parts I and II had been printed before Part IV was available and the first of numerous popular editions was published in 1872. Henceforth to the public William Morris was 'the author of *The Earthly Paradise*'.

To the more observant critic there were a number of features which seemed unsuitable in a poem which claimed the inspiration of Chaucer. The lack of bawdy humour could hardly be mentioned as a fault, but at least one reviewer claimed that by his escape into a romantic past Morris had 'evaded the very conditions on which alone the production of great poetry is possible.'[33] Chaucer's stories had been about real people, contemporaries. Several critics noted another blemish:

an ominous sound which is continually breaking in like the toll of a knell—death! death! death! . . . In the shape of old stories, and in the art of Chaucerian verse, we have modern scepticism goading itself into mere hopelessness as to the value and destiny of human nature . . . And why this 'an empty day'? Has love, has courage, fled the earth since the disuse of mediaeval garments?[34]

It was in explaining this morbidity, the one recurrent reality in *The Earthly Paradise*, that Mackail's fine account of Morris's life was most inadequate. Shortly after its publication Mackail confided in a letter that his 'difficulties over the work itself were great, especially in the constant need for what is called "tact", which is a quality unpleasantly near untruthfulness often; and especially I feel that my account of all those stormy years of *The Earthly Paradise* time and the time following it must be excessively flat owing to the amount of tact that had to be exercised right and left'.[35] In print he confined himself to saying that the late 1860s and early 1870s were 'years of much restlessness and great emotional tension' and brooding after death and that in the verses of the months which frame *The Earthly Paradise* could be found 'an autobiography so delicate and outspoken that it must be left to speak for itself'.[36] But delicacy obscures, and the true cause of tension, in Morris's married life, has only been shown by more recent biographers.

Morris had married Janey for her strange beauty, not for any tangible personality. He had been a young painter then, she flattered to be his model. Since then he had been through many phases. It was hardly surprising that she had been bewildered by his constant changes of interest. No doubt Janey was hurt that Morris no longer painted her, and his kind but strangely wooden letters to her suggest that he failed to win her to his new enthusiasms. Nor was he an easy companion.

5. Jane Morris holding May Morris, from a studio photograph, c. 1865

23

Despite his romantic ideals, Morris typically related to women just as to men in a matter-of-fact manner, often brusque: rarely with open affection, and never with charm. And at this time especially, no doubt in response to his own problems, he seemed socially awkward, almost unkempt, 'corpulent, very careless and unfinished in his dress', with a tendency not just to occasional eccentric rages, but to display a generally 'loud voice and nervous restless manner', and an inability to settle and relax. In the face of all this, Janey retreated into a self-defensive, enigmatic silence, brooding on her own beauty. In 1865 she was ill, possibly following a miscarriage; and since no other pregnancies followed, it is most probable that their sexual relationship then ceased. Thereafter she suffered from intermittent nervous pains and backache. Henry James found her a haunting figure, tall and lean in a long plain dress, with her mass of heaped crisp wavy black hair, her thin pale face and 'strange sad, deep, dark Swinburnian eyes', lying ill on a sofa, a 'dark silent mediaeval woman with her mediaeval toothache'.[37] But she was not only distant to strangers. Morris found himself quite unable to establish any deep relationship with her. Whether she failed to understand him or failed to like him, whether his needs had now changed, and what kind of love he really wanted, remain conjectures. Morris's growing despair is certain.

His feelings are particularly strongly expressed in some poetry of these years which was not published until after his death. There are the suggestive last lines of 'The Doomed Ship':

> Nor have we images of foul or fair
> To vex, save of thy kissed face of a bride,
> Thy scornful face of tears when I was tried,
> And failed neath pain I was not made to bear.[38]

Still more revealing is another poem, in which the woman speaks:

> A childish heart there loved me once, and lo
> I took his love and cast his love away.
>
> A childish greedy heart! yet still he clung
> So close to me that much he pleased my pride
> And soothed a sorrow that about me hung
> With glimpses of his love unsatisfied—
>
> And soothed my sorrow—but time soothed it too
> Though ever did its aching fill my heart
> To which the foolish child still closer drew
> Thinking in all I was to have a part.

But now my heart grown silent of its grief
Saw more than kindness in his hungry eyes:
But I must wear a mask of false belief
And feign I nought knew his miseries.

I wore a mask, because though certainly
I loved him not, yet there was something soft
And sweet to have him ever loving me:
Belike it is I well-nigh loved him oft—. . .

              I knew of love
But my love and not his; how could I tell
That such blind passion in him I should move?
Behold I have loved faithfully and well . . .[39]

Morris in time fought his way to acceptance of the situation:

One thing wanting ought not to go for so much: nor indeed does it spoil my
enjoyment of life always, as I have often told you [he wrote in 1872], to have real
friends and some sort of aim in life is so much, that I ought still to think myself
lucky: and often in my better moods I wonder what it is in me that throws me
into such rage and despair at other times.

As a couple they remained caring, Morris always writing fully to Janey
of his doings when he was away, and responding to her illnesses; while
he conversely found Janey's company was 'always pleasant and she is
very kind and good to me'.[40] By 1874 the better moods were less
frequently broken and he was close to equilibrium: 'I am ashamed of
myself for these strange waves of unreasonable passion: it seems so
unmanly: yet indeed I have a good deal to bear considering how hopeful
my earlier youth was, and what overwhelming ideas I had of the joys of
life.'[41]

    The difficulties of Morris's marriage were in origin internal. But they
were dramatically heightened in these years of crisis through the
intervention of Rossetti. After his wife Lizzie's suicide in 1862, Rossetti
rented a house in Cheyne Walk with Swinburne, devoting himself to
painting luxuriant sensuous women and collecting weird animals,
wombats and armadillos, for his large unkempt garden. He was now a
fat, bald little man who would walk 'with a peculiar lounging gait, often
trailing the point of his umbrella on the ground, but still obstinately
pushing on and making way, he humming the while with closed teeth
. . . Then suddenly he will fling himself down somewhere and refuse to
stir an inch further.'[42] He had his mistresses, as he probably had before
his marriage, but he clung with remorse to the memory of romantic
love. Perhaps nostalgia first drew him back to Janey, whom he had
himself found for Morris. In 1867 she agreed to sit again for Rossetti.

25

Within months he was writing her intense sonnets, she sending him clandestine letters. Janey's heart was moved and opened by his passionate flattery, while Rossetti fell unconcealably in love with her.

Rossetti's letters to Janey at the British Museum, which remained secret until 1964, show the full depth of his feeling. Rossetti writes with an ease and humour which was missing in Morris's letters to Janey, but with clearer frustration. There was now no need for secrecy.

The more he [Morris] loves you, the more he knows that you are too lovely and noble not to be loved: and, dear Janey, there are too few things that seem worth expressing as life goes on, for one friend to deny another the poor expression of what is most at his heart. But he is before me in granting this, and there is no need for me to say it. I can never tell you how much I am with you at all times. Absence from your sight is what I have long been used to; and no absence can ever make me so far from you again as your presence did for years. For this long inconceivable change, you know what my thanks must be.[43]

In 1870 he wrote that 'For the last two years I have felt distinctly the clearing away of the chilling numbness that surrounded you; but since then other obstacles have kept steadily on the increase, and it comes too late.' His passion and his need were clear enough. 'Now everything will be dark for me till I can see you again.'[44] 'I feel so badly the want of speaking to you. No one else seems alive to me now, and places that are empty of you are empty of all life.'[45] But the need could not be satisfied. Several years later he wrote of his 'deep regard for you—a feeling far deeper (though I know you never believed me) than I have entertained towards any other living creature at any time of my life. Would that circumstances had given me the power to prove this! For proved it *would* have been. And *now* you do not believe it.'[46]

The strain proved too much for both of them. Janey collapsed in 1869 and Morris took her for a month in the later summer for a spa cure at Bad Ems in Germany, where she bathed and drank, and he patiently took her for drives and boat outings. But she was still ill the following spring, and this time she spent a month almost alone with Rossetti in a Sussex cottage at Scalands, near Robertsbridge: a discrete, but 'most irregular arrangement'. She was escorted there and fetched back by Morris. Meanwhile Rossetti's own health had deteriorated rapidly after 1868. He could not sleep and became dependent on regular dosing with chloral. In the summer of 1871 he took a joint tenancy with Morris of the Manor House at Kelmscott on the upper Thames, where it was hoped that country air and the company of Janey would help them both. Morris was away for most of the time on his first journey to Iceland. Janey especially seems to have found a new contentment in that

6. Rossetti's 1864 watercolour, 'How Sir Galahad, Sir Bors and Sir Percival were fed with the Sanc Grael; but Sir Percival's sister died by the way', now in the Tate Gallery: suffused with Pre-Raphaelite passion, a return to one of his projected designs for the Oxford Union murals, the time when he first met Jane Morris

Kelmscott summer, partly through rediscovering her own country roots. But it resolved little for Rossetti. Subsequently he decided to break the relationship and then was plunged into bitter gloom. He was suffering from added remorse from having exhumed a bunch of poems thrown into Lizzie's grave, and was deeply shaken by a bitter attack on the sensualism of his work which was published in the *Contemporary Review* in October 1871. Finally in June 1872 he broke down completely with paranoid schizophrenia: hallucinating, hearing mocking voices, believing his friends were conspiring against him, and at least once attempting suicide. He could not be left alone. Later that summer, as he had got somewhat better, Janey looked after him at Kelmscott, helped by a male assistant. 'That Gabriel was *mad* was but too true, no one knows better than myself.'[47] After she left, he stayed on; but he never fully recovered. Morris had found his irregular, languid, moping, gloomy ways intolerable, and avoided Kelmscott when he was there, seeing little of him after 1870. Janey continued to correspond with him, and for the next four years she also visited him, supporting him after further collapses; but she found Rossetti now so depressing, that she then decided to break with him.

Janey's relationship with Rossetti has aroused a wealth of imaginative speculation in recent biographies. Much of this is both misleading and misguided. It reads twentieth-century sexual assumptions into a Victorian situation, and facts into the innuendoes of letters and imaginative verse. We know for certain that Rossetti and Janey loved each other, and that many times they slept under the same roof; no more. We forget how fearful, ashamed, and ill-informed Victorian women were of sex; the real risk of pregnancy; and how there were always servants too under the roof, listening—Janey kept a staff of three maids, a cook, and a boy in the later 1870s. We do not even know much of what she really felt for Rossetti. She deliberately ensured the destruction of many of their letters, including perhaps some of the most passionate. Her own few surviving letters to him, which have been given significantly less attention, are kind and sensible, with flashes of humour, but they show no reciprocated passion. Rossetti's own communications, his flamboyant neurosis and despair, his attempted suicide, strongly suggest an affair that was as unfulfilled as it was intense. And Janey herself, in a moment of rare intimacy with a later friend, was to confide that she had never quite given herself to him.

We are hardly likely ever to know the whole truth. But its importance can be—and in some biographies has been—exaggerated so far as to place Morris's whole life in a false focus. There were millions of cuckolds in Victorian England, and no doubt innumerable homo-sexuals, masochists, and pederasts too. But the significance of William Morris is not that he may have been a cuckold, any more than Gladstone owes his place in history to self-flagellation or Ruskin to loving small girls. What matters is how they overcame the problems and sufferings which in one form or another are common to most human beings, and what they gave through their lives to the wider society. In this sense the fuller understanding which we now possess of the years of crisis leaves Morris as a man enhanced rather than diminished.

Morris had not yet fully reached the views on marriage, sexuality, and the position of women which he was to express in his socialist years. Indeed, since he still maintained a typically Victorian reticence about such intimate matters, we can only infer most of his opinions from his actions. But there can be no doubt that he already shared the rejection, common to his social circle, of the tight-laced Victorian ideal lady. This rejection took many forms. It can be seen, for example, in their immediate and open social acceptance of George Eliot and George

Lewes when they set up together as an unmarried couple; in their efforts, when themselves married, to be tolerant towards unfaithfulness in women as well as men; even in the strange search of the minor Pre-Raphaelite poet, Arthur Munby, for the sexual 'realism' of rough-handed working-class women, which led him to become the sociological observer of the trousered Lancashire pit-head girls, and, secretly, the husband of a domestic servant. The Pre-Raphaelites believed intensely that love must be free of the barriers imposed by law, property and class. Morris had shown this by his very decision to marry a stablehand's daughter in the first place. His early poetry was rare too in its acceptance of women's passion and sexuality, and its powerful sense of the oppressive passivity which choked and constrained them. The same beliefs made the simple, loose gowns which the women of his circle commonly wore not just practical, but also symbolic, gestures towards freedom. And it was in just this spirit that Morris, confronted by crisis in his own life, chose to act.

How did he come through? Firstly, by showing a truly remarkable restraint and generosity. He completely ignored any contemplation of his 'rights' as an 'injured' Victorian husband: such questions at no point became an issue. On the contrary he helped, both with the Sussex cottage, and then through taking the Kelmscott tenancy, to give Rossetti and Janey the time which they needed together without him. To Janey, he showed a continued kindness and caring in his own way, which she returned, and this mutual acceptance was to lay the basis for their subsequent years together. He kept jealousy of Rossetti largely to himself. None of this was without immense strain, although he soon tried to avoid the pain of seeing them together, or even meeting Rossetti. On the house walls Rossetti's new portraits of Janey were being hung; and in humiliation he took down 'La Belle Iseult', his own early painting of her, and gave it away to Ford Madox Brown's son. The anguish comes through in an unpublished poem of these years:

> with hungry eyes
> I watch him as his feet the staircase mount
> Then face to face we sit, a wall of lies
> Made hard by fears and faint anxieties
> Is drawn between us . . .
> Then when they both are gone, I sit alone . . .
> And think how it would be if they were gone
> Not to return, or worse if the time bore
> Some seed of hatred in its fiery core . . . [48]

Here was a friendship turned to agony. Nevertheless, friendship was Morris's second defence. Pencilled in the margin of the manuscript of this poem now at the British Museum is a note—'we two are in the same box and need conceal nothing'. The poem itself is most probably addressed to Georgiana Burne-Jones, whose own marriage was at the same time also in crisis, due to Edward's involvement with a passionate (and also suicidal) Greek beauty, Mary Zambaco. Georgiana and Morris undoubtedly became closely dependent on each other for support, hovering on the brink of mutual love. It was through opening himself to her, and deepening his friendships with other women like Aglaia Coronio, that Morris was able to endure and transcend his difficulties. But equally important was a third response to the crisis: Morris's discovery of a new life-purpose in new interests. His poem *Love is Enough*, written in 1871–2, was an idealization of impersonal love in a strange haunting form, yet quite the reverse of the solution which he was to find himself. On a rare occasion in later life when the subject came up he snatched the volume down from the shelves and rapped it with a paperknife declaring, 'There's a lie for you, though 'twas I that told it! Love isn't enough in itself; love *and work*, yes! *work* and love, that's the life of a man!'[49]

The first new interest was in Iceland. Morris had long been aware of the sagas and had included romanticized versions of Nordic themes in several of his works. But it was not until he met Eirikr Magnusson in the autumn of 1868 that he came to see in the north a separate value of its own, differing from medieval feudal romanticism and chivalry. Magnusson was an Icelander, trained as a pastor, a year older than Morris, who had come to England in 1862 to supervise the printing of an Icelandic New Testament and through a chance meeting on the boat to England had begun a Norse dictionary and a series of translations of Icelandic legend. In 1871 he was to be given a post at Cambridge, where he proved a superb teacher. It is easy to see the appeal to Morris of this stocky fair-haired little man with a bushy moustache, who would pace up and down his room singing northern folk songs in a loud voice, conveying so directly his tremendous enthusiasm for the sagas. Magnusson was equally struck by Morris with his plain, rough appearance and keen eyes and surprisingly extensive information about Iceland. 'Altogether, what with his personal appearance, his peculiarly frank manner, his insatiable curiosity, exuberant hilarity and transparent serious-mindedness, I felt I had never come across a more attractive personality.'[50] He had no hesitation in agreeing to teach Morris.

Morris's method of learning was unusual, although it was close to the

7. Kelmscott Manor House, Oxfordshire, Morris's country home from 1871, at first shared with Rossetti

most advanced modern techniques. He refused to be bothered by grammar. 'You be my grammar as we translate. I want the literature, I must have the story. I mean to amuse myself.'[51] Impatient with waiting, Morris then tried translating before he understood. With his intuitive understanding he was remarkably successful. Together they went through the sagas, meeting some three times weekly for three-hourly sittings. Magnusson would then produce a literal translation, which Morris rewrote for publication. Their first published translation, Gunnlaug's Saga, two weeks' work, came out in the *Fortnightly Review* in January 1869. They went rapidly through the other sagas, Grettis Saga being published later in 1869, Volsunga Saga in 1870. This and other translations were published separately, and it was not until as late as 1890 that Magnusson was able to start a complete scheme in the Saga Library. Of this five volumes (of translations made in the 1870s) were published in Morris's lifetime.

Magnusson was also eager that Morris should write poetry of his own from some of the saga stories and he quickly overcame Morris's initial reluctance. In June 1869 he wrote 'The Lovers of Gudrun' as one of the stories for *The Earthly Paradise*. It is clearly a turning point in his writing, reintroducing some of the tense drama of *Guenevere*. Morris felt it the best of his tales; the rest were 'all too long and flabby, damn it!'[52] There was one other northern story in the final volume of *The Earthly Paradise*, 'The Fostering of Aslaug'. After that there was a pause, while he went to the other extreme of romanticism in his *Love is Enough* and his melancholy sweet translation of *The Aeneids of Virgil* published in 1875. Finally in the autumn of 1875 he started on *Sigurd the Volsung*, which was published a year later. Here his narrative mastery, the swaying rhythmic hypnotism which he had attempted in *Love is Enough* and the grim drama which he had learnt from the sagas, are blended in a poem of rare epic grandeur. *Sigurd* was Morris's poetic masterpiece. He regarded it as his most important poem himself. He wrote no other major poem after it, as if he realized that he could go no further. Yet it was received without enthusiasm by the critics and only some 2,500 copies were sold in twenty years. There can be little doubt that Morris's subsequent standing as a poet has suffered from neglect of *Sigurd the Volsung* in contrast to the contemporary popularity of *The Earthly Paradise*.

Iceland meant more to Morris than poetic inspiration. It helped him to find a new attitude to life. In the summer of 1871 with Magnusson and Faulkner he made a journey to Iceland of which the importance, as Mackail wrote, 'can hardly be overestimated'. They travelled with guides and packhorses, sleeping in tents and cooking their own food. Morris was exhilarated by the rough self-sufficient life. 'You've no idea what a good stew I can make, or how well I can fry bacon under difficulties,' he wrote to Janey.[53] He kept a journal of the trip which shows the deep impact of the northern scenery. Generally in writing of landscape Morris tended to generalize, leaving detail to the imagination, but his descriptions of this journey had unusually vivid realism. There are innumerable small touches, like a camp by the Axewater 'on a beautiful piece of mossy turf close to the water's edge, almost under the shadow of the Great Rift, whose wonderful cliff rose into the moonlit sky a few rods on the other side of the river, and was all populous with ravens that kept crying out and croaking long after we were settled there'; or the valley of the Markfleet, with its strange, high, overhanging cliffs:

They had caves in them just like the mouths in thirteenth-century illuminations; or great straight pillars were rent from them with quite flat tops of grass and a sheep or two feeding on it, however the devil they got there: two or three tail-ends of glacier too dribbled over them hereabouts, and we turned out of our way to go up to one: it seemed to fill up a kind of cleft in the rock wall, which indeed I suppose it had broken down; one could see its spiky white waves against the blue sky as we came up to it . . . We dismounted and scrambled about it: its great blocks cleft into dismal caves, half blocked up with the sand and dirt it had ground up, and dribbling wretched white streams into the plain below: a cold wind blew over it in the midst of the hot day . . . The great mountain-wall which closes up the valley with its jagged outlying teeth, was right before us: . . . often the wall would be cleft, and you would see a horrible winding street, with stupendous straight rocks for houses on either side: the bottom of the cleft quite level, but with a white glacier stream running out of it, and the whole blocked up at the end by the straight line of the master-mountain . . .

His first sight of Iceland from the sea was especially impressive, 'a terrible shore indeed: a great mass of dark grey mountains worked into pyramids and shelves, looking as if they had been built and half ruined; they were striped with snow high up, and wreaths of cloud dragged across them here and there, and above them were two peaks and a jagged ridge of pure white snow': on the east side of the firth was a 'regular Icelandic hillside: a great slip of black shale and sand, striped with the green of the pastures, that gradually sloped into a wide grass-grown flat between hill and sea, on which we could see the home-meads of several steads'.[54]

In this grim setting Morris found a people who still knew their ancient literature, friendly and tolerant, undivided by the acute social inequalities of Victorian Britain. 'I learnt one lesson there, thoroughly I hope, that the most grinding poverty is a trifling evil compared with the inequality of classes,' he wrote later.[55] More immediately important was the stoicism of these hard-worked people in bearing a life so much more difficult than his own, and the help which they found in the old stories. It made his own morbidity seem cowardly. He found a new strength in 'the religion of the Northmen', 'the worship of Courage'.[56] Morris remained an agnostic, as he had been for over a decade, but he had found a way out of the 'hopelessness and unsatisfied Paganism'[57] of *The Earthly Paradise*. 'Surely I have gained a great deal, and it was no idle whim that drew me there, but a true instinct for what I needed.'[58]

> Tale-teller, who 'twixt fire and snow
> Had heart to turn about and show
> With faint half-smile things great and small
> That in thy fearful land did fall,
> Thou and thy brethren sure did gain
> That thing for which I long in vain,
> That spell, whereby the mist of fear
> Was melted, and your ears might hear
> Earth's voices as they are indeed.
> Well ye have helped me at my need![59]

Morris revisited Iceland in 1873. Other travels, to Germany in 1869, Italy in the spring of 1873, and Belgium in 1874, made a slight impression. His crucial journeys in life were to northern France in 1854–5 and Iceland in 1871–3.

When Morris had completed *The Earthly Paradise* in 1870 he had felt 'rather lost at having done my book'.[60] He gave less time to writing in the following years, turning again to more work in the visual arts, throwing himself into the development of the firm. The 1870s were his great years of experiment in design and manufacture. From 1870 the manager became George Wardle, who had been employed by the firm as a bookkeeper and draughtsman since about 1866, and before that had been supplying drawings of paintings and patternwork from old East Anglian church roofs and screens. He remained manager until 1890. The stained-glass market was rapidly recaptured, helped by advertising and lower prices through re-using designs. More fundamentally, there was a sudden expansion in the secular decorative work carried out by the firm. Frederick Leach of Cambridge, who was Morris's favourite decorator, was carrying out two or three jobs a year for the firm between 1867 and 1870. In 1871 there were nine jobs, the next year fourteen, and by 1878 forty-eight. The cost of the work rose from an average of under £200 a year to over £2,000 in 1873 and reached £4,500 in 1878. The key was in the much wider range of products which the firm could now offer. To its own furniture and wallpapers Morris now added reissues of older patterns by established printers, fine imported eastern carpets, and before long, new lines of his own. He designed patterns for machine-made carpets produced by outside firms and in 1873 he began again with wallpapers. In the same year he made his first experimental design for printed textiles, again made by an outside firm, but without success. And the designs themselves, as if reflecting his recovered personal purpose in life, reach forward to a new sense of integration and growth. His patterns designed between 1873 and 1876 are outstandingly attractive, combining a masterly organization with the fresh naturalism of his earliest wallpapers. His fascination for green intertwining levels can also be seen in the illuminated books which he wrote at this time, in the beautiful book cover of 1873 for *Love is Enough*, and in the backgrounds to stained glass from about 1874.

The expansion of the firm brought about an internal crisis. Legally each of the original partners had an equal claim to its assets and profits, although Morris had for several years given far more time to it than any of the others. Burne-Jones continued to supply a large number of stained-glass cartoons. Madox Brown and Webb supplied a few others.

There was less demand for new furniture designs, and with Morris's revived activity in pattern designing his part in the work became even more dominant. At the same time he now relied on the firm to provide his principal income. He therefore asked for a reconstitution of the firm under his sole control. Not surprisingly this produced a bitter dispute with those partners who were unwilling to surrender their speculative profits, Madox Brown, Rossetti, and Marshall. The firm was reconstituted as he wished in 1875, becoming Morris and Company, but he was extremely angry at the difficulty. He finally broke his friendship with Rossetti and was only reconciled to Brown many years later.

Difficulty in obtaining the clear unfading colours which he wanted for his designs led Morris to a close investigation of dyes, at first in the vat at Queen Square and then between 1875 and 1877 at Leek in Staffordshire, where George Wardle's brother Thomas was willing to help with experiments in his works. He was especially excited by these experiments, 'working in sabots and blouse in the dye house myself— you know I like that'.[61] At home he would try new dyes by picking up twigs and boiling them. For two years the post regularly included parcels of experimental dyed pieces from Leek, which he would criticize for colour and scrub and expose to the light to see if they were fast. Once he was confident of the colours, Morris began to design printed textiles rapidly. Three chintzes were designed before 1876, twenty-two more by 1883. They were printed by Thomas Wardle at Leek. At the same time he tried his first woven textile, a silk and linen tissue, manufactured commercially by power loom.

Having explored the technique of dyeing, he now became interested in weaving, and in 1877 a French worker from Lyons was brought over to set up a Jacquard loom in Queen Square. His first designs for heavy handwoven woollens, with archaic birds and dragons inspired by medieval Italian cloths, were handwoven on this loom, but because of lack of space the work remained experimental. Several of the fine woollens and silks which Morris designed in the next few years were woven by other firms on power looms. Morris began experimental carpet weaving in 1878 and tapestries in the next year. At the same time the new coloured silks had given him a revived interest in embroidery design. By the end of the 1870s there were thus a whole series of new techniques mastered, but insufficient space to exploit them in Queen Square, in spite of the fact that Morris had himself moved out to a house at Turnham Green in 1872 and separate sale- and show-rooms set up in Oxford Street in 1877. Morris considered in 1878 moving the firm's works to Blockley in Gloucestershire, and several other more spacious sites were considered before a group of black weatherboard mill buildings were found on the Wandle at Merton Abbey in Surrey. The firm moved there in 1881, at once expanding the production of carpets, woven silks, and woollens. Chintz printing began in 1883. The stained glass, for which there were rather fewer orders in this period, and a small number of tapestries were also produced at Merton. Furniture making was moved to a workshop in Pimlico in 1890. All wallpapers as well as a considerable number of textiles continued to be made by outside firms.

The firm was by now internationally renowned. Its first agent in New York was appointed in 1878, and others followed in Paris, Frankfurt, and Berlin. By the early 1880s Morris was drawing £1,800 a year from the firm, and £4,200 ten years later. But the move to Merton, partly because it was less accessible and partly because of new interests, marked the end of Morris's most active participation in the firm. He continued to design patterns, especially wallpapers, and to visit the works perhaps twice a week, but the business was managed by Wardle, and new designs came increasingly from other hands. May Morris took over the embroidery section in 1885, developing her own vigorous style, while in textiles and stained glass an increasing role in designing was played by John Henry Dearle, who had been taken on as a young show-room assistant in 1878, and was much later to become the firm's art director. Dearle's work was uneven, and much of the stained glass produced in later years is very mediocre, but his best chintz, carpet, and embroidery designs are outstanding. Some indeed have been thought until very recently to be by Morris himself. It is a confusion which vindicates both the standards which he set, and his belief in the creative potential of ordinary working people.

Morris is often portrayed as an unrealistic artist whose firm produced expensive pieces of hand-craftsmanship. It is certainly true that the firm's prices were high (although their products were long-lasting) and Morris was particularly interested in rarities such as tapestries which were individually produced by hand. This was, however, only one aspect of his business. Most of the firm's work after its early years was produced by serial methods rather than individual craftsmanship and machinery took a large part in most processes. In any case more of Morris's designs were produced by outside manufacturers than by the firm itself. In fact the success of the firm had a double basis. Firstly, Morris had created a new type of interior design enterprise, offering a complete range of products unified by style: a concept now familiar from successors like Liberty or Habitat. Secondly, though offering a price range, the firm above all competed through its professional standards. 'You cannot argue from what other businesses do in these matters, because ours is quite a special business,' Morris told Thomas Wardle: 'what I want you to understand is this, that my position depends entirely on my keeping up the excellence of my goods.'[62] This maintenance of quality set the tone throughout. In the Oxford Street showroom Morris would personally advise clients; while in the workshops the pride of his artisans was carefully fostered through impeccable dress standards—striped black trousers and starched collars —as well as above average pay rates. At the same time Morris remained closely aware of price margins. The shrewd business sense with which he negotiated contracts is well seen in his long correspondence with Thomas Wardle. 'As to the price per yard named by you the only thing *we* have to consider is the possibility of our selling the cloths at a profit.' 'I must say though, that I hope at the six months' end you will find it possible to reduce the prices considerably: if not I can't help seeing that the sale is likely to be very limited. The prices are more than double Clarkson's . . . '[63] He could evaluate the selling price of a pattern: 'the extra sixpence per yard falls heavily on a four colour print that doesn't *look* handsomer than the tulip . . . '[64] In the same way, when acting as a salesman for the superb embroideries executed to his designs by Catherine Holiday, he kept the price down, reminding her, 'you know my difficulty . . . with the stingy public', and tried to get her to produce smaller 'more saleable' work.[65] In 1871 Morris had become a director of the Devon copper company which had made his father's fortune. By the time he resigned his directorship in 1876, sitting on his top hat, Morris thoroughly understood the economics of capitalism. It was because he knew what profit meant, and not because he was an unworldly artist, that Morris became a socialist.

When G. F. Watts painted Morris in 1870 he had been a romantic figure, a sensitive face framed in waving dark hair and beard, his eyes vague and distant. The portrait is of course a deliberate exaggeration, and half the look in the eyes came from 'a devil of a cold-in-the-head, which don't make it very suitable'.[66] In those tense years his temper and restlessness were at their most acute. He would never sit still at meals, would pace up and down the room like a caged beast, twist a fork with his teeth or break a chairback or throw a medieval folio at a workman in a moment of anger. Later his outbursts became less dangerous and his restlessness was channelled into his extraordinarily diverse creative activity. It was in the 1870s that the familiar Morris of tradition began to emerge, the jolly figure in an untidy blue suit and old felt hat with a ruddy face and rolling gait who was once mistaken by a passing seaman for the 'captain of the *Sea Swallow*'. In these years frequent hard manual work gave him sound sleep. Dirty with dye, he looked like a rough worker, so much that he was once refused admission by Faulkner's maid. As a pleasant contrast to this London activity he was able, once Rossetti had disappeared and his publisher Ellis had become a co-tenant, to have a relaxing day out of London fishing in the Thames at Kelmscott. 'Please tell Mary to have a many worms ready for me: proper brandlings I must have: they are striped and don't smell nice— that is their sign . . . Don't forget the *worms*.'[67]

Kelmscott came to mean more and more to Morris. The house stood among tall elms and old stone farm barns, unpretentious, wide-gabled with lead gutters spouting out like gargoyles, dark mossy grey stone roofs, creamy roughly plastered rubble walls, and only a small garden with big yew trees. It was built about 1600 in a conservative vernacular style with mullioned windows and a slightly more ambitious east wing was added later in the century with pedimented window surrounds under the gables. Except for the first floor room in this wing, which is lined with a faded blue and brown tapestry of Samson, the rooms are small and low. They are now furnished with Morris hangings, paintings by Rossetti, old chests and chairs and furniture by Webb, but much of this came to Kelmscott after Morris's death; and in the 1960s, the house was thoroughly reconstructed, heated, papered, scraped and refloored. In Morris's own time it was emptier, and very much rougher. One fastidious young lady visitor who called in 1896 found it 'so artistic and grubby' that she dared not accept tea. The only important improvement Morris made was to lay down the plain flagstone floors, in 1895–6. His four-poster bed was in a passage room in the wing, next to the tapestry room. It was the simplicity of Kelmscott which made it 'a house that I love; with a reasonable love I think'.[68]

Behind the screen of tall elms the Thames twisted through open meadows, with ditches lined by willows and low hills beyond. The creek, now cut off, had a boat-house. On the other side of the house is the village, a group of stone cottages and an attractive patchwork medieval church. There are several other fine churches nearby; soft Romanesque and clear early Gothic at Langford, with outside its porch a twisted late Gothic crucifixion and a superb Saxon Christ with long absolutely horizontal arms, big cuffs and robes hanging straight and severe; Fairford with its magnificent late medieval Flemish glass; early Gothic and box pews at Inglesham; other little-restored churches at Longworth and Little Faringdon, and fine spires at Lechlade, Broad-

8. Morris's own bed at Kelmscott, with hangings designed by May Morris c.1893. Lily Yeats was among the embroiderers.

well, and Bampton; and as well as all this, the great stone Gothic barn at Great Coxwell. The villages were still almost all stone-walled and stone-roofed, although tiles and even occasional corrugated iron were creeping in and Morris felt this bitterly, as a kind of terrible disease. He cared equally strongly about the felling of trees and pollarding of willows. At Kelmscott he lived with the seasons, the rooks and owls, herons and moorhens, spring snowdrops, May apple-blossom and buttercups, summer willowherb and purple housemint, October roses and wild scarlet hips, listing them like a psalmist in his letters, taking them for his patterns.

But Kelmscott was a refuge rather than a home. 'I rather want to be in London again for I feel as if my time were passing with too little done in the country: altogether I fear I am a London bird; its soot has been rubbed into me, and even these autumn mornings can't wash me clean of restlessness.'[69] In London he could see more of friends. The Faulkners lived in Queen Square, close to the firm; Burne-Jones had moved to The Grange, a rambling house in North End Road, Fulham, in 1867, and by the 1870s Morris was regularly spending Sunday morning there. Morris himself had moved to Horrington House, Turnham Green, in 1872.

Here something of the old Oxford atmosphere was kept up, Morris declaiming his poetry in the evenings, regularly provoked by practical jokes, and answering with his Dickensian quips and mimicry.

Early in 1878 Morris took his final London home, a plain brick eighteenth-century house which stands in Hammersmith Upper Mall, facing the great bend of the river. It was renamed Kelmscott House. There was enough room to start carpets in a workshop and a tapestry loom in a bedroom until the firm itself had workshops at Merton. Behind the house was a long garden with a soil, according to Morris, mostly composed of old shoes and soot. The principal room was the drawing-room upstairs, lined with the new 'Bird' woven woollen hangings, a Morris machine-woven carpet on the floor, a plain eighteenth-century fireplace with old plates on the mantelshelves and the big Red House settle on one side, and other Webb and Morris chairs, tables and the bright Chaucer wardrobe around it: rich and warm but not overfurnished, giving to the visitor 'a delightful sense of garden-like freshness'.[70] The smaller dining room was papered with the gay wild tulip, more plates were displayed on white shelves, and at one end a huge magnificient Persian carpet was hung like a canopy from the ceiling, with an old chest and Rossetti's brass peacocks below. Morris's study showed his own plain tastes, without curtains or carpet, the walls lined with shelves of massive vellum books, and a fine plain table by Webb with splayed turned legs on which were manuscripts and books, designs, tobacco, ink, and quills. Here he could enjoy the wind and rain, 'the real world bursting into London', and think of the air in the other Kelmscott up the river, clean of 'that sense of dirty discomfort which one is never quite quit of in London'.[71]

When Morris had decided against the Church it had been partly because of the influence of his socially conscious friends. But he had not foreseen any public role for himself. 'I can't enter into politico-social subjects with any interest, for on the whole I see that things are in a muddle, and I have no power or vocation to set them right in ever so little a degree,' he wrote in 1855.[72] For years he remained a passive Liberal. He took less interest than many of his friends either in the later socialist writing of Ruskin or in the Paris Commune of 1870. But by the 1870s, whether he liked it or not, Morris had become a public figure, a popular poet and a fashionable decorator. There were occasional signs that he was unhappy with his position, uneasy that his decorating should be entirely 'ministering to the swinish luxury of the rich'.[73] In a letter of 1874 to Mrs Louisa Baldwin, Georgiana Burne-Jones's sister, he complained:

It seems to be nobody's business to try to better things—isn't mine you see in spite of all my grumbling—but look, suppose people lived in little communities among gardens and green fields, so that you could be in the country in five minutes' walk, and had few wants, almost no furniture for instance, and no servants, and studied the (difficult) arts of enjoying life, and finding out what they really wanted: then I think that one might hope civilization had really begun.[74]

Two years later he was provoked into action, stirred up by Gladstone's righteous indignation against the Conservative government's support of the tyrannical Turkish government. He broke his silence with a thundering letter to the *Daily News* of 26 October 1876:

I whom am writing this am one of a large class of men—quiet men, who usually go about their own business, heeding public matters less than they ought, and afraid to speak in such a huge concourse as the English nation however much they may feel, but who are now stung into bitterness by finding how helpless they are . . . Not even this wretched packed Parliament we have got is sitting. The cry for that was not believed; the members are too busy shooting in the country, and half the nation is dumb, if it were not for the 2000 working men who met last Sunday at Clerkenwell . . . I appeal to the working men, and pray them to look to it, that if this shame falls upon them they will certainly remember it and be burdened by it when their day clears for them, and they attain all, and more than all, they are now striving for . . .

Characteristically, having taken this stand Morris threw himself whole-heartedly into the agitation and became treasurer of the Eastern Question Association, organizing meetings, in May 1877 issuing his appeal *To the Working Men of England* with its prophetic understanding of political class conflict and reliance on the working class, in December making his first impromptu public speech and early in 1878 contributing his first political verse, 'Wake, London Lads!' Although the threat of a pro-Turkish war never materialized, the whole experience was a profound lesson to Morris. His 'shame and anger' at the vacillation of the professional Liberal politicians and the collapse of the Eastern Question Association early in 1878 completely confirmed his initial feeling that a political democrat could hope for nothing except from the working classes. He spent the next five years in spasmodic attempts to develop independent working class radicalism, until he saw a new hope in the socialist movement.

The strain and excitement of this first political venture was testing to a physique already undermined by periodic rheumatic gout, and when he went on holiday to Italy in April 1878 he was crippled by a particularly severe attack. With this vulnerability to disabling pain, his physical strength was never quite the same after this, although until his last years he continued to work extraordinarily hard, waking early in the morning to work at tapestry before breakfast, speaking, writing, designing with irrepressible energy. Moreover, at the same time as the Eastern Question agitation, he had started another public campaign. The provocation this time was the scheme by Gilbert Scott to restore Tewkesbury Abbey in March 1877. He wrote to the *Athenæum*, which had for years attacked drastic restoration work by Scott and other architects, suggesting an association of laymen 'to keep a watch on old monuments, to protest against all "restoration" that means more than keeping out wind and weather, and, by all means, literary and other, to awaken a feeling that our ancient buildings are not mere ecclesiastical toys, but sacred monuments of the nation's growth and hope'.[75] Once again he had grasped from the start that the professionals, clergy and architects, were too involved in the prestige and financial reward of drastic restoration to be relied upon. Within a month the Society for Protecting Ancient Buildings, 'anti-scrape', was formed. Morris remained the dominant member of its committee for his life, although a distinguished body of supporters was soon gathered. During the next few years he often acted as a visitor for the society, advising on restoration schemes, frequently in vain, retiring defeated to the village pub and shaking his fists as the parson passed by, spluttering in fury, 'Beasts! Pigs! Damn their souls!'[76]

Through S.P.A.B. Morris gathered round himself a group of younger men, including W. R. Lethaby and Sydney Cockerell, who were to carry his theories of craftsmanship into the twentieth century. After case meetings the committee would retire to a jovial supper at Gatti's restaurant in the Strand. To raise funds and spread the cause Morris began public lecturing on art, architecture, and design, and so became the public leader of the arts and crafts movement. Lectures, at first on the arts and then on politics, were his most important writing in the next decade. He found the writing difficult; 'I know what I want to say, but the cursed words go to water between my fingers.'[77] Nor was he ever a very popular lecturer, reciting what he had written in the same swaying chant as his verse. Yet the very difficulty in writing, the grit of the text and the penetration of the argument, gives Morris's lectures a special and lasting power. It is a pity that many of his lectures were kept unpublished for decades and most are even now not widely available. He published two small collections in his lifetime, *Hopes and Fears for Art* in 1882 and *Signs of Change* in 1888. Two or three single lectures were published as political pamphlets, but there was no cheap selection until after 1930 and there is still no good selection. On the shelves of second-hand bookshops there are plenty of cheap popular editions of Ruskin but never of Morris's prose.

The lectures, both on art and social history, drew out Morris's historical scholarship. Morris always had a scorn for footnotes and kept his evidence in his head, but the shrewdness of his history is impressive even where it has been overtaken by later discoveries. His analysis of the sources of Byzantine ornament and the interaction of east and west is especially striking. At this time Morris was drawing more frequently on historical examples in his pattern designing and his investigation of carpets and tapestries involved considerable research. There is evidence that his growing knowledge somewhat cramped his style of design in textiles and wallpapers for some years. In the same period he made a close friend in John Henry Middleton, an eminent orientalist and archaeologist who became curator of the Fitzwilliam Museum, Cambridge. In 1877 he began regularly examining textiles as an adviser to the South Kensington Museum. He was also a recognized authority on manuscripts and gave opinions for the Bodleian Library, Oxford. He would run through a pile with extraordinary speed, quickly attributing each book to a monastery and date, apparently with respected accuracy.

To an advanced radical like Morris the Liberal government elected in the 1880 general election failed to bring any satisfaction. Imperial wars and coercion in Ireland continued while reforms at home were minimal. By 1882 he had become very depressed. He had almost stopped speaking. 'I am older, and the year is evil; the summerless season, and famine and war, and the folly of peoples come back again, as it were, and the more and more obvious death of art before it rises again, are heavy matters to a small creature like me.'[78] He had put his hope on the one hand in political radicalism, and on the other in educating the working classes to a feeling for art. Radicalism seemed powerless, while working men took little interest in his lectures, except for his own men from Queen Square, and the bulk of his audiences consisted of his clients. As he sat at home thinking,

with all the aids to a pleasant life around me which mere chance as it seems has given me, and I hear outside brutal and drunken voices, murdering with obscene language and coarse tones the pleasure of the fair spring Sunday, there rises up in me the brutality of my own heart and would stir me into fury against that other brutality if I did not remember that these also are my fellows, merely unluckier than I: not worse.[79]

He was hesitating before socialism, reading Henry George and John Stuart Mill's posthumous papers. At the back of his mind was one recurrent thought, which had come originally from Ruskin:

I could never forget that in spite of all drawbacks my work is little else than pleasure to me; that under no conceivable circumstances would I give it up even if I could. Over and over again I have asked myself why should not my lot be the common lot . . . I have been ashamed when I have thought of the contrast between my happy working hours and the unpraised, unrewarded, monotonous drudgery which most men are condemned to. Nothing shall convince me that such labour as this is good or necessary to civilization.[80]

Finally Mill convinced him, for he came to the conclusion that Mill had given his verdict against the evidence. In January 1883 he joined the Democratic Federation, the only socialist body in the country.

When he joined the socialist movement Morris was prepared to give his whole self to the hope of change in his lifetime.

By union I mean a very serious matter: I mean sacrifice to the Cause of leisure, pleasure and money each according to his means: I mean sacrifice of individual whims and vanity, of individual misgivings, even though they may be founded on reason, as to the means which the organizing body may be forced to use.

It was the 'plain duty' of any socialist to read, to teach and to join 'any body' which was honestly striving for 'Constructive Revolution'.[81] Morris certainly sacrificed much in the cause. He found the formerly friendly press now hostile, complaining that 'he was born to be a dreamer of beautiful dreams, and not a politician, and his voice lost its flute-like notes when he descended into the market-place to bandy paradoxes with the political charlatans of a materialistic age'.[82] Former friends became cool: 'as a socialist I stink in people's nostrils, and I hope by this time most people know what the socialists think of the Khartoum stealers and spreaders of the blessings of shoddy civilization.'[83] He sold his library to raise funds for socialist propaganda; and it may well have been his outdoor speaking that precipitated the breakdown of his health after 1890.

Morris at once set about reading Marx, in French, and Robert Owen, and thoroughly absorbed both, fusing their theories with those gathered earlier from Ruskin. Morris put forward his new view of society in his socialist lectures, in contributions to *Justice*, the socialist weekly, which he also helped with money, and at the socialist open-air meetings, which started in the summer of 1884, again with his help. His creative historical fusion of Marx and Ruskin, his understanding of Marxist economics and the class struggle theory of revolution, and his integration of Ruskin and Owen into a highly significant vision of the future, are set out in full—with a more detailed criticism of his political work—in the chapters at the end of this book.

In these early months socialist ideas seemed to be spreading rapidly, and in November 1884, Morris was predicting an early revolution. 'In all probability England will go first—will give the signal, though she is at present so backward: Germany with her 700,000 socialists is pretty nearly ready . . .'[84] This optimism was shortlived. He quickly became dissatisfied with the essentially Tory-minded leader of the (now) Social Democratic Federation, H. M. Hyndman. Constant quarrelling led to a split and at the end of 1884 Morris, probably unwisely and certainly precipitately, led a majority of the executive to secede and form a separate body, the Socialist League.

During the next five years Morris was travelling the country speaking for the League, indoor and outdoor; writing for its paper *Commonweal*; attending its executive; leading its Hammersmith branch; and marching and speaking in its demonstrations. He kept a diary in 1887, a record of the hard work for small rewards; the audiences in radical clubs who would 'listen respectfully to Socialism, but are perfectly supine and not in the least inclined to move except on the lines of radicalism and trades unionism'; the typical mixed audience of a Sunday street meeting, 'from labourers on their Sunday lounge to "respectable" people coming from Church: the latter inclined to grin: the working men listening attentively trying to understand, but mostly failing to do so: a fair cheer when I ended . . .'[85]

The diary also records the 'usual silly squabbles about nothing' at the League executive. Eventually these were to break the Socialist League: for 1887, when its membership reached about a thousand, was its peak. Morris, suspicious of the corrupting and compromising effects of parliamentary tactics, held the League to a purely educational approach, and lost the support of the able group led by Marx's daughter Eleanor and her husband Edward Aveling. After they left the League in 1888 Morris found himself thrown into the hands of anarchist socialists, and the League went completely out of his control in 1889, disintegrating rapidly. He finally withdrew his support from *Commonweal* in 1890, and the Hammersmith branch was reformed as the independent Hammersmith Socialist Society. It continued to meet in the former coach house of Kelmscott House until Morris's death.

The Socialist League disappeared rapidly after 1890, but it left its mark. It was from its stronghold in west Yorkshire, where an alternative socialist tradition to that of the Social Democratic Federation had been built up, that the Independent Labour Party was to rise in 1892. Nor in any case had Morris's political work been a wasted effort; for the example of a man of his eminence willing to spend his time in the hard dull work of propaganda was an outstanding inspiration to the English socialist movement.

Already before 1890 Morris's hope of an early revolution had faded; the effectiveness of police violence in the struggles for the right to hold outdoor street meetings, the influence of a hostile press, the slow response of the working class and the obstruction of their older leaders, convinced him that change could not come quickly. But he never ceased to hope for a revolution, a fundamental social change, whether it was achieved peaceably through the vote or after a period of violence; nor was he frightened by the realization that socialism would probably begin with 'excesses of utilitarianism' as unpleasant as some of the manifestations of capitalism—perhaps even 'cutting down all the timber in England, and turning the country into a big Bonanza farm or a market garden under glass'.[86] He remained confident that the ultimate future would be worth the pains of transition.

Morris did not give up politics after 1890, although the disappearance of the League and his own declining health greatly reduced his activity. One of the best descriptions of him speaking is of an outdoor meeting in Salford in 1895, only a few months before his health finally broke.

He was speaking from a lorry pitched on a piece of land close to the Ship Canal, his entire surroundings probably distasteful to him. It was a wild March Sunday morning, and he would not have been asked to speak out of doors, but he expressed a desire to do so; and so there he was, talking with quiet strenuousness, drawing a laugh now and then by some piece of waggish wisdom from the undulating crowd, of working men mostly, who stood in the hollow and on the slopes before him. There would be quite two thousand of them. He wore a blue overcoat, but had laid aside his hat; and his grizzled hair blew in wisps and tumbles about his face. As he stood there squarely upright, his sturdy figure clothed in blue, even to the light-blue shirt with turndown collar, and swaying slightly from side to side as he hammered out his points, he looked a man and a gentleman every inch of him.[87]

This was William Morris as the socialists remembered him, and probably as he would have himself wished to be best remembered. Yet politics dominated his activity only for a relatively short period in the mid-1880s. Even then the work of the firm went on. One of the most frequent criticisms of Morris after his conversion to socialism was that it was hypocritical for a businessman to preach a message which he did not practise. Why did he not renounce his own capital, pay himself a weekly wage and share the firm's income with his workmen? Morris had in fact considered a complete scheme of profit-sharing before he became a socialist. Wardle recalled that 'he got the story of Leclaire's experiment and we discussed it. The plan was clearly no solution to the question which was occupying Morris but he adopted so much of it as to give some half-dozen of us a direct interest in the business.'[88] Morris calculated that in 1884 his own income from the firm was £1,800, while Wardle received £1,200 and four others about £500 each. Two of the foremen were also given bonuses. The rest, except for two or three 'lame dogs', were paid by piecework, rather above the trade rates. If he paid himself a foreman's wage he could distribute £1,600 a year to the other workmen, £16 a year each. But the utmost this income could do would be to help 'a few individuals more creep out of their class into the middle class'.[89] True co-operation could never be organized within capitalism; and the gesture itself would cripple the support which he now gave to the socialist cause. Nor was it just to impose the resulting hardship on his family to ease his own conscience. He contented himself with running the factory as well as was possible in a capitalist world, paying generous wages and making the setting of the work pleasant, surrounded by gardens, with an excellent circulating library in the factory. There is no sign that his reputation as an employer ever reduced his standing with the socialists.

Morris returned to poetry after a long gap with a translation of *The Odyssey of Homer* in 1886–7. It was the beginning of the final romantic stage of his writing. In 1886–7 he wrote *The Dream of John Ball* and in 1890 *News from Nowhere*, both visionary dreams with a strong social message. His last long prose romances of the 1890s, *The House of the Wolfings*, *The Roots of the Mountains*, *The Story of the Glittering Plain*, *The Waters of the Wondrous Isles* and *The Well at the World's End*, charming at their best but much less compelling reading, were written principally for pleasure; but they too explore alternative social worlds. Morris had by then ceased to care for the opinions of reviewers, who were exasperated by the strange quasi-archaic vocabulary of the romances.

In the visual arts, on the other hand, his last years especially were rich in achievement. Several of his finest textile and paper patterns date from the 1890s. His direct participation in production, which had already greatly lessened after 1881, was again reduced in 1890 when Wardle retired and the Oxford Street Showroom managers Frank and Robert Smith became partners and managers of the firm. At the same time, however, he began a new enterprise, the Kelmscott Press. His interest in printing went back to the 1860s, when he had dreamed of sumptuous editions of *The Earthly Paradise* and *Love is Enough* illustrated by Burne-Jones, but the immediate stimulus came from a Hammersmith friend and neighbour, Emery Walker. Morris designed the Golden type, a heavy adaptation of Renaissance Italian print, in 1890, and the bold clear Gothic Troy type in 1891. Printing began in December 1890 in a cottage workshop close to his Hammersmith house. Choosing ink and paper, preparing texts, designing borders and initial letters, demanded constant activity in the next five years. The Kelmscott Press books have been perhaps overrated, since they are not as readable as Morris claimed them to be, their technique was archaic, and the realization of the modern book was to come from other designers. But by any account they are a magnificent final gesture.

The strenuous activity of the 1880s, and especially outdoor speaking in wind and rain, weakened Morris, and in 1891 he was again severely attacked by rheumatic gout. Its origins, as with the development of his diabetic tendency, must have been dietary. But this time he was told by his doctor that 'hence-forth he must consider himself an invalid to the extent of husbanding his strength and living under a very careful regimen'.[90] Yet despite new as well as old difficulties, these last years were among his most contented. He indulged himself by collecting expensive manuscripts. From 1892 he had the help first in his library and then as secretary, of a young admirer, Sydney Cockerell, who had escaped from a career in the family coal business, and was later to become the great reforming Director of the Fitzwilliam Museum. Socialism had alienated some of his more respectable acquaintances, but brought him many new friends from the movement. If Janey did not follow him into active socialism, she kept a keen and radical interest in politics, and at this time made a friendship with Jane Cobden, women's suffragist and Progressive London County Councillor. In good company Janey's brooding silence could give way to her 'delicious chuckling laugh', and she remained a 'notable housekeeper'. She could enjoy a quiet moment with Morris too. Cockerell surprised them late one night in the drawing room, Janey on the sofa 'in a glorious blue gown', playing together 'at draughts with large ivory pieces, red and white'. To the young Bernard Shaw, Morris seemed part of a close circle of women friends and family. He read no discord in Janey's silence; and Morris's affection for Jenny was transparent. 'He could not sit in the same room without his arm round her waist. His voice changed when he spoke to her as it changed to no one else. His wife was beautiful, and knew that to be so was part of her household business. His was to do all the talking. Their harmony seemed to me to be perfect.'[91] This was the Morris whom Yeats remembered as 'The Happiest of Poets'.

It was even so a deceptive harmony, won against the odds. Janey and Morris were partly drawn closer by the challenges they faced as parents. The girls were brought up with a relatively open choice between masculine and feminine models. They were sent to Notting Hill High School, a pioneering girls' day school, and May went on to the South

Kensington School of Design. Morris not only taught them to embroider, but would take them fishing and to the theatre, and when away sent them dyestuffs to do their own experiments. His frequent letters to them show him both concerned at their doings and keen to involve them in his own. But his hopes were struck a bitter blow in 1876 when Jenny, 'who had been his pride as a child for her intellectual faculties', developed epilepsy. The condition was then untreatable and misunderstood. Morris wrongly suspected that she had inherited it through himself; while Jenny was treated as mentally impaired, although her mind was not at first affected, and even later principally altered through depression. It was thus left to May to become her father's principal successor: active socialist, professional embroideress, leader of women's arts and crafts, editor of Morris's collected writings, and guardian of Kelmscott. But Morris became increasingly affectionate and protective towards Jenny, enjoying convalescent walks with her, and insisting she should not be sent away to a home. Her attacks were fortunately infrequent, and for the moment she recovered well, so that there were many good times together ahead: musical evenings when Jenny on the mandolin and May on the guitar played duets, for instance, or much more ambitiously, great summer holiday boat journeys up the Thames, right from London to Kelmscott, loaded with friends, with Morris as cook. Nevertheless, if Jenny's seizures were only occasional, they were absolutely unpredictable, and when they came, devastating to the whole family: a constant anxiety hovering in the background. They were the context for Janey's new friendship, with Wilfrid Scawen Blunt. Her letters to him are lively and expressive of feeling, recounting details of her reading and travels, and political news; but they constantly return to Jenny's illness, to being 'angry' at its incomprehensibility, and to her attacks as 'almost a death-blow to me'.[92]

Janey and Blunt's relationship was surprising, and its true nature remained a closely guarded secret until the publication of his biography in 1979. Morris was alert to it, but how much he knew is unclear. Blunt was hardly a worthy successor to Rossetti: a wealthy political maverick, backer of Irish and Arab nationalism, vain and self-important, whose chief hobby was clandestine seduction and adultery. He was a shallow flatterer; but he was a charmer, and a poet too. They met in 1883, a year after Rossetti's death. A year later Janey went to visit him; then he began to woo her with love poems, and she briefly helped him with political lobbying; and in October 1888 he came for the first time to visit her at Kelmscott. He found her at night. 'Mrs Morris slept alone at the end of a short passage at the head of the staircase to the right. All was uncarpeted

9. Wilfrid Scawen Blunt on Shieha

with floors that creaked', and he had to tiptoe past Morris's room with its great four-poster bed: but 'to me such midnight perils have always been attractive'. Janey was emotionally needy, and, now past the menopause, physically less fearful. For her, their brief sexual relationship was intoxicating. Months later she wrote after another visit, 'my soul is in too great a turmoil, whether it will ever calm down again Heaven only knows'; and ten days on, 'I move about in a sort of dream, as if a spell had been cast over me and the whole place. Are you sure you have brought no magic arts from Egypt, and have employed them against a defenceless woman?' But by 1890 their sexual liaison was over, but for one last time in August 1892 when Blunt came to Kelmscott in Morris's absence. 'We slept together, Mrs Morris and I, and she told me things about the past which explain much in regard to Rossetti. "I never quite gave myself", she said, "as I do now".' But what had it meant to her? She gave herself physically, and she told him some of her closest secrets. Yet again, she contrived to hold back. Blunt sensed this. 'She is so silent a woman that except through the physical senses we never could have become intimate.'[93] They never even reached first names; while it had always been Janey and Gabriel. They were lovers; but by no means in the same sense in love.

To some of those who knew Morris only at this time his apparent contentment seemed to be due to a lack of need for fundamental friendship, an absorption in work at the expense of any other feeling. It is true that suffering had hardened Morris and changed his relationship with Janey from lover to companion. Nor did he look for intimacy from many of the new friends who clustered round him in his different activities, the socialists, the arts and crafts and S.P.A.B. men, the printers. To him most of them were simply fellow workers. Towards Shaw his apparent incuriousness was clearly a form of caution which turned out well-founded. Shaw had courted his daughter May until she became serious, and then withdrawn; watched her marry the ineffective Halliday Sparling, socialist journalist and then Kelmscott Press secretary, in 1890; and three years later reappeared as their lodger, to reassert his earlier 'mystic betrothal', and break the marriage. Yet by the time she was divorced and free, in 1898, Shaw was away again, married to another. One may feel that Morris had good sense towards this prospective son-in-law if geniality was as much as he wanted to offer. But this does not mean that he had no deep friendships. Blunt, who first made this accusation, wrote that 'while all the world admired and respected him, I doubt whether he had many friends; they got too little in return to continue their affection. I should say half-a-dozen were all the friends he had.' But he also had good reasons for avoiding intimacy with Blunt. There were others who confided in Morris and found him deeply supportive, like Luke Ionides, who went often to him 'in the depths of misery' and after an hour would leave him 'feeling absolutely happy . . . Until he died I loved and admired him . . . Though he was a strong man he had the delicate feelings of a tender woman.'[94] And Morris had kept his inner circle of real friends for over thirty years. The feeling in his letters to Webb, Georgiana Burne-Jones, and Aglaia Coronio is especially clear.

There was an important positive side to this too. For Morris had reached, in his last years, a new understanding of friendship and sexual relationships. Earlier, he had been seeking for romantic love. By the end of his life, his ideal was a different kind of relationship with a different kind of woman. This had come to him gradually, with his involvement with the socialist movement. Through the influence especially of Engels, Morris now saw the tight Victorian family and men's dominance of women as a consequence of the economic and class system. It was a historical phase, which would be superseded, just as it had evolved itself from wider kin and clan communities in which the sexes had been much more equal. And the existing system did not just oppress women: by allowing them fulfilment only as men's sexual and domestic partners, it distorted their very personality. Edward Carpenter, whom Morris also knew through the Socialist League, was to argue this in his remarkable *Love's Coming of Age*, published in 1896. Morris was now at last able to make full sense of the difficulties of his own personal life in a social and historical context. He used his final prose romances to explore, in imagination, how in another society, with family dissolved into the wider community and women as vigorous as men, sexual fulfilment and fellowship might be reached. But socialism had brought him important direct personal experience too. He had found himself, however briefly, working in public beside and knowing, as colleagues rather than as romantic intimates, a number of gifted, active, out-spoken women, such as Helen Taylor, Annie Besant, Eleanor Marx, and Clara Zetkin. By the end of his life, Morris had long ceased to wish himself the chivalrous courtier of some silent beauty. He treated women as potential fellow-workers. There was a considered philosophy underlying the manner which Blunt—uncomprehendingly —observed: 'He was the only man I ever came into contact with who seemed absolutely independent of sex considerations. He would talk in precisely the same tone to a pretty woman as to a journeyman carpenter.'[95]

Morris in 1895 was thus a fulfilled man, happy in his pattern designing and presswork, happy in the belief that socialism in the end must come, happy in the love of his old friends and his two daughters and the fellowship of artists and socialists who shared his outlook and for whom he was a chief inspiration. He had written, 'Fellowship is heaven, and lack of fellowship is hell: fellowship is life, and lack of fellowship is death.'[96] He could feel that his own life had realized those words of John Ball. A little over sixty, he could look back on years of extraordinary achievement. He had published seven volumes of important original poetry, four of prose romances, six of prose and verse translation, and two of lectures. His designs for patterns for repeated production in wallpapers, textiles, carpets, and tapestry numbered over five hundred. In addition there were many individual designs for embroidery, tapestry, carpets, and stained glass. He had

10. Morris on a visit to Burne-Jones in Fulham, c. 1890

started a private press which in eight years issued fifty-three books, requiring over six hundred separate designs for initials, borders, title pages, and other ornaments. He had supervised the production of more than five hundred stained glass windows, for which he had supplied another two hundred or more figures and pattern designs. He had mastered and revived the largely forgotten techniques of dyeing and tapestry, as well as several other less neglected processes. He had made a financial success of a difficult manufacturing business. He had made a lasting impact on British politics and become one of the few major British political thinkers. In the six years before 1890 he had delivered over two hundred and fifty public lectures. To both art and socialism he had in his prolific years contributed more than any other living man.

Yet by 1895 Morris was an old man, almost exhausted by his own energies. He was weaker and thinner, his blenched hair wisped about a faltering face. He made his last outdoor speech at the funeral of the Russian revolutionary Stepniak in September 1895. His last public meetings in January 1896 were a rally of the Social Democratic Federation, the Sunday lecture at the Hammersmith Socialist Society, and the first meeting of the Society for Checking the Abuses of Public Advertising. By January he was obviously ill and shortly afterwards his diabetes was confirmed by the doctors: exposing his weakening body first to tuberculosis, and finally to kidney failure. Burne-Jones felt 'very frightened . . . the ground beneath one is shifting'.[97] Morris too was losing companions. Faulkner had died in 1891 and now he was shaken by the death of Middleton in the early summer. On his doctor's advice he decided on a sea voyage and set off for Norway with John Carruthers, a socialist engineer. On his return in August he wrote a shaky note to Webb, 'My dear Fellow, I am back. Please come and see me. I saw Throndhjem—big church, terribly restored, but well worth seeing; in fact, as beautiful as can be. It quite touched my hard heart . . . Somewhat better, but hated the voyage; so glad to be home.' He was too ill to move to Kelmscott. To Georgiana he wrote a last note: 'Come soon, I want a sight of your dear face.'[98] She was among those at his bedside when, six weeks later, he died at Hammersmith, on 3 October 1896.

Although most of the socialists stayed away, some for fear of offending Janey by their presence, Morris was buried as he would have wished. The coffin was brought from Lechlade station in a red and yellow farm wagon wreathed in vine and strewn with willow branches. The parson was his old schoolfriend Fulford Adams. It was a wet, blowy afternoon, the hedges and Kelmscott elms dripping yellow and autumn red, the old stone walls glistening in the rain. Webb designed for him a long coped gravestone with a fillet along the top, two sprigs of leaf sprung across, and beautiful spidery lettering. There is another old tomb nearby even more like the long tent of a fighting Norseman. Both are now grey and yellow with lichen.

Morris had made the kind of contribution to life which could not simply disappear with his death. But the sense of loss was felt far beyond his friends. It was best put by Robert Blatchford in the *Clarion*.

I cannot help thinking that it does not matter what goes into the *Clarion* this week, because William Morris is dead. And what Socialist will care for any other news this week, beyond that one sad fact? He was our best man, and he is dead . . . It is true that much of his work still lives, and will live. But we have lost him, and, great as was his work, he himself was greater. Many a man of genius is dwarfed by his own creations. We could all name men whose personalities seem unworthy of their own words and actions; men who resemble mean jars filled with honey, or foul lamps emitting brilliant beams. Morris was of a nobler kind. He was better than his best. Though his words fell like sword strokes, one always felt that the warrior was stronger than his sword. For Morris was not only a genius, he was a *man*. Strike at him where you would, he rang true . . . [99]

Blatchford's verdict still holds true. Ultimately the attraction in Morris is his whole life, his extraordinary versatility, his continuous develop-ment. It is this which still gives life to his work and words. For, as Shaw wrote that same week, 'You can lose a man like that by your own death, but not by his. And so, until then, let us rejoice in him.'[100]

2

ARCHITECTURE

ALTHOUGH he spent less than a year as an architectural pupil and never designed a single building, William Morris is regarded as one of the most important influences in the last hundred years of architectural history. This influence was possible because Morris never ceased to feel the need for architecture as a frame for his thinking and his designs. It was to him 'the synonym for applied art', 'the foundation of all the arts', the supreme example of human co-operation, embracing 'the whole external surroundings of the life of man; we cannot escape from it if we would so long as we are part of civilization, for it means the moulding and altering to human needs of the very face of the earth itself . . . ; it concerns us all, and needs the help of all'.[1] It was the breadth of Morris's conception of architecture, extending from the smallest decorative detail to the landscape itself, which made his ideas important.

When Morris entered the office of George Edmund Street as a pupil in 1856, Victorian architecture was at a crossroads. Already the disintegrating effects of dramatic population growth and rapid industrialization, which had begun in the mid-eighteenth century, had almost broken down the pleasant sensible building traditions of the older, largely rural, pre-industrial England. There had been a sudden expansion in the demand for building, for mass town housing for the workers, railway stations and factories, workhouses and cemeteries, for schools and town churches. There was consequently a shortage of building craftsmen and architects and an opportunity for big block contractors to make fortunes from jerry-building. Worse still, the shortage of well-trained builders and architects occurred at the very moment when the building industry was faced with special problems in design. There was, first, the challenge of new building types, such as railway stations, model workmen's flats, and radiating prisons. Secondly, canals and railways had brought an abundant choice of materials, so that where previously only a few local materials were available, now red and yellow brick; red and blue slates and tiles; limestones, granites, and sandstones in grey and green, golden yellow and pink, became available for buildings all over the country. At the same time new materials had been invented, iron and concrete and plate glass; and manufactured ornaments such as mastic infill and bright encaustic tiles could replace the expensive ornamental work of craftsmen. In iron and glass it was even possible, as the Crystal Palace had shown in 1851, to erect vast buildings at great speed through industrialized prefabrication. All this undermined the old conventions of design. Finally, at the same time the advances of historical scholarship, discovering and defining an extraordinary range of architectural styles, had broken down the very assumptions of architectural taste, by which an architect could evolve his own manner from the broad classical tradition, unrestricted to any one period in his selection of motives and generally unaware of how far he had strayed from the Greek or Roman originals. By 1856 sufficient well-illustrated descriptions of Gothic and Renaissance, Greek and Moorish architecture, in Spain and Germany as well as in Italy, France, and England, existed to give the most ignorant of architects a bewildering choice of styles.

It is easy to criticize the Victorians for not realizing that the industrial

11. Street's former workhouse chapel of 1866 at Shipmeadow, Suffolk: its gothic rationalism equally good for a barn

revolution could only be answered by a wholly new style. Architecture in the past had always been based upon stylistic tradition and to abandon tradition in this moment of chaos appeared to be the final step to anarchy. At the same time the Victorians realized that they must have a style of their own if their architecture was to be alive. Their solution was to build on past styles, borrowing from the storehouse of the past, adapting to new needs and exploiting new materials, and hoping that a Victorian style would emerge. So, in a sense, it did. Underneath its historical trappings the mid-Victorian style is unmistakable in its bold use of brightly coloured materials and contrasting textures, its strong sculptural shapes and coarse simplified detailing. Mid-Victorian architecture at its best has a confidence and originality all of its own, still exciting today, in decided contrast to the grey flat cold archaeological tastes of the 1830s and 1840s.

This High Victorian style led nowhere, because its very boldness meant that in second-rate hands it resulted in especially obtrusive ugliness. By the 1870s the more sensitive and original architects were turning to a more delicately detailed, softly textured historicism, and especially in church architecture they again became cautious in mixing motives from different periods and countries. Victorian architects failed to see that in standardized iron and glass exhibition buildings and railway stations, in plain brick or stone mills, docks, and warehouses, in bridges and railway viaducts, the basis of a functional style already existed. The critics regarded these as mere building or engineering. Pugin and Ruskin had shown that Gothic architecture succeeded because its planning was functional and its materials and structure honestly revealed, but they failed to see the same virtues in Victorian industrial building. It was not until the first years of the twentieth century, and then in Germany and not in England, that the ideas of Pugin and Ruskin were transformed by their application to modern machine craftsmanship instead of medieval craftsmanship, and the modern style was born.

Morris as a thinker in the tradition of Pugin and Ruskin, especially in his wider understanding of the social basis of architecture and the planning of future towns, was a pioneer of modern architecture. His influence on the most advanced architects between 1890 and 1914, W. R. Lethaby and the English arts and crafts men, Henri van der Velde and art nouveau, Walter Gropius and twentieth-century functionalism, was direct and acknowledged.[2] But it was an influence of theory rather than of taste, for in his taste Morris was, in the best sense, wholly Victorian, firmly within the Gothic revival tradition.

As young men both Morris and Philip Webb, whom he found as

Street's senior clerk, were High Victorian in their tastes and they kept something of their early attitude throughout life. They were drawn to Street as one of the most original Gothic revival architects, who was then experimenting with coloured materials, boldly simplifying Gothic detail in his village churches, schools and parsonages. Webb was equally an admirer of William Butterfield's architecture, which was another version of the same approach. It was not entirely accidental that Morris's favourite Oxford building was at that time Merton chapel, newly restored by Butterfield with a brightly painted roof by Hungerford Pollen. Webb was at this time sketching buildings by Butterfield and Morris spent part of his time in Street's office sketching a doorway at St Augustine's College, Canterbury, which Butterfield had rebuilt ten years previously.[3] The architectural style of Webb's first houses, with their high-hipped tile roofs, brick walls, battered chimneys and sash windows, came direct from Street and Butterfield. Red House

12. Cottages at Baldersby, Yorkshire, of c.1855, by Butterfield, whose example strongly influenced Morris and Webb

was characteristic of the best secular Gothic work of the 1850s, Gothic in little more than its straightforward materials and free functional planning. Yet Morris, as we have seen, regarded it as medieval, and probably even saw its circular landing windows as simplified thirteenth-century tracery. When he planned an extension for Burne-Jones in 1864 it was to have been a half-timbered wing enclosing the well court. To modern eyes this would have destroyed the simple excellence of the house, but to Morris it would have emphasized its romantic creeper-covered medievalism. The idea can be seen anticipated in the background to Morris's designs for the St George's cabinet in 1860, where there is a brick doorway under a strainer arch set into the brickwork and filled in with herringbone brickwork, as in designs by Street and Webb, and in the background a half-timbered wing. The taste of Morris and his friends at this time can also be seen in their admiration for Benjamin Woodward, the architect of the bold polychromatic Oxford Museum.

Morris was always eclectic in his own designs, drawing on motifs of many periods and countries and fusing them with his own manner. In this he remained a High Victorian. His early attitudes also survived in his architectural tastes. He preferred the earliest French Gothic to anything later. He was no doubt influenced by Webb, who loved 'a gaunt church', and identified Gothic with the 'strength of what I've *called* barbaric'.[4] Morris, on the other hand, loved the richness of sculpture and ornament and he tended to see buildings more in terms of the styles and texture of their walls than of their internal space. Occasionally he felt a spatial effect deeply. 'I felt inclined to shout when I first entered Amiens Cathedral. It is so free and vast and noble that I did not feel in the least awestruck or humbled by its grandeur.'[5] Lincoln made him feel 'quite happy—and as if one never wanted to go away again . . . : the church is not high inside, though it is long and broad, but its great quality is a kind of careful delicacy of beauty, that no other English minster that I have seen comes up to'.[6] Rheims he felt had 'something amiss with it, I couldn't tell what, except that it seemed *pinched* I mean inside'.[7] But these observations are rare exceptions in the multitude of architectural comments which can be found in his letters. Like most Victorians, Morris was more aware of shapes than spaces. Typically he thought that Salisbury Cathedral 'overdid the lightness of effect'.[8]

In his attitude to architecture other than Gothic Morris had the tastes of a convinced Gothic protagonist. The greatness of Gothic art was founded on its social basis: 'it was common to the whole people; it was free, progressive, hopeful, full of human sentiment and humour; . . . the outcome of corporate and social feeling, the work not of individual but collective genius; the expression of a great body of men conscious of their union.' He could see in archaic Greek temples 'some healthy barbarism', but classic Greek architecture he hated as 'the acknowledged slavery of every one but the great man'. Its sculpture had developed to pedantic naturalism which could tolerate no imperfections in the minor parts of the building, 'so that the inferior parts of the ornament are so slavishly subordinated to the superior, that no invention or individuality is possible in them, whence comes a kind of bareness and blankness'. He dismissed Roman façades as 'plastered sculpture', mere veneer, but praised the plain dignity of Roman engineering and the all-important use of the arch. Byzantine architecture he regarded as early Gothic, with its acceptance of the arch in design and its brilliant fresh ornament, the sign of a new barbarism and freedom.[9]

Post-medieval architecture owed what virtues he saw in it to the survival of Gothic feeling. St Paul's and St Peter's he considered the two

13. Selsley church, Gloucestershire, 1862, by Bodley: the High Victorian setting of the earliest Morris glass

ugliest buildings in the world, 'the very type . . . of pride and tyranny, of all that crushes out the love of art in simple people'.[10] From Verona he wrote that he was quite out of sympathy with the post-Renaissance work of southern Europe: 'in spite of its magnificent power and energy I feel it as an enemy; . . . even in these magnificent and wonderful towns I long rather for the heap of stones with a grey roof that we call a house north-away.'[11] The more ambitious English Georgian architecture seemed 'revolting ugliness', 'stiff-necked follies', 'the feeble twaddle of the dilettantism of the latter Georges', 'foolish upholstery provided by despised drudges for vulgar luxury'.[12] From this nadir the Gothic revival was a recovery, and he continued to regard the mid-Victorian decades as a period in which 'hope was strong', of 'experimental designing—good, very good experiments some of them'. 'None knew better than I do what a vast amount of talent and knowledge there is amongst the first-rate designers of buildings nowadays.'[13]

Nevertheless by the 1870s Morris had changed his attitude to post-Gothic architecture. Like many of the architects who had supported High Victorian originality, he now realized that experiment had produced in lesser hands a popular Victorian style which was 'no longer passively but actively ugly, since it has added to the dreary utilitarianism of the days of Dr Johnson a vulgarity which is the special invention of the Victorian era . . . The ordinary builder is covering England with abortions which make us regret the brick box and slate lid of fifty years ago.'[14]

At the same time Morris had accepted the ultimate implication of Ruskin's discovery that medieval architecture had depended upon the freedom and happiness of medieval craftsmen and had finally understood that modern medievalism was an impossibility. Revivalism produced a constant conflict with the whole contemporary technique of building. A Gothic architect was forced continually to correct and oppose the habits of the mason, the joiner, the cabinet-maker, the carver, etc., and to get them to imitate painfully the habits of the fourteenth-century workmen, and to lay aside their own habits, formed not only from their own personal daily practice, but from the inherited turn of mind and practice of body of more than two centuries.[15]

He could still admire an honest attempt at Gothic like Street's Law Courts, or still more the sensitive Bodley's 'excellent new buildings at Magdalen College', but these were exceptions—'exotics'—and routine late Victorian Gothic he came strongly to dislike as 'dead-alive office work' while a mechanical High Victorian piece like Waterhouse's Manchester Assize Courts now seemed 'an insult to the memory of our forefathers'.[16]

In contrast to this futile effort to copy the past, Morris thought that Georgian architecture had more wisely accepted its technical limitations, 'the division-of-labour workman, and so, indeed, did its best, and had a kind of life about it, dreary as that life was'; and for this reason Morris supported the domestic architecture of the 1870s based on the Queen Anne period, which had still 'some feeling of the Gothic', but was closer to nineteenth-century building traditions. It was also less incongruous to its contemporary social function: 'to step from a very well done outside of Chaucer's time into an interior of afternoon tea and the music of the future is certainly a very prodigious shock; more of a shock, it must be admitted than finding a Queen Anne house inhabited by school-board ladies or gentlemen enthusiastic on sanitary reform.'[17] This fashion of the 1870s had been anticipated by Webb's houses and can be traced back to the enthusiasm of Rossetti and his friends for the Queen Anne period in general. In the early 1860s Warington Taylor was pressing upon E. R. Robson the merits of Queen Anne furniture, china, clocks, and houses. 'Queen Anne brick houses were well suited to their

14. St Paul's American church, Rome, 1873, by Street: Ruskinian constructional colour, and Burne-Jones mosaics within

times . . . No one save Butterfield and Webb has conceived an architecture suited to our times.'[18] Morris praised Robson's own later 'simple but striking' London Board Schools, and also the prettiness of Bedford Park and Norman Shaw's 'elegantly fantastic Queen Anne houses at Chelsea'.[19] Both Robson and Shaw were admirers of Webb.

These changes of view were close to those of the architects who patronized the Morris firm. In the first years the firm's work went into Webb's houses and the bold, original churches of Bodley, Street, and William White. Later the churches, including Bodley's, were more sensitive and correct, while the houses were in the elegant Norman Shaw manner. In his later work Webb also tended to a lighter, whiter style, closer to classical than Gothic tradition, although his church at Brampton in Cumberland is serious Gothic, his subtle originality appearing only in its interesting spatial arrangement. Morris especially admired this church, for which he made one of his finest later windows.

Both Webb and Morris, however, were ambivalent in their attitude towards even the best late-Victorian architecture. They objected not so much to its appearance but to its very success. This was the time when Morris was increasingly uneasy that his own work should consist in 'ministering to the swinish luxury of the rich'. He scornfully referred to the fashionable districts where his patrons lived as 'architectooralooral'.[20] Even the best of styles could not redeem buildings which he was beginning to consider antisocial. 'I doubt . . . the applicability of your old Celtic style to the amenities of joint-stock money-grabbing,' he later told a group of Glasgow socialists.[21] Only under socialism would architecture again become possible: 'until such a change comes about there will be no real modern architecture'. Morris still believed that ultimately the new style would come from the old source. 'There is only one style of architecture on which it is possible to found a true living art, which is free to adapt itself to the varying conditions of social life, climate, and so forth, and that style is Gothic architecture.'[22] But rather than in churches and palaces of art for artists, his faith now lay in common cottages. 'I have a hope that it will be from such necessary, unpretentious buildings that the new and genuine architecture will spring, rather than from our experiments in conscious style.'[23]

Morris thus ended as something of an architectural impossibilist. On the one hand he still rejected the new aesthetic achievements of the industrial age. In 1851 when he had gone to the Great Exhibition he had sat down and refused to go round, declaring it 'wonderfully ugly'.[24] He was as hostile to the building as Ruskin. Some thirty years later he still regarded modern engineering as a 'horrible and restless nightmare' and disliked plate-glass windows because they let in too much light.[25] He still ranked materials in Ruskinian rather than modern terms: 'stone is definitely the most noble material, the most satisfactory material; wood is the next, and brick is a makeshift material.'[26] On the other hand he no longer had any hope for a medieval revival. He could only offer the belief that a socialist society would produce a new healthy architecture. His own anticipation was that this would be some new kind of vernacular tradition.

Although this viewpoint seems in retrospect hopeless, Morris was not alone in holding it. Webb ended with a similar attitude. Building was 'a folk art', architecture consisted in 'building traditionally'. 'I never begin to be satisfied until my work looks commonplace.'[27] In some of the architecture of Webb's disciples, such as Lethaby's thatched rubble Herefordshire stone church at Brockhampton or Earnest Gimson's strange thatch and rock cottages in Charnwood Forest, Leicestershire, or the houses the Barnsley brothers built for themselves at Sapperton, the doctrine can be seen applied. There are also the simple stone cottages at Kelmscott by Webb and Gimson, and the village hall again by

15. Stoneywell Cottage, Ulverscroft, Leicestershire, 1899, by Gimson: the vernacular school

Gimson, built in memory of Morris and Janey. The same spirit—although conceding considerably more to middle-class convenience—was continued in the houses designed by Charles Voysey, like his own 'The Orchard' at Chorley Wood, or 'Spade House' for H. G. Wells at Sandgate. But it is hardly surprising that both Lethaby and Gimson gave up regular architectural practice, Lethaby to teach and Gimson for craftsmanship.

His loss of confidence in the Gothic revival changed Morris's attitude to the treatment of old buildings. When he was young the majority of medieval English churches had been cluttered up with Georgian box pews, pulpits, and tables of the Ten Commandments, and their fabric was generally badly neglected. To repair them soundly, reconstruct parts which had been ignorantly altered, open blocked arches and windows and provide more appropriate fittings, then seemed decidedly desirable. The Morris firm helped with major restorations in the 1860s in three medieval Cambridge colleges. Over a third of the firm's stained glass before 1877 went into old churches and much of this was commissioned as part of restoration schemes. Architects like Butterfield and Street, Bodley and White genuinely believed that a tumbledown medieval building could be improved by reconstruction, the real merits of its architecture revealed, and new tile floors, woodwork, and glass designed which, while honestly Victorian, were close to the spirit of the old work. With the finer buildings they were probably right. It is now easy to forget how much of the fabric of noble churches such as Dorchester Abbey or Amesbury Abbey is in fact Victorian. Sufficient old work survived to make the restoration of the design wholly convincing.

On the other hand Morris was early aware of the dangers of ignorant restoration. Ruskin's writing was full of despairing protests against the senseless destruction of old work. Many of the Gothic revivalists saw this danger and one of the best discussions of the problem came from the prosperous Sir Gilbert Scott. The danger was that 'a barbaric builder, a clerk of works, or an over-zealous clergyman', would cause quite unnecessary alterations:

Not only must substantial repairs be attended to; the foundations under-pinned; the strength of the walls looked to; decayed timbers spliced, or new ones here and there inserted; the most decayed stones carefully cut out and replaced; the covering made reliable; and the fittings put in seemly order, retaining and following every remnant of what is ancient; the stonework cleaned from its thick coatings of whitewash, and the roofs divested of the concealment of modern ceilings; but, beyond this, *everything must be meddled with,*—the seating all taken up, floors removed, plastering stripped from the walls, the whole church left for months at the mercy of the elements by the removal of its roofs; windows which do not please the clergyman or the squire replaced with more pretentious ones; indeed the whole thing *radically re-formed* from top to toe . . . One *perfectly longs* after an *untouched church*, —

for its old tracery with fragments of old glass, its old floor patched with brick and with brass matrixes, the old tool-marks on its stone. What was left was 'a nauseating blank;—neither anything interesting left nor anything good introduced'. Scott suggested that the block contract was one of the worst causes of damage. Instead repairs should be made by day-work 'in a *tentative* and *gradual* manner; first replacing the stones which are entirely decayed, and rather *feeling one's way* and *trying how little will do* than going on any bold system'. Later features should only be removed with the greatest caution and all old fragments should be kept in their original places.

Scott acknowledged his own guilt. 'I do not wish or expect to exempt myself from equal blame where I deserve it. *We are all of us offenders in this matter.*' But it was 'high time that some public protest be made' and he called for local vigilance committees which could watch against over-restoration.[28] This was in 1864. For the moment his suggestion was ignored, but his anticipation of the Society for the Protection of Ancient Buildings indicates how Morris's concern was a common part of the thinking of the Victorian Gothic revivalists. Ironically it was Scott himself, with his scheme for Tewkesbury in 1877, who finally stung Morris into action, and Scott was always the arch-enemy until he became 'the (happily) dead dog'.[29]

By 1877 it was not just bad restoration but the whole concept of restoration to which Morris objected. If a revival of Gothic architecture was impossible without changing Victorian society it followed that any attempts to reconstruct or restore medieval buildings must fail for the same reasons. 'The workman of today is not an artist as his forefather was; it is impossible, under his circumstances, that he could translate the work of the ancient handicraftsman.'[30] Because the nineteenth century had no living style of church architecture, restoration was inevitably a forgery. This was particularly true of the humbler parish churches, and yet it was to these smaller buildings that restorers were paying more and more attention now that most of the major churches had been put in order. The sole interest of many minor churches was in their mellowed texture and haphazard mixture of different periods. To these restoration was destruction. 'The whole surface of the building is necessarily tampered with; so that the appearance of antiquity is taken away from such old parts of the fabric as are left.' That original surface could never be recovered. 'Such an ordinary thing as a wall, ashlar or rubble, *cannot* at the present day be built in the same way as a medieval wall was.'[31]

All this followed from Ruskin's understanding that the life of medieval craftsmen was the foundation of Gothic architecture. Ruskin too gave Morris his conviction that the protection of the past was an imperative social duty of the present. It was 'no question of expediency or feeling whether we shall preserve the buildings of past times or not. *We have no right whatever to touch them.* They are not ours. They belong, partly to those who built them, and partly to all the generations of mankind who are to follow us.' Morris reprinted Ruskin's words in the manifesto of S.P.A.B. But Morris, because of his growing social understanding and hope for change, had come to see the protection of ancient buildings as part of the work for a different future. The time would return when seeing beauty in daily surroundings would once more be a common pleasure, 'almost the greatest of all harmless pleasures'.[32] No private reason could justify the destruction of a beautiful building, and only the strongest public need. 'In destroying or injuring one of these buildings, we are destroying the pleasure, the culture, in a word, the humanity of unborn generations.'[33]

Morris was also more aware than his contemporaries that restoration was an expression of the worst commercial and social forces of the period. Builders found the greatest reward in the utmost destruction; parsons equally required it for promotion and prestige. Morris claimed that S.P.A.B. 'should not be regarded as dangerous, except, perhaps, to the amusements of certain country parsons and squires'.[34] But S.P.A.B. was also part of his campaign for a changed society and frequently the enemies were the same; church authorities like the Ecclesiastical Commissioners whose actions were 'governed by purely commercial principles'.[35] This awareness gave a special force to his letters to the press. 'Is it absolutely necessary that every scrap of space in the City should be devoted to money-making, and are religion, sacred memories, recollections of the great dead, memorials of the past, works of England's greatest architects to be banished from this wealthy City?'[36] In all his work Morris was looking to a simpler future when the public would no longer demand new 'stained glass, and shiny tiles, and varnished deal roofs', but would honour 'as a holy symbol of all the triumphs and tribulations of art . . . the little grey weather-beaten building, built by ignorant men, torn by violent ones, patched by blunderers, that has outlived so many hopes and fears of mankind'.[37]

Having sent his letter to the *Athenæum* in March 1877 calling for a society to protect ancient buildings, Morris threw himself whole-heartedly into the campaign. He at once decided to accept no more commissions for stained glass in old churches unless there were special reasons for doing so. A circular was issued by Morris and Company which resulted in a serious decline in this side of the firm's work. In the first years Morris was secretary and a frequent visitor for S.P.A.B. and he always remained the leading spirit on its committee. His mark was so clear that even fifty years after its formation the S.P.A.B. committee still consisted largely of friends and disciples of Morris and Webb. Although Morris had some early difficulties in organization (one of the first secretaries 'leaving no sweet odour behind him'[38]), within five years over a hundred cases were being handled a year. From the start buildings of all dates were considered and Morris wrote vigorously in the defence of Wren's city churches in spite of his own distaste for them. Through foreign correspondents a certain amount of work was also done in Italy, Egypt, and India.

It is difficult to estimate the influence of S.P.A.B. Certainly clergy resented the intrusion of a society which declared it impossible to treat churches 'as living things, to be altered, enlarged, and adapted as they were in the days when the art that produced them was alive and progressive'. They could hardly accept that their buildings were '*documents*, which to alter or correct is, in fact, to falsify and render worthless'.[39] The Dean of Canterbury protested that his cathedral was not built 'for antiquarian research or for budding architects to learn their art in. We need it for the daily worship of God.'[40] Inevitably too much money was given to transient church furnishings, 'ecclesiastical uphol-stery', and too little to structural repairs which could avert the need for restoration in the future. It is a measure of the successful resistance of the Church that its buildings are still outside the control and protection of the Historical Monuments Acts.

On the other hand the very existence of statutory listing and protection for secular buildings is evidence of the influence of S.P.A.B. Sir John Lubbock, who was responsible for the first of this legislation, was a member of its committee. There is no doubt too that in the twentieth century the treatment of ancient buildings has been much more cautious, even if in recent years the rebuilding of bombed city churches and the wholesale refacing and reconstruction of Oxford suggest a disturbing recovery of courage. It is also true that the appreciation of old textures, which gave S.P.A.B. its nickname 'anti-scrape', has become much more general.

In a number of cases in Morris's lifetime the intervention of S.P.A.B.

may have had a decisive effect. Schemes to add to Westminster Abbey and rebuild Westminster Hall, and to demolish the old school buildings at Eton, a large number of the city churches at York and two fine classical churches in London, St Mary at Hill and St Mary le Strand, were all dropped after protests. An English campaign, organized by Morris's old master, Street, which included a memorial signed by both Gladstone and Disraeli, helped to prevent the rebuilding of the west front of St Mark's in Venice. Through careful watching the late medieval churches at Blythburgh, Edington, and Fairford, and the splendid abbey fragments at Croyland, Thorney, Kirkstead, and Kirkstall, were all repaired rather than restored. Many smaller churches were similarly protected, including Longworth and Little Faringdon close to Kelmscott, and Inglesham, where Morris paid for most of the repairs himself. On the other hand S.P.A.B. could only hope to have a limited impact in a situation in which destruction was so widespread. Over 2,500 churches were restored between 1877 and 1885. In 1878 the society had estimated that there were 750 unrestored churches in England and Wales. How many could survive the century at that rate?

Although its aims were essentially conservative, Morris's social concern gave S.P.A.B. something of the spirit of a modern civic society. It was part of his campaign for a general improvement in the setting of town life. In these years he was also speaking for other comparable bodies, such as Commons Preservation Societies and Kyrle Societies. Morris's lectures for all these societies, both in their broad vision and their sense for detail, are extraordinarily prophetic of twentieth-century environmentalism. It is true that he regarded Victorian towns with open hostility as appalling darknesses on a once beautiful landscape. They made him depressed and resentful. He found that in the East End 'the mere stretch of houses, the vast mass of shabbiness and uneventfulness, sits upon one like a nightmare'.[41] But instead of burying himself in the vision of a Utopia, as he is often thought to have done, Morris produced some extremely practical suggestions for improving urban life.

If people were ever to recover their artistic sensitivity, 'the cleaning of England is the first and the most necessary' step; 'we must turn this land from the grimy back-yard of a workshop into a garden'. It was not a question of just protecting beauty spots; we must 'learn to love the narrow spot that surrounds our daily life for what of beauty and sympathy there is in it. For surely there is no square mile of earth's inhabitable surface that is not beautiful in its own way, if we men will only abstain from wilfully destroying that beauty.'[42] When a new housing estate was built, for instance, a special effort should be made to fit the houses round the existing trees. It was quite wrong to 'begin by clearing a site till it is as bare as the pavement'. Where a park or open space had been secured for the public, it should be kept clean, instead of being left, as so often, strewn with litter 'as if it had been snowing dirty paper'. There was far too much glaring outdoor advertising disfiguring the streets; Morris strongly objected to 'the daily increasing hideousness of the posters with which all our towns are daubed'.[43] Probably most important of all the immediate improvements would be the ridding of towns of smoke pollution. He hoped that with the spread of electric power the dense clouds of smoke poured out of factory chimneys would become as criminal as robbery on the highway. Or possibly even sooner, if the working class would demand it; as he told a Staffordshire School of Art, 'when the day comes that there is a serious strike of workmen against the poisoning of the air with smoke or the waters with filth, I shall think that art is getting on indeed'.[44]

Morris also had a remarkable vision of the type of working-class housing which could be built in big cities where the population densities could not be reduced. Flats need not be 'bare, sunless, and grim bastilles' like those built by Victorian philanthropists. Housing could be built

in tall blocks, in what might be called vertical streets, but that need not prevent ample room in each lodging, so as to include such comforts of space, air and privacy as every moderately-living middle-class family considers itself entitled to; also it *must* not prevent the lodgings having their due share of pure air and sunlight . . . Inside the houses, besides such obvious conveniences as common laundries and kitchens, a very little arrangement would give the dwellers in them ample and airy public rooms in addition to their private ones; the top story of each block might well be utilized for such purposes, the great hall for dining in, and for social gathering, being the chief feature of it. Of course it is understood that public rooms would not interfere with the ordinary private life of each family or individual; they would be there for use, if any one wished to use them.[45]

The grouping of houses into tall blocks would make room for garden space surrounding them. Morris wanted ample garden space in towns, private squares opened to the public, and surrounding countryside generally free to walkers wherever they would not damage crops. 'Every child should be able to play in a garden close to the place where his parents live.'[46]

Beyond these immediate improvements there was the possibility of a radical alteration in the distribution of the population. There was no reason in a reformed society why 'our great cities, London in particular,

16. Millbank Estate, Westminster, 1897–1902, by the London County Council, whose architects were followers of Morris and Webb

were bound to go on increasing without any limit; . . . under the present Capitalist system it is difficult to see anything which might stop the growth of these horrible brick encampments', but in the future thorough decentralization might be possible. 'The development of electricity as a motive power will make it easier.'[47] Morris wanted to see a proper balance between town and countryside, and a limit on urban growth into the 'fields and natural features of the country; nay, I demand even that there be left waste places and wilds in it'.[48]

With this balance, cities could be replanned. Morris believed that the architecture of their principal buildings should 'to a certain extent make up to town-dwellers for their loss of field, and river, and mountain'.[49]

But he did not believe in elaborate planning. The plan should be essentially simple, leaving nature to add complexity.

Contrast such monstrosities of haphazard growth as your Manchester–Salford–Oldham etc., or our great sprawling brick and mortar country of London, with what a city might be; the centre with its big public buildings, theatres, squares and gardens; the zone round the centre with its lesser guildhalls grouping together with the house of citizens; again with its parks and gardens; the outer zone again, still its district of public buildings, but with no definite gardens to it because the whole of this outer zone would be a garden thickly besprinkled with houses and other buildings. And at last the suburb proper, mostly fields and fruit gardens with scanty houses dotted about till you come to the open country.[50]

Model towns had been suggested by a number of Victorian thinkers and a few enlightened mill-owners had attempted to build planned communities round their mills. Morris knew of Robert Owen's New Lanark and Sir Titus Salt's Saltaire. He also approved of Bedford Park, the first garden suburb, which had been begun in 1875. In these lectures he anticipated the garden city. Raymond Unwin, who was to be the planner of Hampstead Garden Suburb and of Letchworth Garden City, was a regular contributor to *Commonweal*, a keen supporter of the Socialist League in the 1880s, and founder of its Manchester branch. Through the League he became fired by the ideals of simple living of Morris, and also of Edward Carpenter on his Sheffield smallholding; but he went on to fuse these with practical northern municipal socialism, evolving an architecture which was designed to satisfy working people not only as producers but as users too. There can be little doubt that the acceptance by socialists of the garden city vision owed much to Morris, and consequently that his influence ultimately helped to produce the post-war new towns.

Morris was therefore an important influence in the development of town planning in Britain—more important than is generally recognized. He was a pioneer of our efforts to protect the countryside, the restriction of advertising hoardings to towns, the protection of ancient buildings, the clean air acts and attempts to control litter, and the garden cities and new towns. In all these he was more evidently a pioneer than in architecture itself, where his influence was more complex. He certainly cannot be regarded as a pioneer of the modern architectural style. In his attitude to building methods and style he was an obstinate Victorian medievalist. On the other hand, his belief in honest construction and frankly used materials, taken from Pugin and Ruskin, which was especially forcibly expressed in his lectures on pattern designing and house decoration, together with his understanding of architecture as a wider framework of society, leading to his suggestions for communal housing and also for town planning, all gave him a profound influence on the future. They lie equally behind the teaching by Lethaby at the Central School of Arts and Crafts of architecture as the art of reasoning, and his attempts to relink artists and craftsmen through the ideal of the guild; and the co-operative workers' building guilds which flourished briefly at the end of the First World War; and more surprisingly, in the visual transformation of the London Underground in the 1930s, when Frank Pick brought in artists to redesign everything from lettering and posters to trains and stations, inspired by the ideal of a subterranean 'Earthly Paradise', which bring a new community unity to the city. Nor was his influence confined to Britain. In America, Frank Lloyd Wright began as a follower of Ruskin and Morris; while transmitted through the writings of Hermann Muthesius, Morris directly influenced the first modern architects in Germany. Thus the Bauhaus was founded by Walter Gropius not only to connect design with contemporary technology, but at the same time to create 'a new guild of craftsmen, without the class distinctions which raise an arrogant barrier between craftsman and artist'.[51] If the claim that Morris was a prophet of the mechanistic modern style which finally emerged is misleading, this does not mean that the admiration of modern architects for Morris is unjustified. The architectural theories which he transmitted and the wider social approach to architecture which he helped to create were as important as stylistic change in the creation of modern architecture: and indeed their relevance will outlast it.

3

FURNITURE AND FURNISHING

OF all Morris's activities, none has had a more persistent influence than his work as a house furnisher. His best-known saying is his maxim, 'Have nothing in your houses that you do not know to be useful or believe to be beautiful.' Yet the maxim, a text for simple living, seems in strange conflict with much of the furnishing work which Morris actually executed. There is a logical development in Morris's work and ideas, but it is not immediately apparent. Let us consider, first what he made—much of which can still be seen; and then, what he said, and the spirit of his message.

17. Furniture: the studio at Red Lion Square, 1856, by Burne-Jones, who is shown looking at the back of a chair designed by Morris which had been decorated by Rossetti; to the right the table by Morris now at Cheltenham, his only surviving design. This was Morris's home from 1856 until 1859

Morris himself designed no furniture for his firm. He designed the rough furniture for his Red Lion Square rooms in 1856, including a round table which is his only design known to survive, and he also appears to have made a hexagonal table for a friend, decorated with carved foliage and fretwork, but both these experiments were distinctly amateurish.[1] On the other hand he supervised the production of Morris and Company's furniture and designed their general schemes of decoration for twenty-five years. Although Webb also took a prominent part in the few decorative schemes before 1870, in the prolific later years the general scheme was almost always by Morris, even if the individual pieces of furniture still came from other hands. The furniture had been first made for the firm by a local Bloomsbury cabinet-maker, but the move to Queen Square in 1865 provided enough room for production directly under Morris's control. In the 1870s the furniture workshop was in Great Ormond Yard, conveniently close to Queen Square. By the 1880s, however, Morris had himself moved, and although the furniture workshop was not moved to Merton in 1881, a larger workshop was bought in Pimlico in 1890. At the same time George Jack, a pupil of Philip Webb, became the firm's chief furniture designer. This must have marked the end of Morris's active part in furniture production, although he was still responsible for the general furnishing schemes. But by this date, as a result of the art lectures which he gave from 1877 onwards, he had become the theorist of a whole school of furnishing—the arts and crafts movement. There are thus two direct phases in Morris's contribution to furniture design, the first of practical example and the second principally of ideas.

Morris's practical work began with the pieces which he designed in 1856, made of big strong planks fixed by protruding pins, in a style that he and his friends thought 'intensely medieval . . . tables and chairs like incubi and succubi'.[2] It was a dramatic assertion of contempt for the typical furniture of the early Victorian period. The same was true of his first decorative scheme at Red House two years later. So what, first of all, was the character of this common furniture so despised by Morris?

It is a mistake to judge the furniture style of the 1850s by the florid extravagances shown at the Great Exhibition of 1851. The pieces shown at exhibitions were specially made to win prestige and were much more inventive and ornate than the everyday furniture of the period. Exhibits were rarely in production. It is now recognized that the period between 1835 and 1860, so far from being chaotic and original, was limited and conservative in its furniture style. It was essentially an undistinguished prolongation of the Regency period. Furniture was still made to personal order, generally by individual craftsmen. Apart from the mechanical-saw very little machinery was used. Innovations such as papier mâché chairs and brass bedsteads were exceptional. Old pattern books continued in use for many years. The fourth edition of Loudon's

Encyclopaedia, issued in 1857, showed little change from the first of 1833, while Thomas King's *Modern Style of Cabinet Work Exemplified*, first published in 1829, was reissued unaltered in 1862. It would seem that the influence of the rapidly growing middle classes in this period, so far from being novel and brash, was staid and conventional.

The furniture of these years was normally in plain mahogany, rosewood, or walnut, rarely inlaid or gilded. Chair backs and chair legs, sideboard backs and sofa backs, were shaped in bold baroque curves. This Victorian rococo style, which was introduced shortly before 1830, was thought to be Louis XIV, but its most characteristic feature, the balloon chair back, was an unconscious Victorian development. Chairs for bedrooms and drawing rooms were given the most gracefully twisted legs and backs. Easy chairs and sofas were completely upholstered in rounded, padded curves; although after 1850 the frames and arms began to reappear from the upholstery. The fashionable colours were light and clear, lilac, yellow and pale clear red. It is a rarely distinguished style, but usually it is comfortably pleasant. The furniture at Hughenden Manor, Buckinghamshire, the house bought by Benjamin Disraeli in 1847, could be taken as a representative example.

It was this common furniture, which he saw in London shops, to which Morris objected. Certainly nothing could have been further from his medieval tastes. But it was not true, as his biographers often assert, that he could not have had suitable furniture made by any established firm. Although the Gothic revival had as yet made little impact on general taste, in the years before 1851 Pugin had designed a number of soundly constructed Gothic tables and chairs for his architectural clients. J. G. Crace, who made many of them, could certainly have executed satisfactory work for Morris. Pugin's designs were generally lighter and more delicate than Morris would have wished in 1856, the table tops inlaid and panels carved with vine leaf patterns and tracery, but in other ways, especially in the strong chamfered legs, low stretchers and curved braces, they clearly anticipated early Morris furniture.

The closeness of Morris's first tastes to those of a Gothic revival architect like Pugin are especially clear in his first decorative schemes, which have much in common with Pugin's work at Lismore Castle. Although the early Morris and Company style evolved from the furnishing of Red House in 1858–60, its character was ecclesiastical rather than domestic. Apart from Red House the only examples of which much remains are the series of decorative schemes traditionally attributed to Morris in churches and two college halls in Cambridge. These are all in the bright primary colours of the High-Victorian period, contrasting with the light soft colours of early Victorian fashion. At Red House the walls were intended to be painted with epic scenes or hung with embroideries of women and gay flowers on dark blue-serge grounds. The ceilings were distempered with coloured patterns and the floors bright with Persian carpets. Except for the oak staircase, the woodwork was black, red, or green. None of the major rooms were lit from the south, so that the effect must have been rich and rather dark.

Certainly the stained-glass windows and darkly coloured walls of All Saints' Church, Cambridge, and the hall and combination room at Peterhouse, are distinctly gloomy today in natural light. At Peterhouse this is chiefly because of the oak roofs and canopied linenfold wall-panelling designed by the architect, George Gilbert Scott (son of Sir Gilbert Scott). But the stencil patterns on the upper walls of the hall and the stained glass only darken the effect. At All Saints' the walls are entirely covered by stencil patterns, formalized roses and monograms in dark red on crimson or dark green on pale green, and there are more varied, lighter patterns on the roofs. It is very sombre.

On the other hand, where there was sufficient light the effect was gay and gaudy. The last important example of the style, Queens' College Hall, Cambridge, which was decorated for G. F. Bodley in 1875, has recently been cleaned and restored. Above the dark eighteenth-century panelling the upper walls are gaily stencilled in two bands of red and green heraldic roses and trailing stems. The rafters and boards of the roof are alternately red and green, covered with gold suns, white flowers and black monograms. The horizontal purlins are black, with white edges and more suns while the braces are dark green, with white and red undersides. A long green leaf pattern runs along the scarlet tie beams, topped by gilded crenellation and edged by mouldings striped black and white like a barber's pole. There is more colour in the exquisitely delicate scenes of the months in the tiles above the fireplace, an earlier commission from Bodley, but these tiles are almost the only delicate note in a dazzling room.[3]

Although the whole colourful effect is eminently High Victorian, comparable with the experiments in constructional colour by Victorian architects in the 1850s and 1860s, it was based (like constructional colour) on medieval precedent. In 1865–6 George Wardle was paid by Morris and Company to analyse the method used in the medieval decoration of screens and roofs in Norfolk and Suffolk churches. Wardle worked out the exact colour combinations and the technique of stencilling, in some cases removing recent layers of paint to examine the original. He sent a large number of drawings. The stencil designs used

1 William Morris aged 23

2 Red House, north front, 1859, by Webb: Morris's home until 1865

3 Kelmscott House, Hammersmith Upper Mall: Morris's London home from 1878

4 'Ministering to the swinish luxury of the rich': the drawing room at Stanmore Hall, Middlesex, decorated by Morris and Company for William Knox D'Arcy in 1888–96. The ceiling pattern and 'Persian Brocatel' woven silk and wool fabric on the walls are by Dearle; the escritoire and stand of inlaid sycamore is now at the Victoria and Albert Museum

5 'Scroll' wallpaper, by Morris, 1872

6 'Acorn' wallpaper, by Morris, 1879

7 'Wandle' chintz, by Morris, 1884

8 'Tulip and Lily' carpet: triple cloth Kidderminster carpet, machine-woven in Heckmondwike, by Morris, c.1875

9 'Clouds' carpet: large handknotted carpet by Morris for Clouds, Wiltshire, now in Cambridge

10 'Woodpecker' high-warp tapestry by Morris, 1885, now at Walthamstow

11 Embroidered wall hanging, designed by May Morris and executed by
Mrs Battye, c.1900, now at Walthamstow

KING HAFBUR AND KING SIWARD,

They needs must stir up strife
All about the sweetling Signy,
Who was so fair a wife
O wilt thou win me then
or as fair a maid as I be?

II

It was the kings son Hafbur
Awoke amidst the night,
And fell to talk of a dream of dread
In swift words nowise light.

III

Methought I was in heaven
Amidst that fair abode,

12 Manuscript of King Hafbur written and illuminated by Morris
c.1870–6, now at the Bodleian Library, Oxford

by Morris, the arrangement of monograms and alternately coloured beams, and even the green leaves and red flowers, are very close to Wardle's drawings.

There were fewer practical precedents for secular furniture, but here again the medieval intention of the firm's early work is clear. It was close to the spirit of Morris's own designs of 1856, although after 1858 Philip Webb rather than Morris designed the pieces. There were two types. The first was that which Morris later called 'state furniture': 'the blossoms of the art of furniture'. Rossetti, Burne-Jones, and Morris had quickly decided to cover the rough planks of the Red Lion Square furniture with 'painted designs of knights and ladies'.[4] Encouraged by the success of this experiment, they began a series of pieces of furniture specially designed for painting. The first was the Chaucer wardrobe, which had huge wooden side panels framed with corner shafts and a crenellated top. Burne-Jones painted it with big blue figures of Chaucer's Prioress and red crowds, turrets and steep roofs. It is disconcertingly like a picture which has been left standing against the wall. Cabinets followed which were raised on simple frames, so that the painted sides were at eye level. One of these, decorated with Burne-Jones's painting 'The Backgammon Players', is in the Metropolitan Museum of Art, New York, but the best-known examples are at the Victoria and Albert Museum, together with the Chaucer wardrobe. The St George's cabinet was painted by Morris himself in 1861, with vivid red and gold scenes on a black background.

The base of this cabinet is in the second style, with thick turned oak legs in castellated bases and strong curved braces at the ends. This was Morris's style for 'work-a-day furniture', which he believed should be of solid joinery construction, 'not be so very light as to be nearly imponderable; it should be made of timber rather than walking-sticks'.[5] Webb's tables had scrubbed oak tops, stout legs, and low stretcher boards. An early example is the round table at Kelmscott, with chamfered splayed-out legs ending in crenellated bases like mailed boots, and boarded sides punched with plate tracery and edged with a wavy chamfer. Settles and side boards usually had decorated sides and backs, but their tall curved overhanging canopies were built in the same solid manner. To stand on the sideboards there were heavy copper candlesticks with big round punched bases designed by Webb in a rather ecclesiastical style.

This early Morris work is important for its consistent quality and vigour rather than for its contemporary influence, which must have been slight. Morris furniture was not well known or widely produced, and all its most striking characteristics can be paralleled in work by other Gothic revivalists. At the 1862 International Exhibition, for example, the firm only displayed its painted furniture, in the medieval court. There was other painted furniture exhibited with it. The Gothic architect William Burges, who had designed his own furniture for several years, had begun making painted pieces at about the same time as Morris. The idea seems to have come independently from cathedral chests which he saw in France, although Burges knew Rossetti. Some of his exhibits are now at the Victoria and Albert Museum. In general shape they are simple and block-like, except for the steeply roofed tops taken from the medieval French chests. They are painted in bright colours with stories, puns, and jokes, set under bold black and gilt-painted arcading.

18. Painted wardrobe and stand, c.1875, by Burges, now at Bedford: both Morris and Burges showed painted furniture at the 1862 International Exhibition

The Museum also owns a superb bookcase which was exhibited in 1862 by Norman Shaw. Its colour comes from a different method, a mottled yellow inlay set in its dark oak frame. Its construction is as massive as anything by Webb, with turned legs, thick chamfered sides and a solid gabled top. Norman Shaw had succeeded Webb as the principal architectural assistant in Street's office. It is clear that both he and Webb owed much of their furniture style to their experience with Street of designing church pulpits and choir stalls. In the 1850s there had been little demand for secular Gothic furniture, so that the development from the lighter Gothic style of Pugin to the solid style of 1862 can only be traced in church work. The transition can be seen, for example, in the strong plain oak furniture designed by William Butterfield for two Oxfordshire churches, Milton and Dorchester, which Webb visited and sketched. There are many similarities in these church pieces to the plainer type of early Morris furniture.

There are also hints as to why the style was short-lived. The pulpit at Dorchester was a controversial experiment, a wooden octagon with broad side panels resting on a ribbed base, big corbels supporting the projecting bookboards and a staircase with the construction exposed as in a ladder. Butterfield was attacked for fixing his corbels with glue, but defended his method as being more honest. Such blocks were to be found if you 'put your hand under any piece of furniture. I have simply used, visibly, that sort of work which is concealed, more or less, in most joiners' work.'[6]

The morality of methods of construction was a source of perpetual argument among the followers of Pugin. Where Butterfield used glue, most medievalists, including Webb, allowed nails and screws. Bruce Talbert in his *Gothic Forms applied to Furniture*, published in 1867, argued that in medieval work 'the wood is solid, the construction honestly shewn, and fastened by tenons, pegs, iron clamps, nails, &c.; it is to the use of glue that we are indebted to the false construction modern work indulges in; the glue leads to veneering, and veneering to polish'. But even so, there was 'the use as well as abuse of all things'.

In short, compromise was inevitable if the style was ever to be practical. Consequently, as Gothic furniture became more popular in the 1860s, so a new high Victorian version evolved. Morris furniture can be seen to reflect this modification. The new fashion was for a heavy semi-Gothic style based on rectilinear shapes which contrasted with early Victorian curves. Surface colour was introduced with small panels of painting, coloured woods, tiles, stamped leather, chased metal, or embroidery. It was rich but sober. At this time the backs of Morris settles were decorated with geometric painted or leather patterns, chequers, trellises and circles mixed with formalized flowers. Some of Webb's furniture followed the fashion for rectangular panels and segment-headed shelves. It is generally less attractive than his more flamboyant earlier pieces, although still close to them in style.

At the same time the medieval Morris style of decoration was gradually adapting to the needs of the time. Morris's clients could not afford to cover their walls entirely with paintings and embroideries and they did not want high-raftered stencilled ceilings. They had flat-plastered ceilings and they wanted wallpapers or silk hangings, carpets and curtains. The firm began to meet these domestic needs, but only slowly. Morris designed his first wallpapers in 1862 and introduced two cheaper types of chair, the rush-seated Sussex chair in about 1864 and the Morris chair with an adjustable back in 1866. Both chairs were based

19. The Morris chair produced from 1866, adapted from a traditional Sussex type found by Warington Taylor in Ephraim Colman's workshop at Hurstmonceaux. Subsequently imitations, mass produced and marketed by mail order, became so popular in America that Bing Crosby's song 'My Honey's Loving Arms' of 1922 ran:
I love your loving arms, they hold a world of
   charms
a place to nestle when I
   am lonely
A cosy Morris chair
Oh, what a happy pair
   . . .

on old country types, but were a response to contemporary demands: at the 1862 exhibition other firms had shown chairs with adjustable backs, and a sculpture by Pietro Magni of a girl reading, sitting on a rustic rush-bottomed chair, had brought cheap rush seats into fashion.

These developments were encouraged by Warington Taylor, who

became the firm's manager in 1865 and in fact discovered the prototype for the Morris chair in 1866. But it was not until the early 1870s when, in addition to these chairs and wallpapers, carpets and textiles designed by Morris were available, that the domestic work of the firm became at all popular. Taylor's letters to E. R. Robson in the early 1860s suggest that a major reason for this slow response to the needs of the time was the taste of Morris and his preference for the work of Webb. Taylor wanted cheap, light, functional furniture. 'It is hellish wickedness to spend more than 15/- in a chair, when the poor are starving in the streets . . . Your Liverpool merchant only loves mahogany because it is heavy like his money and his head.' The need was for 'moveable furniture—light Sir—something you can pull about with one hand. You can't stand fixtures, now there are no more castles . . . Is not Queen Anne furniture more suited to our wants, constructional but light—. . . strongly built

20. The Sussex chair made from 1864 in many variants, all based on a traditional type: one of the firm's most popular products

but with middling thin appearance?' But he was as much against copying Queen Anne as medieval examples. To Taylor the merit of Morris furniture was that 'you cannot say it has any style. It is original, it has its own style: it is in fact Victorian.'

There is no doubt that he found more of these qualities in the furniture by Brown and Rossetti than by Webb. Brown had been a pioneer of light rush-seated chairs, including perhaps the Sussex chair, which Taylor especially admired for its 'poetry of simplicity'. Without doubt the most remarkable piece shown by the firm in 1862 had been a sofa designed by Rossetti, constructed of thin striped poles, which was dismissed by contemporaries as a medievalist absurdity, but now seems extraordinarily progressive. The firm's work seemed to Taylor to be divided: 'the painters like the light, the architects perhaps the massive.' If it was improving, it was because 'Rossetti keeps them up to the point'. The resistance must have come from Morris and Webb, and Morris's preference for Webb's work no doubt largely explains why so few pieces appear to have been produced to the designs of Brown and Rossetti.

It is not surprising that in this period of slow transition from medievalism that the two most important secular schemes by the firm were for public rooms. They were the Green Dining Room at the Victoria and Albert Museum, and two rooms in St James's Palace, both designed by Webb and executed in 1866–7. The Green Dining Room survives intact, but the Armoury and Tapestry Rooms at St James's Palace have been somewhat altered. All the rooms were tall, with flat ceilings. Although original in detail, the layout of the decoration was conventional. Dark panelling was designed for the lower walls, black with painted upper panels in the Green Dining Room, dark green with gilt leaf patterns in the Armoury Room. The upper walls were plastered. In the Green Dining Room they were painted green and patterned in relief, with a dark green frieze of trees and hounds, and a lighter patterned ceiling. There was excellent stained glass in the windows, but this darkened an already dim interior. Thus, although the style was no longer medieval, a certain amount of the Gothic gloom and sombre richness remained.

With the mature Morris style this became rarer. In a typical Morris room of the 1870s or 1880s the division of the walls was often like the Green Dining Room, but the effect was generally less dark. The lower woodwork was sometimes painted white. Occasionally the frieze was painted in bold scrolled foliage or hung with embroideries. More usually the walls were papered or hung with silk, with a white ceiling.

The floors were covered by rugs and matting instead of fitted carpets. The big early Victorian curved mirrors would be replaced by small bevelled mirrors in high mantelpieces with shelves displaying rows of de Morgan lustre pots and blue delft ware. Curtains were made to match the upholstery of the chairs. The colour schemes were subtle combinations, warm and glowing. Reds and yellows were often dominant. The typical drawing room would have cabinets round the walls and frequently a canopied settle by the tiled fireplace. There would be several tables and numerous chairs, some upholstered and buttoned, some with wicker sides and big loose cushions, some Morris adjustable chairs and Sussex chairs. Morris rooms, like most Victorian interiors, were full of furniture and bric-à-brac. The house of A. A. Ionides at 1 Holland Park, which Webb altered and Morris decorated, was filled with his collection of Tanagra figures, majolica, porcelain, prints, and bronzes. Ionides later had the Morris paper in the drawing room 'embossed in silver, overlaid with washes of brilliant transparent lacquer'.[7] A client with sufficient money demanded a very rich effect.

Such was the Morris style in the firm's greatest years, at the moment when, in 1877, Morris began to lecture on art. There is little in these decorative schemes to prepare for the radical challenge to traditional approaches presented by the lectures. Morris's first medieval fervour had been absorbed by contemporary demands for comfort and elaboration and the need to decorate conventionally shaped rooms. The success of his work depended not on an original approach to furnishing, but on his superb sense of quality and detail, pattern and colour.

Certainly there was no sign in Morris's work of the severe simplicity which he demanded as a lecturer. Nor, more surprisingly, was there much evidence of his second theme, his belief, learnt from Ruskin, that art was the expression of men's pleasure in their work. Morris argued that good furniture must be the work of 'a handicraftsman who shall put his own individual intelligence and enthusiasm into the goods he fashions . . . He must know all about the ware he is making and its relation to similar wares.' Furniture could never be a work of art while its makers were each responsible only for a 'minute piece of work, and never being allowed to think of any other'.[8]

This method of working was contrary to the practice of all the leading makers of the time, and Morris and Company were no exception. The firm had in fact followed the general development of the furniture trade away from individual craftsmanship between 1855 and 1880. In these years there had been a rapid growth in the size of firms. From the 1870s machinery became extensively used for shaping and carving wood, and

21. Advanced furniture design of the late 1860s: sideboard of ebonized wood with silver platings and inset panels of Japanese leather paper, now at the Victoria and Albert Museum, designed by E. W. Godwin, c. 1867

even Morris and Company introduced machine-carving.[9] The mass production of furniture for the stock of London sale-rooms began to replace production for personal order, a change which led to the first Furniture Trades Exhibition in 1881. Morris acquired his own Oxford Street showroom in 1877.

These developments increased the division between the debased traditional work of the trade and the advanced tastes of furniture designed by architects and trained designers—a division which summed up the loss of the integrated craftsmanship in which Morris believed. Even if the Morris firm tended to be a little aloof from the tendencies of art furniture, as the advanced taste of the 1870s was called, it was clearly dependent on a similar market and responded to its stylistic influence. Very often, indeed, as in the home which the *Punch* cartoonist Linley

Sambourne and his wife Marion furnished in 1874, Morris products would be mixed eclectically with those of other firms. The typical style of art furniture was usually a lighter version of the rectilinear furniture of the late 1860s. The extreme example was the Japanese style introduced by a Bristol architect, E. W. Godwin. His furniture was built of thin struts of black ebonized wood, creating a remarkably modern effect of cubic solids and voids. Morris was well aware of the Japanese style, if only from the chairs and picture frames which Rossetti left at Kelmscott, but it appears not to have influenced him. Nevertheless the fashion for light black wood rather than plain oak changed the balance of the firm's work. By 1880 Morris and Company were selling comparatively few of Webb's pieces, while the black rush chair had become widely popular.

After Morris began lecturing the gulf between the special well-designed furniture of a few big firms, such as Liberty and Heal's, and the low standard of the majority market continued to widen. Nor was there any fundamental change in the approach of Morris and Company, although there were changes in the firm's style to which we shall return. Nevertheless, Morris's lectures certainly had their effect, for they proved the starting-point and inspiration of the arts and crafts movement. Through the arts and crafts school his theories became a profound influence in modern design, in which the understanding of the needs of materials, the method of production, and the labour process is a fundamental premise. Morris's influence in the movement was mani-fold, extending far beyond the new school of furniture-makers who now began to seek a direct solution to the problems he had posed, through a revival of craft production methods. Morris was equally the inspiration of a whole generation of younger designers who paved the way in Britain and abroad for the new styles which broke free of historicism: architects such as Voysey, Mackmurdo, or Lethaby in England; or Gropius in Germany; Gustave Stickley, furniture-making editor of the *Craftsman*, and Louis Tiffany, exquisite artist-designer in glass and metals, in New York, and the architectural brothers Greene in California; in Norway Gerhard Munthe, like Morris a painter, weaver and Viking enthusiast; or again in Belgium Henri van de Velde, painter, architect, designer of furniture, textiles and papers from his own workshop, and lecturer on the theory of art and society.

But this is looking into the future. The groundswell of the arts and crafts movement was a discontent with the barriers between artists and craftsmen: not only of class, but also, although its leaders were largely blind to this, of gender. The movement gave space to many notable women designers, especially in the feminist 1900s; and one of its first signs was the bringing together in 1884 of various philanthropic groups in the Home Arts and Industries Association, holding annual exhibitions of work at the Albert Hall right through the period, led by and largely representing women. Yet when the Art Workers' Guild came into being in the same year, its core was a group of architects reacting against the professional exclusiveness of the Royal Academy and the Royal Institute of British Architects, and all the founding members were men. The Guild, of which Morris was Master for 1892, remained a male club, and the founding of the parallel Women's Art Guild by May Morris in 1907 came much too late. The Art Workers' Guild nevertheless played a crucial role in launching the Arts and Crafts Exhibition Society in 1888. The London exhibitions, at first annual and later triennial, and also those abroad, proved a principal forum and symbol of the movement, and remained widely influential until the First World War. Morris, at first hesitant that the work would not be good enough or nobody would want to see it, was soon an active supporter, editing the selection from early exhibition catalogues published as *Arts and Crafts Essays* in 1893. In the same year the outstanding new *Studio* magazine began to spread its message to an international audience.

One of the characteristic forms of the movement was the 'guild' which in name, if much more rarely in practice, formed a co-operative association of designers and craftsmen. The name was taken from medieval example not only through the influence of Morris, but also the St George's Guild which Ruskin had formed at Sheffield in the 1870s, of which his museum there remains as a legacy. The first such arts and crafts association was the Century Guild of 1882–8, formed by A. H. Mackmurdo, an architect, with the characteristic aim of restoring 'building, decoration, glass painting, pottery, woodcarving and metal to their right place besides painting and sculpture'. It was less typical in that although the Guild's artists carried out their own carving, painting and metalwork, their furniture was made by an established commercial firm. Mackmurdo also edited one of the first literary artistic magazines, the *Hobby Horse*, which he claimed had spurred Morris by raising the issue of printing as an art.

Of subsequent groups two of the most important were the Guild of Handicraft and the Cotswold school. The former was founded in 1888 by C. R. Ashbee, a writer and East End craft teacher, whose father had been a grand London merchant and, secretly, the foremost bibliographer of Victorian erotica. By the time he left Cambridge Ashbee had discovered not only Morris but also Edward Carpenter, and became a sex-reforming socialist. He arrived at Toynbee Hall in the East End of London inspired by a vision of a cross-class 'new freemasonry' of young men, 'Edward's ideal still burning within me'. The Guild's various wood and metal shops were managed by committees of the workmen. Ashbee saw his whole life *An endeavour towards the teaching of John Ruskin and William Morris*, as a 'practical idealist', designer, teacher and later town planner. His American tours were especially important in spreading Morris's influence there. But unlike Morris he saw class as a personal rather than a political problem, resolvable in the little world of handicraft. Workshop fellowship was to be 'the nucleus out of which the new Society is to be organised'. Morris himself poured 'a great deal of cold water' on Ashbee's scheme, telling him it was 'too small to be of any value' for wider social change; but Ashbee told him, 'I am going to forge a weapon for you.'[10] In its first East End years his Guild worked well. But when in 1902, inspired by Morris's call for a simpler life and the direct example of Carpenter on his smallholding, Ashbee and his entire workforce moved to Chipping Campden in Gloucestershire, they encountered much more serious difficulties: higher transport costs, lack of contact with clients, and little alternative work to fall back on in bad times. The Guild failed in 1907, was restarted, and finally wound up in 1919. Meanwhile the second group of craftsmen, later to be known as

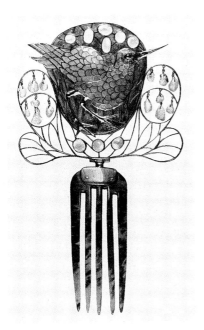

22. Arts and crafts: a jewelled comb in gold, pearls and enamel, made by the Guild of Handicraft to Ashbee's design in the early 1900s

the Cotswold school and led by the architects and furniture designers Ernest Gimson and Sidney Barnsley, had also settled in Gloucestershire, moving to Pinbury in the 1890s, and then in 1903 making their homes and workshops at Sapperton. Smaller in number, they flourished on elaborate, high-quality work for the wealthy. But this twin migration meant that many of the outstanding craftsmen of the movement were in a permanent rural retreat where they could neither assist nor be influenced by metropolitan developments.

There was, nevertheless, a city-based continuation of the arts and crafts movement in the 1900s which formed the seed-bed of a second generation under its influence. In 1902 a craft-encouragement group evolved from the women's page of the socialist *Clarion*. It developed into the Clarion Guild of Handicraft, mounting big national exhibitions, with groups in most industrial cities: a genuine popular campaign. An equally crucial sphere was through new developments in technical education. In London W. R. Lethaby, who had earlier worked in a brief co-operative enterprise with Gimson and Barnsley and like them was a disciple of Morris, became a major influence through his teaching as founder-principal of the Central School of Arts and Crafts. This was in turn inspired by the quality of work of the Birmingham School of Art from the 1890s, whose first two heads, Edward Taylor and Robert Catterson Smith, were again followers of Morris. Further north, more independently developing its own exceptional tradition, was the Glasgow School of Art.

Because they challenged fundamental assumptions about both class and technology it is hardly surprising that the ideals of the arts and crafts movement spread much more rapidly than their practice. There was no pause, for example, in the development of the furniture trade towards the division of labour, the use of machinery, mass production for showroom stock, and the separation of designer and executant. Yet partly because it was in practice never purist, the movement's influence proved remarkably persistent. It was important that its exhibitions always mixed high quality machine products with handwork. It permeated the inter-war campaign to raise commercial standards of design and encourage artists to design for industry, at least until the late 1930s, when with increasing technological complexity the 'artist-designer' began to be ousted by the specialized 'industrial designer'. It was also active—as we shall see in subsequent chapters—in a remarkable range of fields.

In most of them Morris's own hand had left a direct mark, but not in all. He seems to have taken least interest in metalwork. Yet there was a

23. Industrial radicalism: rocking chair of strap brass with gilt inlay, upholstered in plush, made by R. W. Winfield, Birmingham, 1862; a similar chair was shown in the 1851 Great Exhibition

thread, through pre-Raphaelite designs for jewellery back to Pugin's revival of enamelling, which was taken up in Ashbee's exquisite enamelled jewellery, and in the work of Alexander Fisher at the Central School, and Jessie King of Glasgow for Liberty. Equally outstanding was the delicately looped hammered silverware of Ashbee, and Arthur Gaskin's metalwork from Birmingham. One of the most original metalwork designers, however, was W. A. S. Benson, who had hoped to be an engineer, but with direct encouragement from Morris decided to set up his own workshop to produce his sinuous teapots, kettles, and gas- and electric-light fittings. All of his work was machine-made, and by 1887 he had opened a factory in Hammersmith and a Bond Street showroom. His products were also sold by Morris and Company, and after Morris's death he was to become the firm's managing director. A strong believer in commercial production, Benson was one of the founder-members of the Design and Industries Association in 1915.

It was, on the other hand, the ultimate logic of arts and crafts theory that craftsmen should work to their own designs, and in some fields this goal was indeed eventually reached. Art pottery provides a good example of the practical application of the theory. William Morris's potter friend and disciple, William de Morgan, played a role in the revival of pottery design closely comparable to that of Morris himself in the arts and crafts movement as a whole. He had a parallel sense for technique: 'an imaginative mechanic—an imaginative chemist—an imaginative engineer—as well as an imaginative designer . . . '[11] His own skills stretched to tile painting, stained-glass design and cabinet-painting in the early years of the Morris firm. Like Morris, he set his own standards and did not bend readily to the winds of fashion. From 1869, when he set up his own kiln, he supplied the Morris firm with the pottery which it sold. But it was his workmen, not himself, who executed his brilliantly fertile designs for the beautiful lustre which decorated the shelves of Morris houses. The texture of his pots, the drawings of the animals and plants, was precise. His pottery blossomed in a last innovative phase from the 1890s, with new designers like Fred Passenger and Joe Juster using softer grey lustres on a blue base. But craft pottery had begun from the 1870s with the Martin brothers, who worked at their own kiln, and produced much more varied, rougher shapes and textures. During the 1880s several art potteries were started, such as the Elton Pottery at Clevedon Court, impressively represented by the collection in the house today. Others were the Rye Pottery, and the Linthorpe Pottery near Middlesborough. The much simpler stoneware now characteristic of most contemporary craft pottery was, however, only introduced to the movement in the inter-war years, through Bernard Leach. Born in Hong Kong, but sent to school in England as a ten-year-old and trained at the Slade, Leach fused the traditions of two continents. Returning to Japan in 1909, already with the idea of forming 'a group somewhat on William Morris lines', he found himself at a party of potter artists, and was inspired to take up pottery as a craft living. He thus came back to England to set up the crucial St Ives pottery in 1920 steeped in eastern techniques. The revival of English slipware, in which the contrasting colours of the clay are used as a decorative basis, came with Michael Cardew who, drawn to pottery from boyhood by the example of a traditional north Devon local craftsman, Edwin Fishley, 'probably the last vital peasant potter left in England', joined Leach soon afterwards to become 'my first, and best, student'.[12]

Arts and crafts doctrines could be relatively easily applied to pottery. There was no similar transition in furniture. The logic of the theory was scarcely recognized before the 1890s, partly because all the leaders of the movement were architects. Even then, Sidney Barnsley was the only important furniture designer who executed all his own work. Consequently the chief influence of arts and crafts ideas on furniture was not in the development of a school of craftsmen making their own designs, but in the added emphasis on respect for the technique of execution in the training of designers in the art schools. Less necessary, on the other hand, was the failure of British designers to develop simple 'cottage furniture' for the wider market. Gimson regretted this, but believed he could not produce it 'at a price that working class people could afford to pay'. Yet it was successfully developed in Austria and Scandinavia, and finally in Britain too with the Second World War utility furniture scheme, which was led by Gimson's follower Gordon Russell: a realization indeed of Morris's own call for 'good citizen's furniture, solid and well made in workmanship, and in design [with] nothing about it that is not easily defensible, no monstrosities or extravagances, not even of beauty, lest we weary of it'.[13]

Although the arts and crafts movement certainly changed the whole spirit of design in the applied arts, it is less easy to see any precise contribution which it made to modern furniture style. This is partly

24. Arts and crafts furniture, including rush-seated turned ash chairs, designed and made by Gimson for Stoneywell Cottage, Leicestershire, c.1899

because of the diversity of its expression. Certainly there were characteristic features of the period, such as the use of thin uprights with flat square caps, decorative motifs like tulips, hearts or turned leaves, and a general preference for much lighter colours, pink, grey, beige, light blue, and especially white. But the English arts and crafts did not make up a coherent style like the tall linear shapes of the Glasgow craftsmen, or the sinuosity of continental art nouveau, parallel developments which both owed many of their sources to English design in the 1880s, including the work of the Morris circle—and in the case of Belgian art nouveau, to a direct admiration too for Morris's social vision. The English movement was divided between the attractions of plain construction and sophisticated craftsmanship. There was little apparently in common between the styles of Cotswold cottage chairs and the rich inlaid prestige furniture of Ashbee and Gimson, no doubt encouraged by the Dutch cabinet-maker Peter Waals who joined the Cotswold group in 1901: dark woods shimmering in mother of pearl, silver, ivory, and bone. But Grimson was an admirer of Morris, and his simpler work in oak and ash relies entirely on sound craftsmanship for its effect. Some of Gimson's chairs were clearly inspired by the Morris Sussex chair and some of his tables by Webb. Moreover his fine ash chairs with tall ladder backs had been strikingly anticipated by the chair designs of Ford Madox Brown, made as early as 1860.

It is not, however, certain whether this design was later made by Morris and Company, and this uncertainty is revealing. Brown's whole role in the firm's furniture work is rather puzzling. He had designed furniture for his friends in the 1850s and undoubtedly some of his ideas must have influenced Webb and Morris. He probably started the fashion for green stained wood and he may have been responsible for the Sussex chair.[14] The simple green bedroom furniture now in the Kelmscott Manor attics is attributed to him. But little of his work exists and it would appear that not much was produced, unless the Sussex chair was indeed his. Morris and Company seem to have found little outlet for his radical tastes. It was only after he left the firm that he designed the remarkably plain chest of drawers for a workman's cottage which was exhibited at Manchester in 1887 and later at the Arts and Crafts Exhibition. It was of plain deal stained green, and the handles were simply sunk holes, like in the utility furniture of the Second World War. This was much bolder, simpler and more prophetic than any furniture made by Morris and Company.

The contrast between Gimson, who remained a strictly traditional craftsman, and Madox Brown, who was able to achieve a radical

25. Workman's
furniture by Brown,
designed 1861–2 now in
the attic at Kelmscott

simplicity, shows the essentially conservative influence of Morris's
direct stylistic example. It certainly could not be claimed that the style of
C. R. Mackintosh and the Glasgow school of craftsmen owed anything
to Morris. Mackintosh's rectilinear white interiors, with their fitted
cupboards, spare furniture, and complete absence of clutter, were to be
the most important design contribution of Britain to the modern style.
Mackintosh would not have seen the simple light interiors decorated by
Morris in the 1890s for Philip Webb. In any case his style was much
closer to E. W. Godwin's Japanese cubism than to the homely honesty
of Webb. It is more likely that Mackintosh had heard of the room which
Godwin designed for Oscar Wilde in 1884, painted in shades of white
and grey, the furniture all white except for a red lampshade. Followers
of Morris rejected this kind of room as too frigid in its unity, 'needlessly

Spartan—there was a hair-shirt rigour about it, opposed to all geniality or prandial humours'.[15]

The furniture produced by Morris and Company in these later years thus did not represent the most advanced tastes. The best designs were still the two popular chairs and some of Webb's oak furniture, all of the 1860s. After the appointment of George Jack as chief designer in 1890 several new types were introduced. The most attractive were cabinets and sideboards of simple shape, decorated in elaborate marquetry patterns of leaves and foliage. The Victoria and Albert Museum possesses two fine examples in soft brown wood, inlaid in yellow and black with oak leaves and thistles. Another type of cabinet was decorated with sinuous rather unattractive ironwork designed by W. A.

26. Cabinet designed by W.A.S. Benson with characteristic metal details, made by Morris and Company c.1899 of rosewood, inlaid with purplewood, tulipwood and ebony, now at the Victoria and Albert Museum

S. Benson, chiefly interesting because it reflects the shapes of art nouveau. There was also a growing number of designs, some supplied by Mervyn Macartney, which more or less exactly imitated eighteenth-century furniture. Cabinets were often fronted with pretty intersecting tracery. Georgian furniture had returned to fashion in the 1870s. The firm also made some very mediocre neo-Jacobean pieces. In Morris's lifetime there was never any exact reproduction, although after 1905 the firm both sold and reproduced antiques.

This later Morris furniture is very attractive at its best, although it is not as impressive as the best inlaid furniture of Gimson or the Guild of Handicraft. Its foliage patterns, the hallmark of so much Morris work, inspired the honeysuckle marquetry sometimes used by Gimson and the thin climbing flowers on the great oak cabinet by Lethaby which is at the Victoria and Albert Museum. But it had little other direct influence and is of only minor interest in the evolution of English furniture design.

No doubt this was partly due to the small part which Morris himself played in the firm's later work. Where the style was more forward-looking, as in the interiors of the 1890s at Clouds and Standen, the responsibility was Philip Webb's. His work at Clouds has since been altered out of recognition. As in the Morris interiors of the 1870s and 1880s, there were still rich displays of porcelain, but the character of the rooms now came from their essential simplicity. The dining room had plain panelled lower walls and wooden tables with white upper walls and ceiling, like a grand farmhouse kitchen. The drawing room was lined by tall white bookshelves, and the simple white geometry of the mantelpiece and frieze was echoed in the white chair-backs. The colour came from the Morris curtains, cushions, and carpets. Standen, near East Grinstead, has remained unaltered. The Morris wallpapers which line most of the rooms are set off by white woodwork. The whole atmosphere is light and unpretentious. In the gradual evolution of their taste, Webb and Morris had achieved a final style which was the reverse of the dark splendour of Red House.

This final style but slightly supports Morris's claim to be a pioneer of modern style. It is due to Webb rather than to Morris, and in any case these interiors were less advanced than those of Godwin and Mackintosh, and the style of the furniture which filled them was essentially conservative. They would be of slight importance if—like the Morris furniture which can be associated with the arts and crafts school—they did not seem to express an approach much more radical than their style. For these late interiors, together with the earlier furniture which

97

influenced Gimson, are the clearest practical expression of the demand which Morris made in his lectures for a return to simplicity.

This demand for simplicity seems today more immediately relevant to the design and use of furniture than his attitude to craftsmanship, even though it could never have had such a direct influence. In later life Morris not infrequently waved aside his own work with the comment that he would prefer to live 'with the plainest whitewashed walls and wooden chairs and tables' in 'some great room where one talked to one's friends in one corner, and ate in another, and slept in another, and worked in another'.[16]

Although he never went as far as this in a lecture, Morris again and again strongly urged his audiences to make their houses simpler and clear them of rubbish. 'I have never been in any rich man's house which would not have looked the better for having a bonfire made outside of it of nine-tenths of all that it held.' A fireplace would look better without being surrounded by 'trumpery of cast-iron, and brass and polished steel'. A drawing room needed little movable furniture beyond a steady table and several chairs; 'don't have too much of it; have none for finery's sake'. Decoration should be kept to the walls. 'A drawing room ought to look as if some kind of work could be done in it less toilsome

27. The new simplicity: Voysey's own home at the Orchard, Chorley Wood, Hertfordshire, 1900

than being bored.' Medieval art, Morris argued, had been popular art, not the art of palaces; 'rather she fell sick there, and it will take more bracing air than that of rich men's houses to heal her again. If she is ever to be strong enough to help mankind once more, she must gather strength in simple places.'[17] And if art was to begin at home, 'we must clear our houses of troublesome superfluities that are for ever in our way: conventional comforts that are no real comforts, and do but make work for servants and doctors: if you want a golden rule that will fit everybody, this is it: *Have nothing in your houses that you do not know to be useful or believe to be beautiful.*'[18]

In Morris's decorative schemes, as we have seen, there is a gradual evolution from the dark richness of Red House to the white simplicity of Clouds and Standen. There is also, especially in the firm's earliest Gothic furniture, a belief in primitive simplicity. But in these lectures Morris, probably without anticipating how he would be understood, was calling for a much more drastic purging of the Victorian interior, for an economic and modern simplicity. He could do this because he was not merely concerned with art furniture, but with society as a whole, and was as fearless in his approach to each.

This is the key to his lasting reputation in the history of furniture design. There are few of his pieces or decorative schemes which made an important contribution to the stylistic development of the period, and much Morris work is distinctly conservative in spirit. Nevertheless, all his design has a fundamental integrity, a respect for material and a quality of workmanship, which conveyed more than any characteristics of style. Morris was an educated and wealthy man who could have been famous simply as a poet, but who spent the greatest part of his energies in the furnishing crafts. His example gave dignity to these crafts, and encouraged younger architects to take up similar work. His call for simplicity sprang from this same integrity and has proved an equal inspiration.

4

PATTERNS IN TILES AND WALLPAPER

PATTERN-MAKING was the foundation of the art of William Morris. It was his special genius in design. Not only did he design a brilliant series of patterns for a range of repeating fabrics from silk and velvet to common linoleum; patterns were also his instinct in non-repeating work, such as stained glass, embroidery, and tapestry. They even affected his poetry. When he came to formulate his theories of art in his lectures, it was to patterns that he turned for examples.

Yet, in spite of their central importance to his work as an artist, very few biographers of Morris have tried to consider his pattern designs seriously. Apart from the very first biographies by Mackail and Vallance, and the rather unreliable contribution of May Morris, most writing on Morris has been little better than aesthetic hagiography, assuming his pre-eminence as a pioneer of design and embellishing the assumption with anecdotes. The work of Morris's contemporaries was so completely neglected that he came to be seen as an isolated genius. More recently this view has been disproved by the serious study of other Victorian designers and the comparison of their work with Morris. The turning point was the exhibition of Victorian and Edwardian Decorative Arts organized by Peter Floud and the Circulation Department of the Victoria and Albert Museum in 1952. He and his colleagues revealed for the first time the complexity of Morris's relationship with the Victorian period, both as a theorist and a practical artist. In the process a whole forgotten world has been given historical significance. The next two chapters are both concerned with this world of Victorian pattern-making and they are divided merely for convenience. The general theory and practice which is described in this chapter with examples from tile and wallpaper patterns could have been equally well shown from Morris's textile patterns, but textiles introduce the special problems of dyeing and weaving. They are therefore discussed in a separate chapter.

Morris normally began a discussion of patterns with history and it will be easiest to follow him in this. He divided the history of patterns into three stages, each related to the evolution of civilization. In the first, the styles of early art represented the different types of tyranny in the ancient world. Egyptian art was priest-dominated, symbolic, and non-naturalistic. The art of Greece, on the other hand, was naturalistic, the art of perfection of a society of intellectuals. Because intellectual perfectionism resulted in slavery 'mental as well as bodily' for all but the highest craftsmen, Greek decoration was formal, lacking 'the individuality of nature'. Roman imperialism revealed itself in a style of superficial pomp. Its 'great swinging scrolls' of acanthus, borrowed from Greece, were rich and handsome, but without any sense of growth, 'rather stuck together'.

The crucial discovery of continuous growing patterns came with Byzantine art; 'when the Roman tyranny grew sick, when that recurring curse of the world, a dominant race, began for a time to be shaken from its hold, men began to long for the freedom of art.'[1] The great age of pattern-making followed in the work of the free craftsmen of the Middle Ages. Ruskin had seen in the wilful gargoyles of the cathedral front the freedom and pleasure of the medieval sculptor. Morris saw the same lesson in medieval weaving and pottery, made for common household use by craftsmen who created their own patterns in their own handiwork. 'There was little division of labour among them; . . . a man knew his work from end to end, and felt responsible for every stage of its progress.'[2]

Although threatened by the expansion of commerce, pattern-making of this kind still survived in many parts of the world. In Europe it had been finally destroyed by the combined effects of the Renaissance with its reassertion of intellectual perfectionism and the factory system with its division of labour:

All the heaped-up knowledge of modern science, all the energy of modern commerce, all the depth and spirituality of modern thought, cannot reproduce so much as the handiwork of an ignorant, superstitious Berkshire peasant of the 14th century; nay, of a wandering Kurdish shepherd, or of a skin-and-bone oppressed Indian ryot.[3]

His interpretation of the history of the decorative arts was eventually to lead Morris to the conclusion that the only hopeful future for art was in a society of free craftsmen comparable to the Middle Ages. His view was taken up by the crafts movement, with its belief that a designer should execute his own work. It therefore comes as a surprise to realize that in his own pattern-making Morris was little influenced by this theory. Apart from some tapestry and a few early experiments in other techniques, he executed none of his own pattern designs. He did not even produce the majority of them under his own supervision. All his wallpapers and many of his carpets, silks, and chintzes were made by other manufacturers. It is true that in many cases the method used was hand production rather than machinery, but this did not in any way resemble the free handwork of medieval craftsmen. In most of his manufactures Morris used a pre-Victorian process, but it was always organized in the workshop on a serial basis, with different craftsmen responsible for different parts of the sequence and none of them making an individual contribution to the design. The only important exception was in embroidery, although a very limited discretion was also allowed to the glass painters and tapestry weavers.

Wallpapers provide a characteristic example of the kind of work involved. Nearly all Morris papers were handprinted from wood-blocks. The advantage of this method was that colours could be printed separately block by block and thus given time to dry. In machine

28. The work process: chintz printing by hand at Merton Abbey Works, from a Morris and Company catalogue of 1909

printing the colours are printed together and must therefore be quick-drying. Quick-drying colours were thin and liable to fade quickly. Morris tried printing his first paper with metal plates but was dissatisfied. All the rest of his designs were therefore handprinted from wood-blocks by Jeffrey and Company of Islington until 1930, when the blocks were transferred to Sanderson's. It is a skilled but extremely boring process, monotonously repetitive, putting down the block on the paper and making sure each time that it fits exactly and no joins are visible. Machine-printing, involving the control of the rollers, the regulation of the colour consistency, and the tension of the paper, is in fact closer to Morris's ideal of work. It requires intelligent judgement and gives the worker more sense of overall control.

Morris and Company's own work methods were very similar. Tile painting, which was quite an important activity in the first years of the firm, may be taken as an example.

Chiefly through the efforts of Pugin, encaustic tiles, imitations of medieval tiles with patterns of inlaid clay, had been revived by Minton's of Stoke-upon-Trent. Morris, however, preferred the commoner modern process of painting on plain white tiles. Most firms printed outline patterns onto the tiles which were then coloured in by unskilled labour, but Morris objected to printing, believing that the character of

29. The work process before the Morris firm: tablecloth printing by T. Welch at Merton in 1852, from the *Illustrated Exhibitor*

tiles came from delicate brushwork. Morris and Company designs, whether subtle scenes such as Beauty and the Beast or the Months, or mere repeating patterns of swans or daisies, were copied onto the tiles by highly skilled draughtsmen first in outline and then in colour. They were fired in the firm's glass kiln. This difficult and slow work was often executed by the families of the partners, especially Kate and Lucy, the sisters of Charles Faulkner. The result was that Morris tiles cost five times as much as they would have if printed outlines had been used, and after the first years of the firm not many were produced. It is true that they have a delicacy unlike most Victorian tiles, but this was a mixed advantage in view of their customary use in fireplaces. The two finest series are both in Cambridge, at Peterhouse and Queens' College, and only the latter, which is unusually placed on the hood of the chimney, is properly preserved. Morris tiles were of no use for flooring, where tiles were most frequently needed. Had Morris been less inclined to favour handwork, he might have seen that tiles were most obviously suited to bold patterns and colours, arranged in abstract geometric mosaics. His arrangements were like watercolours on a white background, the design crossing the joints between the tiles as if they were irrelevant. Other designers exploited tile shapes, squares, triangles and rectangles being made up into elaborate diamonds, chequers, or zigzags. A fine example also in Cambridge is the floor of the crossing in Jesus College Chapel, designed by G. F. Bodley.

Tiles were perhaps an extreme example of mechanical handwork. When the quality of the product would not be impaired Morris was very willing to use machinery, particularly for heavy work. Shaw recalled a visit with Morris to Merton when he dared to say, 'You should get a machine to do that.' Morris replied, 'I've ordered one.'[4] There was plenty of machinery in the factory already, as any photograph shows, and Morris would certainly have liked more. He regretted, for example, that 'in my small business I am obliged to refrain from doing certain kinds of weaving I should like to do because my capital can't compass a power-loom'.[5] Morris emphasized in his political teaching that in an ideal society 'machines of the most ingenious and best approved kinds will be used when necessary, but will be used simply to save human labour'.[6] Morris believed that both individual creativity and collective mass production would be needed under socialism.

Equally, Morris never pretended that the firm's methods were medieval. On the contrary, he knew that they could not be in an industrialized capitalist economy.

I have got to understand thoroughly the manner of work under which the Art of the Middle Ages was done, and that that is the *only* manner of work which can turn out popular art, only to discover that it is impossible to work in that manner in this profit-grinding society. [It had been] impossible to do more than to ensure the *designer* (mostly myself) some pleasure in his art by getting him to understand the qualities of materials and the happy chances of the processes.

Except with a small part of the more artistic side of the work, I could not do anything (or at least but little) to give this pleasure to the workmen, because I should have had to change their method of work so utterly that I should have disqualified them from earning their living elsewhere.[7]

For the moment the best that he could and did do was to ensure that as a designer he himself understood the labour process; and that as an employer he taught his craftsmen—many of whom were started as unskilled boys, including some recruited as deprived orphans—the full method of production giving them as much responsibility as the process and their developing skill would allow, up to the point, most notably in the case of Dearle, of becoming themselves designers. Morris's practice nevertheless remains in some conflict with his theory. His dislike of machinery and the industrialism which it symbolized, combined with his love of patterns, seems to have overpowered any realization that monotonous hand copying of other men's patterns was a servile type of work. Thus he would impose repeating patterns on work such as embroidery where they were technically quite unnecessary. Morris also held the characteristic Victorian view that the most elaborate techniques were the best. He saw textiles as a hierarchy from printed chintz to tapestry. This helps to explain his lack of interest in plain handweaving, which Ruskin was attempting to revive, and which was to be the modern craft weaver's method. For the same reason, although he fully understood the kind of patterns suited to machine processes, he never accepted that patterns were by their nature mechanical or that the simplest were often the best. 'Set yourselves as much as possible against all machine-work . . . But if you have to design for machine-work, at least let your design show clearly what it is. Make it mechanical with a vengeance, at the same time as simple as possible.'[8] He seems never to have recognized that designing such mechanical patterns might be his supreme achievement.

A similar paradox may be found in Morris's principles of design, again characteristic of the theoretical tensions of the Victorian period. In his art lectures, which he began in 1877, Morris told students to 'follow nature, study antiquity, make your own art'.[9] These three principles could be hard to reconcile. With his delight in the countryside, Morris wanted patterns to be the 'visible symbol' of nature, clothing 'our daily and domestic walls with ornament that reminds us of the outward face of the earth, of the innocent love of animals, or of man passing his days between work and rest'.[10] But the realistic naturalism which would seem to follow from this could not be found in old work, from which Morris drew his principal rules of design. He regarded the study of old examples as 'a positive necessity' to modern design. He told the Royal Commission on Technical Instruction in 1882 that permanent museum exhibitions should be linked to design schools

so that one can come day after day and see the same thing; so that a man who is a lecturer can take his class to the museum and give a lecture on such and such an article, or that a manufacturer, like myself, can take a designer to the museum and say, I want the thing done in such and such a way.

Londoners had such a collection at South Kensington, 'and perhaps I have used it as much as any man living', but new museums were needed in many provincial towns, linked to the local industry. In Nottingham, for example, he advocated a collection of sixteenth- and seventeenth-century designs and examples to help designers in the lace industry.[11]

From these old examples Morris learnt three fundamental rules. First, 'never forget the material you are working with . . . The special limitations of the material should be a pleasure to you, not a hindrance.'[12] A designer should study the technique of manufacture, where possible visiting a workshop to 'learn the practical way of carrying out the work for which he designs; he ought to be able to weave himself'.[13] The quality of the material and the technique of manufacture determined how close to naturalistic realism the design should come. All materials required some conventionalizing of nature, but the coarsest needed the most symbolic approach. Thus of textiles tapestry should be closest to pictures, carpets to symbols. But Morris denied that any material called for wholly abstract patterns. 'I, as a Western man and a picture-lover, must still insist on plenty of meaning in your patterns; I must have unmistakable suggestions of gardens and fields, and strange trees, boughs and tendrils.'[14]

Secondly, there were certain general principles in pattern-designing. Thus, 'the more obvious the geometrical structure of a pattern is, the less its parts should tend toward naturalism.' 'All growth must be capable of explanation logical and clear.'[15]

Rational growth is necessary to all patterns, or at least the hint of such growth; and in recurring patterns, at least, the noblest are those where one thing grows visibly and necessarily from another. Take heed in this growth that each member of it be strong and crisp, that the lines do not get thready or flabby or too far from their stock to sprout firmly and vigorously; even where a line ends it should look as if it had plenty of capacity for more growth if so it would.[16]

There were more rules for modelling and colour. Both should be sharp and clean. Shading, for example, should be used for explanation, and not to make an object look round, while any two areas of colour should be separated by a thin dividing line of a third colour, which would play the part of shadow in natural colour harmonies.

Thirdly, old examples contained numerous stylistic hints which could contribute to a style of one's own. 'Don't copy any style at all, but make your own; yet you must study the history of your art, or you will be nose-led by the first bad copyist of it that you come across.'[17] In effect a personal style should consist of a blending of traditional pattern structures and themes from nature within the limits imposed by the material.

This theory of design was very similar to that of other leading Victorian designers, such as Pugin, Owen Jones, and Christopher Dresser, whose views had been widely influential from the 1850s. Nor did Morris solve the essential problem that they had failed to answer: where should the balance be drawn between natural and conventional form, between tradition and originality?

In practice Morris, like his contemporaries, moved between one position and another. The phases of his design can be best followed and related to his contemporaries in his wallpaper patterns, because they extend over the longest period of his activity, from 1862 until 1896, and also because they can be accurately identified and dated from the Patent Office records. These records show that altogether Morris designed 41 patterns, but that several commonly thought to be his are by other designers, chiefly his pupil J. H. Dearle. Ten Morris and Company wallpapers before 1896 and 31 subsequently were not by Morris.

Before Morris began designing wallpapers the design reformers had already brought about an important change of taste. They had justly derided early Victorian wallpapers for their realistic drawing, bouquets of flowers shaded in high relief and coloured in bilious maroons and bottle greens. The reformers argued that wallpapers should be highly conventionalized geometric patterns, absolutely flat, in light bright colours. Beginning with Pugin's designs for the House of Commons, there had been a remarkable revolution of taste in the 1850s, so that by 1860 the most fashionable patterns were austere diapers, formal fleur-de-lis, and acanthus, in almost heraldic colours.

Morris accepted the common argument of the critics that wallpapers should be flat. But he wanted 'to be reminded, however simply, of the close vine-trellis that keeps out the sun by the Nile side; or of the wild-woods and their streams . . . or of the many-flowered summer meadows of Picardy'; and, moreover, as he told Warington Taylor in 1863, he 'disliked *flowers* treated geometrically stiffly in patterns'.[18] So his first small group of wallpapers, which were issued in 1864–6 after several experiments, were in fact astonishingly old fashioned—'so jolly and no conventionalism', as Taylor put it. His 'Trellis' was a realistic piece of woodwork with prickly climbing roses and birds and insects carefully drawn by Philip Webb. 'Daisy' and 'Fruit' were flatter, but they had no geometric pattern at all, clumps of daisies and columbines and sprays of apples and pomegranates scattered all over the wall surface—very like the tile patterns which the firm was producing at the same time. Their attractiveness lies in the fresh naïve charm of their realism. It was in effect a return to the naturalism of the 1840s. 'Daisy' was to remain a very popular design until the twentieth century, and because of Morris's later reputation as a design reformer it came to be considered in some way a turning point. It was not. The first Morris designs were completely ignored by contemporary designers and they did not sell well for some years. The earliest public comment on them which has been found comes from a sentimental novel of 1872, which praised the 'eye-comforting' realism of their 'blooming fruits'.[19]

Because of the limited sale of these first designs, no more were added before 1871. It is interesting that the first which were then issued, 'Diaper', 'Indian', and 'Venetian', were adaptations of old geometric patterns and much closer to the formalism which was still the fashion. But they were unimportant in comparison with the tremendous group of seventeen patterns which Morris designed between 1872 and 1876. This was in fact his finest group of wallpapers. Their rare combination of life with clear pattern has rightly remained a recurrent inspiration to subsequent generations of designers. They are quite as naturalistic as the first, but now generally based on a subtly concealed but strong underlying pattern which gives their easy curves the reality of growth. They do not look absolutely flat, but rather as if arranged within a depth of about an inch. The drawing and colours are clear and fresh, conveying an extraordinary immediacy. One untypical client, a small tradesman, conveying to a visiting East End clergyman his 'great delight in the Morris paper with which his room was covered', put his finger on it: 'seems as if it was all-a-growing.'[20] One can almost smell the 'Jasmine' or touch the stiff blue and green fronds of 'Branch', the delicate double-swishing leaves of 'Marigold'; one longs to reach into the blue and take the orange-flecked fruit of 'Apple', or to pick the bunches of grapes that glisten against the luxuriant dark leaves of 'Vine'.

By 1876 the naturalism which had been so conservative was no longer unfashionable. The change had begun in 1871, just before this second series of Morris papers, when Jeffrey and Company reintroduced some asymmetrical naturalistic designs. By 1874 these had become the advanced fashion. Some designers, such as Bruce Talbert and E. W. Godwin, were strongly influenced by Japanese naturalism, while others, such as Walter Crane and J. D. Sedding, drew on motives from Renaissance scroll work. Although Morris was out of sympathy with both sources, his own designs now became much more admired by the leading designers. The period which followed was one of exceptional liveliness and quality. Some of the motives which were developed, such as Walter Crane's linear swirl and blob, and the floating seaweed effect, were to be important sources of the Art Nouveau style of the 1890s.

Yet Morris only participated for a brief moment in this new naturalism. By 1876 he was turning in a contrary direction, towards historicism and formalism. Characteristically, this change was due to a cross-influence from a new enthusiasm—his study of woven textiles at this time. He was impressed by their sharply emphasized mirror-wise repeats and their bold conventional drawing, and although there was no technical reason for this kind of design in wallpaper, it affected nearly all his subsequent work. Sometimes formalism was thoroughly justified, as in a stately paper like 'Acanthus', designed in 1875 and elaborately printed from sixteen blocks, or 'St James', specially produced for St James's Palace in 1881. Among simpler, less ambitious papers 'Acorn' (1879) has a compelling miniature tracery structure, but in others formalism could too easily arrest the feeling of life and growth in the patterns.

The most striking example of historicism was in a group of designs inspired by a seventeenth-century velvet, which was acquired by the Victoria and Albert Museum in 1883. They closely follow its framework of diagonal twisting stems. 'Wild Tulip' (1884) is a delightfully fresh design on this basic pattern, but 'Bruges' (1888) is the most formalized of all Morris's papers, sombre silhouettes of rich leaves which simulate the texture of a brocade.

It may be that Morris's wallpaper designs between 1877 and 1890 suffered from his preoccupation with textiles. Several of his designs in these years were used for both chintz and paper. After 1890, when his wallpapers again outnumbered his textile patterns, he produced a striking last group of designs, in which something of the natural ease of his earlier work is recaptured. They are of no set type, and indeed 'Triple Net' is an exceptionally rigid design, while the pretty naturalistic details of 'Blackthorn' are set in a formal structure 'Compton', long thought to be Morris's last pattern, is in fact by Dearle, and has rather conventional detail arranged in a natural way. Surprising combinations of this kind occur in most of these late patterns. Several patterns combine naturalistic and formal detail, often with a background powdered with dots and tendrils behind larger leaves; 'Wallflower' and 'Double Bough' are examples. 'Bachelor's Button' is perhaps the most satisfying late design, boldly setting large, simply drawn flowers among sweeping acanthus leaves. It is at the same time unaffected and majestic, qualities which few but Morris could have combined.

Morris's wallpaper designs cannot therefore be regarded as a straightforward stylistic development related to a consistent theory. His changes in style simply represent his fluctuating influences. Nor do they bear a close relationship to the main development of English wallpaper style from Pugin and the early Victorian reformers to Voysey and the first modern designers. Yet his patterns, because they were never responses to fashion, have held their appeal for far longer than the work of his contemporaries. Jeffrey and Company's wallpapers in the 1900s include designs which are very obviously inspired both by the naïve naturalistic 'Daisy' and by the later rigid patterns. Today some thirty Morris and Company wallpaper patterns, over half by Morris himself, in more than a hundred different colour versions are in production by Sanderson's. His designs have proved adaptable to an extraordinary variety of furnishing fashions. The explanation is less that they anticipate the modern style than that, unlike the historically more significant and sometimes very striking designs of his contemporaries, the best Morris papers have a classic, timeless independence.

5

PATTERNS IN TEXTILES

THE relationship between theory and practice in work and in style which
we have examined in the preceding chapter could have equally well been
shown in Morris's textile patterns. Indeed, although these cover a much
shorter period, the great majority being designed between 1875 and
1885, they provide still more striking examples of Morris's manufacturing technique and of his responsiveness to historical influence.

Wallpaper printing was a relatively simple process which could be
mastered without a study of ancient examples. Morris appears to have
been satisfied by the colours available, and in any case he was more
interested in the linear patterns of his papers than in their colour. Most
of them were available in several different colour schemes, some of
which seem somewhat careless. But textile patterns always had to be
based on colour, because linear patterns could not be seen properly in
folded hangings or upholstery.

Morris was at once so dissatisfied with the commercial dyes available
for his first printed cotton, that in 1874 he began his investigation of the
art of dyeing, which in turn led to his study of weaving and to the
setting up of his own looms not only for silks and serges, but also for
carpets and tapestries. The study of his textiles is therefore of technical
as well as aesthetic interest.

Once again it will be convenient to begin with history. Morris
asserted that the secret of the ancient art of dyeing had been the
vegetable palette, and that its deterioration was due to the introduction
of chemicals (anilines). The dyes used in Europe from the sixteenth to
the eighteenth century had consisted principally of blue indigo, a
vegetable dye; red kermes, an insect dye, and red madder, a vegetable
dye; weld yellow from wild mignonette, and a variety of other
vegetable yellows from poplar, willow, birch, and heather; and brown
from walnut husks or roots. The wood dyes were less permanent than
kermes or indigo. Other colours were made up by combinations; indigo
and weld for greens, indigo and kermes for purple, and so on. Until
1800 the only additions were some red and yellow American wood
dyes, yellow quercitron being the most important, and an American red
insect dye, cochineal, which tended to replace indigo as a basis for black.

The first important change, Morris argued, came with the introduction

30. Folk art
contemporary with the
Morris firm: a
patchwork quilt of
c.1851

of Prussian blue in about 1810, a chemical dye on an iron basis. Other chemical dyes followed, such as a solid acid green in 1835, as a substitute for the soft blueish green of weld on indigo. The gaudy mauve and purple coal tar dyes to which Morris especially objected, were discovered in 1856. They completed the disruption of the old vegetable palette.

Although the collapse of colour harmony was evident enough, this was a less fair picture of the major technical advances which had been made not only in the range of colours, but in their permanence, and in the processes of dyeing and printing colours. Most of the new colours produced had been perfectly satisfactory. Moreover the mid–nineteenth-century developments were the fruit of chemical experiments which went back to the late seventeenth century. Iron had been long used as a basis for black. And when vegetable dyes were used, it was often necessary to use a chemical mordant, generally alum, to fix them. A colour which would dye easily, would not always print; or would not print easily on particular cloths, such as cotton or linen. It might then be best to print the mordant, the fixing chemical, as a pattern on the cloth, so that after dyeing the colour could be soaped out of the parts which were not mordanted. It was because the most permanent dyes, as James Haigh observed in *The Dyer's Assistant* of 1778, were generally the most difficult to use, 'that the true knowledge of chemistry, to which the art of dyeing owes its origin, is of so much use'. Alternatively, with a dye which fixed easily, a resist might first be printed as a negative of the pattern.

Morris was fully aware of these facts. His own dye shops were to make full use of chemical mordants and resists, and for a few of his designs even used chemical dyes—in the delightful 'Daffodil' chintz, for example.[21] As a dyer it was his eye for colour, rather than his technique, which distinguished him from his contemporaries. But learning the complex and often ancient techniques of dyeing excited him, becoming not merely a practical exercise, but a romantic rediscovery of a lost world.

This was especially true of indigo, which he feared would be the most important victim of the chemical dyes. Indigo was a particularly difficult dye to use, because it was soluble only when hydrogenated. When exposed to the air it quickly became oxidized and fast. In spite of the discovery in the eighteenth century of chemical methods for delaying oxidization ('pencil blue') or for dissolving and oxidizing indigo after it had been printed on the cloth ('china blue'), it was not until the end of the nineteenth century that a wholly satisfactory method of printing with indigo was finally developed. Until then the cloth was more easily dyed, with a printed resist producing the pattern. Even dyeing was far from simple, whichever method was used in preparing the vat. The hot vat, for example, required three days' preparation, sealed from the air to prevent oxidization, and the moment for dipping was known by its smell, which, according to James Haigh, was 'sharp, and resembles that of stinking meat roasted'. It was important to dip the cloth evenly, because near the vat surface the indigo became partly oxidized and dyed less strongly. Because of these difficulties Morris thought the indigo hot vat 'a ticklish job, and requires, I should say, more experience than any other dyeing process'.[22] Not surprisingly, it fascinated him.

Morris began his experiments with his own small dye house at Queen Square. Then he decided to investigate the whole process at the dye works of Thomas Wardle, brother of Morris and Company's manager, at Leek in Staffordshire. Wardle, who had learnt the old processes from his father, was already an experimenter himself. His special interest was in Indian textiles, and he travelled widely there and in the Middle East collecting patterns and arranging imports from local manufacturers; while for new work, he used the leading English designers. Their mutual influence is shown in Morris's chintz design 'Indian Diaper' of 1875. He had gone up to Leek that February. His letters were written in a hand 'shaky with doing journeyman's work the last few days: delightful work, hard for the body and easy for the mind'. Most of Wardle's work was in the commercial chemical dyes. 'The copper-pots in the dye-houses, full of bright colours where they are dyeing silks, look rather exciting, but alas! they are mostly aniline: our own establishment is very small.'[23] Morris worked especially at the indigo vat, covering himself with blue so that he 'wanted pegs to keep my fingers one from the other'. He expressed his exasperation with a typical fit of temper; 'I wish I hadn't been such a fool; perhaps they will turn me out to-morrow morning, or put me in the blue-vat.'[24]

The visit proved a success and was the first of several during the next three years, while Wardle tried to start regular production of the dyes which Morris approved. A lengthy correspondence between the two men ensued. Morris was continuing his own experiments all the time, with walnut peel, with a blue dye taken from the eighteenth-century French writer Hellot, with a handful of poplar twigs out on a fishing expedition at Kelmscott. He sent Wardle copies of the old treatises on dyeing; Hellot, Philemon Holland's Bliny, Gerard's herbal, the sixteenth-century Swiss Fuchsius, and Venetian Matthiolus. Wardle sent back parcels of trial fents, which Morris soaped, criticized for colour, and exposed to the sunlight to test their fastness:

The fents have just come; in 1032 the greens are well matched to 967; but the yellow mossing is too dark and especially red; . . . 1034 is not much use, it looks dead and washed out: and 1031 for 964 is also no use being too bright and crude . . . ; in green 968 a lighter colour might be a little fresher; this fent washed very badly, the darkening of the yellow in soap obviously making the evil worse;

and so through the parcel.[25]

At first the results were discouraging, because Wardle's printer seemed incapable of

even the simplest matching, and it all is a matter of luck how things go: I believe he thinks we can't do without him and that he can do anything he pleases: I don't suggest sacking him at once in face of all the present orders, but we can't be for ever under his hippopotamus thumb . . . The fact is the man's mind is in a perfect muddle.[26]

Morris considered getting advice from France, even from Constantinople. Blues and greens were the most serious difficulty and the indigo

114

vat was not started until 1876. Wardle then replaced his printer and Morris found the blue 'quite a success now; I am very pleased and congratulate you on it'.[27] Gradually the other dyes were worked out in turn.

The first patterns to use the new dyes were six designs for chintzes which Morris sent for production by Wardle. The most ambitious was the 'Honeysuckle' pattern, which 'cost us a lot in blocks, and is one of the most important we are likely to have'.[28] The difficulty in matching this seems to have brought about a crisis. Morris had already been arguing Wardle to cut down his prices, which were double those of Thomas Clarkson of Bannister Hall, the printer of Morris's first experimental 'Tulip and Willow' chintz in 1873:

Of course we both hope and think that, when all goes smoother, you will be able to do the cloths as cheap as other people: meanwhile we have known the cloths long enough to find that people start at the present prices we are obliged to charge. I must also remind you how much we suffer from imitators. These will be all agog as soon as they hear of our printed cloths being admired, and we must try not to give them the advantage of grossly underselling us.

The prices could only be justified by the quality of the goods, and the fact that the colours were fast. 'I don't think you should look forward to our *ever* using a machine. As to the mercantile branch, that is quite out of *our* way: but I see no reason why *you* should not try it, if you think it would pay; and I should be happy to help if you wanted any help in the designing way.'[29] Clearly Wardle was not satisfied with the rewards which could be won from dyeing for an exclusive art furnishing firm. Morris on his part was stretching his standards, trying to buy as many cloths as possible: 'I have always strained my artistic conscience to the utmost in dealing with doubtful cases and have kept many pieces which, if I were dealing merely in a business way, I should have refused; as a result we have a good deal of stock which is only half useful to us.' The crux of the problem was 'the lack of constant artistic supervision on the spot'.[30] He had already invested too much in the printing to drop it, so he offered to buy Wardle out if he did not want to carry on. Although this proved unnecessary for the moment, Morris probably decided at this point that he must eventually print his own chintzes from his own dyes. His last patterns for Wardle were simpler, less dependent on exact shades and 'very nice balance of colour'. He attempted to allow for the unevenness of the indigo pencil blue: 'when I come down we must talk about what is the best kind of *design* for these *printed* indigos.'[31]

Meanwhile Wardle had also started dyeing for woven textiles. After 1876 he dyed the yarn for the Morris Kidderminster carpets which were machine-woven at Heckmondwike, Yorkshire; previously the yarn had also been dyed at Heckmondwike. He was delighted by a trial carpet in red wool: 'nothing could be better both as to tone and relief of colour—so that is settled'.[32] Similarly arrangements were made with J. O. Nicholson of Macclesfield to weave silks dyed by Wardle. Morris had first used silk dyed in France but found that it faded badly. A start was also made with woollen serges and Utrecht velvet.

Difficulties in these arrangements for exploiting the new dyes turned Morris's attention to weaving. 'I wish I had my own looms, which would mend it all,' he wrote in the autumn of 1876.[33] He had once previously bought a loom, but had failed to work it, in spite of help from some Spitalfields weavers. He now encouraged Wardle's wife to attempt some experimental carpet weaving, and in the spring of 1877 he decided to try both carpets and woven silks himself.

The silk was started first. With Wardle's help a French weaver from Lyons was engaged for a year to set up a Jacquard loom. Morris was 'dazzled at the prospect', looking at old silks and 'studying birds now to see if I can't get some of them into my next design'.[34] Although his Oxford Street showroom was opening, 'I can't say I am much excited about it, as I should be if it were a shed with a half dozen looms in it.'[35]

In weaving the distinction between power-weaving and hand-weaving was less important than that between the traditional draw loom and the Jacquard loom. The fabric of all woven textiles is essentially made up of warp, which is a foundation set of parallel threads, and weft, which is interwoven across the warp. The variety of colour and texture in woven fabrics depends on the materials used, and which materials are presented on the surface of the cloth, and whether, as in velvet, the threads are caught up to form a pile. Carpet weaving is not essentially different, although a carpet often has a complex structure—as, for example, a Kidderminster three-ply, which is composed of three interwoven fabrics, each with its own warp and weft. Pile carpets, such as Brussels, are made like velvet. Not all carpets are woven, however; hand-knotted or tufted carpets are made by tying worsted or silk into a coarse foundation which is generally itself constructed as the work progresses. Chenille (patent Axminster, invented in 1839) and Axminster (invented in 1876) carpets are woven imitations of hand-tufting.

Most textiles, including carpets, could be woven on a Jacquard loom, an invention of 1802 introduced to common use in the 1820s. Previously for all but the very simplest geometric patterns the weaver had required the help of a draw boy. Each warp thread needed for the pattern was tied to a lash by a series of cords and pulleys. (One advantage of a repeating pattern was that a series of warp threads across the loom could be tied to a single lash.) The lashes for each line in the design were grouped together and pulled by the draw boy, while the weaver threw the shuttle carrying the weft through the resultant 'shed' of warp threads. The Jacquard loom replaced the cords and the draw boy, using cards punched in advance and set up on the loom. There were two consequences for the designer from this change. Because the new method was swifter and more accurate, more ambitious patterns could be woven than on the draw loom at the same cost. On the other hand, it was no longer possible for the craftsman to spontaneously choose, for example, to repeat a line to make the effect more solid as the pattern was being woven.

There was therefore no element of aesthetic judgement in weaving by the Jacquard loom, and it made no difference whether it was worked by power or by hand. In practice outside contractors used power looms for Morris textiles, while the Merton Abbey Jacquard looms were hand-operated. But Morris did not use power simply because he was producing small quantities of textiles for a limited market, and 'because my capital can't compass a power loom'.[36] It is perhaps surprising that he never experimented with the earlier draw loom, which was to be the basis of the Ruskinian revival of cottage hand-weaving in Cumbria and elsewhere from the mid–1880s. Very likely one reason was its association with tedious child labour.

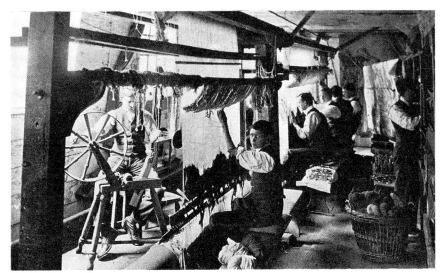

31. Weaving at the Merton Abbey Tapestry Works in the early twentieth century. In the foreground an apprentice: the boys were lodged next to the works under the care of a housekeeper

After some initial difficulties Morris soon mastered the Jacquard loom. At the start Bazin, his French weaver, muddled his pattern cards; 'these weavers don't understand much about getting a pattern together: they can just weave, and that is all.'[37] But with the help of an old English weaver from Spitalfields difficulties were sorted out, and, once started, the chief difficulty in expanding the firm's weaving before the move to Merton in 1881 was simply lack of space.

Morris decided not to weave carpets on the loom. He had been studying and buying oriental carpets, and in 1877 had seen an ancient Persian carpet 'that fairly threw me on my back. I had no idea that such wonders could be done in carpets.'[38] In the following year, with the help of a hand-weaver from Glasgow, he set up carpet frames in the stables of his Hammersmith house. This work was also restricted by lack of space until the move to Merton. At Merton handtufting, according to an approving visitor, took place in a large low room:

In the middle sits a woman finishing off some completed rugs; in a corner is a large pile of worsted of a magnificent red . . . On the windowsill are pots of musk . . . The strong, level afternoon light shines round the figures of the young girls seated in rows on low benches along the frames, and brightens to gold some of the fair heads. Above and behind them rows of bobbins of many-coloured worsteds, stuck on pegs, shower down threads of beautiful colours, which are caught by the deft fingers, passed through strong threads (fixed uprightly in the frames, to serve as a foundation), tied in a knot, slipped down in their place, snipped even with the rest of the carpet, all in a second of time.[39]

A girl knotted two inches of carpet in a day. It was a typical example of the semi-skilled handwork used by Morris for many of his products.

So, to a surprising extent, was tapestry, Morris's culminating venture in weaving, which he also started at Hammersmith and moved to Merton. Inspired by a sale of tapestries in Paris in 1877, he began to work out this last technique from an eighteenth-century French book of *Arts et Metiers*. In 1878 he set up his own loom in his bedroom. He would work at it in the early mornings and completed his first piece, the 'Cabbage and Vine' tapestry, in May 1879. The Merton loom was based on an ancient example which he had found at Gobelins.

Morris did not regard tapestry as suitable for repeating patterns. 'The noblest of the weaving arts is Tapestry, in which there is nothing mechanical: it may be looked upon as a mosaic of pieces of colour made up of dyed threads.' The weaver must be an artist, drawing with the coloured threads; otherwise he would 'turn out nothing but bungles, disgraceful to everyone concerned in the matter'.[40] It seems obvious that this view of tapestry requires the artist to weave his own designs. Yet

Morris, once he had mastered the art, trained boys in the work who had no previous experience even of drawing and were given only a very limited freedom in interpreting the designs which they had to copy. He was even prepared to offer Thomas Wardle designs of leaf and flower greeneries for commercial manufacture. The new textile firm of Arthur Lee, which started weaving high quality fabrics at Warrington in 1888, using leading arts and crafts designers, and set up its Tapestry Works at Birkenhead in 1904, produced luxurious tapestries and embroideries for the world market. It organized its mainly female workforce, rising to 500, with a classic paternalistic hierarchy of labour, as its workers themselves clearly remember; but the firm not unreasonably claimed its founder's inspiration in Morris himself.[41]

In most of Morris's manufactures there is little reason for thinking that the tensions between his theory and practice inhibited his designs. In tapestry it proved a disaster. Technically the revival of the art was one of his greatest triumphs. Apart from the Royal Tapestry Works at Windsor, which started in 1876 on eighteenth-century French lines and were never very successful, no important English workshop had woven tapestries for over a hundred years. Unlike most of his contemporaries, Morris saw that tapestry had been one of the great medieval arts, with its rich colours, its strong contrasts of tone, its use of silhouette as the basis of design, and its abundant clear, imaginative detail. 'You really may almost turn your wall into a rose-hedge or a deep forest, for its material and general capabilities almost compel us to fashion plane above plane of rich, crisp, and varying foliage with bright blossoms, or strange birds showing through the intervals.'[42] He condemned realistic Renaissance design as 'wholly unfit for tapestry' and regarded the Gobelins practice of copying old masters as the final degradation of the art.[43]

Nevertheless, instead of himself weaving a few tapestries which drew out his own unrivalled sense of colour and imaginative detail, he contributed little more to most of the firm's tapestries than designs for the background. The figures were usually by Burne-Jones. None of them showed any real feeling for tapestry. The 'Adoration of the Kings' tapestry in Exeter College Chapel, Oxford, for example, is ruined by his bent, sickly figures. The 'Angeli Laudentes' and 'Angeli Ministrantes' tapestries were adapted from a window design for Salisbury Cathedral and several other adaptations from paintings by Burne-Jones were made after 1900. The figures in the 'Orchard' were copied from the roof of Jesus College Chapel, Cambridge, an early work of the Morris firm. 'Primavera' was taken directly from Botticelli. The charming 'Forest' is marred by incongruously realistic animals and birds by Philip Webb. 'Flora' and 'Pomona' succeed because the background dominates, and the most convincing of the tapestries, the 'Woodpecker' at Walthamstow, was woven in 1885 from a design for once entirely by Morris, with no figures, simply two bright birds among the apple branches of a strong brown-trunked tree, wrapped about by a magnificent blue acanthus. It makes one realize how much Morris might have achieved on his own.

Morris regarded carpets as 'somewhat of the nature of Tapestry', but his designs for them were much more successful, if only because they were straightforward repeating patterns.[44] Although he insisted that carpet patterns must have 'plenty of meaning', he took the common view of the Victorian design reformers that they should not be realistic. In Christopher Dresser's words, carpets should be flat, 'for nothing can be more uncomfortable to walk over than a rough and uneven surface of land and water, bestrewed with bushes and other large objects which cast massive shadows, interspersed with Louis-Quinze ornament'.[45] For Morris this meant that 'the designs should always be very elementary in form, and *suggestive* merely of forms of leafage, flowers, beasts and birds.'[46]

The carpet manufacturers had already responded to criticism before Morris made his first designs in the early 1870s. Charles Eastlake's *Hints on Household Taste* of 1868 illustrates a fine Kidderminster carpet by the architect E. J. Tarver. But since there is neither any representative collection nor any published study of English carpets after 1860, it is not easy to compare Morris with his contemporaries, despite the clarifying recent work of Linda Parry on his own development. Even his designs for commercially made carpets must be assessed from a very few examples. Morris is known to have designed in the 1870s for all the principal types of Victorian commercial carpet: Kidderminster, Wilton and Brussels pile, patent Axminster and Axminister—over twenty patterns for Wilton alone. Some, have completely disappeared, most are known only through designs or photographs, and only a very few examples for machine-woven carpets have survived. They are ingenious, tight designs, with only three or four colours and a close, interlocking repeat. The best known is the Kidderminster three-ply 'Lily', whose black and green flowerheads nod restlessly across bands of white and yellow. There was also a blue and white 'Daisy' pattern. The Victoria and Albert Museum have a charming Wilton carpet of 'Bellflowers', in blue and green. These interesting designs are all surprisingly naturalistic.

32. Hammersmith handknotted rug, designed by Morris, 1880s

The hand-knotted carpets made by Morris and Company after 1878 were very different, much closer to oriental abstract patterns. The colours, which could show a much more subtle range, were generally based on red and blue rather than green. These changes reflected Morris's study of ancient examples in the mid–1870s. The smaller rug designs were duplicated and a large number of examples survive. At their best they are extremely attractive, with their broad flat stems and twigs in soft colours and charming criss-cross knotting at each end. But others are over-naturalistic; the patterns are sometimes upright and perhaps intended as wall hangings. More successful small rugs were soon to be made by the arts and crafts designers who followed Morris; some, such as those by George Walton, were purely geometric; others, made by Liberty's, exploited the woolly roughness of handmade rugs with bold non-repeating designs. Morris's finest designs were for much larger, unique carpets, made for ambitious decorative schemes like those at Clouds and Naworth Castle. As with the smaller rugs he used repeating patterns, although there was no need for repeats, but with a confident splendour which quite overcame the difficulty of their naturalism. Some are based on complex ground covers of intertwining leaves, others on central medallions; some patterns read from each side, others from only one. A magnificent example is the 'Clouds' carpet now in the Regent House, Cambridge. A border of huge buff leaves patterned over with white sprays, with paler leaves and red bell-flowers behind them, provides a most beautiful framework for the long central pattern of brownish pink and green stalks, darker leaves and great heraldic flowerheads intertwined on a bright blue ground.

The problem of identification is less serious with Morris's designs for other woven textiles, but as with carpets incomplete information hampers an assessment of his designs. No systematic collection exists. The firm's catalogues and sample book were compiled after 1900 and, like the list made by May Morris, they attribute to Morris designs now known to be by J. H. Dearle. Only nine designs can be dated through their registration at the Patent Office. Eight of the designs in the sample book are unknown elsewhere and the fragments are too small to put together. Nor is it known where many of them were manufactured. The first silks and woollen fabrics designed in 1876 were woven by McCrea of Halifax and by Nicholson of Macclesfield on power looms. Nicholson probably also wove the 'Oak' and 'St James' silks of 1881, in view of the quantity produced. The finest woollen hangings, the 'Bird' and 'Peacock and Dragon' were specially designed in 1878 for hand-weaving on the newly acquired Jacquard loom, but the others were power-woven either by Dixon of Bradford or by Alexander Morton of Darvel, Ayrshire, who also produced the 'Madras' muslin of 1881. But practice varied and it is rarely possible to be certain about any particular piece.

Apart from a few early designs such as 'Anemone', Morris patterns for woven textiles are very closely related to medieval examples. He was especially inspired by the thirteenth- and fourteenth-century woven silks of Palermo and Lucca, with their sharply drawn, clearly repeating patterns of mythical beasts, vine leaves, 'the lions drinking at the woodland fountain', or pairs of long-tailed birds turning their heads to peck fruit.[47] Some of these patterns were based on vertical twisting lines, or on interlacing lines forming ogival patterns. These structures became more emphatic in the later north Italian and Spanish silks and damasks which also strongly influenced Morris. These were much more formal, with heraldic patterns based on thistles and artichokes. Morris had long been aware of these patterns from George Wardle's drawings of East Anglian church screens where the saints wore robes of both kinds. He now also studied the fine collection at South Kensington.

Some of the patterns were taken directly from old examples. The 'Mohair' cotton damask of 1876, for example, was adapted from a formal fifteenth-century Rhenish printed linen, simply by replacing the birds in the original with flowers. Dearle's popular silk and wool 'Rose and Lily' pattern of 1893, until recently thought to be the last of Morris's woven textile designs, was similarly taken from a sixteenth-century Venetian silk, also formal; the only change was a rose in the place of a crown.

The remaining designs are of two types. There are those with birds. 'Dove and Rose' is a silk and wool of 1879 of a very medieval spirit, but the finest are the heavy rough woollen fabrics of 1878–9, such as 'Bird and Vine', and 'Peacock and Dragon'. The great archaic pairs of birds, clawing, pecking and fluttering in the stiff foliage, in warm reds, orange, brown, and blue, are among the noblest of all Morris's designs.

The foliage designs without birds are rather less successful and sometimes quite close to printed patterns. The most interesting are the most heraldic and formal: the 'Granada' velvet of 1884, the 'Oak' and 'St James' silks and among the heavy woollens, 'Ispahan', now known to be by Dearle. In the more naturalistic patterns the rigid framework seems an uneasy constraint. The more formal designs also benefit from a simplicity in colour; the silks were in blue on dark green and pink on red respectively. But fine though they are, they are less striking than some of the still more formal silks designed by Owen Jones in the early 1870s and woven by Benjamin Warner of Spitalfields. In Jones's severe pink and black silks the ogival framework is brilliantly integrated into a pattern of brittle, thrusting, but completely formalized leaves. Morris was incapable of this ruthlessness. His woven textiles, like his wallpapers, seem immune from the vehemence of his contemporaries. This explains how the 'Oak' silk came recently to be accidentally reproduced as an antique damask.

Morris's patterns for printed chintz are the most numerous group of his textile designs. Because of the Patent Office records they are also the best dated. Consequently Morris's chintzes, like his wallpapers, provide

33. Silk by Owen Jones, c. 1870

a good opportunity for comparing his work with that of his contemporaries. Again it has emerged that his designs did not have the solitary pre-eminence often ascribed to them. English printed floral cottons, dominated by London copperplate printers in the mid-eighteenth century and by Lancashire wood-block printers between 1780 and 1820, had fallen from their high standards in the 1830s. The decline was due to dominance by the cheap export market as well as the disruption of the colour palette through the introduction of chemical dyes and the replacement of woodblocks by progressively cheaper engraved roller-printing. A nadir of harsh colours and vulgar realism was reached between 1850 and 1870. The influence of Owen Jones and Pugin's criticisms was slight in this field and the rare attempts at more formal designs were unimpressive. But shortly after 1870, when the leading designers had again become generally interested in floral patterns, an astonishing recovery of commercial standards began. The change came through designers outside the trade, but by the 1890s and 1900s these had been joined by professional designers trained in art schools, such as Lindsay Butterfield and Sydney Mawson, together raising the standard of the best trade designs to the highest level ever reached in this country. The first stage of this revival was undoubtedly dominated by Morris, whose established reputation and power as a designer provided inspiration for a whole school of designers. Thus the choice of flowers preferred by designers reflected changing tastes in gardening, with the bright new exotic mid-nineteenth-century discoveries from the east like fuchsias and rhododendrons now giving way to quieter colours. But it was Morris who led the return to British flowers, many wild from the country hedges, in parallel with the rise of the partly wilder, flower-filled garden, reflecting the changing seasons rather than the efficiency of the greenhouse. The revival certainly

34. Chintz by Bruce Talbert, 1873

depended upon his liberating thought and example. It was not, however, begun by him. Already in the early 1870s Bruce Talbert was designing extremely attractive floral chintzes, influenced by the organization of Morris wallpaper patterns but deriving their sensitively conventionalized detail from Japanese sources. Nor was Morris in the long run the most important stylistic influence. His own work, with its superbly balanced colours, its combination of sensitively observed naturalism with rich, strongly-controlled pattern, set a splendid standard. It was the starting point for later designers like Walter Crane,

Arthur Mackmurdo, and Charles Voysey. But it was closer to traditional textiles than that of most designers, and the later development of original Art Nouveau and abstract patterns began with the sinuous designs of Crane from the 1870s and Mackmurdo in the 1880s. Thus Morris's chintzes, like his wallpapers, made their mark because of their classic quality rather than their stylistic invention, and this remains their chief attraction.

Morris designed his chintzes in three phases. They were all block-printed and the essential approach is very similar throughout; the repeats of the patterns are clear, frequently arranged with formal symmetry, and the detail is conventionalized. The first group of designs was made for outside production, the unsuccessful 'Tulip and Willow' of 1873 by

35. 'Tulip' chintz, by Morris, 1875

Thomas Clarkson of Preston and some six others of 1875–7 by Thomas Wardle at Leek. Most of these patterns are particularly formal, but they tend to retain something of the careful drawing and vague suggestion of depth of the wallpapers. The noblest is 'Honeysuckle'; the Victoria and Albert Museum Circulation Department have a large piece with a sea-blue ground, the leaves standing out pale bright blue, and the flowers and twisting stalks white, with touches of pink. On this scale the formal pattern of the stalks looks much more natural. 'Tulip' is also a beautiful design, successful in several colour combinations.

The second phase of designing, between 1881 and 1885, was for the chintzes printed at Merton from 1883. The great majority of Morris chintzes, over twenty, come from these years. Partly because of printing difficulties but also as a result of his studies, Morris had concluded that his patterns should be flatter, with less line drawing and simpler, almost naïve detail, 'made up of spots and stripes and flecks of broken colour'. Chintz was 'decidedly an Eastern manufacture . . . you cannot well go wrong so long as you avoid commonplace'.[48] Of his first group of designs 'Snakehead', a bright, intricate pattern with black, brown and blue forming a dark background to flaring white and yellow flower-heads, pleased Morris most: 'I don't know that I don't like it best of all that we have done.'[49] 'Flowerpot' and 'Eyebright' are very much in this style. Equally naïve, but livelier, are the chintzes in which Morris introduced birds and animals such as 'Rose', 'Brother Rabbit', 'Bird and Anemone', and the well-known 'Strawberry Thief'. These gay and charming designs are very closely modelled on the medieval Sicilian and north Italian woven silks.

Other designs are more formal in feeling, closer to late medieval designs. The diagonally structured Italian velvet acquired by the Victoria and Albert Museum in 1883 influenced a group of chintzes as well as wallpapers. 'Kennet', which hangs in the Green Room at Kelmscott Manor, is a pretty example: 'Cray' and 'Corncockle' are still better in their fresh blue, white, and pink. Another diagonal pattern, 'Wandle', has brightly striped barber's-pole stalks.

Only a few more designs were added after 1885. Some patterns, like the later wallpapers, combine naturalistic and formal detail. Several are organized around a sinuous vertical stalk. With them Dearle's 'Daffodil', designed in about 1891, is one of the most beautiful of the Morris firm's patterns, a dark blue ground across which are thrown daffodils, leaves and sprays of pink flowers, between wavy dotted bands lined with tiny black and white flower stems; it is enchantingly suggestive of spring.

Chintz is the last group of Morris's manufactured textiles which we must consider. One final branch of textile design remains, which at first appears to be unrelated to the rest. But although embroideries were quite differently produced, they made an equally successful use of Morris's dyeing, and, apart from the very first examples, Morris's embroidery designs were remarkably close to his other patterns.

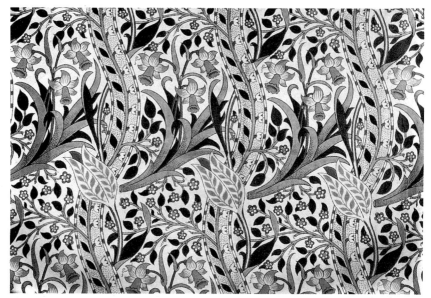

36. 'Daffodil' chintz, by Dearle, 1891

For Victorian women of the middle and upper classes, kept innocent of sex, generally debarred from public life, relieved of the children and cookery by servants, embroidery provided a rare and essential creative outlet. Although commercial work was developing in the nineteenth century, embroidery was one of the crafts least affected by the Industrial Revolution. Inevitably the character of design reflected the tastes of the period, but the quality of workmanship often remained high, so that some traditional types of Victorian embroidery, such as whitework smocks and patchwork quilts, are as fine as any ever produced. Morris, however, was not interested in these traditional types but in fashionable embroidery, in which the quality of design was much more variable.

From the 1830s until the 1870s the most fashionable form of embroidery was Berlin woolwork. Tens of thousands of coloured patterns were published for stitching designs onto canvas for fire-screens, bags, slippers, and upholstery. The colours were in bright wool and the designs were realistic pictures with shading. As with other textiles, this approach was attacked by the Victorian design reformers, who argued that designs should be more heraldic and formalized and that instead of an even pictorial surface, varied types of stitch and silk and gold thread as well as wool should be contrasted to give texture.

They pointed to the rich patterns and conventionalized linear drawing found in medieval and seventeenth-century English embroidery. As a result, from the 1840s there was a marked change in church embroidery, Pugin leading the Roman Catholics and the Ecclesiological Society the Anglicans. A number of church architects began to design altar frontals, sedilia hangings and vestments. G. E. Street was among them and it was probably due to his influence that Morris began designing and studying embroideries in about 1856. Street's designs are extremely interesting, flowers thrusting from knobbly crosses rather in the style of wrought iron spikes. Nothing of this kind by Morris is known, but the embroideries of about 1860 designed by G. F. Bodley, showing sweet graceful female saints, are remarkably close in style to the first surviving Morris work, the panels of twelve illustrious women made for Red House by Janey. These are fresh and charming, mixing wool and silk, blue-green and orange, similar in feeling to some early Morris stained glass. One fragment also survives from the bedroom hangings at Red House, with simple repeating motifs of trees, birds, and mottoes rough-stitched in bright thick wool on a dark serge ground. The early work of the firm was probably in both styles, but although there were certainly numerous commissions no examples have been traced.

The earliest Morris altar frontal known today was made in about 1870 for Busbridge church and is in a very different style, a spreading pattern of delicate leaves like a Morris wallpaper of the early 1870s. As so often with his designs, Morris allowed the influence of other work which was absorbing his interests to affect his style. In about 1875, when he had been planning an illustrated edition of *Love is Enough*, he designed some embroideries like woodcuts, fine lines of brown silk on linen. A splendid wall-hanging designed for Rounton Grange in about 1880 has all the characteristics of a carpet, a repeating pattern in four quarters with big buff and blue diagonal fronds turning to yellow, pink, and blue flowers, and a background of grey tendrils on white linen. It looks equally well from any direction although it is a vertical hanging. Other embroideries seem to have been conceived as tapestries and of these some, because of their lively texture and colouring, are more successful than Morris tapestries. Examples are the Rounton Grange frieze of 1874–82 at the William Morris Gallery, now faded to soft shimmering browns touched with blue, with fresh Burne-Jones figures in the spirit of Botticelli and backgrounds of landscape or foliage pattern: or the 'Pomona' embroidery of 1885, formerly at Alfred Pemberton and Sons, a pretty orange figure standing surrounded by swirling silvery grey acanthus on a dark blue ground, directly copied for a Morris tapestry.

Nor was the stylistic influence in a single direction, for in some of his later paper and cotton designs Morris used patterned leaf motives taken from seventeenth-century English embroideries.

Morris's interest in embroidery was especially strong in the 1870s when his experiments in dyeing produced exciting new silks. Morris and Company sold designs with specially dyed silks as well as finished articles. Morris also designed for the Royal School of Needlework, founded by a group of aristocratic ladies in 1872, where Janey's sister Elizabeth Burden joined the staff: the teaching significantly was in execution, not design. In the next few years a large number of other societies were formed which issued patterns, such as Mrs Thomas Wardle's Leek Embroidery Society. Through these bodies Morris, and other designers including Bodley, Norman Shaw, and Walter Crane, carried the reformed style of church embroidery into secular work. It became known as 'art needlework' and in the 1880s the fashion completely replaced Berlin woolwork. It was suitable for hangings and coverlets but not for upholstery, so that an absurd custom started of draping loose embroideries over furniture. The bright Berlin wools were replaced by more sombre silks, and exotic flowers by more conventional sunflowers, wild roses, lilies, berries, and brambles. Morris patterns were one of the most popular sources of inspiration. Japanese naturalism, asymmetrical, with clouds and blossom above, waterplants and ducks below, was also influential. There are some interesting embroideries by Rossetti at Kelmscott in a strange Japanese style, but Morris considered that Japanese work had 'no architectural, and therefore no decorative, instinct. Their works of art are isolated and blankly individualistic.'[50] His own designs are usually strong patterns, however monotonous the repetition must have been to the embroideress. Yet their quality depended as much upon the executant as the designer and it is no coincidence that by far the finest of Morris's embroideries are those which were specially designed for execution by Catherine Holiday, wife of the stained-glass designer. Morris left the colouring to her, dyeing silks himself to patterns which she sent him. The Victoria and Albert Museum have a wonderful coverlet of about 1876, embroidered by her in silks on a blue linen ground. The design hinges on a buff furry stem which sprouts at both top and bottom from a soft pink root. From these roots a pattern of madder stalks and white flower outlines runs round the edges of the coverlet, while the two ends of the stem throw out a tremendous wheel of great umber brown leaves, with white veins and edges, paling as they approach the centre, where the stems meet in a big, simple central flower, glowing like a sun, soft yellow, buff and a light burnt sienna. Its colour is incredibly subtle, yet the pattern is as powerful as an oak.

Morris made few designs for embroidery after 1880, but in 1885 the firm's embroidery section was taken over by May Morris. It continued to produce fine work for many years. New designs were added by J. H. Dearle and by May Morris. May Morris had her own style of bright blossoms on spindly pale tree stems and naïve animals, as in the Battye hanging at Walthamstow; these were non-repeating vertical designs. Dearle's work was also vertical, and used white flowering frothy trees, but with more of the strength of Morris, especially in his choice of leaves. A fine *portière* designed by Dearle, which was worked by Mrs Battye in about 1900, hangs in the great parlour of Wightwick Manor, Staffordshire. An exact record of the work produced by the firm between 1892 and 1896 survives in May Morris's day book. There were nearly a thousand items, but most were small cushions and screen panels, for which Morris's 'Flowerpot' design was popular. Two altar frontals and two large *portières* were made, and two more *portières* were started for completion by clients. Embroideries were also supplied for work bags, nightgown bags, tablecloths, chair seats, bookcovers, tea cosies and photograph frames. The average charge was £1, but a completed *portière* cost £95. There is also a record of the work on William Morris's bed hangings at Kelmscott, which was designed by May Morris. Much of the work was executed by Lily Yeats, sister of W. B. Yeats, who later ran her own embroidery school in Ireland; and altogether it took over forty weeks.

It reminds one of the great gulf between Morris's vision and the work which he could achieve as a designer and manufacturer. In embroidery work he never challenged its association with an image of feminine submission and meekness. It needed the later arts and crafts work of May Morris herself, Mary Nevill her Birmingham associate, Phoebe Traquair of Edinburgh, and Jessie Newbery and Ann Macbeth of Glasgow, for embroiderers to claim their place as artists; and its spread to women of other social classes through the Women's Co-operative Guild, and its symbolic use for the banners of the suffrage movement, to give it a new radical message. Morris's own work contributed directly to none of this: but it nevertheless fulfilled part of his vision.

Morris's ideas, his belief that men and women's work should be creative and satisfying, that design should be based on respect for material and technique, are still immediate today. His designs contributed only indirectly to the development of the new twentieth-century style. They were mostly made in small quantities for wealthy clients, and produced by monotonous work processes, whether by factory artisans or by bored Victorian ladies. They must be enjoyed, not as mere precursors of the present, but for their intrinsic qualities as expressions of both the deeply-grounded understanding and the outstanding skill of their designer: for recent criticism of William Morris, while reinterpreting his historical significance, has categorically reasserted his claim to be the greatest pattern designer of all time.

6

STAINED GLASS

ALTHOUGH English churches were no doubt once filled with medieval glass as fine as much of that abroad, by the beginning of the nineteenth century the Protestant preference for white interiors purged of Gothic saints and symbols had destroyed the great majority of this old glass. The very techniques of stained glass making had been forgotten. It was one of the most remarkable achievements of the Victorian Gothic revival that the art of stained glass making was rediscovered and a considerable number of windows produced which can be compared in quality with the surviving medieval work. The glass of Morris and Company was the climax of this achievement.

The technical development of medieval glass had resulted in two principal styles. The first, which was perfected in the twelfth and thirteenth centuries, was the style of Chartres and Canterbury. The glass consisted entirely of either 'pot metal' or 'flashed' glass. Pot metal is the pure white or coloured glass taken from the kiln. It is taken out on the end of a long pipe and blown into a bubble. The bubble can be banged, shaped by tools, or blown out inside a mould, so that it becomes a long cylinder. As it cools it is slit down one side and tapped off the pipe onto a flattening stone, on which it unrolls. A flat sheet of glass is thus produced, marked by the texture of the stone if it is rough. Red or blue glass was produced by dipping or 'flushing' the white pot metal bubble in red or blue glass before blowing it out into a cylinder. In early glass the very uncertainty of the technique helped to produce varied colour. The glass was thick, so that the colour was dark, but it was uneven, giving the colour an attractive streaky effect. Some of this texture could come from the rough flattening stone. Often a kiln slightly dirty from a previous firing would give another variation to the colour.

This thick, rough, deeply coloured glass was cut up into pieces by trailing a red hot iron across the sheet and then snapping it. The edges were worked into the required shape by a notched iron called a 'grozing iron'. The designs were then painted with a pigment ground up with powdered flint glass, so that it could be put back into the kiln and fused onto the pot metal. Finally the pieces were fixed together with lengths of grooved lead, soldered together, tied to iron frames and fitted into the window.

In early glass the pieces used were relatively small, so that the dark colours showed as a bright jewel-like mosaic against the black pattern of the leading. The painting on the glass had to be bold in order to show and the limited colour range meant that realism was impossible. The figures were stylized, special prominence given to features like the hands, and the settings were symbolized, a house signifying a town or a tree the countryside. The colours were chosen as pattern, without any realistic intention.

The later medieval style developed from this technique. Windows were larger and more light was required, so that more white glass was used. Pieces became gradually larger, and the reduced amount of leading made colours look less bright. Lighter pot metals were introduced, a more silvery blue, a fresh green, and a golden yellow. In the early fourteenth century it was discovered that silver nitrate applied to white glass would fuse into a beautiful translucent golden stain and this 'yellow stain' became increasingly popular as a substitute for yellow pot metal. All these lighter colours meant that painting could become more elaborate, and in the late fourteenth century a new technique of stippling was introduced, which produced more realistic effects than shading by lines. Another method was 'matt' shading, in which a flat wash was brushed off except in the deeper parts of the shadow. In the process of firing it would become lighter. It could be repainted and refired two or three times, producing subtle effects. Stipple shading could be brushed and refired in a similar way. Glass in this later medieval style is relatively common in England. The cathedral and city churches of York have an outstanding collection. A fine fourteenth-century example is at Eaton Bishop, Herefordshire.

A further technical development in the mid-sixteenth century finally removed the limitations which had obliged early glass to be conventional and symbolic. Medieval shading had been confined to brown or black. Enamel colours were now produced by grinding coloured glass to powder and mixing it into paint, so that white glass could be painted in any colour. Painting became a substitute for coloured pot metal. A special danger was that in firing, in order to melt the paint before the white pot metal, a flux was commonly used, borax, which has proved especially vulnerable to the wet English climate. Consequently much later glass has decayed badly.

Enamel colours meant that stained glass could be treated like painting. Several coloured stains were also introduced, which could be etched off with acids to produce diapers and patterns. More and more glass came to be designed realistically, often by professional painters. Relics of the old techniques can still be seen in the pieces of pot metal used along with enamel colours by artists like Van Linge or Peckitt of York in Oxford college chapels in the seventeenth and eighteenth centuries, but much more typical was the realistic small-scale domestic Dutch glass of the great painted cartoon effect of the west window of New College, Oxford, by Sir Joshua Reynolds.

The Gothic revival inevitably renewed the demand for stained glass, but it was some time before medieval techniques were again understood. Even after 1850, some firms continued to produce glass in large sheets with very little leading and a large picture painted in enamel colours, essentially by the same method as Reynolds. It must have been dissatisfaction with this pictorial approach which caused the use of the very reverse techniques in a few early nineteenth-century windows designed as abstract colour patterns. A very pretty window at Lympsham in Somerset has an emerald green ground crossed by red diapers, with stars, circles, and shields in mauve, blue, and orange.

From the early nineteenth century a few artists, such as Thomas Willement, were learning through repairs of old work how it could be copied. Because early glass was rare the later medieval style was more generally imitated.

In the 1830s a London lawyer, Charles Winston, began a close study of old glass. In 1847 he published his *Hints on Glass Painting*, which for the first time distinguished the different styles of medieval glass in different periods, and emphasized the need for leading and conventionalized painting rather than the cartoon approach.

At the same time important practical advances were made by Augustus Welby Pugin, the dedicated architectural leader of serious Gothic revival. In 1837 Pugin met John Hardman, and together they formed a joint enterprise, Pugin designing at his studio in Ramsgate for glass which was made at Hardman's works in Birmingham. They reintroduced the use of pot metal. They exploited the imperfections of rough streaky textures, which had come to be avoided by other makers as blemishes. Pugin used conventionalized drawing and medieval symbolism rather than naturalistic shading and realism in colour.

Pugin's glass varies in quality, but it is the first really good glass of the Gothic revival. The glass made by Hardman for Pugin's ambitious church at Cheadle is especially interesting and very varied, single figures mixed with scenes in deep blue roundels, set under gay canopies, with patterned backgrounds of monograms, fleurs-de-lis and garters, deep blue, rich ruby red, bright viridian green and madder, red and yellow stars, and vine leaf borders. Pugin's understanding that the vitality of medieval glass came as much from its borders and backgrounds was the key to his success.

Pugin also worked with other makers, including William Warrington of London, Michael O'Connor, and William Wailes of Newcastle. O'Connor was a pupil of Willement and his first commission after he set up his English workshop in 1842 was for the glass at St Saviour, Leeds, under Pugin's direction. The rows of glittering canopied saints in the great east, north, and south windows, glowing blue, violet, crimson and gold, are a brilliant contrast to the subdued adjacent later windows by Morris. Wailes's work for Pugin in Newcastle-upon-Tyne Catholic Cathedral is also good and no doubt Pugin's influence helped towards the many acceptable minor windows with pretty vine leaf borders which Wailes made in the later 1840s.

Thus by 1850 the essential method of painting on pot metal and the bold symbolic style of the old work were more generally understood. The biggest technical barrier remained the quality of the pot metal. Pugin was never satisfied by the colour of Hardman's glass. In 1849 he made a special visit to Chartres, bringing back some fragments which he tried to get Hardman to match. Soon afterwards Winston began to analyse medieval pieces at the Whitefriars glass works of James Powell and Sons. This factory had existed since the seventeenth century for making clear flint glass and had been bought by the Powell family in 1834. It was managed from 1840 until 1894 by Arthur Powell, an unusually able and imaginative manufacturer. As a result of Winston's experiments the firm in 1853 began to produce thick streaky glass of the early medieval kind. Before long it was fully imitated by other makers.

The new streaky glass made imitation of early medieval glass more possible. In the 1850s and 1860s Wailes, Willement, Hardman and, after 1858, Clayton and Bell, were capable of archaic but lively designs in deep primary colours, mixed with gold, mauve, and green. Hardman's north transept window at Hereford is an outstanding example and many cathedrals have convincing glass by Clayton and Bell, such as the east window at Oxford or the south windows of the Salisbury retrochoir and lady chapel.

Although the best glass of this kind is very successful in old buildings, the Victorians could not be content with mere imitation. Imitation was in any case devalued by the increasing commercialization which exploited the demand from restorers and church builders. In glass-making a distinct division of labour already existed in the Middle Ages. Attending to the kiln, blowing the glass, painting, cutting and leading, were different skilled crafts. By the eighteenth century the designer, who had probably been the painter in the Middle Ages, was often a cartoonist with no part in the execution. Organization was now taken a step further. Different glass painters would specialize in particular styles or even particular parts of a window. Some apprentices would be taught to draw goggle eyes and crinkled draperies, others Gothic canopies in different period styles. Consequently the variation in the work of one firm could be astonishing. At Halewood in Lancashire, a church with several Morris windows, two large transept windows are signed by W. H. Sullivan of Liverpool. The first, of 1869, is in the pictorial eighteenth-century technique; Naaman in his chariot with a big thick palm tree and a pale vista of desert and sky. The second, only two years later, is in the early medieval style, well leaded, in bright primary colours. Equally disturbing contrasts can be found within many windows. Often the pictorial panels are in a semi-realistic manner, while the surrounding borders and foliage work are in a lively early style.

Dissatisfaction with common commercial work led a number of Gothic revival architects, including William Morris's master George Edmund Street, to design many of their own windows. Charles Winston believed that standards could be raised if better artists were commissioned to design windows. He was again able to win the support of Powell's. At his suggestion first Rossetti and then, at Rossetti's recommendation Burne-Jones and Madox Brown, were invited to produce designs for windows. The invitation was enthusiastically taken up. Winston was entirely justified by the results.

Only one piece of glass designed by Rossetti for Powell's has survived, but it suggests that he had quickly grasped the intrinsic interest in stained glass. It is not very well balanced as a whole and is marred by two big etched mooning angel's eyes, but there are interesting effects in the leading and some splendid pieces of streaky red and bright speckled green glass are used.

Burne-Jones's first cartoon was also interesting, but because of the jagged, irregular pieces which he suggested, it was impossible to make. Many of his early windows, like the fascinating St Frideswide window at Oxford Cathedral (1859), are also marred by disconcerting disparities of scale. Very soon, however, he achieved a remarkable success in the 1857 window of the old chapel (now dining hall) at Bradfield College. The window consists of three lancets. In the centre is a scarlet tower of Babel with a mass of tiny disputing figures in purple and blue. In the left lancet are Eve, sitting with long golden hair holding a child in her arms, and Adam, crouched among sunflowers and bright grass, weeding, with long bare arms and a blue shirt. In the right lancet are King Solomon and the Queen of Sheba, with tight sad early pre-Raphaelite faces, bright medieval robes and head-dresses, surrounded by bearded, censing eastern priests and trumpeters. Above the lancets is an extraordinary sexfoil, a St Andrew's cross of green wood on blue, surrounded by flaming foliage tongues licking out into the foils, sometimes ending in snakes' heads, mauve, green, and white, with scarlet roses at the top. The whole window is brilliant and exciting, its hot colours characteristic of the 1850s.

The climax of Burne-Jones's designs for Powell's was the Waltham Abbey east window commissioned by William Burges and made in 1861. It is one of the best of all Burne-Jones's windows. There are three big lancets surmounted by a roundel. In the lancets is the stem of Jesse, with gorgeously robed figures against a background of peacock blue. The tree is dark brown and the figures are clothed in bright scarlet, mauve, and straw yellow. They stand among flowers, clusters of apples, and odd random lettering of a kind favoured by Burges. The roundel is a Christ in Majesty surrounded by scenes of the creation in seven circles. The first three of these circles are the best; a pale whirlpool of water and flickering flame in the first; in the second the waters separating, crested green waves, brown and blue; and the third of five trees silhouetted against the sky, with ploughed furrows and ripe fruit in the bluish grass. The colouring of the window is far bolder than anything which was to be made by the Morris firm. It is set in a coarse bold wall designed by Burges, which through sheer vigour makes an effective east end to the Norman abbey church. With its glass it is characteristic of the best High Victorian work.

When the Morris firm was founded in 1861, Burne-Jones had become an accomplished stained glass designer. In 1859 he had given a course on glass painting at the Working Men's College. Madox Brown and Rossetti had also a little experience of designing for Powell's, and Morris had been inspired by his friend's success to try some cartoons himself in 1857. Webb in his years with Street must have learnt a good deal not only of the designing of glass but also of how to fit it into an architectural setting. It was Webb who tested out George Campfield, the firm's first glass foreman, after Morris had found him at the Working Men's College. It is thus not surprising that excellent windows were produced by the firm from the very beginning. It is much more remarkable that although all but one of the partners contributed to the glass-designing in the first years, often a single window being the work of several hands, the glass had from the first a coherent style.

138

The reason lay in the organization of the firm. Morris and Company was in fact an extreme example of the division of labour in glass work. To begin with, the firm never made its own glass. The white and coloured pot metal was chosen by Morris from Powell's stock. It was a little time before he began to insist on glass which was sufficiently thick. The only colour added by the firm was yellow stain, which could produce a range of colour from pale lemon to rich copper, and when applied to blue pot metal resulted in equally varied greens. At a later date a reddish enamel wash was also used for flesh colour, probably the firm's only deviation from medieval techniques.

The colouring of the windows was always entirely left to Morris. In the early 1860s the designers usually showed lead lines in their cartoons, but in later years the leading was also worked out by Morris.[1] The cartoons were then divided among the glass painters, who worked in a long corridor at the back of the house in Queen Square. The most skilful draughtsmen, such as Campfield or Fairfax Murray, were given the face and hands.[2] Morris insisted on close fidelity to the original cartoons, except in the choice of patterning on draperies, which he allowed to be selected by the painter from a book of medieval examples. The glass was fired in the basement kiln and then assembled for Morris to review, an extremely difficult task for the larger windows, because they had to be passed in sections in front of a workshop window, each section remembered as part of the whole. Nevertheless Morris made this assessment very thoroughly, often insisting on substantial alterations to the final window. After any unsatisfactory piece had been remade, the glass was ready for leading and fixing. The unity of effect thus came from the specialization of each painter and the complete control by Morris of the colouring.

There was also a less exact but equally important division of responsibility in the designing. Figures and scenes were designed by most of the partners, but the backgrounds in which they were set were designed by either Webb or Morris. Webb was responsible for the layout of all the most important early windows, as well as heraldic and architectural details and the notably clear style of lettering. He insisted on thick iron bars between the panels and probably at first helped Morris with the leading. In the later 1860s and early 1870s Morris tended to replace Webb as the designer of the layout and background.

The effect of this method of work was to reduce the distinction between the different cartoonists. It is only on close examination and with the help of the numerous surviving signed cartoons that the contribution of each artist can be estimated.

The designs by outside artists, who included Arthur Hughes and Val Prinsep, were too few to make any special impact. The most important of them is the great pale frieze of the tribes of Israel across the east window at Middleton Cheney, which was designed by Simeon Solomon. With their golden heads and firm pre-Raphaelite jaws the figures are close to the style of Rossetti. Of the partners, Faulkner contributed no designs, Marshall scarcely any, and Webb chiefly details.

Rossetti was responsible for thirty identifiable designs and almost all of these were made in 1861–2, although some were repeated in windows made more than ten years later. Ten of the designs were for domestic glass, including two panels of the Tristram and Iseult series at Bradford Art Gallery, and Music and six panels of the Story of St George at the Victoria and Albert Museum. Music, with the auburn-haired King René leaning over a barrier of organ pipes passionately kissing his new Queen, shows the contrived poses and intense gestures of Rossetti's style at its best. He was less at home with religious scenes and significantly one of his most successful panels was the Visitation at Selsley, with a rather merry Virgin and olive and apple trees, distinctly secular in spirit.

Morris himself was at one time thought to have designed very few figures or scenes for glass, but in fact some 150 subject designs can be attributed to him. He had a distinctive, rather strong, stiff style and his most popular figure design was a St Peter, first used in the east window of All Saints', Cambridge in 1866, and repeated ten times. Four of the best panels in the Sir Tristram series are by him and so is one of the most dramatic scenes at Selsley, the Annunciation, the glowing bronze-robed angel and white and yellow Mary with bowed heads against a red chequer fence. Other good windows of 1862 by Morris are the three Maries at the Sepulchre, facing a strong-faced angel seated on the panelled tomb, at St Michael's, Brighton; and the Feast of Cana at Cranbourne, the sharp-bearded bridegroom and bride with posies surrounded by guests, pages, tall ochre and red pottery, and leather jugs.

Although Morris designed other good scenes after 1862, including the outstanding Guernsey Tree of Jesse, they became less frequent. After 1868 there were very few and after 1873 none. The reason for this was the same difficulty and lack of patience which caused him to abandon painting, his uncertainty with figure design and movement. It is significant that the most beautiful of all the windows which he designed, the Creation at Selsley, contains few figures. Morris left the circle of Adam and the beasts to Webb, although the elegant Adam leaning against a tree with Eve lying in the grass is his own work. The contrasts between the circles with figures and the bold abstract circles, the tide of vertical waters dividing from rays of light like lily stalks, or the flat waters with specks of flame and smoke-blue sky, and the splendid colouring of the whole, the rich olive and sea greens, the clear blue and flashes of red, make this one of the very best of all the Morris windows. The glass is excitingly set in the bold plate tracery west window of a church by Bodley, whose steep saddleback tower rises from a promontory of orchards; one of the most memorable places associated with Morris.

Ford Madox Brown also contributed about 150 designs, chiefly in 1862–4 and 1869–74. He produced none after the reconstitution of the firm in 1875. Brown believed that windows required 'invention, expression and good dramatic action'.[3] His cartoons were always forceful and masterfully organized. Except at the very beginning when he tried to medievalize, his compositions tended to rely on complex diagonals within a square, as in the arrangement of his paintings. Unfortunately they were often too complicated to register at a distance. The fine window at St Oswald, Durham, is meaningless until one is within two yards of it. No doubt the colour contrasts used by Morris are partly to blame, but Brown certainly had not visualized the scenes in the simple terms of glass patterns. It is symptomatic that where his cartoons indicate leading, the jagged irregular lines ignore any technical limitations. This lack of feeling for glass, together with lack of co-ordination between cartoonist and colourist, explains why none of the windows designed by Brown are as a whole among the very best Morris windows. On the other hand, the panels which he designed are invariably excellent in detail and usually worth a much closer look than those by Rossetti or Burne-Jones. Nothing at Selsley is more intense than his stumpy, painful, straggling-bearded Christ on the cross. The finest group of his designs is in the apse at Meole Brace, where the three windows date from 1870. Most of the Old Testament scenes in the left window are by Brown; Adam and Eve expelled from Eden, two almost bare, bent figures driven before the lifted red wing of the angels; the old woman finding Moses's cradle among the clear drawn reeds and bright blue water; dancing figures round the golden calf; scenes of sacrifice, thunder, and rocks. They have the intensity of sixteenth-century Flemish primitives. They are strikingly different from the much more Gothic and hierarchical pairs of figures, angels and crucifixion of the central window. Brown's example must have inspired the small panel scenes which Burne-Jones frequently combined with larger figures in the 1870s and 1880s.

Burne-Jones had very soon become the most prolific of all the firm's glass designers and after 1875 figure designs came entirely from him. He was at the height of his powers in 1862. At this time he was strongly influenced by the Gothic Siennese painting which he had seen on visits to Italy in 1859 and 1862, and also by his master, Rossetti. His designs had a fresh medieval simplicity, together with a forceful posing of figures learnt from Rossetti. His Adam and Eve at Selsley are enchanting, standing among thick foliage, very youthful—Adam elegantly spare, innocent; and Eve softly rotund with knee-length golden hair. His Annunciation at Dedworth is of exquisite delicacy, reminiscent of Rossetti's early painting. Rossetti's later style is reflected in some of the languorous singers of the Song of Solomon at Darley Dale.

Other fine windows of 1862 by Burne-Jones are at Lyndhurst, in an ambitious and fantastic church of white, yellow, and red brick by Street's friend William White. There are two Morris windows: the east window, of magnificently robed, red- and golden-haired angels, and the south transept window, consisting of more angels, mostly by Burne-Jones but some of very similar design by Rossetti, and a series of panels by Burne-Jones. These panels have the vitality of Burne-Jones's windows for Powell's, especially the battle sequence—sunrise at the tents, the praying soldier, the fighting and the wounded, masses of spears and splendid armour; or prophets of Baal, a frieze of ecstatic fair-haired white and yellow figures crowned with flowers and raising their arms to a flaming sacrifice.

Few of Burne-Jones's later windows have this feeling. His development was more in the direction of the nobly graceful angels. One of the first windows which entirely relied on this skill of his was made for Bicester in 1866. Large slender female figures of Faith, Hope, and Charity in delicately patterned white robes stand against dark blue and red backgrounds. They are saved from sentimentality by the odd frightened little oafish figures of the vices which they crush below their feet. Yet with its big, unemotionally beautiful figures and large areas of clear colour this window anticipates his later work. Burne-Jones was falling under the influence of the Florentines, of Botticelli and Michelangelo, and at the same time he was losing the warmth he had learnt from Rossetti. His mature style evolved during the 1870s. The west window at Middleton Cheney shows it at its most effective, three youths caught up in a mass of wreathing hot yellow flames. Much more characteristic are the pale stylized figures in Oxford Cathedral, tranced figures in swirling drapery, dependent on their soft bright yellows and greens for life.

This development of Burne-Jones's style combined with changing types of setting to produce four phases in early Morris glass. The earlier settings were designed by Webb. The very first windows at Selsley have little background of any kind. The panels either fill the windows or are surrounded by mainly transparent quarry glass. But even here Webb designed canopies for the apse windows. There are other canopies in several early windows, including a delightful series at Cheddleton. With their gay primary colours and late medieval Gothic detail they help to bring the effect quite close to old glass, although Webb's High Victorian liking for bold shapes appears in their simplified detail and stumpy thickness.

Equally medieval in origin was Webb's geometric patternwork, which became the commonest setting for glass in the first five years. Sometimes, as in the fishscale grisaille at Christchurch, Sunderland, or the grey quarries set in deep green borders and circles at Kentish Town, the imitation seems very literal. At Dedworth the brilliant green and blue patchwork relies on colour rather than pattern; but soon Webb was inventing patterns. Some of the first are at St Martin's, Scarborough, with borders of a brilliant mosaic of corn ears, initials, and pieces of red.

These canopies, patterns, and borders, and the patchwork of primary colours, helped to create the distinctly medieval effect of the first Morris style. Sometimes, as in the west windows of St Michael's, Brighton, and St Martin's, Scarborough, the mosaic of colour completely breaks up the figure designs, so that the glass gives the effect of fragments put together. It is perhaps not so surprising that the firm's exhibits at the 1862 International Exhibition were attacked by rival makers as being merely old work patched up. A piece like the faded crucifix, sun and moon against a deep red in the tracery at Rodbourne (1862) might easily be mistaken for a fragment of medieval glass today.

Very quickly, however, a new style was reached in which the patchwork of primary colours gave way to the dominance of green, used with slate blue and pale yellow, with the strongly coloured panels surrounded by white and palely coloured quarry glass, some opaque and some clear, articulated by the thin lines of Webb's geometric patterning. His patterning becomes more boldly original at this stage. Langton Green and Henley-in-Arden, for example, have strange patterns of small circles like bottleglass. His use of clear and opaque glass, together, was often echoed in the panels, which were executed with great delicacy, etching away the yellow stain to transparency, as in late seventeenth-century Dutch glass. The general effect was cold, but strongly held within its framework of patterning. One of the finest windows of this kind is at St Edmund Hall, Oxford (1864).

The third style emerged more slowly. Webb's experiments in patterns reached a climax in the diagonal black letter inscriptions at All Saints, Cambridge, and Henley-in-Arden, which alternate with a patchwork of quarry glass, some white, some shades of pale blue-green, some with delightful flowers, and edged with borders of initial letters, signs of the zodiac and specks of bright blue-green. But by 1868 his backgrounds were becoming less common. In many windows the figures began to be set directly in plain quarries. This method was rarely attractive and accounts for the first undeniably second-rate windows made by the firm, such as those at Antingham (1865) or Fawley (1868). It also explains the weakness of the more ambitious windows at Llandaff. A more successful background introduced at the same time, and also used very frequently for several decades, was a dark red or blue scrolled brocaded effect. The characteristic later Morris background of foliage was not yet used, but several windows made a partial use of foliage, beginning with soft sea green palms at Amington in 1864 and the wonderfully varied waving leaves in the Middleton Cheney east window. A few striking experimental backgrounds, such as the flaming stars at Tilehurst, occur in the late 1860s.

These new backgrounds combined with the lighter, more elegant designs of Burne-Jones and a changing use of colours to produce the third style. Dark blue and red were still used, but with larger areas of pale blue, pale sea green and bright light yellow. Green and white no longer dominate. The effect is of even, clear, light, but warm colour. The east windows of Middleton Cheney (1865) and Bloxham (1868) are splendid examples. These windows are essentially transitional. They still have the forceful variety of the earlier windows, and their layout of pairs of kings and saints still owes something to medieval precedent, but the colour effect is now wholly original.

Finally, with the development of Burne-Jones's larger Michelangelesque figures, all dependence on medieval glass is lost. Colour is used in broad areas, dark red and slate blue frequently contrasted with clear yellow. The colour in some windows of just before 1870 is sometimes very intense. An extreme example of the richness which could be achieved is at St John, Cardiff. But generally Burne-Jones's anaemic, unemotional figures were set in subtler, paler colours, as in the series in Oxford Cathedral.

The evolution of the Morris style up to this point had been a legitimate development of the technique of stained glass. It has been away from the deep glitter of early glass towards the lightness of late medieval and sixteenth-century work, but the quality of the material had not been ignored or sacrificed. After 1870, however, both in design and in colouring Morris glass began to rely on effects which show much less feeling for the nature of the medium. Morris was never able to experiment with his own pot metals and after the firm moved to Merton in 1881 the firing of painting and stains was entrusted to outside firms. No doubt this lack of involvement in the whole technical process helps to explain Morris's growing disregard for the material.

From about 1872, Morris began to introduce patterns of intertwining stalks and leaves as backgrounds filling whole windows. Some are spare and open, like the delightful pale vine with creamy grapes at Brown Edge or the strange, knobbly, Celtic patterns at Alderley Edge. Elsewhere the effect depends on a shimmering mass of foliage, as in the splendid east window of Rotherfield, subtly varied with grass green, blue green, olive green, and touches of yellow. In some of the most beautiful windows the foliage is mixed with fruit and flowers, pineapples, pomegranates, and roses. One of the first is at Leigh (1874). At Allerton the two transept windows are like high summer and autumn, the south with fiery red and orange flowers in its bright varied foliage, the north with darker greens, more olive and brownish greens, and purple berries and brown fruit. In the east window at Brampton the angels stand on a dark cone covered with red and blue flowers, a rare and brilliant effect with the pale blue, pink and crimson of the figures.

The best of these windows are magnificent, but they succeed through their colour and not through the linear patterns. Patterns of this kind are quite foreign to leaded glass, which is by its nature a patchwork. Undoubtedly they reflect Morris's growing preoccupation with textiles and wallpapers.

At the same time the colouring of the windows was coming closer to the streaks and subtle tones of watercolour cartoons, pale blue merging into inky blue, pale pink into dark crimson, instead of forming patterns of sharp contrast. The window at Salisbury Cathedral, which combines these colours with intertwining foliage, was copied in tapestry with no apparent difficulty. With an earlier Morris window this would have been impossible.

Undoubtedly some of these later windows have impressive qualities. This was because of a new force which appears in some of Burne-Jones's designs. The 1870s had been years of personal crisis for him and uncertainty and indecision seem also to have infected his designing: often his scenes tended to empty sentimentality. Sometimes they can be moving, as the crucifixion at St Michael, Torquay. More commonly Christ and the Evangelists are effete and sickly. But from the 1880s increasingly Burne-Jones tried to overcome this through an exaggeration which comes close to expressionism, jungle sprouts of tree and sweeps of sky. Morris responded with melancholy colouring, gritty blues and pallid greens, and emphatically linear leading. The change can be well seen at Allerton (from *c.*1880). Burne-Jones's work on the mosaics of St Paul's church, Rome, commissioned by Street in 1881, brought him under the influence of early Christian mosaics. Their stately elongated figures are the source of Burne-Jones's final style, of which the finest examples are the windows at Birmingham Cathedral and Hawarden, completed in 1897.

These were the last important windows made by Morris and Company, although the firm continued to make stained glass until its dissolution in 1940. The old designs were often repeated with fair success, but nothing was made to compare in quality with the best work before 1880. The cause of this failure lay directly in the style of the firm's later work. In the hands of Morris and Burne-Jones its inherent defects were usually concealed by the quality of the colour and the inventiveness of the design. In lesser hands its technical lifelessness was manifest.

This weakness was apparent even in Morris's lifetime. Poor windows produced by the firm before 1870 are very rare. In the 1870s there was a considerable amount of mediocre work. After 1880 it was common. This reflected both the development in style and the increasing delegation of responsibility by Morris. He found that satisfactory background foliage could be produced by the firm's draughtsmen. Much of the later work was designed by W. E. Pozzi. It is decent, but lifeless. After the workshops had been moved to Merton in 1881 it is probable that the colouring of some windows was left to the discretion of the foreman glass painter. J. H. Dearle, who after Morris's death became entirely responsible for the artistic direction of the firm's stained glass, said that at Merton Morris 'very seldom saw a window before it was finished; and, so imbued was the pupil with the feeling of his master, that it was by rare exception if the glass failed to pass muster'.[4] Today the more mechanical later windows, executed with such cursory supervision by Morris, seem empty of interest.

Morris stained glass thus came to a disappointing conclusion. What then was the significance of this work in the history of English glass? Stained glass is one of the few fields in which neither Morris's theory nor his work can be said to have anticipated modern design. His glass can only be understood and enjoyed in a Victorian context. It was a direct product of the Victorian Gothic revival. Apart from the domestic sets of medieval stories made in 1862 and the glass for Peterhouse of

1870–4, secular commissions were never important. The overwhelming majority of Morris glass is to be found in churches built or restored by the Victorians. Nor was it by any means an isolated phenomenon, unique in its quality.

Morris glass is in fact far closer to Victorian glass as a whole than is often believed, especially in its best early years. For by 1860 there were several makers who had sufficiently absorbed medieval imagery and technique to be ready, like Morris, to use the old methods with fresh imagination. A number of windows can be found which are comparable with Morris glass both in colour and in the arrangement of the design.

In some instances their designers have only been recently identified through the renewed interest in Victorian glass, and the makers of some of the best windows are still undocumented.[5] It is difficult to know how many windows of real quality exist forgotten in country churches or obscured by urban dirt. At Winscombe, in Somerset, for example, the designer of the east window was unknown, although he was suspected to be associated with William Burges. Kings, sibyls, and prophets stand rich and enchanting among squares of apples and leaves and random lettering. Its maker has now been established as W. G. Saunders,[6] whose little-known firm also produced two first-rate sets of windows for Burges at Skelton and Studley Royal, Yorkshire. Some of the early work of Clayton and Bell for Street, at Howsham in Yorkshire (1860) and Denstone, Staffordshire (1861), is again of notable quality. But it is scarcely possible to guess how many windows by a prosperous firm like Heaton, Butler and Bayne are as good as the great south transept window at St Mary, Nottingham. Here the wide colour range, of scarlet, blood brown, slate blue, violet, amber, peacock blue, and olive green, is characteristic of the daring of the 1860s; very different from Morris, but certainly as exciting.

Burne-Jones had himself used a comparable colour range in his last window for Powell's at Waltham Abbey. More is known about the subsequent work of Powell's than of most makers. The firm also commissioned the painter Albert Moore who designed for them an outstandingly fine window at Thursford, Norfolk, in 1862: brown, slate blue, and violet figures against irregularly leaded vivid red back-grounds, and wonderful skies of suns and stars. They then invited a friend of Burne-Jones, Henry Holiday, to succeed him as cartoonist, and during the next thirty years Holiday designed many of their windows, and proved a strong influence on their work in general. His stylistic development was strongly influenced by that of Morris. At first he used bright dark colours, jewel-like borders, Gothic canopies, and geometric patterning. Fine windows of this type are at Mere in Wiltshire (1865) and Bletchley (1868). Soon, however, he was introducing paler colours. His window in the south nave aisle of Westminster Abbey (1868), recently cleaned, has figures and scenes in white, pale green and yellow, coppery brown and pink madder set against inky blue. It is quite as impressive as any by Morris and quite different. Many windows made by Powell's in the 1870s use this attractive madder pink, with dark browns, blue-greens, scarlet, and violet. There are two delightful examples at Codford St Peter, Wiltshire, with berries, and vine and olive leaves. Several of Holiday's windows show the influence of Morris foliage backgrounds. A charming window at Ockham, Surrey, made by Powell's to a design by T. G. Jackson, has a background of trailing vine stems, grey-blue leaves, and white grapes. Holiday also eventually followed Morris in designing large single figures in broad pale colour schemes, as in the apse windows of St Luke, Kentish Town, which were made by Heaton, Butler and Bayne.

Powell's must have been influenced by the later work of Burne-Jones in their rather frothy style at the end of the century. In general, however, Morris glass was not influential after 1875. There are a few exceptions, such as the windows by Sir William Richmond at Holy Trinity, Sloane Street, or by Selwyn Image at High Cross, but they were not very fruitful. In commercial work the leading influence was now the sweet, late medieval style of C. E. Kempe; while the modern style in stained glass was to evolve from yet other influences.

First, there was a reaction against the Victorian division of labour in glass-making, of which Morris and Company were themselves an example. Nevertheless this came from artists who had been influenced by the general theory of craftsmanship of Ruskin and Morris, although usually only as far as closer supervision of the execution of their designs. Thus Henry Holiday set up his own glass workshop in 1891, from which he produced his notable west window of Southwark Cathedral in 1893. Younger arts and crafts artists made similar experiments, chief among them Christopher Whall. A Hammersmith neighbour of Morris, and teacher at the Central School of Arts and Crafts, he was the leading exponent of arts and crafts glass, his pupils including a number of women glass artists. His own windows are full of bright jewels of colour, mixed with rough matt shading and foliage which is wrought into prickly canopies, very like Art Nouveau decoration. Good examples are at Holy Trinity, Sloane Street (1905), and Haversham, Buckinghamshire (1897).

In spite of their detail, Whall's windows are essentially late medieval in effect. In style the modern movement was to return to the colours of early glass, again in opposition to the practice of Morris. An interesting pioneer in the late 1890s was Oscar Paterson of Glasgow, who made his own pot metal. He insisted that glass should be a rough mosaic. He was influenced in his design by contact with Germany.[7] The earliest mature window in the new style was made for St Mary, Slough, by A. A. Wolmark in 1915, a glittering abstract pattern of purple, orange, red, and dark green.

Thus although modern glass was based on the nineteenth-century revival of the art, it owes little directly in style or in technique to the work of the Morris firm. But the nineteenth-century revival from which it sprang was itself one of the most original achievements of the Victorian period. The Morris windows which may be seen in impressive quality all over England were its culmination, and remain as its outstanding attraction.

7

BOOK DESIGN

IN his book design the lives of William Morris as a designer, author, and art reformer come together. And a popular author has a unique opportunity for affecting taste through the design of his books. A classic example, directly due to contact with Morris, was the influence of Bernard Shaw's book style of plain Old Caslon type with off-centre title pages, beginning with his *Plays: Pleasant and Unpleasant* in 1898. Yet although at the end of his life Morris was designing, printing, and publishing his own books, he never achieved a direct influence of quite this kind. How was this?

Morris's interest in book design started with his discovery of the illuminated medieval manuscripts of the Bodleian Library when he was at Oxford, and for many years he was much more concerned with written than with printed books.

He himself began illuminating in 1856. Little of his early work survives. Its style was thoroughly Gothic, modelled on the late medieval manuscripts in the Bodleian, with coloured borders, angular lettering, and rich initials, and Rossetti wrote that it was 'quite unrivalled by anything modern that I know—Ruskin says, better than anything ancient'.[1] But Morris quickly became absorbed by other interests and it was not until 1869 that he returned to illumination, this time in a different style. All his principal illuminated manuscripts were written during the next six years.

The most obvious change of style was in the handwriting, which was now in a legible Roman script, so that the whole effect of the manuscript was much lighter. But the decoration had also broken from the medieval precedent. Among the first of the new manuscripts was 'A Book of Verse', a selection of Morris's poetry which expresses the fear and anguish of his love at this time, written out in 1870 and given to Georgiana Burne-Jones. It is now at the Victoria and Albert Museum. The decoration was a co-operative work. The delicate miniature watercolours were painted by Burne-Jones and Fairfax Murray, and they include a head of Morris with reddish beard and tousled hair, and a portrait of Morris and Janey surrounded by white blossom. The coloured initials were by George Wardle, who also executed some of the ornament. This was designed by Morris and consists of wonderfully fresh foliage, soft green and yellow, with pale blue and red flowers and fruit, running down the margins and between the lines. Some of it is loosely powdered, like the first naîve Morris wallpapers, but the finest pages have superb intertwining running patterns, which anticipate the series of wallpapers begun by Morris in 1872. In fact this 'Book of Verse' is crucial evidence of the great turning point in Morris's pattern designs. The Bodleian manuscripts of 'The Story of the Dwellers at Eyr' and 'Sigurd of the Volsungs', probably written in about 1871, also have some loose powdering, but Morris then abandoned it for the running patterns. The 'Omar Khayyám' at the British Museum, illuminated for Georgiana Burne-Jones in 1872 and again painted with miniatures by Murray, was the culmination of this style of ornament, although it makes a less attractive manuscript than the 'Book of Verse' because the rich running foliage and fruit is a little too heavy for its small pages.

The first manuscripts had been written on paper, but 'Omar Khayyám' was on vellum bought in Rome. Anxious as always to improve his work, Morris was studying the manuscripts in the British Museum to find the secret of their success. He was experimenting with honey and white of egg in mixing his paints, just as he would soon try to rediscover the old vegetable dyes for textiles. And these studies, as with dyeing, subjected him to historicist influences. His foliage patterns had so far had little in common with old manuscript ornament. There was some general precedent in the intertwining ivy leaf patterns common in late medieval illumination, but none in detail. In the last manuscripts, finely represented by the 'Odes of Horace' begun in 1874, now in the Bodleian, most of the motifs have clearly recognizable sources. Naturalistic flowers and fruit have usually been replaced by a conventional motif like a flower gone to seed, a gold dot surrounded by thin rays, which was commonly used by fifteenth-century French and Italian illuminators. Like Morris, they also mixed this type of foliage and seed ornament with scrolled acanthus leaves. Morris's fine initial letters, which are interlaced by knobbly stalks, depend very closely on the white vine stem ornament which is found in fifteenth-century Italian manuscripts and also in romanesque illumination. The Italian humanists revived this motif which had been first applied to the initial in northern barbarian illumination, perhaps because they believed that the romanesque manuscripts in which they found it represented classical tradition. Morris studied examples from both romanesque and Renaissance manuscripts. Thus as an illuminator Morris's technical scholarship gradually diminished his originality.

Contrary to what is probably the common impression, Morris's venture in illumination was not in itself exceptional. The tradition, however debased, had never died out in formal documents such as addresses and charters. Its revival was a natural offshoot of the Gothic revival and of the growth of monasticism in the nineteenth century. In addition, illuminating became a popular middle-class Victorian hobby, more attractive to men than embroidery, but equally time-consuming. It was practised by the most influential of Victorian designers, Owen Jones and Pugin, and was the subject of a fine volume published by Digby Wyatt in 1860, *The Art of Illuminating*. A year later the much less tasteful but most popular book on the subject appeared, G. and A. Audsley's *Guide to the Art of Illuminating and Missal Painting*, which had reached some twenty editions by 1900 and was reissued with very little alteration as late as 1911. To '*the true illuminator*, who toils, yet knows it not, day after day, in every spare hour, and through the night far into the hours of morning for the love of the glorious art itself', it offered a characteristic mid-Victorian contradictory theory of design. 'The great principle in all decorative ornament is conventionalism'; but, 'should we be asked by the eager student where and from what source may conventionalism be studied, we should tell him, that nature must be his school'. To complete the reader's confusion, the authors then presented a scientific theory of colour harmony, complete with a diagram for calculating the effect of any combination possible from the 'set of illuminating colours, in powder, of great strength and brilliancy', which were specially produced by Rowney's.

It is impossible to say whether much worthwhile work was inspired by these books. On the other hand it is certain that, although Morris's illuminated manuscripts are the only examples of the period which can now be readily seen, they had little contemporary influence. Morris never lectured on contemporary illumination and his work was 'known only to the elect'.[2] Nevertheless, in later life he became something of an influence as a collector of manuscripts and a recognized authority on the art. As such his direct influence was chiefly historicist. His own superb collection contained very little modern work and in his limited patronage of contemporaries he did not encourage much originality. The *Studio* in 1896 singled out the manuscripts of three designers, Edmond Reuter, a competent copyist of late Gothic work, Phoebe Traquair, who freely used late Gothic foliage with striking pre-Raphaelite miniatures, and W. B. MacDougall, whose style was a Celtic type of Art Nouveau. It was Reuter who had been commissioned by Morris.

Illumination had in any case a limited future. In the long run the importance of Morris's manuscript work was in his calligraphy, even though this was less accomplished and intended to be less noticed than the ornament. His early manuscripts had been in a 'rather cramped and uncertain' Gothic hand,[3] but when he took up the art again his handwriting, although still not very sophisticated, was in a pleasant legible light roman script. It would be interesting to know what caused this important change. Was it simply that he wanted the text of his own expressive verse to be easily read? Could it have been suggested by Burne-Jones, with his enthusiasm for fifteenth-century Italy? Or did Morris take the script from the fine lower-case lettering devised by Philip Webb for the firm's stained glass?

Whatever the source, Morris worked at the style of his handwriting in the next few years. He learnt to cut a quill moderately well and he studied both romanesque calligraphy and the revived roman of the fifteenth-century Italian humanists. The beautiful cursive italic writing of the Italians especially appealed to him. He possessed copies of the four early manuals of handwriting: Ludovico Arrighi's *La Operina* and *Il Modo*, Sigismondo Fanti's *Thesauro de Scrittori*, and Giovantonio Tagliente's *La Vera Arte de Scrivere*, all published in the 1520s. He also later owned two fifteenth-century Italian manuscripts which he may have bought at this time[4] and he is known to have studied similar work in the British Museum. His attempts at both roman and italic scripts are revealed by a trial leaf for his 'Virgil' manuscript, begun in 1874, in which he seems to talk to himself: 'let us try some hands now this is not right good but rather shaky tis somewhat of a puzzle to know how to set to work about it: tis between pointed and round . . .' He tries a very sloped fast cursive italic, but comments, 'a good piece of work is not to be done with such a very broad nibbed pen upon vellum with only common ink'. Then a more careful italic, including the name of Arrighi and his second manual: 'Con le varie Sorti de lettere ordinato per Ludovico Vicentino In Rome nel anno no good at all: it all ran together . . .'[5]

In spite of his difficulties, Morris managed to develop an attractive handwriting in his last manuscripts. The 'Odes of Horace' are written in a beautiful light semi-italic, quite small, while there are other manuscripts written in a larger, bolder hand with a broader nib. These scripts use the diagonal hairline upstroke of italic cursive, and the letter shapes are close to the Italian manuals, although the 'Horace' script suggests a slightly earlier late fifteenth-century model. If the letter shapes are mediocre by modern calligraphic standards, they are certainly a great step forward from the excessively vertical and awkward individual letters with which he started in 1870. His ordinary style of writing was also greatly improved from this date. Morris kept his interest in calligraphy, and indirectly became a crucial influence in the revival of the art at the end of the century. Mary Bridges, who published the first modern manual of italic calligraphy, *A New Handwriting for Teachers*, in 1898, was closely associated with the arts and crafts movement. Between the wars school calligraphy was especially advanced by Marion Richardson's methods of teaching through writing cards and the learning of patterns before letters. By then a London schools inspector, she had been brought up in a poor Birmingham family and won a scholarship to the Birmingham School of Art. Her teachers there included Catterson Smith, who had himself worked with Morris at the Kelmscott Press, while she was 'taught writing by a pupil of Edward Johnston'. Johnston, who became the first great modern calligrapher and teacher of the art, decided to make it his profession because of the encouragement of three followers of Morris: Sydney Cockerell, Harry Cowlishaw, an architect who was interested in calligraphy, and W. R. Lethaby, principal of the Central School of Arts and Crafts, who advised Johnston which models to study, gave him his first commissions, and put him in charge of his first class in 1899. One of his earliest pupils was Eric Gill whose decision to abandon the architectural profession for lettering was made through his reading of Morris. Johnston himself started with the belief that '*method* is to be sought in the old work',[6] but his understanding of letter shapes became so fundamental that in 1916 he designed the absolutely plain sans serif lettering still used by the London Underground. Thus although Johnston never met William Morris, through Johnston the whole modern movement in calligraphy, the italic style now taught to thousands of schoolchildren, the international Society for Italic Handwriting, even the most severely functional of modern display letters, can be traced back to Morris's pioneering efforts in the 1870s.

During his period of illuminating Morris was also interested in the design of bookbindings. While at Oxford he had some books bound in white vellum with heavy brass clasps and knobbly bosses, but he later came to dislike them, probably because of the vulgar versions of such knobbly bindings which became popular. In the 1860s Rossetti designed a number of remarkably simple bindings with thin spare asymmetrical line decoration, no doubt reflecting his Japanese interests, and although Morris designed nothing so plain he must have been influenced by their simplicity. His 'Omar Khayyám' manuscript at the British Museum has an attractive red cloth binding covered with close clumps of gold tooled daisies and thistles. Still more striking was his binding for *Love is*

37. *Love is Enough*, cover binding, by Morris, 1873

Enough, designed in 1873, a green cloth cover with the title set in a single band of light interlacing gold willow leaves. This was not the last binding designed by Morris, but it was the last of any importance. The Kelmscott Press books were bound either in white vellum, which made them floppy and difficult to hold, or with plain grey-papered millboard sides. Although these were not strong no margin was allowed for rebinding in leather. Morris's lack of interest in binding in later years was also shown by his attitude to T. J. Cobden-Sanderson, a barrister

Love is Enough.

THE MUSIC.

OVE is enough: though the world
be a-waning,
And the woods have no voice but
the voice of complaining;
Though the sky be too dark for
dim eyes to discover
The gold-cups and daisies fair
blooming thereunder,
Though the hill be held shadows,
and the sea a dark wonder,
And this day draw a veil over all deeds passed over,
Yet their hands shall not tremble, their feet shall not falter;
The void shall not weary, the fear shall not alter
These lips and these eyes of the loved and the lover.

THE EMPEROR.

The spears flashed by me, and the spears swept round,
And in war's hopeless tangle was I bound,
But straw and stubble were the cold points found,
For still thy hands led down the weary way.

THE EMPRESS.

Through hall and street they led me as a queen,
They looked to see me proud and cold of mien,
I heeded not though all my tears were seen,
For still I dreamed of thee throughout the day.

THE EMPEROR.

Wild over bow and bulwark swept the sea
Unto the iron coast upon our lee,
Like painted cloth its fury was to me,
For still thy hands led down the weary way.

38. Trial page for *Love is Enough*, 1871; cherubs by Burne-Jones, borders and initials by Morris, who engraved all the woodcuts

who decided to dedicate himself to bookbinding, setting up his own Doves Bindery. He led its revival as an artistic craft which proved especially popular with women, with scope to carry out their own designs; May Morris among them. Cobden-Sanderson's covers were undoubtedly beautiful. But he recorded in his diary in 1885 that Morris 'thought my work too costly; bookbinding should be "rough"; did not want to multiply the minor arts(!); went so far as to suggest that some machinery should be invented to bind books'.[7]

It is a great pity that Morris never looked at his own work in printing with an equally savage eye. Both his unsuccessful projects of 1866–72 and his successful launching of the Kelmscott Press in the 1890s would have been greatly helped by a more cautious assessment of the development of Victorian printing, and especially of the social value of good printing by cheap methods.

Morris's first printing projects were for illustrated editions of *The Earthly Paradise* and *Love is Enough* which were planned in 1866–8 and 1871–2. Burne-Jones designed about a hundred woodcuts for the first scheme and some of these are first rate in their simplicity of line and bold economic modelling. The second scheme went as far as some interesting trial pages, delightfully decorated with a big leafy initial L and borders of apples and cherubs. It is not properly balanced, because the borders are too heavy for the type, but the effect is far lighter and much more readable than anything which Morris produced later.

According to Mackail, these projects were abandoned because of the technical defects 'in both typography and woodcuts' of the trial proofs printed by the Chiswick Press:

The art of producing books had sunk to a deplorable condition, and it became evident that the proposed work was impossible without the organized labour of years. The poet and the designer were prepared with their part; but the type-founder, the compositor, the printer, the wood-engraver, had all to be educated.[8]

This statement, typical of many of Morris's biographers in its assumption that every art which he had not yet mastered was decadent, is completely untrue.

The technical standard of printing in the 1860s was still high. The gradual introduction of machine presses, machine-made paper and mechanical type-casting had not altered the basic method, which remained close to that of Caxton in the fifteenth century. The work of the Chiswick Press was of a particularly high standard, and combined good presswork with a tradition of good design; indeed, under the management of Charles Whittingham the younger, who had retired as recently as 1860, it had for twenty years produced some of the most distinguished books ever printed in England. For the publisher William Pickering, whose hallmark was a beautifully simple brief title-page in small capitals, Whittingham had printed a remarkable group of distinctive books, including the fifty-volume Aldine Edition of British Poets and culminating in the editions of the Book of Common Prayer of the 1840s, printed in red and black, some in Gothic type and some in the Caslon Old Face type revived by Pickering. For Joseph Cundall the Chiswick Press printed the charming Home Treasury series of children's books, launched by the design critic Henry Cole in 1843.

Whittingham also printed the superbly illustrated books of Henry Shaw, published by Pickering, which combine coloured wood-blocks and hand-coloured lithographs and are probably the finest of all Victorian colour books. But in book illustration the Chiswick Press had closer rivals than in presswork. The mid-century was the great age of coloured lithography, pioneered by Owen Jones at his own press and splendidly used by Pugin in his *Glossary* of 1844 and *Floriated Ornament* of 1849, both printed by Michael Hanhart. In addition there was an excellent tradition of copper and steel engraving, and the superb proficiency of Victorian wood-engravers can be readily confirmed by a glance at the weekly *Illustrated London News*.

The true reason for Morris's failure was that he was not yet sufficiently interested in book design as a whole. His prejudice in favour of dark rather Gothic woodcut ornament created difficulties in layout and typography which he was unable to solve and he was unwilling either to try a lighter style, which would have gone admirably with Chiswick Press printing, or to investigate the problem thoroughly. His lack of a sustained interest in typography and undecorated printing at this time is indicated by the fact that, although his early publications, *The Oxford and Cambridge Magazine*, *Guenevere*, and *Jason* had all been well printed by the Chiswick Press, his books published by F. S. Ellis after 1868 were printed in an inferior style with inferior presswork by John Strangeways. They are indeed 'plain, clean, inconspicuous, well-mannered'; but certainly less distinguished. There is no sign that Morris resisted this change. He did continue limited experiments, with limited runs of two dozen copies of an edition specially printed on hand-made Whatman paper, with bigger margins and board or vellum hand-sewn bindings. These were intended for friends. Rather than indicating, as has been recently argued, that Morris 'showed every concern for the printing of his books' throughout, they suggested that he had put the problem aside for the time.[9]

It remained at the back of his mind for some years yet. The marking of four hundred years of English printing by the 1877 Caxton Exhibition in London aroused new public interest in early printed books. The old Fell types were revived by the Oxford don Henry Daniel who ran his own pioneering private press, again from the 1870s. But it was not until 1888 that Morris himself became fired with enthusiasm for printing as an art in its own right. Mackmurdo, editor of the *Hobby Horse*, later claimed that the turning point was a conversation when he explained to Morris all his difficulties in getting good materials and good design, so as to produce 'a page of printed text that was a pleasure to look at'. Morris 'instantly saw what could be done. "Here is a new craft to conquer and to perfect. A new English type needs to be founded".'[10] Whatever the truth of this memory, certainly in practical terms it was Emery Walker who opened the path for him. A reticent man with a passion for early printed books, a process-engraver by profession, Walker had become a riverside neighbour at Hammersmith in 1883. The crucial event was a lecture on printing which Morris attended, given by Walker at the Arts and Crafts Exhibition on 15 November 1888, illustrated by enlarged photographs of letter shapes. He indicated precisely the whole range of changes which would be needed to recreate a handsome page. Afterwards, as they went home together, Morris asked Emery to help him design a new typeface. The lecture was later printed, its text worked up with Morris, enlarged, made more historical and polemical, in *Arts and Crafts Essays* and, together with Morris's paper on 'The Ideal Book' given to the Bibliographical Society in 1893, it lays down the main principles in book design which Morris hereafter followed. They are principles which still make excellent sense.

The key to good book design was not decoration. 'I lay it down, first, that a book quite unornamented can look actually and positively beautiful, and not merely un-ugly, if it be, so to say, architecturally good, which by the by, need not add much to its price.' The chief points of architectural arrangement were that, 'first, the pages must be clear and easy to read; which they can hardly be unless, secondly, the type is well designed; and thirdly, whether the margins be small or big, they must be in due proportion to the page of letter'. Pages must be designed as they opened, in pairs, and not singly. The narrowest margin must be inside, the next at the top, the third on the outside and the widest at the bottom. 'The modern printer, as a rule, dumps down his page in what he calls the middle of the paper, which is not really the middle, as he measures his page from the headline, if he has one, though it is not really part of the page, but a spray of type only faintly staining the head of the paper.' The spacing of words and lines should be tight, with only the minimum of white needed to separate them; 'if the whites are bigger than this, it both tends to illegibility and makes the page ugly'. It was especially important to prevent rivers of white meandering across the page; the aim should be to knit the page together, like solidly bonded brickwork. On the other hand the lateral compression of the letters themselves, with the resulting over-thinning of their shapes, must be avoided. Finally, good materials and clean presswork were necessary; 'the white should be clear and the black black'. and, if hand-made paper could not be used, the machine-made paper 'should show itself for what it is . . . I decidedly prefer the cheaper papers that are used for the journals, so far as appearance is concerned, to the thick, smooth, sham-fine papers on which respectable books are printed.'[11]

One might expect these principles to lead to the simple, well-designed, mass-produced, cheap book, and certainly through other designers, many of them directly inspired by Morris, this hope was to be fully realized. For the moment, however, although he told press reporters that 'I wish indeed that the cost of books was less', his aim was to demonstrate how a printed book could be a real work of art. Cheap books for all could have hardly met this immediate purpose. Rather, the best should be shared: 'You see if we were all Socialists things would be different. We should have a public library at each street corner, where everybody might see and read all the best books, printed in the best and most beautiful type.'[12] Hence Morris himself did not advance towards Penguin Books; he moved backwards, towards the first Gothic printers, towards the medieval illuminated manuscripts with which his interest in books had begun.

The first product of his new interest was the design of *The House of the Wolfings*, published in December 1888, which was printed by the Chiswick Press in Basle Roman, an adaptation of an early sixteenth-century type which had been cut by Whittingham in the 1850s. Morris was delighted with the results, although it is easy to understand the reviewer whose 'eyes smarted and dazzled in the most uncomfortable fashion',[13] for it is in fact much less legible than Caslon Old Face, the type previously used in his books. Morris quickly saw room for improvement, especially in the spacing of the words, and told his publisher that 'if ever I print another book I shall enter into the conflict on this side also'.[14] He took his opportunity in *The Roots of the Mountains*, published in November 1889, in which he altered the 'e' in the Basle Roman type, used shoulder notes at the top of the margins instead of headlines to the pages and printed 250 special copies on Whatman hand-made paper. Because of their type, neither of these two books seem very successful today, but their general layout and the proportioning of the margins is excellent and in this they were as influential as anything to be produced by the Kelmscott Press.

At the end of 1889 Morris decided to set up his own printing press. He asked Emery Walker to be his partner, and although Walker refused he was closely associated with the work throughout. Morris's aim was 'to produce books which it would be a pleasure to look upon as pieces of printing and arrangement of type', easy to read, but with a 'definite claim to beauty'.[15] The Kelmscott Press did not begin printing until over a year later, in the spring of 1891, because of the care with which Morris prepared for it. First he searched for suitable hand-made paper, and, failing to find any, he arranged for it to be specially made by Joseph Batchelor at Chart in Kent. It was based on a fifteenth-century north Italian pattern, made wholly of linen, and even the wire moulds were hand-woven to give a slightly irregular texture. A limited number of copies were printed on vellum, which Morris persuaded Henry Baud of Brentford, Middlesex, to produce for him. Both the special paper and the vellum continued to be made for several decades. His ink was made by Jaenecke of Hanover, since no English maker would use linseed oil. Morris insisted that the oil should be freed from grease with stale bread and raw onions rather than chemicals, mixed with boiled turpentine, and matured for six months, after which the organic animal lampblack was ground into the mixture.

The types used were new designs by Morris himself. The Golden type was a roman letter, based on the face used by Nicholas Jenson in 1470 and another type of Jacques le Rouge, a fellow Venetian printer of the same period. Both these models were heavy, and unlike most designs based on Jenson (such as the beautiful Centaur of Bruce Rogers) the Golden type is no lighter. Morris regarded the slighter sixteenth-century Aldine types as decadent, Plantin as 'poor and wiry', and eighteenth-century types like Baskerville and Bodoni as 'sweltering hideousness'.[16] He intended his letters to be solid and square, and certainly they are. The Golden type took a year to design and Morris would keep a matchbox in his pocket with specimens of the latest letters. He used enlarged photographs of Jenson, le Rouge, and Golden to criticize and compare their subtlest details.

Golden was followed in 1891 by the Gothic large Troy and smaller Chaucer types, two sizes of the same design. Morris wished 'to redeem the Gothic character from the charge of unreadableness which is commonly brought against it', and consequently his black letter is based on the clearest model which he knew, the Mainz Bible printed by Peter Shoeffer in 1462, which was 'simpler, rounder, and less *spiky*' than most Gothic scripts.[17] Morris's design is still clearer, almost classical in its simplicity, and quite close in feeling to Golden. Several of the capitals are based on roman rather than Gothic models, and Morris printed it with arabic numerals, and without medieval tied letters and contractions.

The three types were cut by Edward Prince and machine cast, since Morris could see no advantage in casting by hand. Some use was also made of new methods in the ornaments. Burne-Jones's pencil sketches were first redrawn in ink and then transferred to wood by photography in a two-stage process devised by Walker. The borders and initials were designed by Morris. The title pages and initial words were printed from woodblocks, but—with Walker's persuasion—recurring initials and ornaments from electrotypes. Otherwise the old methods were used, with Morris closely watching, cross-questioning, until he fully understood them:

> He talked and listened to compositors, his intent eye taking in every movement of their hands, and every detail of their tools, until he knew as much as they did of spacing, justification, and all the rest of it. With pressmen he spent hours, familiarizing himself with every particularity of their doings, from the reason for damping paper in a given way, and to a given degree, to that for a lingering 'dwell' when the type had been brought into touch with it. But, again, he never stood at a case or pulled a sheet; his trusted fellow-craftsmen were there for that.[18]

The foreman compositor was the socialist Thomas Binning, who had previously been in charge of *Commonweal*. When printing was started, in a cottage in Hammersmith Mall, he became father of the union chapel and forced the London Society of Compositors to accept their first woman member, a Mrs Pyne. But the Kelmscott Press had little other popular importance. A few books cost as little as 2s. 6d., but the great majority cost more than a guinea and were produced in limited editions, providing a fine opportunity for speculative collectors. Altogether 18,234 volumes were printed of 53 books. The first few were published by Reeves and Turner and then by Bernard Quaritch, but most of the remainder directly by Morris, or by his trustees after his death. The press was wound up, after completing several books started by Morris, in March 1898.

In spite of Morris's belief in legibility, there is no denying that the Kelmscott volumes were books to be collected, not to be read. In effect Morris persuaded himself that his own decorative instincts did not conflict with his functional principles; that his heavy types, his cramped-up spacing, his bright black ink were legible, even that it was better to sit up with a heavy book than to fidget with a small one—'a big folio lies quiet and majestic on the table'.[19] Certainly the best of his books look splendid on a table; above all the great volume of *The Works of Geoffrey Chaucer*, with its splendid rhythm of groups of plain pages of black-letter text and rich pages with black borders of acanthus and vine, initial words wrapped in woody bench-end foliage, and Dantesque scenes by Burne-Jones.

Most of the books are much simpler than this, although there is little

Sold by William Morris at the Kelmscott Press.

39. Kelmscott Press colophon

variation in the type of ornament. Borders were either black frames of formal foliage in a classical manner or lighter outlines of stems and leaves, very similar to fifteenth-century German woodcuts, generally used for corners or for a single margin. Generally these outline borders are the more attractive variety; the black of the others is too dense. The initials were chiefly of three kinds, whether Roman or Gothic; letters interlaced with white vine stems, based on manuscript sources; letters set in a Germanic kind of Renaissance scroll-work; and letters decorated with foliage, sometimes with a pleasant woodenness, sometimes interestingly sinuous and seaweedy. All three kinds were in use by 1892, and whether Gothic or Roman they were used indiscriminately with the three Kelmscott Press types.

Because their design tends to heaviness, the most attractive Kelmscott books are generally those which are relatively short and lightened in some way. This could be by decorative woodcuts, as in *The Glittering Plain* or *The Shepheard's Calendar*; by a generous use of red, as in *The Book of Wisdom and Lies* or in the enchanting *Laudes Beatae Mariae Virginis*, by red and blue; or because there was less type on each page, as in volumes of poetry, such as those of Rossetti, Herrick, and Blunt, and

163

Morris's own *Guenevere*, all set in Golden, or the delightful *Sire Degrevaunt*, and the splendid *The Floure and the Leafe and the Boke of Cupid*, set in Chaucer and Troy. These are simple enough to be quite pleasant to read, even though the form of the stanzas is frequently obscured by the big initials.

The great importance of Morris's work as a printer was not in his style but in his example. Kelmscott books were not the foundation of modern book design. Their decorative style was medieval, still in the manuscript tradition, and their type faces were too hard on the eye to come into general use. Even Mackail in his biography and May Morris in the *Collected Works* preferred other types. In technique the Kelmscott Press was archaic, at a time when printing was being revolutionized by the introduction of machine-composing, photographic block-making and photographic illustrations. It was expensive, providing for the literate minority of the past rather than for the educated majority of the future. The Kelmscott style could lead nowhere, because it was not intended to be relevant to the printing industry as it then existed; and consequently its direct influence on style was generally bad, whether in the illegible elaboration of the new typefaces designed by C. R. Ashbee for his Essex House Press, which had taken its equipment and three workmen from the Kelmscott Press itself, in the commercial parodies, or George Allen's editions of Ruskin (printed by Ballantyne), or in the incongruity of the Everyman endpapers.

But in starting the Kelmscott Press Morris had not merely created a style; he had shown, as only an artist of his reputation could have shown, that printing could be a great art, and its details worth infinite trouble. Book design, after he had taken it apart and stripped it to its essential principles, took root in an entirely new way. In the late 1890s and 1900s a great revival of printing began. In England a whole series of new private presses with artist-proprietors blossomed: among them the Ashendene Press founded in 1895 by St John Hornby, 'brimful of enthusiasm for Morris'; the Vale Press of Charles Ricketts, who claimed that Morris wept on his deathbed at the beauty of their books; the Eragny Press of Lucien and Esther Pisarro, stimulated by Ricketts; and within a stone's throw of Morris's own Hammersmith home by the Doves Press of Emery Walker and T. J. Cobden-Sanderson. The movement carried directly through to the outstanding Golden Cockerell Press of the 1920s for which Gill and Eric Ravilious designed, leading the modern English woodcut revival. Meanwhile several new publishing firms founded in about 1890, including Joseph Dent, Fisher Unwin, Grant Richards, Methuen, John Lane, and William Heinemann, began to produce excellently designed books, and some authors, notably George Bernard Shaw, imposed their own standards. Morris was also 'progenitor' of the parallel American revival, inspiring the careers especially of Daniel Updike, founder of Merrymount Press, and Bruce Rogers of Riverside Press, of Frederick Goudy and Will Ransom of Village Press in the 1900s, and even of William Diggins, who led American trade design in the interwar years with his work for Knopf. The direct influence of Morris also reached Europe, especially the Netherlands and Scandinavia. 'The extraordinary impact of his work spread with a rapidity that has never been properly appreciated.'[20] Morris might not have chosen the modern tradition which they created, lighter, more elegant, more simply functional, more classical than his work, but he undoubtedly played a crucial role in the making of it.

8

LITERARY CRITIC

WHEN Morris was invited to stand for the Professorship of Poetry at Oxford in 1877, he refused on the ground that 'though I have read a good deal and have a good memory, my knowledge is so limited and so ill-arranged that I can scarce call myself a man of letters . . . It seems to me that the *practice* of any art rather narrows the artist in regard to the *theory* of it.'[1]

There was certainly sense in this excuse. Morris's attitude to literature shares none of the theoretical importance of his views on the arts, and his tastes are interesting chiefly for the light which they throw on his character and his writing. Morris wrote criticisms of Browning's poetry in 1856 and of Rossetti's in 1870, and introductions to some of the Kelmscott books and the saga translations, but generally he regarded criticism as an undesirable and parasitic occupation. Once his own reputation was established he took little notice of reviewers and disliked literary discussion of his work. He angrily demanded of a critic in the *Athenæum*, 'why the devil doesn't he *do something* himself instead of writing about what somebody else has done?'[2] When a Professorship of English Literature was proposed at Oxford in 1886 he wrote to the papers to

protest emphatically. For the result would be merely vague talk about literature, which would teach nothing. Each succeeding professor would strive to outdo his predecessor in 'originality' on subjects whereon nothing remains to be said. Hyper-refinement and paradox would be the order of the day . . . Philology can be taught, but 'English literature' cannot.[3]

Morris was content that his own judgements should be instinctive. In disapproving Swinburne's poetry, for example, he admitted that 'I may be quite wrong, and the lack may be in myself: I only state my opinion, I don't defend it.'[4] Even this degree of diffidence was unusual. He described Coleridge as 'a muddle-brained metaphysician, who by some strange freak of fortune turned out a few real poems amongst the dreary flood of inanity which was his wont'. There was 'absolutely no difficulty in choosing, because the difference between his poetry and his drivel is so striking'.[5] In short, in his literary judgements Morris was something of an anti-intellectual, making no effort to disguise his own prejudices.

The essential framework of Morris's taste was formed by the time that he left Oxford. It was, at that time, a relatively progressive taste, reflecting the main currents of the romantic movement of the late eighteenth century, which by 1855, although almost exhausted, had not quite broken up. The romantic movement had been a reassertion of human individuality and emotion, a protest against oppression, whether by despotic government, rigid rules of taste, hypocritical social and religious convention, or industrial squalor and distress. It was moved by a common belief in simpler life. But this belief could either be held in hope of the natural goodness of mankind, a hope encouraged by the vision of revolutionary France and of free Greece, or held in despair of change, preferring the inspiration of a more romantic and heroic past, an escape to the pleasanter world of dreams. By 1855 hope had all but dried up. 'We were born into a dull time oppressed with bourgeoisdom and philistinism so sorely that we were forced to turn back on ourselves, and only in ourselves and the world of art and literature was there any hope.'[6] Morris's tastes therefore tended to medievalism and escapism. Romantic protest, it is true, was the common element in Blake ('the part of him which a mortal can understand'),[7] in Tennyson's *Maud*, in Cobbett, Carlyle, and Ruskin; and romantic hope in Byron and Shelley. All these Morris admired, but he was still more strongly drawn to romantic escape, which he found in Keats and Coleridge, in Scott's novels (which he started at the age of four), in Rossetti's *The Blessed Damozel* (which he had read in the pre-Raphaelite paper, *The Germ*) and Tennyson's *The Lady of Shalott*, in the old stories collected in Thorpe's *Northern Mythology*, and Malory's *Morte d'Arthur*. Probably he was also attracted to Browning's poetry because of his medievalisms, and he enjoyed Dickens and Chaucer for their entertaining humour rather than their social realism.

Although Morris tired of none of these early enthusiasms, the balance of his interests was greatly changed in later years. He liked very little poetry written after 1855; in particular he felt little sympathy for later Tennyson, later Browning, or Swinburne. The important exception was Rossetti, whom he first met in 1856. Probably he also enjoyed Matthew Arnold's pastoral poems, although he never acknowledged his influence. But after Morris had published his own last major poem in 1876, he developed an attitude of pessimistic impossibilism towards poetry which parallels his final view of architecture. He thought that simple language and direct emotion had been the secret of the great poetry of the past. But things had 'very much changed since the early days of language: once everybody who could express himself at all did so beautifully, was a poet for that occasion, because all language was beautiful. But now language is utterly degraded in our daily lives, and poets have to make a new tongue each for himself.'[8] Similarly, Victorian society, with its combination of conventional suppression and intense introspection, had no place for straightforward romantic emotion. Morris could not bear Browning's colloquial style of poetry, 'with its subtle psychology and abrupt formless methods'; but he was equally dissatisfied with Swinburne's artificial style 'founded on literature, not on nature', for he knew that in poetry, 'there is no room for anything which is not forced out of a man of deep feeling, because of its innate strength and vision'.[9] Hence his blunt ultimate conclusion that 'poetry was tommy rot'.[10] He meant modern poetry.

In compensation Morris's enthusiasm for medieval poetry increased as his knowledge of it grew. Caedmon and the Anglo-Saxon lyrics, medieval ballads, 'Omar Khayyám', *Piers Plowman*, and Dante came to rank with Chaucer. His liking for epic poetry and ancient stories developed still more strongly. He enjoyed later medieval story collections such as *The Thousand and One Nights* or Boccaccio's *Decameron*, but he preferred the earliest, above all Homer, Beowulf, the Volsung Saga, and the Old Testament. 'They cannot always be measured by a literary standard, but to me are far more important than any literature. They are in no sense the work of individuals, but have grown up from the very hearts of the *people*.'[11]

Morris also developed a strong liking for novels. His shelves were full of cheap yellow-backs bought for train journeys. He read for entertainment and his favourites were George Borrow, Defoe, Dumas, Scott, Victor Hugo, Thomas Love Peacock, Robert Surtees, and Dickens. Morris declared 'that I yield to no one, not even Ruskin, in my love and admiration for Scott: also that to my mind of the novelists of our generation Dickens is immeasurably ahead'.[12]

Morris predicted that Dickens would be chiefly remembered for 'his fashioning a fantastic and unreal world for his men and women to act in'.[13] He would use Dickensian quips, such as the unanswerable disapproval of, 'Bring him forward, and I'll chuck him out o' winder', and especially liked to imitate the mannerisms of Joe Gargery and Mr Boffin, commonly greeting friends with Gargery's 'Wot larks!' or Mr Boffin's 'Morning, morning!' Dickens provided part of his dream world, for use in situations where Sigurd or Tristram would have been unimaginable.

It was certainly the humour rather than the realism of Dickens which appealed to Morris. The novels which he enjoyed most had the qualities of medieval stories, with their 'rude joviality, and simple and direct delineation of character'.[14] He succeeded in reading Tolstoy's *War and Peace* 'with much approbation but little enjoyment', but decided not to 'tackle *Anna Karenina*; I want something more of the nature of a stimulant when I read'.[15] He much preferred simpler books, like *Uncle Remus* or *Huckleberry Finn*. He was prepared to argue that a successful author must 'qualify or soften the ugliness and sordidness of the surroundings of life in our generation'. But he seemed scarcely more satisfied to read a dramatic story set in just this way. Hardy's novels, for example, were

supposed to represent scenes of modern life . . . But do they? I say they do not; because they take care to surround those modern scenes with an atmosphere of out-of-the-way country life, which we ourselves never by any chance see. If you go down into the country you won't see Mr Hardy's heroes and heroines walking about, I assure you.[16]

Morris, as he grew older, and increasingly aware of the social tragedy of industrialization and urbanization, could no longer find in major contemporary novelists the pleasure which he wanted from fiction. The great writers of the late nineteenth century were either false, or depressing. Thus Zola's *Germinal*, while 'part of a true picture of the life which our civilization forces on labouring men', was hardly a subject for art; while there was still less to be said for Henry James, 'the clever historian of the deadliest corruption of society, the laureat of the flirts, sneaks, and empty fools of which that society is mostly composed, and into whose hearts(?) he can see so clearly'.[17] This kind of writing might be useful propaganda for the criticism of existing society, but it was not good literature, because it offered no hope to the spirit.

His attitude to the theatre was similar. In the early days of his friendship with Rossetti, Morris had been an enthusiastic follower of Robson and Kean, but by the time that he had to take his daughters to plays he could scarcely tolerate anything produced, and would mutter in an embarrassingly loud voice as the heroine appeared, 'damned little pink TOAD', or dismiss a hero as 'a pink pig squealing into a wool-sack'. He thought that the theatre should be symbolic, not realistic; scenes and costumes should be represented by simple conventional symbols, and actors should wear masks 'to simplify and detach the persons of the drama'.[18] There should be no deaths on the stage and no soliloquies. 'In my opinion modern tragedy, including Shakespeare, is not fit to be put upon the modern stage: Shakespeare's genius has consecrated by its poetry and insight what was really a very bad form of drama, and has enslaved play-wrights ever since.'[19] Consequently, although he thought Ibsen's *A Doll's House* 'a piece of the *truth* about modern society clearly and forcibly put', and 'another token of the new dawn', he could not really admire it as a play.[20]

Thus while his enthusiasm for ancient literature grew, Morris's favourites in modern literature remained little changed from the point which he had reached in 1855. When in 1886 he contributed his list of 54 best books to a series in the *Pall Mall Gazette*, his bias in favour of the past, his preference for the Gothic north rather than any kind of classicism, and above all his feeling that literature should be a pleasurable entertainment rather than a challenge, resulted in a selection of apparently undesirable eccentricity. Thirty-seven of his choices were ancient and medieval, although he denounced several Latin authors and excluded Virgil and Ovid as being of purely 'archaeological value'. The whole period between the end of the Middle Ages and the romantic movement was represented only by More's *Utopia*, Shakespeare's poetry, Bunyan, and Defoe. At other times he conceded an admiration for 'the keen-eyed, cool-headed Gibbon',[21] but the omission of Marlowe, Jonson, Dryden, Milton, Pope, Swift, and the eighteenth-century novelists was undoubtedly intentional. Of Milton he said that 'the union in his work of cold classicalism with Puritanism (the two things which I hate most in the world) repels me so much that I *cannot* read him'; while the eighteenth century he dismissed as 'a few word-spinning essayists and prosaic versifiers'.[22] The remaining thirteen modern books consisted of Grimm's *Teutonic Mythology*, and the works of Carlyle and Ruskin, five romantic poets, and five modern novelists. There was no mention of Tolstoy, Dostoevsky, Balzac, or Zola, of the poetry of Verlaine or Baudelaire, or of the entire French and English theatre.

Morris had formed his original escapist tastes as a reasonable reaction to a world which he abominated. But by 1886 an author was 'confronted by the rising hope of the people', the socialist movement into which Morris had thrown his own energies. He believed that this hope could add 'backbone' to literature.[23] But he was perhaps too old for this belief to alter his basic tastes. He failed to see that social realism might be transformed by political hope; that the conventional Victorian view that literature should have a moral purpose, which he had rejected when that purpose was conventional moralizing, might lead in a new context to great realistic fiction and drama making its own contribution to change. This obstinate attachment to the past perhaps stunted his own final development as a writer. Nevertheless Morris did, in his own inimitable fashion, set out to create a new moral and collective drama in his later prose romances, *News from Nowhere* and *The Dream of John Ball*. It is in the context of this positive vision of the future that his tastes must be understood: his belief that literature, like art, should spring from the people. This was why he preferred sagas and folk literature to the anguished and hopeless individualism of the nineteenth-century middle-class novel. This was why he wanted to purge the English language of its ruling class Romanisms and reconstruct it on its Saxon vernacular base. And why he had so little patience for the parasitic specialists of literary criticism.

9

PROSE WRITING

THE consequence of Morris's conviction that literature should provide a pleasurable world of escape, and that modern society could not be a successful subject for literary art, are immediately apparent in his prose writings. These are sharply divided. On the one hand there is the straightforward style of his utilitarian prose, used for letters and lectures, composed but undecorated; on the other hand the specially created and symbolic manner of his prose romances, ornamented as art. Inevitably the style of one influenced the other, so that there are archaic tricks in his letters and moments of immediacy in his romances, but the two kinds of prose need to be approached in quite different ways.

Today Morris's utilitarian prose is his most easily enjoyed writing. This is above all because it so clearly reveals his personality, whether in private letters or in public lectures. Inevitably the letters are less carefully written; they tend to be more abrupt, often inventories of terse comment on politics, weather, and art with no more stylistic co-ordination than the antiquated conjunctions, 'to wit' and 'item'. Many have already been quoted in previous pages, so that a reminder of their style will suffice here: a letter to Janey after a visit to Kelmscott in December, where he 'had fine but very cold days; this morning brilliant but white-frosty: the river had been much flooded, but was lower the first day, & I caught two good pike: I should like to have sent you one in a letter'; and then a return to London in August: 'I can't say London looked pretty when I got there: item the house smelt of cat.'[1] The style is so blunt that it scarcely bears quoting, yet it conveys his feeling very well.

A few letters, chiefly written about journeys or to friends whom he hoped to convert to socialism, are rather more sustained and approach the careful and continuous argument of the lectures. Even in these letters, as in the lectures themselves and also in Morris's socialist articles for *Justice* and *Commonweal*, it is not so much the style which impresses, but the content; the observation of people and scenery, the clear bones of Morris's logic, the forceful illustrations and the pervading warmth of feeling. The language has no purple patches; the vocabulary and syntax are always simple, so that the message comes across directly. There are few attempts to build up any elaborate effects in scenic description; a

scene is evoked in a few brief common words rather than by exact
verbal realism. Neither in argument nor in description can any prose of
Morris compare with the rhetoric and visual imagery of Ruskin. This
does not mean that Morris gained consistent clarity in compensation.
His prose was not easily written; he thought himself a bad letter-writer,
and found the composition of his first lectures extremely difficult. He
hammered out his thoughts with a bare bluntness so condensed that it is
difficult to read continuously, and it is only in rare moments that his
feeling breaks through strongly enough to make the simplicity of the
language in itself impressive.

The lectures, like the letters, are frequently quoted in other chapters
(especially Chapter 12), but it is worth giving two substantial extracts of
Morris's prose style at its best. The first comes at the end of 'The Lesser
Arts', the first of his lectures, given in London in December 1877.

I do not want art for a few, any more than education for a few, or freedom for a
few.

No, rather that art should live this poor thin life among a few exceptional
men, despising those beneath them for an ignorance for which they themselves
are responsible, for a brutality that they will not struggle with,—rather than
this, I would that the world should indeed sweep away all art for awhile, as I
said before I thought it possible she might do; rather than the wheat should rot
in the miser's granary, I would that the earth had it, that it might yet have a
chance to quicken in the dark.

I have a sort of faith, though, that this clearing away of all art will not happen,
that men will get wiser, as well as more learned; that many of the intricacies of
life, on which we now pride ourselves more than enough, partly because they
are new, partly because they have come with the grain of better things, will be
cast aside as having played their part, and being useful no longer. I hope that we
shall have leisure from war—war commercial, as well as war of the bullet and
the bayonet; leisure from the knowledge that darkens counsel; leisure above all
from the greed of money, and the craving for that overwhelming distinction
that money now brings: I believe that as we have even now partly achieved
LIBERTY, so we shall one day achieve EQUALITY, which, and which only, means
FRATERNITY, and so have leisure from poverty and all its griping, sordid cares.

Then, having leisure from all these things, amidst renewed simplicity of life
we shall have leisure to think about our work, that faithful daily companion,
which no man any longer will venture to call the Curse of labour: for surely
then we shall be happy in it, each in his place, no man grudging at another; no
one bidden to be any man's *servant*, everyone scorning to be any man's *master*:
men will then assuredly be happy in their work, and that happiness will
assuredly bring forth decorative, noble, *popular* art.

That art will make our streets as a beautiful as the woods, as elevating as the
mountain-sides: it will be a pleasure and a rest, and not a weight upon the spirits
to come from the open country into a town; . . . for as nothing of beauty and
splendour that man's mind and hand may compass shall be wanting from our

public buildings, so in no private dwelling will there be any signs of waste, pomp, or insolence, and every man will have his share of the *best*.

It is a dream, you may say, of what has never been and never will be; true, it has never been, and therefore, since the world is alive and moving yet, my hope is the greater that it one day will be; true, it is a dream; but . . . it lies at the bottom of all my work in the Decorative Arts, nor will it ever be out of my thoughts: and I am here with you to-night to ask you to help me in realising this dream, this *hope*.[2]

For pure style, this is one of the most striking passages in the lectures, but even here, in spite of the simple language, the sentences are not all easily understood, and the climaxes tend to slip away.

Quite a different extract comes from the journal which Morris wrote of his first visit to Iceland, with publication originally in mind. The account of his day in the Faroes on the voyage out is one of the best of many unusually vivid descriptions in the journal.

The ship had steamed into the little fishing harbour of Thorshaven in the cold early morning. Morris watched the passengers landing after 'a great deal of kissing on deck', and a boat carrying the governor, rowed 'by the queerest old carles' dressed in the Faroese style of caps, stockings, and knee-breeches. The passengers disembarked after breakfast and first looked round the little town of black wooden turf-roofed houses. Morris found the women 'not pretty, but not horrible either', and the men quite handsome, although with 'a curious cast of melancholy on their faces, natural I should think to the dwellers in small remote islands'. Then they set off to walk across the island, climbing up from the meadows into the open peaty fells, with a view back to the town below.

We turned a corner of the stony stepped grey hills, and below us lay a deep calm sound, say two miles broad, a hog-backed steep mountain-island forming the other side of it, next to which lay a steeper islet, a mere rock; and then other islands, the end of which we could not see, entangled the sound and swallowed it up; I was most deeply impressed with it all, yet can scarcely tell you why; it was like nothing I had ever seen, but strangely like my old imaginations of places for sea-wanderers to come to: the day was quite a hot summer day now, and there was no cloud in the sky and the atmosphere was very, very clear, but a little pillowy cloud kept dragging and always changing yet always there over the top of the little rocky islet . . . . All the islands, whether sloping or sheer rocks, went right into the sea without a handsbreadth of beach anywhere; and, little thing as that seems, I suppose it is this which gives the air of romanticism to these strange islands. Close by the sea lay the many gables (black wood with green turf roofs) of the farm of Kirkinbœ (Kirkby), a little whitewashed church being the nearest to the sea, while close under the basalt cliff was the ruin of a stone mediaeval church: a most beautiful and poetical place it looked to me, but more remote and melancholy than I can say, in spite of the flowers and grass and bright sun: it looked as if you might live for a hundred years before you would ever see ship sailing into the bay there; as if the old life of the saga-time had gone, and the modern life had never reached the place.

We hastened down, along the high mowing-grass of the home-field, full of buttercups and marsh marigolds, and so among the buildings: the long-nosed cadaverous parson who guided us took us first to the ruin, which he said had never been finished, as the Reformation had stopped the building of it: in spite of which story it is visibly not later than 1340 in date, which fact I with some qualms stoutly asserted to the parson's disgust, though 'tis quite a new fault to me to find local antiquaries post-date their antiquities: anyway it was, or had been, a rich and beautiful 'decorated' chapel without aisles, and for all I knew had never been finished: thence we went into the more modern church (such a flowerbed as its roof was!) which was nevertheless interesting from its having a complete set of bench-ends richly carved (in deal) of the fifteenth century, but quite northern in character, the interlacing work mingling with regular fifteenth-century heraldic work . . . ;

and so back into Thorshaven, to sail after dinner.

It was a fine evening, so the ship left by a sound called the Westmannafirth. The water

was quite smooth clear and green, and not a furlong across: the coasts were wonderful on either side; pierced rocks running out from the cliffs under which a brig might have sailed: caves that the water ran up into, how far we could not tell, smooth walls of rock with streams flowing over them right into the sea, or these would sink down into green slopes with farms on them, or be cleft into deep valleys over which would show crater-like or pyramidal mountains, or they would be splintered into jagged spires, one of which single and huge just at the point of the last ness before we entered this narrow sound, is named Trollsfinger; and all this always without one inch of beach to be seen; and always when the cliffs sank you could see little white clouds lying about on the hillsides. At last we could see on ahead a narrow opening, so narrow that you could not imagine that we could sail out of it, and then soon the cliffs on our right gave back and showed a great land-locked bay almost like a lake, with green slopes all round it . . . where lay the houses of a little town, Westmanna-haven; they tell us that the water is ten fathoms deep close up to the very shore in here, and that it is as it looks, a most magnificent harbour. After that on we went towards the gates that led out into the Atlantic; narrow enough they look even now we are quite near; as the ship's nose was almost in them, I saw close behind us a stead with its homefield sloping down to the sea, the people running out to look at us, and the black cattle grazing all about, then I turned to look ahead as the ship met the first swell of the open sea, and when I looked astern a very few minutes after, I could see nothing at all of the gates we had come out by, no slopes of grass, or valleys opening out from the shore; nothing but a terrible wall of rent and furrowed rocks.[3]

Without much doubt this is the most impressive prose description written by Morris, but it is his excitement which carries the reader through. The phrases are strung together monotonously, and the words used are not themselves interesting, except for some words formerly common but by then obscure, which would have been better avoided. It is successful as a whole, rather than impressive when examined in detail.

In Morris's prose romances the content is less immediately compelling, and the difficulties of his style less easily forgotten. He wrote two groups of romantic prose stories, the first in 1855–6 for publication in the *Oxford and Cambridge Magazine*, and the second in 1888–96. Both consist of dreams of a simple, generally medieval world, with unspoilt landscape and uncomplicated people. The earlier romances have an element of brutality and sinister magic which gives a special interest to 'Lindenborg Pool'. As with his first poems they already show Morris's ability to bring, in momentary flashes, past into present.

The later prose romances are nearly all very long, and different in tone. W. B. Yeats was one of the rare contemporaries who really enjoyed them: they were 'the only books I was ever to read slowly that I might not come too quickly to the end'.[4] Yeats described Morris's intention as

a dream indeed, but a dream of natural happiness . . . It was his work to make us, who had been taught to sympathise with the unhappy till we had grown morbid, to sympathise with men and women who turned everything into happiness because they had in them something of the abundance of beechen boughs or the bursting wheat-ear . . . All he writes seems to me like the make-belief of a child who is remaking the world, not always in the same way, but always after its own heart . . . He has but one story to tell us, how some man or woman lost and found again the happiness that is always half of the body.

Yeats liked the women of the romances, mothers and housewives to whom 'love was less a passion for one man out of the world, than submission to the hazard of destiny', the changes and chances of life to be accepted as gladly as the seasons. Morris 'may not have been, indeed he was not, among the very greatest poets, but he was among the greatest of those who prepare for the last reconciliation when the Cross shall blossom with roses'.[5]

To Yeats the prose romances had a different meaning than they are likely to have to most modern readers. For most it is very difficult to keep an interest in what seems an unreal world of human goodness and fulfilment, lacking not only psychological pain, but satire and comedy too. The shortest tale, *The Glittering Plain*, is brief enough to sustain a sense of primitive wonder, but the shallowness of characterization, the frequent use of magic, and the general obscurity of purpose makes the longer stories to many almost unreadable. *The House of the Wolfings*, in which the narrative and speeches are alternated with sections in verse, is one of the most difficult of all. Morris intended it 'to illustrate the melting of the individual into the society of the tribes', and the tales certainly do contain interesting imaginative explorations of Morris's vision, not just of language, but also of sexual relationships. If formally in the past, they are also a dream of a future society: of the dissolution of the constricting nuclear family into a wider kin and community, of fulfilled sexuality, of women who are no longer ambiguously seductive, silent and pale, but brown, strong, and active. These female heroes, some ruthless fighters, culminate in Birdalone of the final *Water of the Wondrous Isles*. In literature they are a rarity, and were one reason why in the late 1960s and 1970s the prose romances found a new Anglo-American readership: a generation of young men and women also optimistic of the innate goodness of human beings, feminist, and seeking worlds of escape and alternative social relationships in fellow-ship and communalism. Nevertheless, Morris wrote these dreams as much for his own pleasure as to convey explicit messages, and he publicly protested when *The Wood Beyond the World* was interpreted as a socialist allegory.[6]

The unreality of the later romances was increased by specially created language, which combines a relatively simple syntax with a strange archaic vocabulary, which only Morris could easily comprehend. It certainly had a valid purpose. He understood that language is intrinsic to every social culture, so that one world can never be adequately conveyed by the diction of another. His solution was to forge a new form, foreign yet understandable, which pulls the reader out of the contemporary world. But while some critics greeted this language as a new form of literary art, a commoner reaction was mere exasperation. What did Morris mean by a phrase like 'Come hither and handsel him selfdoom for my fool's onset'? What exactly was a 'shut-bed' or the 'haysel'? How did one 'swink' or 'staunch'?[7] As Quiller-Couch commented, archaisms were difficult enough in poetry, but in prose

the whole mediaeval vocabulary and apparatus began to look like an old and played-out bag of tricks . . . Affectation of this kind may creep under the wide shield of poetry, but in prose it is only preserved from general derision by the author's evident and pathetic conviction that he is doing the right thing, odd as it may appear.[8]

The later prose romances were never popular and Morris probably did not think of an immediate audience when he wrote them. They were Gothic fancies of his old age, created for his own pleasure and perhaps for the society of the future, like the Kelmscott Press where he had most of them printed. But they cannot be dismissed as mere eccentricities for two reasons; first, because they represent the culmination of some tendencies which are present in most of Morris's writing; and secondly, because with them must be grouped two stories which Morris wrote as serials in *Commonweal* in 1886–7 and 1890, *The Dream of John Ball* and *News from Nowhere*.

These two stories are among the most successful pieces which Morris wrote. Both are dreams, the first of medieval Kent and the second of a socialist England, set in a world of simple, happy people close to nature, very similar to the unreal world of the prose romances. Yet both succeed because reality breaks through into the dream, creating a dramatic tension which is absent in the prose romances. In each story this tension is centred upon the narrator, whom Morris thus uses as the interpreter of the dream. In *The Dream of John Ball* the confidence of the rebel preacher, with his medieval aims and message, is challenged by a glimpse of the future: a future in which his aims will have been won, only to lead to another slavery; and so he is shown his part in the long struggle of the people. In *News from Nowhere* the narrator is constantly remembering the reality to which he must return, so that the simple ideal world becomes a socialist allegory. *News from Nowhere* was never intended to be a literal picture of a socialist utopia, but it was meant to convey a set of socialist values which were distinct from those of a mere rationalized state capitalism. This it does very well. Of the two stories *The Dream of John Ball*, because of its medieval setting, is probably the less well known, but in some ways it is the more effective; the talk in the village inn before John Ball arrives, his great sermon on Fellowship at the village cross, and the confrontation with Morris himself in the church at night, are among the most dramatic scenes in all his writing.

There is no doubt that the challenge of his socialist audience helped to bring out the best in Morris. It stimulated his only interesting later poem, *The Pilgrims of Hope*, and even led him into an entertaining attempt to put his odd dramatic theories into practice, *The Tables Turned, or Nupkins Awakened*, written as a socialist fund-raiser in 1887. Morris played the part of Archbishop of Canterbury himself, dressed in a symbolic pair of bands and black stockings, 'presenting his own person to the audience like a lantern with the light blown out'. Shaw remembered the wild laughter of the audience, 'a motley sea of rolling, wallowing, guffawing Socialists . . . There has been no other such successful first night within living memory.'⁹

This awareness of his audience gives a real value to these two socialist dreams, his socialist poem and play, but it did not enable Morris to escape from the basic methods which he thought appropriate to any literary work of art. And paradoxically, the most striking example of these methods was not in his original work, but in his prose translations of the sagas. The sagas, so critical in rescuing Morris from mere morbid romantic escapism, were the source of the archaic dream language of the prose romances.

Morris's co-operation with Magnusson in the translation of the sagas has already been described. They would begin by reading through the saga together; Magnusson would then produce a prose version, which Morris would polish for publication. Morris's alterations now seem distinctly for the worse, for he would twist back the English towards the word order of the original and replace common English words by archaisms closer to the Icelandic. Many of these archaisms were pure inventions. The trick had started when they were reading together, and Morris would invent words which were helpful 'towards penetrating the thought of the old language'. Thus 'kvaenask', to marry, from 'kvan', a woman, he translated as 'to bequeen one's self'. This enjoyable way of working was incomprehensible to anyone who was unaware of these connections, but Morris saw it as a way of creating a special type of English, more Teutonic, which could accurately preserve the spirit of the sagas. He built up a new vocabulary; some words, such as 'by-men' (byjarmenn), meaning 'townspeople', and 'shoe-swain' (skosveinn), meaning 'page', were based on Icelandic; while others, such as 'stead' for 'farm', or 'cheaping' for 'market', were based on old English.

The result was a cramped, inverted style, difficult to read. Morris's very desire to reproduce the old sagas faithfully, to give his translations the artistic quality of the originals, destroyed their essential directness and made the popularity of his versions an impossibility. With some of their translations Morris and Magnusson were breaking entirely new literary ground. The Volsunga Saga had never previously been translated into English. Yet the method which they used wasted a great opportunity of presenting the literature of the north, which both admired so much, to the wide audience it deserved.

Morris as a prose writer thus presents a paradox. His very failings spring from his significance as a writer. For his perpetual seeking of escape from social reality, his dreaming can be read both as 'an account of the agony of holding the mind together' in an intolerable present, and as uniquely constructive imagination of a communal future. John Lucas writes:

Morris creates a revolutionary literature because he discovers forms which dramatize the tensions of the revolutionary mind. And I don't know any other writer in English who does that. These forms included the very basis of social communication. He took immense pains to reach a vernacular simplicity of language. His words and syntax reflected both his analysis of society, and his belief that imagination must be grounded in history. Yet in much of his writing this very form cut him off from any wide audience. Nevertheless it is the very creative struggle for expression, the battle for straightforward meaning, which gives to some of his later work, *News from Nowhere*, the socialist lectures, an unforgettable conviction.[10]

10

POETRY

In his lifetime William Morris was more famous as a poet than as an artist. As 'the author of *The Earthly Paradise*' he was a respected public figure, and his reputation was hardly increased, probably in some minds even diminished, by his activity as a 'poet-upholsterer'. In sheer volume his production of poetry is an astonishing achievement. Yet today it is as an artist or a socialist rather than a poet that Morris is most admired. His work as an artist has worn well, and most of his designs are a pleasure to look at, but his poetry has suffered much more from fashion, and much of it is little read. How justified is this neglect?

The sequence of Morris's publication of poetry and its reception by the reviewers has been described in the context of his life, but a recapitulation at this point will be helpful. His first volume, *The Defence of Guenevere*, appeared in 1858 and received a few generally hostile reviews. Morris suddenly became one of the most popular of Victorian poets with the publication in 1867 of *The Life and Death of Jason*, followed in 1868–70 by the stories of *The Earthly Paradise*, for which *Jason* had originally been written. In spite of this popularity his last major poems, *Love is Enough* and *Sigurd the Volsung*, published in 1872 and 1876, were relatively coolly received. Subsequently Morris wrote the socialist poetry of 1884–6, *Chants for Socialists* and *The Pilgrims of Hope*, and in 1891 published a collection of extracts from the latter together with earlier poems in *Poems by the Way*. In addition Morris wrote verse translations of *The Aeneids of Virgil* (1875), *The Odyssey of Homer* (1887) and *The Tale of Beowulf* (1895), as well as sections of verse for the Icelandic saga translations of 1869–75.

Not surprisingly, the main interest is in his original poetry. Morris's verse translations, like his prose versions of the sagas, miss the essential qualities for success, clarity, and readability. They are accurate translations, but so carefully kept to the original lines and order of phrases that they are difficult to read. For the *Aeneids* and the *Odyssey* Morris relied on his own Greek and Latin, but for *Beowulf* he had the help of a Cambridge scholar, A. J. Wyatt. It is perhaps the worst thing he ever wrote, quite incomprehensible without a glossary.

The saga verse shares these faults, but it has a special interest, for its odd, evocative, compressed style has a hint of original poetry which

Morris never wrote, that might have fulfilled the early promise of *The Defence of Guenevere*. Where the meaning is clear it can be strangely striking:

> Brethren shall fight
> And be bane of each other,
> Cousins moreover
> Kinship shall spill:
> A hard while in the world,
> A while of great whoredom;
> An axe-age, a spear-age;
> Shields shall be cloven;
> A wind-age, a wolf-age
> Ere the world sinketh.[1]
>
> Go, look on Sigurd,
> On the ways that go southward,
> There shalt thou hear
> The ernes high screaming,
> The ravens a-croaking
> As their meat they crave for;
> Thou shalt hear the wolves howling
> Over thine husband.[2]

For there is no doubt that *The Defence of Guenevere* is by far the most provocative of Morris's books of poems. Contemporaries disagreed strongly on its merits. John Parker, the editor of *Frazer's Magazine*, thought it made up 'of the most obscure, watery, mystical, affected stuff possible', and the *Athenæum* dismissed it as a pre-Raphaelite 'curiosity which shows how far affection may mislead an earnest man towards the fog-land of Art'. Swinburne, on the other hand, asked defiantly, 'where among other and older poets of his time and country, is one comparable for perception and expression of tragic truth, of subtle and noble, terrible and piteous things?'[3] And although this early poetry is now regarded as Morris's most significant, modern opinion is still sharply divided.

To bring out their full value the poems must be read slowly, with each syllable given its full value, avoiding any strong rhythmic beat. Read like this, the apparently naïve defects in the poems, the odd deviations from the normal iambic beat, the unexpected rhymes and the curious overlapping of the lines, become masterly devices for creating tension, for suggesting a deeper meaning. In the opening lines of the book, for example, a secondary rhythm drags against the weakened primary metre, so that a purely physical description of Guenevere takes on a sense of sexual shame:

But, knowing now that they would have her speak,
She threw her wet hair backward from her brow,
Her hand close to her mouth touching her cheek,

As though she had had there a shameful blow,
And feeling it shameful to feel ought but shame
All through her heart, yet felt her cheek burned so,

She must a little touch it . . .

The fourth line, clumsy according to conventional metrical standards, is here brilliantly effective. Morris had in fact created a new verse form, like stammering direct speech, which parallels the effects of Gerard Manley Hopkins to break through conventional metre with the sprung rhythm of *Piers Plowman*. These two experiments in medievalism were both important steps towards the freedom of modern verse.

Morris had also succeeded in using with striking reality themes and images which other poets had used to create a distant, languid dream-world. His Oxford friend Canon Dixon recalled that Morris 'understood Tennyson's greatness in a manner that we, who were mostly absorbed by the language, could not share. He understood it as if the poems represented substantial things that were to be considered out of the poems as well as in them.'[4] In Morris's poems symbols and reality are interpenetrated as in all the greatest poetry. The images of emotion are physical, and the description is full of symbolic suggestion. The bright colours, the heraldry, the counting of numbers, the parts of armour, the details of dress and architecture, add up to make the feverish tense atmosphere of 'The Defence of Guenevere', of 'Sir Peter Harpdon's End' as a prisoner of the French, and of the trapped lovers in 'The Haystack in the Floods'. The words are plain, but in their stiff, crabbed, broken-backed lines they become powerfully evocative. Guenevere speaks of her love:

And in the Summer I grew white with flame,
And bowed my head down—Autumn, and the sick
Sure knowledge things would never be the same,

However often Spring might be most thick
Of blossoms and buds, smote on me, and I grew
Careless of most things, let the clock tick, tick,

To my unhappy pulse, that beat right through
My eager body . . .
So day by day it grew, as if one should

Slip slowly down some path worn smooth and even,
Down to a cool sea on a summer day;
Yet still in slipping was there some small leaven

Of stretched hands catching small stones by the way,
Until one surely reached the sea at last,
And felt strange new joy as the worn head lay

Back, with the hair like sea-weed; yea all past
Sweat of the forehead, dryness of the lips
Washed utterly out by the dear waves o'ercast

In the lone sea . . .
I was half mad with beauty on that day . . .

I dared not think, as I was wont to do,
Sometimes, upon my beauty; if I had

Held out my long hand up against the blue
And, looking on the tenderly darken'd fingers,
Thought that by rights one ought to see quite through,

There, see you, where the soft still light yet lingers,
Round by the edges; what should I have done,
If this had joined with yellow spotted singers,

And startled green drawn upward by the sun?
But shouting, loosed out, see now! all my hair,
And trancedly stood watching the west wind run

With faintest half-hearted breathing sound—why there
I lose my head e'en now in doing this . . . [5]

The mixture of Gothic remoteness and direct physical violence and
sexuality is particularly remarkable in 'Concerning Geffray Teste
Noire', the attraction and terror inextricably expressed in the lines:

I saw you kissing once, like a curved sword
    That bites with all its edge, did your lips lie,
Curled gently, slowly, long time could afford
    For caught-up breathings; like a dying sigh . . .

The same kind of image is used in 'Golden Wings' when the love-crazed
knight 'kisses the long wet grass'. A wasp hangs dying in an apple,
caught by the fangs; and colours heighten the strangeness—the red
walls, the purple bed, the green moat.[6] Still more striking for its
singular use of colour and sense of menace is 'The Wind':

So I will sit, and think and think of the days gone by,
Never moving my chair for fear the dogs should cry,
Making no noise at all while the flambeau burns awry.
For my chair is heavy and carved, and with sweeping green behind
It is hung, and the dragons thereon grin out in the gusts of the
    wind;
On its folds an orange lies, with a deep gash cut in the rind.

Wind, wind! thou art sad, art thou kind?
Wind, wind, unhappy! thou art blind,
Yet still thou wanderest the lily-seed to find.

If I move my chair it will scream, and the orange will roll out far,
And the faint yellow juice ooze out like blood from a wizard's
    jar;
And the dogs will howl for those who went last month to the
    war . . . [7]

The evocative refrain is another recurrent device. Morris began 'The Blue Closet', a poem in honour of a painting by Rossetti, with the chant of the damozels:

> Lady Alice, Lady Louise,
> Between the wash of the tumbling seas
> We are ready to sing, if so ye please;
> So lay your long hands on the keys;
>   Sing, '*Laudate pueri*'.
> *And ever the great bell overhead*
> *Boom'd in the wind a knell for the dead,*
> *Though no one toll'd it, a knell for the dead.* [8]

At times the poetry is so odd that it comes close to nonsense; yet it grips the imagination, matter absorbed into metaphor until it becomes magic. Should one ask for disillusionment in understanding what Morris himself really intended in these poems? Does it matter? In one sense not; whatever Morris thought he was doing, his instinct was making him write real poetry, which we should be thankful to enjoy. But it is worth looking still more closely, for to understand how Morris wrote *The Defence of Guenevere* is to come some way towards an explanation of his complete transformation in *The Earthly Paradise*.

The truth is that *The Defence of Guenevere* was something of an accident; a vividness of expression which stumbled out of Morris's unconsciousness almost in spite of himself. He never felt satisfied with these early poems. To his friend Cormell Price he apologized for his odd rhymes; 'it *is* incompetency; you see [if] I must lose the thought, or sacrifice the rhyme to it, I had rather do the latter and take my chance about the music of it'.[9] He destroyed a great many of his early poems very similar to those published, and when *Guenevere* was reissued in 1875 he proposed alterations which would have ruined the poems. He would have smoothed and padded out the rhythm and replaced the startling direct images by conventional poetizing. The two versions of some of the stanzas of 'The Chapel in Lyoness' make a disconcerting comparison:

First version
> There I pluck'd a faint wild rose,
> Hard by where the linden grows,
> Sighing over silver rows
> > Of the lilies tall.
> I laid the flower across his mouth;
> The sparkling drops seem'd good for drouth;
> He smiled, turn'd round towards the south,
> > Held up a golden tress.

Proposed revision
> There in my rest I plucked a rose
> Where neath the lime a garden blows
> And winds run through the trembling rows
> > Of lilies slim and tall.
> I bore him water for his drouth,
> I laid the flower beside his mouth,
> He smiled, turned round towards the south,
> > Held up a golden tress.[10]

In short, Morris wanted to take away the very best things in these stanzas—the faint wild rose, the sighing linden; even the flower was to be laid beside instead of across his mouth, taking all the force out of the symbolic act. Could he have wanted these changes if he had understood the real merits of the poetry?

There is other disturbing evidence that apparently masterly devices in the poetry were the result of chance. When Morris was asked the meaning of the haunting spell, '*Two red roses across the moon*', he explained, 'But it's the knight's coat-of-arms of course!'[11] The queer blunt speech in the poems seems to have been an attempt to imitate the knightly directness which he found in Malory. The dramatic opening of *Guenevere* was pure luck, due to a mistake by the printer, who started with the second page of the manuscript. In general the abruptness of the stories was chiefly due to Morris's inexperience with narrative, and to his lack of interest in the psychology of his characters. He used none of the underlying technique of a plot, with its hints, connections, and surprises; instead he presented a series of vivid visual scenes, like a medieval fresco painter or illuminator. Morris's grasp of physical reality was always more striking than his depiction of character, but once he had mastered the art of narrative he never told a story in this crude way.

The simplest technical explanation of *The Defence of Guenevere* is that it represents an innocent but brilliant fusion of the metaphors of pre-Raphaelite painting and poetry: on the one hand the visual symbolism of intensified colour, abundant flowers, distortions of space and size; on the other, Tennysonian imagery, understood literally and physically,

combined with mannerisms taken from Browning, and set in the broad
form of medieval ballads. Tennyson's land of *The Lady of Shalott* is close
to that of Morris's knights and castles, but more faintly sensed:

> Willows whiten, aspens quiver,
> Little breezes dusk and shiver
> Thro' the wave that runs for ever
> By the island in the river
> > Flowing down to Camelot.
> Four grey walls, and four grey towers,
> Overlook a space of flowers,
> And the silent isle embowers
> > The Lady of Shalott . . .
> She left the web, she left the loom,
> She made three paces thro' the room,
> She saw the water-lily bloom,
> She saw the helmet and the plume,
> > She look'd down to Camelot.
> Out flew the web and floated wide;
> The mirror crack'd from side to side;
> 'The curse is come upon me', cried
> > The Lady of Shalott.

Morris wanted to give this dream-world the reality which he admired
in the broken conversational verse of some of Browning's early poems.
In his review of Browning's *Men and Women* he quoted from 'Andrea del
Sarto', where the painter, 'made alive again', talks 'calmly' of himself
and his art. Spoken slowly, it sounds a little like Morris:

> I do what many dream of all their lives,
> —Dream? Strive to do, and agonise to do,
> And fail in doing. I could count twenty such
> On twice your fingers, and not leave this town,
> Who strive—You don't know how the others strive
> To paint a little thing like that you smeared
> Carelessly passing with your robes afloat,
> Yet do much less, so much less, someone says,
> (I know his name, no matter) so much less!
> Well, less is more, Lucrezia! I am judged.
> There burns a truer light of God in them,
> In their vex'd, beating, stuff'd and stopped-up brain,
> Heart, or what'ere else, than goes on to prompt
> This low-pulsed forthright craftsman's hand of mine . . . [12]

So he broke up his ballad stanzas with gruff speeches, constructed his
dream castles with solid masonry. The result is highly original poetry.
Partly this is because of the nature of the dream itself; an ability to
penetrate the barriers of time, to bring past into present, present into

future, in intensely personal experience. In this Morris had from the start a unique vision to convey, and it was to recur in changing forms throughout his imaginative writing. In particular, he already stood out among contemporary poets in his portrayal of women. He conveys an intensely erotic and passionate female sexuality, absolutely without shame; and at the same time an overpowering sense of their condemnation, by a conventional passivity and helplessness, to suffocating constraint and senseless suffering. The morality of his Guenevere was consciously different from Tennyson's. In his whole development, however, the early poetry stands with the furniture he built for his Red Lion Square rooms at the same time, an expression of the same intensely medieval passion, constructed with the same crude carpentry. Its strength was the enthusiasm, the tension of youth, and the roughness of inexperience. And as Morris reached maturity as a poet, both in his technical command and his own emotional experience, he seemed to lose the secret of *The Defence of Guenevere*.

The intermediary stage can be seen in the unfinished 'Scenes from the Fall of Troy', and in the first draft of the prologue to *The Earthly Paradise*. The style is more fluent, but something of the early abruptness remains. Then, with *The Life and Death of Jason* and the published version of *The Earthly Paradise*, the transformation is complete. Morris's manner is now expansive, reflective, elegiac. The style is mellifluous, the narrative is organized with mastery, and the meaning always clear. Page after page is wonderfully decorative. Nothing could be easier reading. Nevertheless, there must have been hundreds of Victorian wives who, as they sat in the evening listening to a benevolently declaiming husband, found themselves, like Georgiana Burne-Jones, 'falling asleep to the steady rhythm of the reading voice, or biting my fingers and stabbing myself with pins in order to keep awake'.[13] *The Earthly Paradise* is an excellent way of passing a train journey, but it is not always easy at the end of the journey to remember what was in it. Why is this?

Primarily because Morris was too successful in realizing his own aims. *The Earthly Paradise* consists of a set of stories, taken from medieval and from classical sources, told by a group of wanderers who have fled from a plagued city to an Atlantic island where Greek and north European cultures intermingled. The wanderers are purely a device for linking the stories; unlike Chaucer's pilgrims, their precedent, they completely lack individual character, and never affect the style of narrative. The purpose of the stories, as Morris wrote in the opening and closing verses of the book, was to provide an escape from the unsettled present into a secure, slow-changing past, which would make reality easier to bear:

> The heavy trouble, the bewildering care
> That weighs us down who live and earn our bread,
> These idle verses have no power to bear;
> So let me sing of names rememberèd,
> Because they, living not, can ne'er be dead,
> Or long time take their memory quite away
> From us poor singers of an empty day . . .
>
> Then let the others go! and if indeed
> In some old garden thou and I have wrought,
> And made fresh flowers spring from hoarded seed,
> And fragrance of old days and deeds have brought
> Back to folk weary; and all was not for nought.
> —No little part it was for me to play—
> The idle singer of an empty day . . . [14]

And so, come with the wanderers:

> Forget six counties overhung with smoke,
> Forget the snorting steam and piston stroke,
> Forget the spreading of the hideous town;
> Think rather of the pack-horse on the down,
> And dream of London, small and white and clean . . . [15]

One should not too readily dismiss this escapism as misguided evasion. Morris's view of the ancient story-tellers as men who lightened the bitterness of life was perfectly tenable. For the Victorians, frightened by the upheaval which their own energy was producing, shaken in their religious confidence by scientific discovery, personally insecure in an age of ruthless economic competition, witnessing an unprecedented transformation and degradation of the landscape, the desire for a permanent, secure land, the desire to forget the emptiness of death, was a real and deeply rooted emotion. This desire was especially strong in Morris, to whom the poverty and ugliness of Victorian civilization seemed at that time irredeemable:

The hope of the past times was gone, the struggles of mankind for many ages had produced nothing but this sordid, aimle. ., ugly confusion; the immediate future seemed to me likely to intensify all the present evils by sweeping away the last survivals of the days before the dull squalor of civilization had settled down on the world. [16]

In addition, *The Earthly Paradise* was written in years darkened for Morris first by a terrible brooding on death, and then by the crisis of emptiness in his marriage.

These real emotional needs are honestly reflected in the poem. By reading Morris's own sufferings, not only into the framing verses but the characters in the tales too, intense personal meanings can be found in it. The entire *Earthly Paradise* indeed is paradoxically a poem driven by 'scourged hope, even despair': a confrontation with loss, fear and mortality, shifting between a cynical fatalism and the affirmation that man can leave something for the future in artistic creation. A perceptive critic can observe too how its elements are organized in a complex design, a 'sophisticated structure' of notable 'architectonic power', in which the cycle of the seasons is linked to the fate of passion, and stories within stories set faces of mood against each other.[17]

The difficulty is that so little of this disturbs its surface. The background of the poem has a classic calm, far removed from the feverish atmosphere of *Guenevere*, and far more soothing. The reapers

> Cast down beneath an ancient elm
> Upon a little strip of grass,
> From hand to hand the pitcher pass
> While on the turf beside them lay
> The ashen-handled sickles grey,
> The matters of their cheer between:
> Slices of white cheese, speckled with green,
> And green-striped onions and ryebread,
> And summer apples faintly red,
> Even beneath the crimson skin;
> And yellow grapes, well ripe and thin,
> Plucked from the cottage gable-end.[18]

Even the plague-stricken town from which the wanderers fled is conveyed without any sense of horror:

> I turned, and saw the autumn moonlight fall
> Upon the new-built bastions of the wall,
> Strange with the black shadow and grey flood of light,
> And further off I saw the lead shine bright
> On tower and turret-roof against the sky,
> And looking down I saw the old town lie
> Black in the shade of the o'er-hanging hill,
> Stricken with death, and dreary, but all still
> Until it reached the water of the bay . . . [19]

The poem revolves with the seasons, but is essentially in the mood of late summer, days when the story-tellers lay

> . . . well at ease,
> And watched the poppies burn across the grass,
> And o'er the bindweed's bells the brown bee pass
> Still murmuring of his gains . . . [20]

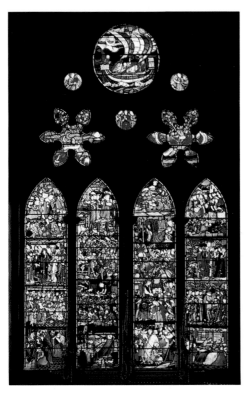

1 (*left*) Oxford Cathedral, Latin chapel, St Frideswide window, designed by Burne-Jones for Powell's, 1859

2 (*below*) All Saints' Selsley, detail of the rose window at the west end of the nave, possibly designed by Morris himself

3 Roundel, angel with harp by
Burne-Jones, 1873

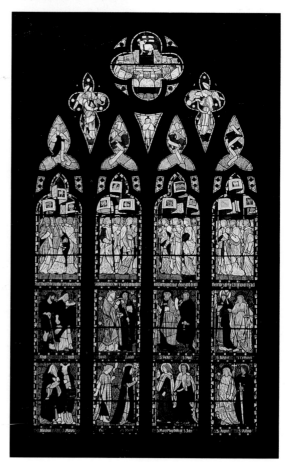

4 Middleton Cheney east window,
1865

5 Middleton Cheney, detail of
Abraham and Moses, by
Simeon Solomon

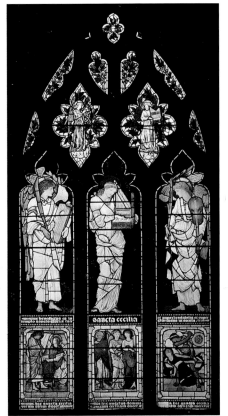

6 Oxford Cathedral, St Cecilia window,
by Burne-Jones, 1874

7 Liverpool, All Hallows Allerton, south transept, by Burne-Jones, 1879

8 St George's cabinet, 1861, of oak, designed by Webb and painted by
Morris, now at Victoria and Albert Museum

9 Cattistock, Dorset, by
Morris, 1882

10 'Fruit' wallpaper, by Morris, 1864

11 'Jasmine' wallpaper, by
Morris, 1872

12 'Snakehead' chintz, by
Morris, 1876

13 Design for 'Honeysuckle' chintz, by Morris, 1876

14 'Cray' chintz, by Morris, 1884

15 'Peacock and dragon', woven woollen hanging, by Morris, 1878

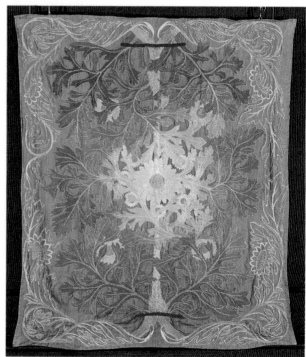

16 Coverlet, designed by Morris and embroidered in silks by Catherine Holiday, *c*.1876, now in Victoria and Albert Museum

But it is not a land of perpetual sunshine and happiness like that of the later prose romances. In this sense the pastoral vision which Morris first presents in *The Earthly Paradise* is transitional; earthly, tales of action, yet sung in a transient moment of idleness, caught still—before death knocks at the door. For winter and death are always imminent, kept at bay by the tales:

> Be merry, masters, while ye may,
> For men much quicker pass away.[21]

> In the white-flowered hawthorn brake,
> Love, be merry for my sake;
> Twine the blossoms in my hair,
> Kiss me where I am most fair—
> Kiss me, love! for who knoweth
> What thing cometh after death?[22]

In the same way the verses between the tales are used to contrast the simple romance of the stories with the empty pain of his own experience.

> From this dull rainy undersky and low,
> This murky ending of a leaden day,
> That never knew the sun, this half-thawed snow,
> These tossing black boughs faint against the grey
> Of gathering night, thou turnest, dear, away
> Silent, but with thy scarce-seen kindly smile
> Sent through the dusk my longing to beguile.

> There, the lights gleam, and all is dark without!
> And in the sudden change our eyes meet dazed—
> O look, love, look again! the veil of doubt
> Just for one flash, past counting, then was raised!
> O eyes of heaven, as clear thy sweet soul blazed
> On mine a moment! O come back again,
> Strange rest and dear amid the long dull pain!

> Nay, nay, gone by! though there she sitteth still,
> With wide grey eyes so frank and fathomless—
> Be patient, heart, thy days they yet shall fill
> With utter rest—Yea, now thy pain they bless,
> And feed thy last hope of the world's redress—
> O unseen hurrying rack! O wailing wind!
> What rest and where go ye this night to find?[23]

The fundamental defect in *The Earthly Paradise* was that, although Morris introduced these reminders of reality, he overbalanced the poem towards the contrasting lulling dream. Most of the stories are far too drawn out. As one exceptionally critical reviewer complained, 'the natural languor of Mr Morris's style makes his verse at once diffuse and tedious. An incurable habit of gossiping causes him to loiter in his narratives, when he should be swift and stirring.' Morris himself was embarrassed by the 'elephantine bulk' of the finished poem.[24]

This difficulty was aggravated by his avoidance of open suffering, brutality, or forceful emotion in the poems. In *Jason*, for example, Medea is softened and idealized and the cruelty of her revenge given justification. In 'The Lady of the Land', in which a maiden has been turned to a dragon and can only be rescued from the spell by a kiss, the lecherous cowardly sailor of the original story becomes a chivalrous semi-hero. In 'Acontius and Cydippe', Acontius, Morris admitted, 'is a spoony, nothing less'.[25] Again and again, in order to avoid pain, passion is subtly reduced, and to prevent offence to Victorian sensibility, sexual events are bowdlerized. It is hard to imagine a more acceptable form of rape than the tingling drowsiness which Jove imposes on Danaë in 'The Doom of King Acrisius'.

In the same way there is little drama in the scenery, which has a strange uniformity for all its superficial variety. The cumulative effect of all these devices is too often an atmosphere of such soothing unreality that it can become hard to feel interest in the characters or their adventures. This does not apply to all the tales; the romantic heroism of 'Ogier the Dane' with its grey Parisian scenes, or the picturesque medieval morality of 'The Proud King', are attractive in their way, and 'The Lovers of Gudrun', the turning point in Morris's poetry to which we must return later, is a story told with real force and drama. But with far too many stories, especially the Greek tales, the poetry sinks into a static, moody monotony.

These faults are exaggerated by Morris's poetic method. We have seen how in *The Defence of Guenevere* he used physical images to convey emotion, thus avoiding introspection, and his settings were built up with words of symbolic suggestiveness, rather than closely realistic description. In a moderated form he continued with both tendencies. There is more careful development of character in *The Earthly Paradise*, but never any real inner complexity. In this Morris's method was appropriate enough for the mood which he wanted in the poem; but without the tension with which it was used in *Guenevere*, the method becomes tedious. In the same way his descriptive technique lost its attraction when the symbolism became more straightforward. The settings in *The Earthly Paradise* are written in an intentionally limited vocabulary of relatively common words which Morris used as symbols to provoke an imaginative vision of the scene. His flowers are roses, lilies, and sunflowers, rather than those whose names were themselves evocative, like ragged robin or old man's beard, amaracus, or asphodel. His sea was plain green or blue, calm or tumbling; one never finds the acute realism of Tennyson's sound, 'Break, break, break, on thy cold grey stones'—or of Arnold's 'Dover Beach':

> Only, from the long line of spray
> Where the sea meets the moon-blanch'd land,
> Listen! you hear the grating roar
> Of pebbles which the waves draw back, and fling,
> At their return, up the high strand,
> Begin, and cease, and then again begin . . .

Nor does one find in Morris the wonderful sense of colour and growth which Ruskin and Hopkins conveyed. The best Victorian naturalism has the acute observation of a scientific age combined with an intense concern; for here was the heart of their doubt; did they see the wonder of God's creation, or the terror of the struggle for existence? Morris deliberately turned his back on both interpretations, in order to create a placid calm from common symbols. But inevitably it lacks the interest of the tenser writing of his contemporaries:

> Sir, please you to look up and down
> The weedy stretches of our stream,
> And note the bubbles of the bream,
> And see the great chub take the fly,
> And watch the long pike basking lie
> Outside the shadow of the weed.
> Withal there come unto our need
> Woodcock and snipe when swallows go;
> And now the water-hen flies low
> With feet that well-nigh touch the reeds,
> And plovers cry about the meads,
> And the stares chatter; certes, sir,
> It is a fair place all the year.[26]

Thus length, painlessness, simplicity of character and landscape, all weaken the poem's effect, until the most sympathetic reader can tire. As Swinburne complained, 'his Muse is like Homer's Trojan women; she drags her robes as she walks . . . my ear hungers for more force and variety of sound in the verse'.[27]

Yet this is perhaps not the most serious criticism of Morris's method in writing *The Earthly Paradise*. Morris wrote the poem too quickly, and he gave it too little of his concentration. Its 42,000 lines were written over six years, but much of the work was crowded into short bursts. On one occasion he wrote 750 lines for *Jason* in a single day: on another, 310 in an evening. It is true that much of the poem was redrafted and many variant versions of the stories survive, but Morris rarely worked at a manuscript. His method was to think out a poem in his head while he was busy at some other work. He would sit at an easel, charcoal, or brush in hand, working away at a design while he muttered to himself, 'bumble-beeing' as his family called it; then, when he thought he had got the lines, he would get up from the easel, prowl round the room still muttering, returning occasionally to add a touch to the design; then suddenly he would dash to the table and write out twenty or so lines. As his pen slowed down, he would be looking around, and in a moment would be at work on another design. Later, Morris would look at what he had written, and if he did not like it he would put it aside and try again. But this way of working meant that he never submitted a draft to the painful evaluation which poetry demands. He did not even possess a dictionary until the year before his death. So far from seeing the danger of this method, Morris was convinced that poetry could be written in no other way. Indeed, his view sprang directly from his social vision; his hostility to the narrow and socially isolated specialism of a literary and critical intelligentsia, and contrasting belief in popular, collective culture and literature. This was why he strongly opposed any exclusive concentration on poetry, argued that all poets should be part-timers, and declared that 'if a chap can't compose an epic poem while he's weaving tapestry he had better shut up'. Poetry was 'a mere matter of craftsmanship';[28] by which Morris meant that it should be pleasant work, which would be spoiled by intellectual perfectionism. In fact one can say that he wove his poems like tapestries, limiting his vocabulary like the colour range of his wools, conventionalizing and symbolizing his subject matter to meet the limitations of the material—limitations which in *The Earthly Paradise* were not inherent but imposed, and coarsened its quality. But on the other hand it is important not to forget that this is itself a retrospective critical judgement. In its own time, socially, *The Earthly Paradise* did prove an unequalled popular success.

It was no accident that his next poem, *Love is Enough*, which was technically his most elaborately contrived work and a remarkable experiment, caused Morris an unusual 'maze of re-writing and despondency'.[29] It is a symbolic verse play with a medieval dramatic structure of receding planes of action representing different levels of consciousness. The outer frame is a pair of rustic lovers, Giles and Joan; the second plane the Emperor and Empress; the central plane Love herself; the fourth, the main action, the freeing of King Pharamond, who puts aside his crown for love; and the innermost, the chorus of Music. Each plane has a different metre: simple eight- and ten-syllable couplets for the outer planes, a heroic decasyllable for Love, alliterative unrhymed verse for the main action, and haunting rhymed dactylics (long-short-short) for the Music. The metre of the main action was an experimental attempt to break away from conventional classical metres and return to old English rhythms. It depends on accents, not feet, and is knit together by alliteration instead of rhyme. It was based on some of the saga poetry and on *Piers Plowman*, but Morris doubled the length of the line used in *Piers Plowman* and varied the alliteration by spreading it over a third line and introducing slighter alliterations in the track of the principal. The effect is very interesting, even if not fully convincing. Pharamond speaks to the wind:

> O sweet wind of the summer-tide, broad moon a-whitening,
> Bear me witness to Love, and the world he has fashioned!
> It shall change, we shall change, as through rain and through
>   sunshine
> The green rod of the rose-bough to blossoming changeth . . .[30]

The difficulty lies partly in the subject-matter, the idealization of the idea of love, which is better suited to the hypnotic swaying of the Music:

> LOVE IS ENOUGH: though the World be a-waning
> And the woods have no voice but the voice of complaining,
>   Though the sky be too dark for dim eyes to discover
> The gold-cups and daisies fair blooming thereunder,
> Though the hills be held shadows, and the sea a dark wonder,
>   And this day draw a veil over all deeds passed over,
> Yet their hands shall not tremble, the fear shall not alter
>   These lips and these eyes of the loved and the lover.[31]

In *Love is Enough* Morris pushed the exploration of the idealized world of the *The Earthly Paradise* still further towards escape and inaction. It is an evocation of love in hopeless devotion; an expression of his own personal despair in these years of crisis. It represents the extreme triumph of symbolism over reality in his writing. Its finality was marked by the fact that he did not start work on another poem until four years after its completion. When he did, he took up a completely different approach, the dynamic, tragic reality of Icelandic legend.

The Icelandic stories had already inspired Morris to write the best of the stories of *The Earthly Paradise*, 'The Lovers of Gudrun'. It makes an interesting comparison with 'The Fostering of Aslaug', which although published in the last volume was written earlier. 'The Fostering of

Aslaug' is based on a Norse story, but it is gentle and softly voluptuous. Aslaug is a romantic heroine, who bathes naked and white in the cold lake. When the wandering sailors first saw her

> She stood; one gleaming lock of gold,
> Strayed from her fair head's plaited fold,
> Fell far below her girdlestead,
> And round about her shapely head
> A garland of dog-violet
> And wind-flowers meetly had she set;
> They deemed it little scathe indeed
> That her coarse homespun ragged weed
> Fell off from her round arms and lithe
> Laid on the door-post, and that a withe
> Of willows was her only belt . . . [32]

'The Lovers of Gudrun' still retains a great deal of this romanticism, and Gudrun herself is described in pre-Raphaelite terms, but the atmosphere of the poem as a whole is very different. The story is of two friends, Kiartan and Bodli, who both love Gudrun. Gudrun is betrothed to the more forceful Kiartan. Before marrying, Kiartan decides to go to Norway for fighting and plunder, and he stays there too long, allowing Bodli to return first and persuade Gudrun to marry him by telling her that Kiartan has deserted her. Kiartan then returns to find them married, and in his disappointment marries another woman. Gudrun, dismayed by the treachery of Bodli and the disloyalty of Kiartan, makes Bodli's life an empty misery, and provokes a quarrel between the former friends, which leads to Bodli ambushing and killing Kiartan, and Bodli being killed in vengeance by one of Kiartan's family. The story is told with real drama by Morris; the characters and not the landscape, as so often in other tales, dominate; Kiartan is an exceptionally attractive and strong character, especially towards the end; and the pathetic emptiness of Bodli's life is conveyed with the bitterness of Morris's own experience. The story rises to its tragic climax with the murder of Kiartan and Gudrun's attempt to prevent the burning of his body, and then ebbs away with the old age of Gudrun, and her sore memories: 'I did the worst to him I loved the most.' Morris's version lacks the terse roughness of the original legend. He introduced much more explicit emotion and to some extent gave this emotion the tone of chivalrous honour and romantic love. This was certainly intentional. Morris meant to retell the story in his own way and not to produce a mere verse translation. But he kept sufficient Norse grimness to make the story thoroughly convincing, and with the advantage of his clear narrative organization 'The Lovers of Gudrun' is a fine tragic poem in its own right. As such it towers above the other tales of *The Earthly Paradise*.

The story of 'The Lovers of Gudrun' came from the Laxdaela Saga, which Morris and Magnusson had translated but never published. In 1869 they had also made the first English translation of the Volsunga Saga, which they described as the noblest and grandest of all the northern legends, 'the Great Story of the North, which should be to all our race what the Tale of Troy was to the Greeks'.[33] Morris wrote to his friend Professor Norton:

The scene of the last interview between Sigurd and the despairing and terrible Brynhild touches me more than anything I have ever met with in literature; there is nothing wanting in it, nothing forgotten, nothing repeated, nothing overstrained; all tenderness is shown without the use of a tender word, all misery and despair without a word of raving, complete beauty without an ornament, and all this in two pages of moderate print. In short it is to the full meaning of the word inspired.

At the end of this letter, which shows how perfectly Morris understood the effectiveness of the saga method of story-telling, he mentioned that he had thought of writing an epic of it, 'but though I still hanker after it, I see clearly it would be foolish, for no verse could render the best parts of it, and would only be a flatter and tamer version of a thing already existing'.[34] It was not until October 1875 that he found the courage to begin *Sigurd the Volsung*. The result was the greatest of all his poems.

Morris did not attempt to handle *Sigurd* with any important changes in his poetic method, and it is possible to criticize the poem in the same way as his earlier tales. But with *Sigurd*, unless prolonged literary research has dimmed the drama of the story itself and led to an excessive preoccupation with textual hints and details, criticism must yield to admiration.

As in his other poems, Morris limited his vocabulary, but his avoidance of Latinized words was appropriate here. As always he wrote loosely, so that few sections of the poem will stand close criticism; but this lack is to a great degree compensated by the splendid rhythm of the lines, the wonderful chant which carries the reader onward through the poem. It is, Alfred Noyes wrote, an 'unending sea of song, swelling and dying and surging again like the wind in some mighty primaeval pine-wood'.[35] It has an irregular rhythm of six beats, mostly written in anapaests, with a stop in the centre of the line. Like the experimental metres of *Love is Enough*, it was based on medieval forms, but combined with a wholly new freedom. Morris wrote it in rhymed couplets, binding the long lines with frequent alliteration. Listen to its sound in the last battle of old Sigmund, Sigurd's father, a few moments before his death:

> On went the Volsung banners, and on went Sigmund before,
> And his sword was the flail of the tiller on the wheat of the
>   wheat-thrashing floor,
> And his shield was rent from his arm, and helm was sheared
>   from his head:
> But who may draw nigh him to smite for the heap and the
>   rampart of dead?
> White went his hair on the wind like the ragged drift of the
>   cloud,
> And his dust-driven, blood-beaten harness was the death-
>   storm's angry shroud,
> When the summer sun is departing in the first of the night of
>   wrack;
> And his sword was the cleaving lightning, that smites and is
>   hurried aback
> Ere the hand may rise against it; and his voice was the following
>   thunder.
> Then cold grew the battle before him, dead-chilled with the fear
>   and the wonder:
> For again in his ancient eyes the light of victory gleamed
> From his mouth grown tuneful and sweet the song of his
>   kindred streamed;
> And no more was he worn and weary, and no more his life
>   seemed spent:
> And with all the hope of childhood was his wrath of battle
>   blent . . . [36]

Once into the swing, one can read a whole book of the poem without wandering—an achievement unique in Morris's poetry.

Equally, although Morris altered this story like all others which he put into verse, and some of the alterations were certainly for the worse, in *Sigurd* the changes are justified by the final result. The task of giving a satisfactory shape to the epic was by no means easy. The saga had only been finally committed to writing in the later Middle Ages, after generations of embellishment and divergent versions had reduced it to a noble ruin rather than a coherent story. The more primitive stories of Sigurd's ancestors, in which magic and violence and cruelty overshadow the characters, are the earliest part. Probably the original Sigurd was in fact one of his ancestors, Sigmund or Sinflioti. The early life of Sigurd, his contending with the magic evils of the sword-smith and the dragon Fafnir, his victory through the ancestral word and his horse Greyfell, and his discovery of Brynhild on the fire-ringed summit of Hindfell, represent a second layer. The newest part is the main story. Sigurd comes to the House of King Gunnar of the Niblungs, whose intriguing mother drugs Sigurd to forget his betrothal to Brynhild. He is married to Gunnar's sister Gudrun, and then wins Brynhild for Gunnar by riding through the fire again and sleeping a night with her with a sword laid between them in the bed. Only after the wedding does he recover his memory and realize his tragic mistake. The magic used in this part is reduced to a device, and the interest is entirely in the terrible situation of the characters, the fury of Brynhild, the ambivalence of Sigurd, the futile efforts of Gudrun and Gunnar to keep husband and wife. The climax comes when Sigurd offers to put away Gudrun and fulfill his broken promise to Brynhild, and she in her pride rejects him—'I will not wed thee, Sigurd, nor any man alive.' His death alone will satisfy her. When she has had him murdered, she kills herself, so that she can be burnt beside him on the same funeral pyre. The story then breaks up in a confused mixture of fragments, some very primitive, telling of Gudrun's revenge and the extermination of her entire family.

Morris thought that this 'curious entanglement of the ages' was part of the attraction of the story.[37] But the differences in development of character and the importance of the supernatural in the various parts, the scale of the prelude in relation to the main story, and the ragged, over-lengthy ending, were all different problems. Nor could he possibly write a successful epic poem with the mere terse hints or suggestive silences which was all the original saga gave of motive and emotion. Some modern critics, notably Dorothy Hoare, have suggested that Morris killed the tragedy of the story by giving it clarity, expression, and logic; real tragedy should come from a clear sky—'a flash, and the heart of darkness is exposed'.[38] Morris rightly avoided writing a pseudo-primitive tragedy, which would have been little better than a parody.

His solution was to preserve the separation of the major sections of the story, but to shorten the prelude and cut off some of the appendages at the end, and to clarify and fill out the central story of Sigurd and Brynhild. Certainly one may regret some of the savage episodes which he chose to omit, such as Sigmund's biting out of the wolf's tongue when he is clamped to the stocks in the wood, or the death of Gudrun's daughter Swanhild, trampled by horses with her head tied in a bag. Prudery, as much as the need for brevity, may well explain some of the omissions. But it is absurd to treat these as the heart of the tragedy, and their loss is counterbalanced by scenes such as the bitter dialogue between Brynhild and Gudrun as they bathe in the river, which were originally so brief as almost to escape notice.

Morris wisely retained a contrast between the prelude and the main story, keeping the characterization of the ancestors admirably blunt. Signy, Sigmund's sister, sits at her wedding banquet beside her husband:

> Ruddy and white was she wrought as the fair-stained sea-
>   beast's tooth,
> But she neither laughed nor spake, and her eyes were hard
>   and cold . . . [39]

Brynhild and Gudrun on the other hand are articulate, fully developed women, even if a little pre-Raphaelite in appearance, and their passion for Sigurd is real. Morris too could read into the bones of the story the destructive violence of struggles for material and sexual possession, which he understood too well, both from subsequent history and his own time. Consequently he was able to draw out the growing tension in the household of Gunnar with an emotional drama beyond the range of the original saga:

> There now is Brynhild abiding as a Queen in the house
>   of the Kings,
> And hither and thither she wendeth through the day of queenly
>   things;
> And no man knoweth her sorrow; though whiles is the Niblung
>   bed
> Too hot and weary a dwelling for the temples of her head,
> And she wends, as her wont was aforetime, when the moon is
>   riding high,
> And the night on the earth is deepest; and she deemeth it good
>   to lie
> In the trench of the windy mountains, and the track of the
>   wandering sheep,
> While soft in the arms of Sigurd Queen Gudrun lieth asleep:
> There she cries on the lovely Sigurd, and she cries on the love
>   and the oath,
> And she cries on the change and vengeance, and the death to
>   deliver them both
> But her crying none shall hearken, and her sorrow nought shall
>   know
> Save the heart of the golden Sigurd, and the man fast bound
>   in woe: . . .
> But of Gunnar the Niblung they say it, that the bloom of his
>   youth is o'er,

And many are manhood's troubles, and they burden him oft
  and sore.
He dwells with Brynhild his wife, with Grimhild his mother he
  dwells,
And noble things of his greatness, of his joy, the rumour tells;
Yet oft and oft of an even he thinks of the tale of the night,
And the shame springs fresh in his heart at his brother Sigurd's
  might;
And the wonder riseth within him, what deed did Sigurd there,
What gift to the King hath he given: and he looks on Brynhild
  the fair,
The fair face never smiling, and the eyes that know no change,
And he deems in the bed of the Niblungs she is but cold and
  strange;
And the Lie is laid between them, as the sword lay awhile
  agone . . .

In the hall sitteth Sigurd by Brynhild, in the council of the Kings,
And he hearkeneth her spoken wisdom, and her word of lovely
  things:
In the field they meet, and the wild-wood, on the acre and the
  heath;
And scarce may he tell if the meeting be worse than the
  coward's death,
Or better than life of the righteous: but his love is a flaming
  fire,
That hath burnt up all before it of the things that feed desire.

The heart of Gudrun he seeth, her heart of burning love,
That knoweth of nought but Sigurd on the earth, in the heavens
  above,
Save the foes that encompass his life, and the woman that
  wasteth away
'Neath the toils of a love like her love, and the unrewarded day:
For hate her eyes hath quickened, and no more is Gudrun
  blind,
And sure, though dim it may be, she seeth the days behind:
And the shadowy wings of the Lie, that the hand unwitting led
To the love and the heart of Gudrun, brood over board and bed;
And for all the hand of the hero and the foresight of the wise,
From the heart of a loving woman shall the death of men arise. [40]

And so the story moves relentlessly to the inevitable tragedy, to
Gudrun's terrible loss and pitiful lament:

O ye, e'en such was my Sigurd among these Giuki's sons,
As the hart with the horns day-brightened mid the forest-
  creeping ones;
As the spear-leek fraught with wisdom mid the lowly garden
  grass . . . [41]

Morris was able to add important verbal expression to the story. He also, as one would expect, added some worthwhile background, such as his opening description of the hall of the Volsungs, or his picture of Hindfell rising from the clouds. But it is impossible to do full justice to *Sigurd* in quotation, for the poetry relies on its context. Undoubtedly this is a real weakness of the poem, due to Morris's method with language. Another serious fault is that the first and third books of the story are more powerful than the second and fourth, so that the ending is a little lame. This is in spite of Morris's pruning, and his use of the Nibelungen Lied version of the legend, in which Gudrun actively incites the killing of her kindred instead of being the helpless victim of her second husband's avarice and trying to protect them, as in the saga.

Nevertheless, *Sigurd the Volsung* is a great poem, an epic of truly heroic stature. Today it is acknowledged, but little read. Unlike *The Defence of Guenevere*, it has not been defended against the damaging criticism made of it by some scholars. Probably this is a matter of time. *Guenevere* is historicist poetry of the earlier type, original because its medievalism was naïve and superficial, like the Gothic of eighteenth-century architecture and decoration. *Sigurd* corresponds to the serious Gothic revivalism of the age of Ruskin, which is only slowly being revalued. It is more difficult to judge, because its originality is so closely interwoven with historicist accuracy.

Sigurd is a difficult poem to assess, because it is both a close rendering of a Norse story and an original Victorian epic. It is set in the world of the sagas, but its values are those of Morris, not of the Norsemen. It celebrates the conquest of loss and fear through social courage which with their help he had now found. Like any imaginative work with a historical setting, it needs to be judged in its own right, not historically. The poem is undoubtedly an achievement scarcely rivalled in modern times. It was justly described by the *Athenæum* as 'far ahead of anything of equal length that has appeared in this century',[42] and by Shaw, with less justice but an enthusiasm that may in time seem reasonable, as 'the greatest epic since Homer'.[43] It is the work on which, in the long run, Morris's standing as a poet must depend.

There is little need to linger over the poetry which Morris wrote in the remaining twenty years of his life, for only *The Pilgrims of Hope* deserves attention. Apart from some short poems and ballad translations written earlier, its extracts are the only interest in *Poems by the Way*. *The Pilgrims of Hope* had been written in instalments for *Commonweal*. Morris did not consider it good enough to publish independently, although he allowed a small private reprinting. Certainly it is unequally written, but it has a genuine interest as a description of the socialist movement. The picture of a socialist speaking at a radical club is frankly autobiographical:

> Dull and dirty the room. Just over the chairman's chair
> Was a bust, a Quaker's face with nose cocked up in the air;
> There were common prints on the wall of the heads of the party
>   fray
> And Mazzini dark and lean amidst them gone astray.
> Some thirty men we were of the kind that I knew full well,
> Listless, rubbed down to the type of our easy-going hell.
> My heart sank down as I entered, and wearily there I sat
> While the chairman strove to end his maunder of this and of that.
> And partly shy he seemed, and partly indeed ashamed
> Of the grizzled man beside him as his name to us he named.
> He rose, thickset and short, and dressed in shabby blue,
> And even as he began it seemed as though I knew
> The thing he was going to say, though I never heard it before.
> He spoke, were it well, were it ill, as though a message he bore,
> A word that he could not refrain from many a million of
>   men . . .
> But they sat and made no sign . . .
>   I rose ere the meeting was done,
> And gave him my name and my faith—and I was the only
>   one.[44]

But undoubtedly the best part of the poem is 'The Message of the March Wind', where Morris returns to the old world which had so often inspired him before. The wind blows from London:

> Hark! the March wind again of a people is telling;
>   Of the life that they live there, so haggard and grim,
> That if we and our love amidst them had been dwelling
>   My fondness had faltered, thy beauty grown dim.
>
> This land we have loved in our love and our leisure
>   For them hangs in heaven, high out of their reach;
> The wide hills o'er the sea-plain for them have no pleasure,
>   The grey homes of their fathers no story to teach . . .
>
> Come back to the inn, love, and the lights and the fire,
>   And the fiddler's old tune and the shuffling of feet;
> For there in a while shall be rest and desire,
>   And there shall the morrow's uprising be sweet . . .[45]

Nothing reveals more clearly than *The Pilgrims of Hope* the real limitation of Morris's poetry. It was not that he failed to deal with modern events or real problems. Historicisms and escapism were so real to him that they provided the warmest note in this poem about the present. The pervading weakness of all Morris's poetry was that it was written with insufficient care. He wrote three great poems—*The Defence of Guenevere*, *The Lovers of Gudrun*, and *Sigurd the Volsung*. But he was not a consistently great poet; and paradoxically the explanation lies in the very source of Morris's greatest strength, his social vision. Morris wished to bring back poetry into everyday life. And he did succeed not only in writing some great poems, but also in reaching a popular audience, while remaining a craftsman of manifold skills. But the cost of this success was that Morris as a writer was uneven, at other times writing principally for his own pleasure and relaxation; and in finding such satisfaction from the pen, reducing poetry to the level of craftsmanship in verse, to the pleasant way of work which he regarded as the fundamental right of mankind.

POLITICS

THAT William Morris as a romantic poetic should have been concerned with politics was not surprising. From the French revolution to the Spanish civil war there runs a long tradition of political poets; Blake, Shelley and Byron, Yeats and Spender: even to some degree Tennyson and Arnold. Some of these made sacrifices of health and comfort more dramatic than Morris. What is unusual about Morris is that he became a genuine political leader, and made a real impact on the English political scene.

Although Morris's political activity did not start before 1876, his step-by-step development began while he was at Oxford. He went up there as the wealthy elder son of a family newly risen to the gentry, poised to become a Tory gentleman. His High Church views and medieval enthusiasm might well have led him to a benevolent paternalistic concern for the working classes, a romantic Victorian feudalism, but this would have been distinctly hostile to political radicalism. He was saved from this standpoint by his introduction to the circle of Birmingham friends at Pembroke. Their radicalism, founded on a real experience of the terrible conditions of the industrial population, helped him to interpret the social criticism which he found in Carlyle, Ruskin, and Kingsley, so that he 'got into my head therefrom some socio-political ideas which would have developed probably but for the attractions of art and poetry'.[1] With his practical turn of mind Morris could sympathize with radicalism, but he knew that his own talents lay elsewhere; 'I can't enter into politico-social subjects with any interest, for on the whole I see that things are in a muddle, and I have no power or vocation to set them right in ever so much a degree.'[2]

So he became politically passive, voting Liberal and occasionally attending public meetings, but never speaking or writing for the party. The new friendships which he made after Oxford no doubt helped to keep him a radical at heart. Ford Madox Brown was a fervent democrat—his painting 'Work' is, in fact, an allegory of the dignity of labour in which Carlyle and the Christian Socialist F. D. Maurice take key positions. Through Rossetti, whose family were revolutionary refugees, Morris was introduced to continental radicalism. Probably as a member of the Artists' Corps of the Citizen Volunteers in the early

1860s he had felt a patriotic pride in the encouragement given by Palmerston's England to revolutionary movements abroad. Perhaps he then even shared the mid-Victorian confidence that freedom and commerce must together triumph over tyranny and stagnation throughout the world. Certainly it was a foreign issue very much in the Palmerstonian tradition which brought him into active politics in 1876. But at the same time there had been a process of subconscious rumination going on in his mind about his own role as an industrialist. He had come dangerously close to bankruptcy at one point, and only won through by learning to run his business like any other capitalist, calculating profits and driving bargains. He had been forced to buy out his partners in 1875 at the cost of the friendship of Brown and Rossetti. He had even, in a last effort to protect his declining inherited income, accepted a directorship of the Devon Great Consuls Company in 1871. Probably this struggle brought its own reaction when his position was at last secure. Morris must have been ashamed as well as angry about the quarrel in 1875, unhappy with his constant need to look at art with the eye of an economist, uneasy in his role as a prosperous manufacturer of fashionable luxuries. He had also been turning over the contrast between the ugly inequality of Victorian England and the still poorer, yet somehow more wholesome, society which he had found in Iceland. 'I learnt one lesson there, thoroughly I hope, that the most grinding poverty is a trifling evil compared with the inequality of classes.'[3] This lesson was, no doubt, very much in mind when, in January 1876, he resigned his Devon Consuls directorship and defiantly sat on his top hat.

He was finally stung into open public action by the Eastern Question. This was a cause directly in the tradition of Byron—a nationalist revolt in the Balkans against Turkish rule. Following the Greek example of the 1820s, the Serbs, Montenegrins, and Bulgars had risen in 1875–6, and in June 1876 reports had been published of appallingly savage suppression, by Turkish mercenaries, of the Christian population in Bulgaria. Disraeli's government, so far from wishing to encourage the rebels, regarded the integrity of a friendly Turkish government as an essential strategic protection of the newly opened Suez Canal route to India. Gladstone, who had retired disillusioned from politics after his defeat in the 1874 general election, realized that this was a perfect issue with which to rouse the conscience of the middle-class electorate. On 6 September he published his famous pamphlet, *The Bulgarian Horrors and The Question of the East*, which not only fiercely opposed any suggestion that the British government should support the Turks if Russia seized the excuse of the persecuted Bulgarians for a push south to the

Mediterranean, but demanded the evacuation of the Turks, 'bag and baggage', from the whole Bulgarian province. It was the idea of British intervention against the Turks, of a war with 'a just and honourable aim', which stirred Morris to his great letter to the *Daily News* of 26 October and his subsequent part in the agitation. His cry was, 'The Turkish Government to the Devil, and something rational and progressive in its place.'[4]

The subsequent course of the crisis itself over the next two years is less important here than Morris's experience in the agitation. He found himself supported in his stand by many fellow writers and artists— Ruskin, Carlyle, de Morgan, and Rossetti—as well as by Liberal clients of the firm like George Howard of Naworth. Morris was quickly persuaded to become treasurer of the Eastern Question Association. But from the start he showed more confidence in the radical working-class leaders than in the parliamentary Liberal party. His letter to the *Daily News* contrasted the members of 'this wretched packed Parliament' away on their autumn shoots with 'the 2000 working men who met last Sunday at Clerkenwell'. In May 1877, when Russia had actually declared war on Turkey and the danger of English intervention on the wrong side seemed most acute, he issued his appeal *To the Working Men of England*, in which he frankly described the issue as a struggle between the capitalists and the people:

Who are they that are leading us into war? . . . Greedy gamblers on the Stock Exchange, idle officers of the army and navy (poor fellows!), worn-out mockers of the clubs, desperate purveyors of exciting war-news for the comfortable breakfast tables of those who have nothing to lose by war . . .

Working men of England, one word of warning yet: I doubt if you know the bitterness of hatred against freedom and progress that lies at the hearts of a certain part of the richer classes in this country: their newspapers veil it in a decent kind of language; but do but hear them talking among themselves, as I have often, and I know not whether scorn or anger would prevail in you at their folly and insolence:—These men cannot speak of your order, of its aims, of its leaders without a sneer or an insult: these men, if they had the power (may England perish rather), would thwart your just aspirations, would silence you, would deliver you bound hand and foot for ever to irresponsible capital . . . [5]

It was in this spirit that Morris worked hard on the Association committee, joined in delegations to stir up Liberal politicians, made his first impromptu public speech, and wrote his 'Wake, London Lads!' for a great demonstration organized by the Workmen's Neutrality Committee at Exeter Hall in the Strand on 16 January 1878. This was at the height of the final crisis, when Russian troops were advancing victorious on Constantinople and British intervention again seemed inevitable. Morris was 'really astounded at the folly that can play with such tremendous tools in this way; and more and more I feel how entirely right the flattest democracy is'.[6] His song was sung by a choir from the stonemasons' trade union procured by Henry Broadhurst, and Morris himself tried to speak, 'but was so hoarse from excitement that he could scarce utter a word'.[7]

Less than a month later the Eastern Question Association had collapsed. A wave of popular anti-Russian jingoism had swept the country. Even at the Exeter Hall meeting the noise of the enemy's roughs outside had been 'like the sea roaring against a lighthouse'.[8] Within a fortnight jingoes were breaking up meetings and even smashing Gladstone's windows. The parliamentary Liberals took fright, Gladstone decided to discontinue the agitation for the moment, and the Eastern Question Association faded away, only Broadhurst remaining firm to the end. Morris was 'full of shame and anger at the cowardice of the so-called Liberal party', although at the time he did not blame Gladstone for the retreat.[9] Disraeli was in fact able to secure his aims through bluff alone. At the Congress of Berlin in July 1878 Bulgaria was divided, and the Russian bridgehead on the Mediterranean removed, while Britain secured a new naval base in Cyprus.

In spite of this disillusionment, Morris did not withdraw from politics. In 1877 he had also begun his series of art lectures and launched the Society for the Protection of Ancient Buildings, both part of his campaign to stir up demand for a better world.

I have more than ever at my heart the importance for people of living in beautiful places [he wrote in 1880]; I mean the sort of beauty which would be attainable by all, if people could but begin to long for it. I do most earnestly desire that something more startling could be done than mere constant private grumbling and occasional public speaking to lift the standard of revolt against the sordidness which people are so stupid as to think necessary.[10]

Besides lecturing to art students and art workmen, Morris kept in touch with Broadhurst and the working class radicals. In 1879–82 he joined in two efforts to form pressure groups from the trade unions and working men's radical clubs, and for the first, the National Liberal League, he again acted as treasurer. He got it to take up anti-imperial issues, but not social reform, and the failure of both these attempts undermined his earlier confidence in radicalism.

His faith in Gladstone was finally shaken by the performance of the Liberal government elected in 1880. As Prime Minister, Gladstone not only evaded any radical reform at home, but seemed unable to keep out of imperialistic ventures as objectionable as those of Disraeli. The spectacle of a Liberal government imposing coercion on Ireland and invading Egypt completed Morris's disillusionment with Liberalism.

The Liberal party was scarcely in a position to satisfy Morris in either home or foreign questions. The Egyptian invasion was a perfect case for demonstrating its helplessness in the face of the remorseless force of commercial advances abroad. Free trade had been forced on Egypt by Palmerston in about 1840, in the then confident belief that liberal social reform would follow commerce. In fact commerce had simply destroyed Egyptian society. The Khedive could not balance trade, and was forced to borrow at high interest, and finally in 1876 went bankrupt. Britain and France then took over financial control of the country, and undermined its whole social structure by turning the Khedive into a foreign debt-collector and forcing him to tax the wealthy landed and military classes on whom his regime had depended; the result was a nationalist revolt in 1881 and riots in Alexandria. In order to protect the Suez Canal and British credit, and also to forestall a French invasion, the Liberal government was persuaded to intervene; and having invaded and defeated the Egyptians and finally destroyed all local authority, it could not withdraw its garrisons for fear of leaving chaos behind. Worse still for Gladstone, the defeat of the Egyptian army had allowed the Sudanese to rebel, and the stability of Egypt could therefore only be secured by an excursion into the Sudan. The attempt to withdraw from the Sudan was to lead to the death of Gordon at Khartoum in 1884. Against this seemingly irresistible chain of events mere sentimental protest was helpless; a fundamentally different approach was the only answer.

Such a change could hardly be expected from a political party which relied for its funds on businessmen. Nor, for the same reason, could the Liberal party be readily transformed into an instrument of rapid social reform. In the last thirty years of the nineteenth century the Liberal party was in fact in a very awkward position. It had won its position as the advanced progressive party through its support of parliamentary reform, religious tolerance, and free trade. These policies had made it the party of the professional and commercial classes. But after the franchise reform of 1867 it needed to appeal to the growing working-class electorate. There were parts of the country, especially in the north and west, where the strength of Nonconformity among the more prosperous skilled workers drew them naturally to the Liberal party, but in the generally irreligious big cities other policies were needed to win working-class support. The danger was that these policies would alienate the middle-class voters and especially those businessmen and traditionally Whig families whose money was essential to maintain the party organization and fight elections.

In these years the party situation was unusually fluid. The Conservatives were traditionally the party of church and aristocracy, but once a degree of commercial freedom, religious tolerance, and franchise reform had been accepted, they were in a position to compete with the Liberals for the support of the expanding prosperous middle class of the towns. They could also court the working class with a strong foreign policy (in defiance of the Nonconformist-Liberal conscience) and with trade union, factory, and health legislation interfering with the freedom of Liberal industrialists. The Conservative party's anxiety to adapt to the widening electorate was well shown in the early 1880s by the campaign of Lord Randolph Churchill for 'Tory Democracy'.

The shifting situation was clearly illustrated by the political career of the outstanding radical politician of the 1880s, Joseph Chamberlain. Having made his fortune from a Birmingham screw factory, Chamberlain had entered politics on a typically Nonconformist issue, the objection to levying rates to pay the fees of poor children attending church elementary schools. By 1873 he had realized 'that there is not enough force in the Education question to make it the sole fighting issue for our friends . . . The assistance of the working classes is not to be looked for without much extension of the argument.'[11] He proposed a new programme of Free Land (easy land purchase), Free Schools (abolition of elementary school fees), Free Church (disestablishment), and Free Breakfast Table (no food duties). He combined this with a programme of civic improvement in Birmingham, buying out the gas and water companies, extending the drainage, and pulling down a central slum to build a new street of shops and offices, and with a campaign to rouse the still voteless rural labourers against their Tory landlords, supporting the rural vote, agricultural labourers' trade unions, and schemes for smallholdings. The chief addition to this programme in the next ten years was graduated house and death duties. The whole attack, which rose to a climax in 1885, was on the parasitic aristocracy (Whig as well as Tory), on landlords and monopolists of essential services; there was no recognition that the interests of the urban working classes and the wealthy middle classes and industrialists might also be in conflict. He demanded, 'What ransom will property pay for the security which it enjoys?' and he was confident 'we shall sweep the country with free education and allotments, and the Tories will be smashed and the Whigs extinguished'.[12] He failed. In 1885 the Liberals made great gains in the rural constituencies where the labourers were voting for the first time, but in the towns there was a disturbing swing to the Conservatives. Chamberlain was again forced to change tack. The slogan 'three acres and a cow' had worked in the country, but 'the "urban cow" is the great difficulty. I put my money on free schools, but, judging by London, the electors do not care much about it.'[13]

The Liberal failure could be attributed to three causes; the inefficiency of the party organization, which would only be improved by more money—from the wealthier Liberals; the economic depression and unemployment, which could only be countered by a much more advanced urban social programme; and the anti-imperialist Gladstonian policy of Irish Home Rule. It was the last which decided Chamberlain:

I am convinced, from personal observation, that the workmen will not stand much more in the way of Irish conciliation or concessions to Parnell . . . The more I look at the thing, the less I like it. Whatever we do we shall be smashed for a certainty. The question is whether it is better to be smashed with Mr Gladstone and the Parnellites or without them. I believe the anti-Irish feeling is very strong with our best friends—the respectable artisans and the non-Conformists.[14]

So he led his Birmingham radicals out of the Liberal party; and ten years later was the progressive reformer in a Conservative cabinet.

This was the background to Morris's personal campaign. It was clear enough that the changes which he wanted, a progressive anti-imperialism abroad and the eradication of poverty and squalor at home, could hardly come from either party. If he had come to this conclusion before 1882 he would have probably seen no alternative to a return to silence—'it needs a person of hopeful mind to take disinterested notice of politics'.[15] But in that year there was a sign that hope might lie in another new quarter: the socialist movement.

English socialism had been quiescent since the mid-Victorian decades as a result of the collapse of the Chartist movement and the general increase in prosperity, but interest in collectivist ideas had revived with the onset of prolonged depressions and widespread unemployment in the 1870s. For the intellectual inquirer who could not tackle Marx in French or German there was little satisfactory reading, for the best English discussions were still the hostile Mill and the eccentric Ruskin of *Unto this Last* and *Fors Clavigera*. Among the working class, however, Chartist memories had not disappeared, and in London the old embers were rekindled by contact with socialist refugees from the continent, so that by the early 1880s a small number of socialists could be found among the speakers at radical clubs, the campaigners for land reform, and those who were calling for a radical realignment independent of the Liberal ministry.

It was from these dissatisfied radicals and socialists that the Democratic Federation, which as the Social Democratic Federation (S.D.F.) was to become the first English socialist party, was founded in 1881. It was typical of the confused political situation that, although formed on the initiative of the *Radical*, it quickly passed to the leadership of a socialist: H. M. Hyndman, a widely travelled man of independent means, aged nearly forty, a Cambridge graduate, who was temperamentally a radical imperialistic Conservative, but had been converted to socialism by reading Marx's *Capital* in French in 1880. The new party was a negligible force, soon losing the radical clubs which had first joined it, but in 1882 it received a great stimulus from the arrival of the American land reformer, Henry George, for an English campaign tour. George was no socialist, but his arguments against land monopolies set off a widespread revival of interest in socialism, which did not fail to impress Morris.

For a few months Morris hesitated; he read Henry George's *Progress and Poverty* and Mill's posthumous papers, and decided that Mill had given his verdict against the evidence; he sat in his study listening to the drunkards outside, wondering where his allegiance lay.

In looking into matters social and political I have but one rule, that in thinking of the condition of any body of men I should ask myself, 'How could you bear it yourself? what would you feel if you were poor against the system under which you live?' I have always been uneasy when I had to ask myself that question, and of late years I have had to ask it so often, that I have seldom had it out of my mind: and the answer to it has more and more made me ashamed of my own position, and more and more made me feel that if I had not been born rich or well-to-do I should have found my position *un*endurable, and should have been a mere rebel against what would have seemed to me a system of robbery and injustice. Nothing can argue me out of this feeling, which I say plainly is a matter of religion to me: the contrasts of rich and poor are unendurable and ought not to be endured by either rich or poor.[16]

Finally, in January 1883, he joined the Democratic Federation.

It was a dramatic step for both sides. Two old friends of Morris, Webb and Faulkner, followed him and worked hard for the socialist movement, but the majority, including Burne-Jones, were dismayed by his desertion of Liberalism. He found himself largely isolated among his social equals, disapproved by the formerly friendly Press, and working with new working-class associates some of whom his wife disliked intensely. For the Democratic Federation on the other hand, Morris was the most impressive adherent they had so far gained, inevitably challenging the dominance of Hyndman. An incident at the first meeting which he attended was prophetic. Robert Banner, a Scots bookbinder, passed a note to his Austrian refugee friend Andreas Scheu, 'The third man to your right is William Morris.'[17] Scheu turned to glance at the plainly dressed, earnest-looking figure. A few minutes later a resolution in favour of artisans' dwellings was proposed, and Scheu proposed to amend it to 'people's dwellings', on the ground that not only artisans needed housing. Hyndman, as chairman, was about to brush the amendment aside, when Morris rose to second it with a few brief words, and it was carried unanimously.

Morris had no ambition to oust Hyndman from the leadership, although he accepted a place on the executive in May—'I don't like to belong to a body without knowing what they are doing.'[18] His first anxiety was to master the new creed. He started immediately with Robert Owen and Marx, in French. He was at once gripped by *Capital*, 'bubbling over' with enthusiasm for the 'great work' which he was to thoroughly dissect more than once again in the future. He knew no economic theory and had never opened Adam Smith or even heard of Ricardo, so that 'whereas I thoroughly enjoyed the historical part of "Capital", I suffered agonies of confusion of the brain over reading the pure economics of that great work'.[19] But that French translation became a treasured copy, later specially bound for him by Cobden-Sanderson. In any case he knew enough of the workings of profit and the meaning of exploitation from his own commercial experience, so that although he accepted the surplus value theory, it was not the most important addition to his political understanding which he gained from *Capital*, even if it explained what he had much earlier perceived.

Much more critical to his development was the influence of Marx's historical theory of the class struggle as the instrument of change. From this point onwards he saw quite differently the means by which social chapnge could be won. Morris had, it is true, seen himself as a preacher of discontent, but as late as March 1883, he was speaking in favour of efforts 'to bridge the gap between the classes' with measures like industrial co-partnership, education, and art galleries.[20] By the summer he was writing in quite different terms. Education was useless when 'people have only slavish work to do', and was anyway geared to 'breed tyrants and cowards' for the existing social situation. And it was the business of critics of 'this earthly hell', not 'to try to climb up out of it, as your thrift-teachers, tell you, but to make an end of it . . . to destroy it'. Nor could much come of the 'isolated acts of a few persons of the middle and upper classes':

The basis of all change must be, as it has always been, the antagonism of classes: I mean that though here and there a few men of the upper and middle classes,

MONOPOLY,

OR

HOW LABOUR IS ROBBED.

The "Freedom" Library.

VIVE LA COMMUNE!

The "Freedom" Library.

BY

WILLIAM MORRIS.

PRICE ONE PENNY.

OFFICE OF " FREEDOM,"
127, OSSULSTON ST., LONDON, N.W.

LONDON: W. REEVES,
83, CHARING CROSS ROAD, W.C.

40. Socialist propaganda: a cheap edition of a lecture Morris gave frequently in 1887–8. He regarded it as 'my best lecture'; 'suitable anywhere'. The pamphlet was issued in 1896, along with Morris's *Useless Work versus Useless Toil* as the 'Freedom Library' by the anarchist Freedom Press. Some of its printing equipment came from the Socialist League. The typography owes nothing to the influence of Morris, but the engraving celebrating the Paris Commune is a design by fellow Socialist Leaguer Walter Crane; this is itself an adaptation of the famous Delacroix of 1830, 'Liberty on the Barricades'. Crane's design was first printed in *Commonweal*, 10 March 1888.

moved by their conscience and insight, may and doubtless will throw in their lot with the working classes, the upper and middle classes as a body will by the very nature of their existence, and like a plant grows, resist the abolition of classes: neither do I think that any amelioration of the poor on the only lines which the rich *can* go will advance us on the road; save that it will put more power into the hands of the lower class and so strengthen both their discontent and their means of showing it: for I do not believe that starvelings can bring about a revolution. I do not say that there is not a terrible side to this: but how can it be otherwise? Commercialism, competition, has sown the wind recklessly, and must reap the whirlwind: it has created the proletariat for its own interest, and its creation will and must destroy it: there is no other force which can do so.[21]

Morris was not originally expecting early change; the weakness of the Democratic Federation made that unlikely. He believed their immediate task to be educational, 'the founding of a religion, towards which end compromise is of no use, and we only want to have those with us who

214

will be with us to the end'. They needed a body of men as determined as he described himself to an audience—'I stand before you, one of the most fortunate of this happy class, so steeped in discontent, that I have no words which will express it: no words, nothing but deeds, wherever they may lead me to, even [if] it be ruin, prison or a violent death.' Above all, 'what we want is real leaders themselves working men, and content to be so till classes are abolished', rather than seeking assimilation into the middle class. [22]

He threw himself wholeheartedly into this work. He helped to launch the first socialist weekly *Justice*, in January 1884, selling it in the streets, writing two or three articles a month for it, and paying its weekly deficit. He toured the country, lecturing in Birmingham, Leicester, Manchester, Edinburgh, and Yorkshire. He spoke at the first regular socialist outdoor meetings in Hyde Park in the summer of 1884. He formed a branch of the Federation in Hammersmith.

In these months the Federation seemed to be making unexpectedly rapid progress. New middle-class supporters included Edward Aveling, a Darwinian chemist and secularist leader, and H. H. Champion, who resigned his army commission to join the movement. Equally encouraging, there was now a nucleus of working-class leaders: James Macdonald, a Scots tailor; Harry Quelch, a city-warehouse packer; Jack Williams, an unskilled dock labourer who had been brought up in a workhouse; and John Burns, a Battersea engineer who had been a temperance speaker and had a voice like a bull's. At the beginning of 1884 Macdonald and Williams went up to speak during a cotton strike and secured a foothold in Lancashire. At its 1884 conference socialist objectives, a basic programme, and the title of Social Democratic Federation were adopted. That week Morris wrote in *Justice* that 'undoubtedly the *hope* is spreading, and even far more speedily than some of us would have thought possible a little time ago; and it is clear that when the *hope* is once received into the hearts of the mass of our people, the beginning of the new day is at hand'. [23]

This apparent success brought to a head the different tactical views of Hyndman and Morris. Hyndman wanted to convert the Federation into an election-winning party as quickly as possible, and was prepared to combine political compromise with revolutionary bluster to do so:

His aim has been to make the movement seem big; to frighten the powers that be with a turnip bogie which perhaps he almost believes in himself: . . . hence the founding of branches which melt away into mere names, the neglect of organization for fruitless agitation. [24]

Morris wanted the emphasis to be on education. He recognized the need for an immediate party platform, but he saw its main purpose as educational, much as he wanted to see some of it implemented. There was no better way of inducing radicals 'to lay aside this worship of names', this senseless shouting after faithless leaders, than 'to accept *themselves* a little responsibility for themselves, for the dreary wretched lives which they and their brethren lead; to ask themselves if they have all they want except the franchise'. Radicals should press their leaders

on such points as free education, and the eight hours working day; push them on to attacking the railway monopoly, the vested interests of property in typhoid or cholera, and you will find that you will either force them into avowed Conservatism of the modern cynical type, which allows that slavery is bad for the working man, but will uphold it all the same, or into nameless groups of philanthropic varnishers; you will either force them into avowed tyranny or conscious and obvious hypocrisy.[25]

Nevertheless Morris was confused about the usefulness of this tactic. At times he had no hope of gaining any of these objects; the eight-hour day was 'good as a cry, but again how can a bourgeois government ever think of that?' But a few weeks earlier he had thought that 'the most important thing to press upon the notice of the people at present is the legal reduction of the working day: every working man can see the immediate advantage to him of this: the Trades Unions *may* be got to take it up: and I doubt if the Government dare resist a strong cry for it'. Concessions like this would be 'tubs to the whale cast out first by one party and then the other', their very efficacy strengthening the working class. But again, could partial remedies bring any real gain in living standards? Morris accepted the simplified interpretation of the 'iron law of wages' then common among socialists, and believed that capitalism would instinctively 'meet every attempt at bettering the condition of the people with an attack on a fresh side'.[26] So was there any purpose in confusing socialist principles with futile short-term policies?

Finding a satisfactory balance between purism and practical agitation was to be the fundamental problem of Morris's whole work as a socialist. Hyndman's position was equally ambiguous, but he was not worried by inconsistency. The real difference between the two men was temperamental. Morris recognized the need for compromise. 'To be "politic" and not able to say exactly as one thinks is a beastly curse, . . . but I cannot yet forgo the hope of our forming a Socialist *party* which shall begin to act in our own time, instead of a mere theoretical association in a private room.'[27] Compromise was, however, a nasty necessity, and Morris was particularly anxious to avoid the dangers of electioneering before a strong party had been formed. Hyndman, on the other hand, revelled in political manœuvre and was was anxious to put up candidates as soon as there was an opportunity.

The S.D.F. conference in 1884 had decided not to fight parliamentary elections and had replaced Hyndman as President by a rotating chairman of the executive. But Hyndman was quite unwilling to work as an equal with his colleagues and he continued to press his own views through his position as editor of *Justice* and his influence over the S.D.F. secretary. When the executive demanded control over the contents of *Justice* he refused to co-operate, despite the fact that the paper was kept going by Morris's subsidy. Two opposing groups developed on the executive, and Morris was gradually forced into the leadership of the opposition. Seeing that Hyndman was 'determined to be master, and will not accept any other place, and he cannot change his nature and be otherwise than a jingo and a politician even if he tries',[28] Morris decided that it was a waste of energy to stay quarrelling, and in December 1884, approved by the personal backing of Engels, with whom he was at this time in regular consultation, he led a majority of the executive out of the S.D.F. to set up a new party, the Socialist League.

There can be little doubt that in choosing to walk out thus abruptly Morris threw away the strength of his position in the conflict. Probably he underestimated Hyndman. Certainly Hyndman seemed to have none of the qualities needed for a successful socialist leader. He was both a poor strategist and an ingrained conservative. He succeeded in quarrelling, not only with Morris, but with Marx and Engels, and with Champion, Burns, and Tom Mann, the ablest of his colleagues. He scorned the eight-hour day campaign, dismissed trade-union leaders as 'the most stodgy-brained, dull-witted, and slow-going time-servers in the country',[29] and in later years opposed both syndicalists and suffragettes. He was a persistent anti-Semite, became a violent anti-German, supported the Ulster Unionists, and backed allied intervention against the Russian revolution. But for all this he was a determined man, whose confidence and authority on theory gave him a strong hold over his working-class followers.

Hyndman was to keep at the agitation for another forty years, and the S.D.F. under his leadership, although often in spite of his advice, was to establish a significant following in Lancashire and London: a following based on its unemployed agitation, its lead in the free-speech struggles, its part in the great trade-union expansion of 1889–92 and particularly in the Gasworkers' Union, its pioneering campaigns for subsidized housing, labour exchanges, free school meals, and universal secondary education, and its activity in local politics—notably George Lansbury's work in humanizing the Poplar workhouse and the great civic improvement scheme of the first Labour town council in the country, led by the S.D.F., at West Ham in 1898.

Hyndman and the S.D.F. have been too easily dismissed by historians as an insignificant minority sect. Undoubtedly they failed in the long run and their failure to work with the new Labour Party in the 1900s was a fatal mistake, but they were not insignificant; they won a membership of over 10,000, and they had their part in building the Labour Party.

Morris likewise underestimated the dogged determination of Hyndman and his followers. Before the split he made no attempt to keep the rank and file informed and he did not even make sure that he had a list of S.D.F. branch-secretaries' addresses. Consequently he left Hyndman in much the stronger position, with probably three-quarters of the S.D.F. membership of about 500, and its best workers, Burns, Williams, and Champion. Still worse, the split had been so sudden and ragged that Morris was not even left with a group with a coherent standpoint.

In 1885 the differences in the League had not crystallized and the question of electoral activity did not seem imminent. Moreover the blunder of the S.D.F. at the 1885 general election in using 'Tory Gold' to sponsor three candidates produced a general feeling of disgust. Nevertheless from a very early stage the leaders of the Socialist League fell into two groups. On the one hand, led by Joseph Lane, an East End carter who had pioneered the radical land agitation in the late 1870s, was a group which was anarchist rather than socialist, strongly hostile to central authority and political discipline. They included Charles Mowbray, a London tailor; Sam Mainwaring, a London engineer; and Frank Kitz, the jolly, rebellious son of a German exile for whom Morris found work as a dyer at Merton Abbey. On the other hand there was the rather more impressive group which had accepted the general aims of the S.D.F., but refused to submit to the authority of Hyndman. These were the League's secretary, John Mahon, an engineer; Thomas Binning, a London compositor; Tom Maguire of Leeds; and three middle-class intellectuals, Ernest Belfort Bax, an elegant, but misogynistic and somewhat humourless philosopher-musician, Karl Marx's still vivacious theatrically-minded younger daughter Eleanor, and Edward Aveling. Aveling, whose unscrupulous swindlings and cheque-bouncings off other comrades to support secret sexual liaisons were soon to make him a notorious handicap to any party, had begun to live with

Eleanor in a free Bohemian marriage in 1884. His double-dealing was eventually to make a tragedy of both their lives and ultimately both committed suicide. For the moment they were a powerful political couple. The Avelings and Bax were in intimate contact with Engels, whose hostility to Hyndman made him anxious to see the Socialist League built up into an alternative party.

Morris was anxious to avoid any direct rivalry with the S.D.F. He told its Hammersmith branch that 'he hoped as soon as possible we should bury the hatchet. He had nothing to say against his former associates but he disagreed with their tactics.'[30] During the next few years he was in fact remarkably successful at keeping the two socialist bodies working alongside each other without collision. He was helped by a broad geographical division of strength, the League developing in Scotland, west Yorkshire, and Norwich, the S.D.F. in Lancashire, the Midlands, and London. Outside Glasgow and London there was little rank and file friction, and even in London the League stronghold was in west London, where the S.D.F. was weak.

Morris helped this distinction by strongly emphasizing the educational role of the League. On 6 January 1885 he told the *Daily News* that he wanted an educated movement.

Discontent is not enough, though it is natural and inevitable. The discontented must know what they are aiming at when they overthrow the old order of things. My belief is that the old order can only be overthrown by force; and for that reason it is all the more important that the revolution . . . should not be an ignorant, but an educated revolution. What I should like to have now, far more than anything else, would be a body of able, high-minded, competent men, who should act as instructors of the masses and as their leaders during critical periods of the movement. It goes without saying that a great proportion of these instructors and organizers should be working men.

The statement of the Socialist League executive at the same time emphasized that it had 'no function but to educate the people in the principles of Socialism, and to organize such as it can get hold of to take their due places, when the crisis shall come which shall force action upon us'.[31]

This view went with a confidence that such a crisis was inevitable in the near future. At the first League conference Morris spoke of his certainty that things would change. 'For my part, I believe we shall see much of it in our own time.' In this situation they would merely risk losing their leaders by trying to send them to 'our sham parliament, there to become either nonentities, or perhaps our masters, and it may be our betrayers'. In his weekly *Commonweal* notes Morris interpreted the shifting political scene as 'contemptible trifling, which is unparalleled by anything save the Court changes in the worst periods of the Byzantine empire'. He predicted that the two parties would soon amalgamate into a new united capitalist party, to which the only possible opposition would be extra-parliamentary revolutionary discontent. 'Let all *our* efforts be directed towards giving it something to repress', rather than in wasting energy over palliative measures of dubious value.[32] Even Home Rule, which he thought the one serious Liberal policy, would simply 'clear the ground for sowing the seed of Revolution' in Ireland, and he rightly predicted that in that isolated, priest-dominated country the road to socialism might be a long one; independence under Parnell would lead, 'it seems to me, to founding a nation fanatically attached to the rights of private property (so-called), [a] narrow-minded, retrogressive, contentious, and unhappy' country of peasant proprietors. 'Nationalism and socialism', he told Blunt, 'have nothing in common.'[33] Even if any good was to be had from other legislation, it was more likely to be wrung out of the ruling classes by fear than 'wheedled and coaxed out of them by the continual life of compromise which "Parliamentary socialists" would be compelled to live'.[34]

It was some time before the impracticability of this standpoint became apparent. The League launched its paper *Commonweal* as a monthly in February 1885, and by May 1886 it was strong enough to become a weekly. This was against the advice of Engels, who thought the move 'absurd in every respect'. Nevertheless, it became the best socialist journal in Britain in these years, and succeeded in reaching an average circulation of between 2,000 and 3,000. It contained excellent theoretical articles by Bax and Aveling, articles by Binning and Maguire on trade unionism, and regular notes, articles, and poetry by Morris. Its overall tone was perhaps too theoretical, not enough concerned with the day-to-day struggle, but its quality was undeniably high. Some of Morris's pickings from the news, such as 'The husks that the Swine do Eat', a report of a starving man sentenced to a month's hard labour in prison for begging the scraps from soldiers' plates as they took them to the swill tubs, still make horrifying reading today.[35]

Meanwhile a second issue, both tactical and fundamental, was being confronted by Morris as *Commonweal* editor: the 'woman question'. The League was committed to equality between the sexes, in an abstract and general sense. But it was reluctant to back the immediate cause of women's equal citizenship and the right to vote, or to launch any public challenge to family attitudes. The League's male members were themselves seriously divided on these questions, which they saw as secondary, and potentially damaging diversions. Given his hostility to electoralism, Morris's disinterest in women's suffrage was logical. 'To speak plainly my *private* view of the suffrage matter is that it is no use until people are determined on Socialism,' he had told Jane Cobden; he favoured abstentionism 'till we have a national convention to settle things on a new basis'. He believed that there was little hope of winning the vote for women through parliament, for even with the radicals, 'tis nothing but a sham fight between the parties. They don't *mean* anything.' But much more inconsistent was his deliberate muting of debate on the family in *Commonweal*. He would not publish an essay on the future of marriage offered by Shaw, but in April 1886 he did print a vitriolic attack on suffragists and feminists by Bax, which although pruned of the assertions of female genetic and mental inferiority which Bax published elsewhere, comes close to condoning child- and wife-battering. Privately Morris told protesters that he had 'often fallen foul' of Bax on such points. But partly because he was at that moment particularly dependent on the explosive Bax as the League's Marxist theoretician, and partly because of the confusion to which he feared general debate would lead, he decided against 'cutting the dam of the waters of controversy'.[36] No rebuttals of Bax appeared in *Commonweal*. This betrayal of his own personal views now seems one of Morris's most damaging political misjudgements.

By the summer of 1886, however, with open air propaganda well established, membership had grown to about 700. Good branches were formed in Leeds and Bradford, Norwich, Glasgow, and Edinburgh, and six other provincial towns, as well as nine London branches, of which Hammersmith and Bloomsbury were the best. The Hammersmith branch rose to over a hundred members, held outdoor meetings with regular audiences of 200, organized Sunday lectures and a reading room, and helped to form other branches in nearby districts.

To this pioneering work nobody gave more time than Morris; at Hammersmith branch meetings and lectures his attendance was frequent; at outdoor meetings he spoke, took collections, carried banners, sold literature, acted as chairman; he was treasurer of the League, and the most influential member of its executive, and edited *Commonweal*; he toured Lancashire and Yorkshire, Scotland and East Anglia, and visited Dublin, speaking for the cause, altogether lecturing 120 times for the League in 1885–6.

Morris's optimism at this progress was short-lived. By 1887, although membership had reached a peak of about 1,000, and several more branches had been formed, others were lapsing. *Commonweal*'s circulation was stationary. The League's organization was weak, and too many of the smaller branches, like the League's executive, wasted their energies in quarrels, 'metaphysical subtleties' and 'bombastic revolutionary talk'.[37] In the meantime there had been a frightening indication that events might move too fast. In February 1886 a demonstration of the unemployed organized by the S.D.F. had marched down Pall Mall and Piccadilly and smashed some club and shop windows, and Hyndman, Burns, and Williams had been arrested. In fact their trial, which ended in an acquittal, proved a fine opportunity for propaganda, but Morris was thoroughly disturbed, and he wrote a serious warning in *Commonweal*:

I have said that we have been overtaken unprepared, by a revolutionary incident, but that incident was practically aimless. This kind of thing is what many of us dreaded from the first, and we may be sure that it will happen again and again while the industrial outlook is what it is; but every time it happens it will happen with ever-increasing tragedy. It is above all things our business to guard against the possible consequences of these surprises. At the risk of being misunderstood by hot-heads, I say that our business is more than ever *Education*.

Aimless revolt would lead only to disillusionment and counter-revolution:

We must be no mere debating club, or philosophical society; we must take part in all really popular movements when we can make our own views on them unmistakably clear; that is a most important part of the education in organization. Education towards Revolution seems to me to express in three words what our policy should be.[38]

These three words were not so easy to translate into practice. In January 1885 Aveling had proposed that the League's policy should include assisting trade unions and co-operative societies and working in local elections with the aim of forming a Socialist Labour Party. This was rejected. In the next two years the League decided to support the agitation against Irish coercion and the war in the Sudan, and it worked with the S.D.F. in the struggle to protect outdoor meetings from police prosecution. It was an incident in this struggle in September 1885 which led to Morris's reproof in the dock of the Thames Police Court for hustling a policeman. There is no doubt that the League gained strength from its involvement in these issues. But it took no part in trade-union and industrial agitation, and apart from the Norwich branch, which held demonstrations of over 1,000 strong, it did not follow the S.D.F.'s extremely successful example in organizing the unemployed.

There were signs in 1887 that Morris's purism was modifying. In an article in *Commonweal* on 19 February, 'Facing the Worst of It', he argued that revolution might be delayed by a European war, or a commercial recovery, or possibly the government's provision of 'a kind of utilitarian sham Socialism' of moderate social reform. 'History has shown us over and over again that retribution is halt-foot.' This at any rate showed greater realism. At the same time he began to take more interest in industrial struggle. He had earlier believed that trade unionism, because higher wages could only cut profits and thus lead to unemployment, must be 'defeated by its own success: as all attacks of the workmen on capital must be defeated that are not international in character'. Now he saw more clearly the importance of strikes as 'part of the great labour war' and was permanently impressed by his own visit to Northumberland in April during a miners' strike where Mahon had been organizing socialist meetings. At a great open air demonstration there Morris spoke of the eventual possibility of a general strike. There were also signs of a less uncompromising view of electoral work, no doubt due to the pressure of the Avelings and Bax. He admitted

that at some future period it may be necessary to use parliament mechanically: what I object to is *depending* on parliamentary agitation. There *must* be a great party, a great organization outside parliament actively engaged in reconstructing society and learning administration whatever goes on in the parliament itself.[39]

Morris held this view until about 1891 and was not, as has often been suggested, shaken in it by the Trafalgar Square battles in November

41. The battle of Trafalgar Square: 'Bloody Sunday' demonstration on 13 November 1887

1887. These culminating incidents in the free-speech struggles had started with police interference with S.D.F. unemployed meetings in the early autumn of 1887. The Socialist League decided at first on a policy of non-intervention, in spite of protests from the Glasgow branch, but this attitude was quickly dropped when the police cleared a whole series of meetings in October and finally on 8 November banned all meetings in the Square. There was a tremendous rallying of all shades of radical and socialist opinion to the defence of free speech and a Law and Liberty League was formed with Morris an active committee member. A massive demonstration was organized for 13 November, with processions converging on the Square from several directions. It was remorselessly dispersed by the police, who charged like soldiers on an enemy, and two men subsequently died of their injuries.

Morris's immediate reaction was an outburst of fury at the brutality with which harmless citizens 'were beaten and trodden underfoot; men were hauled off to the police courts and there beaten again . . . The very Radicals have been taught that slaves have no rights.'[40] And popular indignation was made equally plain. A week later an immense combined protest demonstration of radicals and socialists was held in Hyde Park. A minority, who directly challenged the official ban against meetings in the Square, were again remorselessly charged and batoned by the police. Amongst those who fell was a mere passer-by named Alfred Linnell, acutely wounded. His subsequent death made him a popular political martyr. He was buried on 16 December with the largest funeral demonstration which had been seen in London since the death of Wellington. As the procession wound its way through the city towards Bow Cemetery, Morris walking beside the hearse plainly inscribed 'Killed in Trafalgar Square', it swelled to a crowd of over ten thousand. 'There was to me something aweful (I can use no other word) in such a tremendous mass of people, unorganized, unhelped, and so harmless and good-tempered.'[41] And after the burial in the fading light and rain, the immense, dense, drenched crowd beside the grave sang the 'Death Song', sold for Linnell's orphans, written by Morris for the day.

Morris was not, like Bernard Shaw, shaken by the easy victory of the police against an unarmed demonstration. He predicted that it was the beginning of a period of 'rougher work than languid "constitutional agitation"'. But he did conclude that in the face of state violence 'mere numbers without drill or organization are useless', and that socialists would need to learn 'the proper way to defend a position in a large town by a due system of scouts, out-posts and supports'.[42] The implication was that an easy revolution was not round the corner. He did not believe, in the immediate aftermath, like Eleanor Marx, that one more demonstration could be the turning point: 'Last Sunday the troops had ammunition ready and stood with fixed bayonets. Next Sunday I think it very possible they will actually fire. That would be *very* useful to the whole movement here. It would complete the work some of us have been doing this long while past . . . ' To Morris this was mere self-indulgence. 'The revolution cannot be a mechanical one . . . Why then should we swagger about violence which we know we cannot use?'[43] In the end the experience of 'Bloody Sunday' thus served to confirm Morris's growing feeling that revolution was not to come as rapidly as he had thought. It made him realize the strength of capitalism, of the police, and the Press, and the weakness of a small and divided socialist movement. In *News from Nowhere*, which he wrote in 1890, the change comes by revolution, but the date is 1952.

1887 proved the watershed of the League's fortunes. At the annual conference Bax's Croydon branch proposed a motion in favour of putting up parliamentary candidates. It was eventually withdrawn in favour of a similar resolution by Mahon; which was supported by Leeds (Maguire) and Bloomsbury (Binning and the Avelings), but defeated 17–11. Mahon left the Socialist League at the end of the year, taking with him a considerable following which he had built up in the north. Bax and the Bloomsbury branch followed after a second defeat at the 1888 conference. The result was to throw Morris into the hands of the revolutionary anarchists in London, while in the provinces, apart from the militant Bradford and Leeds branches which were kept going by Maguire, the League's strength was everywhere declining. The branch at Norwich, where Morris spoke to a crowd of over 7,000 in the market place in August 1888, was weakening under anarchist influence, while Glasgow, the other stronghold, was being led by Bruce Glasier towards vague escapist idealism. In London more and more time was wasted in quarrelling. The Hammersmith branch was still strong enough to start new branches and carry on vigorous outdoor propaganda, but the Sunday lectures at Kelmscott House had become fashionable and intellectual.

Morris was becoming throughly disheartened. He was subsidizing the League and *Commonweal* at the rate of £500 a year, more than he could afford. The paper's sales had now declined as other more practical rivals, such as Keir Hardie's *Miner* and Champion's *Labour Elector*, began to appear. It no longer contained any trade-union articles and only mentioned Hardie's crucial campaign as an independent labour candidate at the 1888 Mid-Lanark by-election as 'a great Whig triumph'.

Morris complained that 'the *active* (?) members in London mostly consider themselves Anarchists, but don't know anything about Socialism and go about ranting revolution in the streets, which is about as likely to happen in our time as the conversion of Englishmen from stupidity to quick-wittedness'.[44]

The disintegration of the League was in fact only a matter of time. The Yorkshire branches, which alone made any important contribution to the great wave of trade-union strikes and organization in 1889, were now virtually independent, kept in the League by personal loyalty to Morris. They found it better to sell other papers than *Commonweal*, which was containing more and more anarchism. It was by no means all unsympathetic to him, for the anarchists provided some of the most cogent criticism of the dangers of state socialism. But even this was not enough for the anarchists, who ejected Morris from the editorship at the 1890 conference. Morris sent his last article in November and then withdrew the Hammersmith branch, renaming it as the independent Hammersmith Socialist Society. Without his money and restraining influence the League quickly broke up into revolutionary groups. *Commonweal* ceased to appear regularly after a few months and its new editors ended up in prison with the Walsall bomb case of 1892.

Mackail described 1890 as the end of Morris's activity as a propagandist; 'the weary work of militant socialism was now over for him'.[45] This was not true. He continued to speak for the lively Hammersmith Socialist Society, which drew regular outdoor audiences of 300, and to chair its lectures and committee. He also spoke at outdoor meetings in other parts of the country, on several occasions for the S.D.F. In these last years his reputation with socialists of all kinds, due to his obvious integrity and scrupulous avoidance of personal fighting, enabled him to speak for any organization and write for any paper without suspicion. He used this reputation to bring about negotiations for a united English socialist party in 1892–3, although the effort proved a failure. It is certainly true that as an unattached socialist after 1890 his propaganda work was less frequent, but the reason was not a loss of interest or disillusionment with the movement, but the serious decline of his health which began in 1891.

At about the same time he evolved his final view of the correct tactics for the socialist movement. As early as 1888 he had conceded that 'perhaps we Leaguers have been somewhat too stiff in our refusal of compromise. I have always felt that it was rather a matter of temperament than of principle; that some transition period was of course inevitable, I mean a transition involving State Socialism'—and that 'towards this State Socialism things are certainly tending.'[46] He was even prepared to welcome the victory of the Progressive (Liberal) party at the first L.C.C. election in 1889, 'though I don't suppose that the County Council can do much directly as they are now constituted: yet they may become Socialist in feeling, and so make a rallying-point for a kind of revolt against the Parliament'.[47] But at this point he put his chief hope in the development of a militant trade-union movement, inspired by the success of the great Dock Strike of 1889. He wanted the trade-union movement to make a 'plan of campaign', so that instead of scattered skirmishes there should be 'the whole mass standing shoulder to shoulder in all strikes'.[48] At the time of the 1890 miners' strike he described 'an universal strike' as 'one instrument for the winning of freedom'. 'If the miners act well together, and if they are supported by the sympathy of their brother workers, even those who will suffer by the strike, they will now for the first time understand their power, and a weapon for the hand of revolution will be fashioned, which will be irresistible.' It might be necessary to use Parliament in the last stages of the revolution, but it was a 'hopeless enterprise' to try to jockey it into socialism. 'The true weapon of the workers as against Parliament is not the ballot-box but the *Boycott*. Ignore Parliament; let it alone, and strengthen your own organizations to deal directly with your masters.'[49]

By 1892, however, the trade-union movement had been checked by the downturn of the economy and the resistance of the employers, while the possibility of real advances through electoral activity, which had until recently seemed so slight, had become distinctly hopeful. The change was due to both socialist and trade-union agitation. The socialist propaganda of the 1880s had begun to make its mark and win a distinct following among the more rebellious and politically-minded younger generation of working men, so that when the dramatic expansion of trade unionism to the semi-skilled and unskilled workers took place in 1889–92 many of its leaders were socialist—John Burns, Tom Mann of the Engineers, Ben Tillett of the Dockers, and Will Thorne of the Gasworkers. Under this socialist leadership the new unions at once entered into politics, not as socialists, because the majority of their members would have resented this, but as independent 'labour' men. They stood for local councils, School Boards, and Boards of Guardians, and with the extensive backing of their members they secured some startling victories. Once their strength was clear the Liberals tried to avoid conflicts with them. In London 'labour' candidates were supported by the radical *Star* and at the 1892 L.C.C. election the

Progressives found seats for an independent 'labour bench' of twelve members. Morris was impressed and

pleased on the whole. It is certainly the result of the Socialist movement, it is a Labour victory, as the affair was worked by the Socialist and Labour people . . . Of course I don't think much of gas and water Socialism, or indeed of any mere mechanical accessories to Socialism; but I can see that the spirit of the thing is bettering, and in spite of all disappointments I am very hopeful.[50]

In the general election of the summer of 1892 the first three Independent Labour M.P.s were elected to Parliament along with the victorious Liberals, and in his comments on the election in the *Hammersmith Socialist Record* in August Morris wrote that 'this obvious move forward of the class-feeling is full of real hope'. There was value in the fight for limited reforms, provided that they were properly understood.

Rise of wages, shortening of hours of labour, better education, etc., all these things are good, even in themselves; but unless they are used as steps towards equality of condition, the inconvenience they will cause to the capitalists will be met by changes in the markets, and in the methods of production, which will make the gains of the workers mere games.

In August 1892 in a lecture on 'Communism', he linked this view to the equally careful statement that

I cannot fail to see that it is necessary somehow to get hold of the machine which has at its back the executive power of the country, however that may be done, and that the organization and labour which will be necessary to effect that by means of the ballot-box will, to say the least of it, be little indeed compared with what would be necessary to effect it by open revolt.[51]

Morris remained thoroughly aware of the dangers of being drawn, through political action and concessions won, into a mere semi-socialistic reformism, confusing the mere 'machinery' of socialism with its 'essence'. The good in schemes for improving town life, raising wages and shortening hours, improving housing and education, was plain enough. But he saw clearly, as we shall see—as did few others of his time—how they might simply lead to a modified welfare capitalist society, in which equality remained as distant as ever. For this reason, 'great as the gain would be, the ultimate good of it, the amount of progressive force that might be in such things would, I think, depend on *how* such reforms were done—in what spirit?' The way forward towards socialism therefore lay, not in standing back from the struggle for reforms, but through entering them, seeking 'to raise their aims . . . to give form to the vague aspirations which are in the air about them': by a combination of day-to-day struggle with education to socialism.

It had taken Morris a long time to reach this position. 'Some of us I say once believed in the inevitableness of a sudden and speedy change. That was no wonder with the new enlightenment of Socialism gilding the dullness of civilization for us. But if we must now take soberer views of our hopes, do not reproach us with that . . . '[52] Certainly one must recognize that Morris's failings as a political tactician were due to the inexperienced enthusiasm of a pioneer. But even so, it is hard to deny that his interpretation of the situation was wrong in 1884–5 and that he was still a step behind events in 1892–3.

In making this criticism one should, however, remember how few of the socialists with whom Morris was in contact saw what was to be the way ahead and how the movement might have been influenced. The Independent Labour Party, which was forming in the north in 1892–3 and was within a decade to bring trade unionists and socialists together in the Labour party, was unable to secure more than a foothold in London before 1905. London socialism continued to be dominated by the contrasted attitudes of the S.D.F. and the Fabian Society. Although there was some successful co-operation between local S.D.F. branches and trade unionists which led to political successes, as a whole the S.D.F. held rigidly to the ideal of a purely socialist parliamentary party.

The Fabian Society, on the other hand, was at this time advocating what Morris rightly condemned as 'the fantastic and unreal tactic' of permeation—the infiltration of the existing political parties and using them to enact socialism without their realizing what was happening. The Fabian claims to victories by this method were so brilliantly described by Bernard Shaw and other Fabians that for many years it was genuinely believed that they did indeed succeed in manipulating the Liberal party associations and the radical *Star* newspaper, and in foisting the Newcastle programme on the Liberal party as its 1892 election platform, municipal socialism on the Progressive party, and the 1902–3 Education Acts on the Conservative government. Recent historical research has shown that these claims are unjustifiable. The more important of them can hardly have been seriously believed by their propagators. In truth the main political effect of the Fabian Society was to assist the S.D.F. in holding up the formation of a Labour party in London, and to confuse the Labour movement by evading the economic problems and social resistance which a socialist government would face. 'They hope for a revolution, which is not *the* Revolution, but a revolution which is to ignore the facts that have led up to it and will bring it about,' Morris commented. 'Revolution without the class struggle . . . is an absurdity and an impossibility.' Socialism would only come when the working class demanded it.[53] Here Morris certainly had the more realistic understanding. One should remember that the Webbs did not come round to accept the need to work for change through the working-class movement until 1912.

The Socialist League failed, split on the rock of tactical misunderstanding. But had it all been a waste of time? Would Morris have better confined himself to expounding his socialist criticism of Victorian Britain and his vision of the future?

The Socialist League disappeared, but it did leave a permanent mark. Its significance was in establishing from an early stage in the socialist movement an alternative to the S.D.F. other than the Fabian Society, which apart from its unrealistic strategy had the disadvantage of being largely composed of middle-class Londoners. Had Morris succeeded in ousting Hyndman from the leadership of the S.D.F. this might not have been necessary, but having decided not to attempt this it was important to provide an alternative tradition. This the Socialist League achieved, for there is a marked continuity, both geographical and personal, between the League and the early Independent Labour Party.

In London this was a disadvantage, since the handicaps of personal quarrelling, anarchist infiltration and the animosity surrounding the Avelings continued. But even here it is noticeable that the strongest areas were west London and Woolwich, which both had Socialist League rather than S.D.F. traditions.

In Hammersmith itself a Socialist Leaguer formed a branch of the Independent Labour Party, but Morris's followers did not pursue any common policy after the break-up of the League. Others worked with the radicals, standing as vestry candidates, and bringing the local radical clubs into general support of the Labour movement. The middle class Leaguers more commonly joined the Fabian Society, which later formed an active Hammersmith group under the chairmanship of Emery Walker. This disunity, together with the fact that Hammersmith was an exceptionally well-organized Conservative constituency, meant that Morris's local efforts were not followed by any electoral successes for socialism, but the fact that the Liberal party decided to put up Labour candidates for the constituency in the 1892 and 1895 general elections was an indication of the tendency of local opinion.

Much more important was the legacy of the League in the north, for it was from the Socialist League's stronghold in west Yorkshire that the Independent Labour Party sprang. The League's Leeds and Bradford branches had been among its most successful, throwing their whole energies into the trade-union agitation in 1889. In Leeds Tom Maguire and Alf Mattison organized a builders' labourers' union and led it through a successful strike; formed a tailoresses' union of 1,500 members; and started the gasworkers' agitation, holding demonstrations of over 5,000, forming a branch in Halifax, and leading the Leeds gas strikers to their dramatic victory in 1890. Ben Turner of the General Union of Textile Workers joined the branch in 1889. The Bradford Socialist League, which included the future leader of Bradford socialism, Fred Jowett, was active in similar work. In these towns the League branches were the pioneers of socialist propaganda, and this was the cradle of the Independent Labour Party. This fact alone means that, although Morris failed in his own aims, his political activity made a vital contribution to the British socialist movement.

Even apart from this important achievement, Morris's political activity was of immense value to the socialist movement simply as an example. Of all the eminent men of his generation who showed sympathy with socialism, he was the only one to throw himself into the active struggle. However mistaken his strategy may have been, he showed that conviction must be expressed in deeds and not just words, and he was willing to break across class and cultural barriers to do this. It was not easy. He felt the social difficulties of different ways of thinking just as any middle-class Fabian socialist did—the 'great drawback that I can't talk to them roughly and unaffectedly'.[54] But he was willing to find the patience necessary for communication and the tolerance essential for co-operation, for he had no hesitation, once he had concluded that the great dynamic of political progress was the class struggle, in aligning himself in that struggle with the working class. '[In] the mist of words and names there are but two camps; one is the camp of those who are the exponents of the change which is taking place; the other of those who are striving to insure Society against that inevitable change.'[55] And having chosen the first camp, 'how can we of the middle classes, we the capitalists, and our hangers-on, help them? By renouncing our class, and on all occasions when antagonism rises up between the classes casting in our lot with the victims.'[56]

In understanding Morris's practical contribution to socialism one must not just count the direct achievement, the small group of hard-won converts; one must imagine the symbolic value of this celebrated poet and great designer marching with common working men, spending his evenings speaking in dingy lecture rooms, exhausting his health in preaching the message at street corners in rain and wind. Consider, for example, a day's work such as one which he described in a letter in April 1887, when he went to Newcastle to help John Mahon during the Northumberland miners' strike, and guess at the lasting memories it must have left with the miners as well as Morris:

Early the next morning we started off for the collieries, and alighted from the train in a wretched-looking country enough; not smoky, for alack the collieries are not working, but so waste and desolate looking like—well a back yard on a large scale. The roads of course were black and presently we had to strike off onto a railway which was also a footpath and went through one of the collieries; this brought us out presently into the village where the pitmen lived called Seghill where Mahon had a great following, and then we went into one of our friends' houses. The family were all in, a man, his wife and daughter; they were very nice people, the man intelligent and pleasant, talking with that queer Northumbrian smack that makes the talk sound like that of foreigners: poor man, he had lost one eye in an accident and damaged the other; the house was as clean and neat as a country cottage, and indeed they all seemed like that; most of them as we passed their open doors showed a swell but ugly bedstead in the place of honour: Well Donald and I sat and talked there while Mahon went to make arrangements for these people to march to the field where the meeting was to be: and after about an hour we went to the railway station and Mahon and I set off for Blithe where we were to pick up another detachment: when we all got to the station there we found quite a crowd waiting for us who followed us to the market-place, and as Mahon again had some arrangements to make they brought a trolly to the place and I got up and amused them by a speech of some half hour or more: then we set off, rather a draggle-tailed lot because we couldn't afford a paid band, and so hadn't got one there, and not more than half the men in the market place followed us, and we straggled a good deal.

Blithe is a sea-port, and as we came in I could see the masts of the ships there: and as we plodded on through the dreary (O so dreary) villages, and that terrible waste of endless back-yard, we could see on our left a strip of bright blue sea, for it was a beautiful sunny day. At last at one village we saw a crowd drawn up and a band and a banner, and then we fell into some sort of order and rolled up rapidly, so we went on till we mounted the crest of a low hill after a six mile march and had some 2000 at our heels by then. We came onto the meeting field where the two other detachments had already come, and besides groups of men and women streaming up the field from all about: the crowd was thick about the waggon we were to speak from . . . all near the waggon the men all sat down on the ground to give the others a chance to hear: we had to stand on a rather perilous plank above the rail of the waggon, and I was for simply coming to the front without mounting on the plank but some of them sung out from the side, 'If yon man does na stand on the top we canna hear him!' So up I had to climb: however some one turned a poled notice board up for me and I leaned on that and so was pretty comfortable. It was very inspiriting to speak to such a big crowd of eager and serious persons, and I did pretty well and didn't stumble at all.[57]

According to the *Newcastle Chronicle*, Morris told the crowd:

They were connected with a great struggle. Into the details of the strike he would not enter. He quite understood that they were at present in such a position that they could scarcely live at all. Their struggle was for a position in which they would be able to live a life which people called tolerable. (Hear, hear.) He did not call the life of a working man, as things went, a tolerable life at all. When they had gained all that was possible under the present system, they would still not have the life which human beings ought to have. (Cheers.) That was flat . . . What was their life at the best? They worked hard day in, day out, without any sort of hope whatever. Their work was to work to live, in order that they might live to work. (Hear, hear, and 'Shame'.) That was not the life of men. That was the life of machines . . .

He went on to urge them to fight and organize, not just for their immediate ends, but for a better life.

Not a little more wages here and leave to work for six days instead of four. He wished they only worked two days and got the same wages or more. Six days a week for the work they had to do was a great deal too much for men of ordinary body and strength. What, he asked, was a life of real happiness? Work for everybody who would work. For him who would not they could not say that Society had rejected him: he had rejected Society. The masters had rejected Society. He wished that the men might have a life of refinement and education and all those things which made what some people called a gentleman, but what he called a man (Cheers.) That was the victory he wished for. Nothing short of that would be victory. And yet every skirmish on the road and every attack on the position of the masters brought them nearer. They must go on until all the workers of the world were united in goodwill and peace upon earth. (Loud cheers.)[58]

Nor was this the end of the day. In the evening, after he had got back to Newcastle, he was out speaking in a Tyneside recreation ground until well after dusk. The miners did not forget Morris. Nearly fifty years later, in the great slump, Harold Laski found copies of *The Dream of John Ball* and *News from Nowhere* 'in house after house of the miners', even when most of the furniture had been sold.[59] They named streets after him too. Sheer hard work like that day in 1887 made Morris stand out from passive well-wishers, made him an inspiration to socialists of all types; so that his portrait was hung beside that of Marx in the clubrooms of the S.D.F., his name was taken for socialist halls and even for Labour churches, Socialist Sunday School children were made to sing his chants and read *News from Nowhere*, and the Clarion movement took him as the prophet of their future *Merrie England*. He became a symbol beyond Britain too—although we know less about this—as far, for example, as the working-class William Morris Clubs of San Francisco. More diffusely, aspects of campaigning ideas made a deep mark on middle-class English socialism, with its tastes for unpretentious and wholesome living, for craft products along with his own patterns, its attachment to the countryside and concern for conservation, and its repeated commitment to peace movements. These have been crucial characteristics of its distinctiveness within the international socialist movement. And this whole current of thinking equally clearly leads through to the new Green politics of the present: 'of the social critics affected by the love of nature, William Morris was perhaps the most perceptive and also the most important of the socialist revival'.[60] But it is significant that the most immediate and direct spreading of his vision came through the Clarion movement. For with its hopes for reconstructing the city beautiful combined with enthusiasm for 'communion with nature', mountain-climbing and country walking with craftwork, its evangelical clubs of cyclists spreading the new faith out into the villages, it was then the cultural lifeblood of urban English working-class socialism.

Undoubtedly the true picture of Morris as a politician has suffered from the desire of wishful-thinking hagiographers to claim him for their causes. He has even become something of an inspiration to anti-Marxist state socialists and anti-socialist simple-lifers with whom he would have had scarcely any sympathy. But to those who care to read it, the real story of his political work can still be inspiring, and one can understand the tribute of a Lancashire branch of the S.D.F. at his death—among the most moving of them all—'Comrade Morris is not dead there is not a Socialist living would believe him dead for he Lives in the heart of all true men and women still and will do so to the end of time'.[61]

12

PAST AND PRESENT

WILLIAM Morris remains one of the great original socialist thinkers. Why is this? It was not because of the elements of which his thought was fashioned. There are parallels or antecedents for most of his key ideas in Carlyle, Ruskin, Marx, or elsewhere. He possessed the technical skills of neither a historian like Thorold Rogers, nor an economic philosopher like Marx. Nor has time proved Morris more right than them. Nevertheless, his vision still stands as a whole, prophetic and compelling.

This is for two reasons. Firstly, Morris was centrally concerned with what have proved the fundamental insights of his time: the nature of work, human consciousness and alienation; and the relationship between class conflict and historical development. He also perceived exceptionally acutely the fragility of both nature and human culture worldwide to the advance of commercial exploitation. He grasped the importance of these problems in a very personal and sometimes remarkably independent way. Morris's own deep understanding of the 'dialectical' pattern of historical progress, for example, can be shown not merely through the striking parallels between a key passage in Engels's *Feuerbach* and Morris's *The Dream of John Ball* published *earlier* in the same year ('I . . . pondered how men fight and lose the battle, and the thing that they fought for comes about in spite of their defeat, and when it comes turns out to be not what they meant, and other men have to fight for what they meant under another name'). It can be traced back much earlier in his work: to a lecture of 1884, for example, where he speaks of history 'moving forward ever towards something that seems the very opposite of that which it started from and yet the earlier order never dead but living in the new, and slowly moulding it to a recreation of its former self'.[1] Or even, in a more embryonic sense, to the interwoven exploration of past, present, and future in his first poetry and romance.

Secondly, Morris put together his ideas in a vision which as a whole is entirely his own. It is unique in its fusion of the romantic tradition and Ruskin with the systematic historical analysis of Marx. It is unique in its pervasive grasp of *moral* values. And it is unique in its imaginative leap into a future with a new morality and a new society.

The evolution of Morris's theory cannot be studied at length because his theoretical writing is almost entirely confined to the years after 1877, when he began lecturing. Throughout his life he was deepening his understanding, absorbing not only 'modern historical research' but also new interpretations of the stages of development of primitive culture, and mythology.[2] But already, in 1877, it was almost complete; his initial ideas from Ruskin and Carlyle had been matured by fifteen years of practical experience as a designer and manufacturer. His first lectures concentrated on the social basis of art. Their message was little altered in subsequent years. Meanwhile, his activity as a politician developed his theory of social change, leading towards his acceptance of socialism. He was already fully conscious of the existence of class conflict in 1877, but it was not until 1883, when he first read Marx, that he saw it as a positive force for change. The final stage in his thought was the grafting of socialist thinking onto his own previous theory to produce his vision of the future. His theory of revolutionary practice we have already discussed with his political activity in Chapter 11, and we shall come to his concept of a future socialist society in Chapter 13. Our concern here is Morris's interpretation of the meaning of human history.

Morris started most of his lectures with history, rather than any basic definitions of formulae. His definitions are never very satisfactory. He invariably subsumes both women and men under the generic 'man': a usage of his time which at this point we shall have to follow. He spent little time in analysing concepts like 'society', 'morality', 'pleasure', or even 'beauty'; he simply observed them in practice. Art, for example, he described as 'man's embodied expression of interest in the life of man; it springs from man's pleasure in his life; pleasure we must call it, taking all human life together, however much it may be broken by the grief and trouble of individuals'. Anything made by man 'must be either beautiful or ugly; beautiful if it is in accord with Nature, and helps her; ugly if it is discordant with Nature'. This kind of simplification is scarcely satisfying. But it has to be seen as in itself an expression of Morris's fundamental philosophy. It was through doing, through making their lives, that men created their own consciousness. To start with theoretical philosophizing was thus to turn reality on its head. When one realizes that Morris as he wrote was watching craftsmen of the past at work, identifying art with the people who made it, one can understand his meaning. His whole faith was founded on the evidence of history, rather than of abstract concepts:

I know that men's natures are not so changed in three centuries that we can say to all the thousands of years which went before them: You were wrong to cherish Art, and now we have found out that all men need is food and raiment and shelter, with a smattering of knowledge of the material fashion of the universe. Creation is no longer a need of man's soul, his right hand may forget its cunning, and he be none the worse for it. Three hundred years, a day in the lapse of ages, have not changed man's nature thus utterly, be sure of that . . . [3]

Modern civilization, Morris argued, was the result of the transformation of primitive society through the 'antagonism between individual and social interests'. Once the original savage could see that he could do more than merely satisfy his immediate daily needs for food and shelter, he formed a co-operative group with his blood-relations. Intermarriage with other groups resulted in tribes, which were loosely grouped in peoples. The ethic of this primitive society was one of social responsibility; 'every freeman had certain necessary duties to perform', such as sitting on juries to adjudicate disputes, or exacting vengeance as in blood feuds. The assertion of private interests 'would have been looked upon as a crime'. There was no central executive, but local officers appointed personally. Religion consisted of ancestor-worship, and art in ceremonies and the decoration of implements connected with getting food. All land was held in common by the wider family group. Without private property, and little specialization of tasks, men were not yet dominant over women. It was only with the growth of private wealth, when the prime importance of motherhood gave way to that of property inheritance through men, that 'the world historic defeat of the female sex'—as Engels put it in *The Origin of the Family*—was to occur. And Morris noted that even in semi-feudal early Icelandic society some such earlier attitudes survived.

The greatest men lent a hand in ordinary field and house work, pretty much as they do in the Homeric poems . . . The position of women was good in this society, the married couple being pretty much on an equality: there are many stories told of women divorcing themselves for some insult or offence, a blow being considered enough excuse.[4]

Outside the early family group, however, wealth was the prize of war. War therefore developed leaders, who were rewarded with wealth, and once the agricultural stage was reached it produced a slave class (previously captives had been killed). Thus the start of class oppression coincided with that of women by men. This was the final development of barbaric tribal society.

Political life and systematic religion began with the rise of cities, and their federation into larger and larger units, culminating in the Roman Empire. The idea of the community was abstracted and the city itself was worshipped. The 'splendid ideal of equality of duties and rights' was applied only to freemen, while the slave class was rapidly and ruthlessly developed. Slaves were treated as mere property, forbidden to marry, or to give evidence except under torture, and when a debtor was handed over to his creditors as a slave 'they could cut him up in pieces and carry away each his dividend to do what they pleased with'. Slave labour gradually took over agriculture and craft work so that the middle class arose which did not feel the comradeship in rough work, which barbaric tribes felt for their slaves; they were thus more brutal—'the highly cultivated Greek citizen, who was mostly a prig; or . . . the energetic public-spirited Roman, who was mainly a jailer'. With the increasing gulf between wealthy and poor freeman, Roman society in its last stages consisted of

a privileged class of very rich men, whose business was war, politics and pleasure; and money-making as an instrument of these enjoyments: of their hangers-on forming a vast parasitical army; of a huge population of miserable slaves; and of another population of free men (so-called) kept alive by doles of food, and contented with people's palaces in the form of gladiatorial shows. That is, the free citizen had become an idler, either a rich luxurious one, or a pauper, and the work was done by men under the most obvious form of compulsion.

Art and literature were 'galvanised corpses'. Morris regarded the later Roman Empire as the complete triumph of individual self-interest, within a framework which was 'a terrible example of over-organiza- tion,' and which should be a warning to Fabian municipal socialists.[5]

This corrupt society was overwhelmed by barbarians 'fresh from their tribal communism, and once more the antagonism of individual and common rights was exemplified in the two streams of Barbarian and Roman ideas' which formed medieval society. To Morris this was a great precedent—'so shall we be our own Goths, and at whatever cost break up again the new tyrannous Empire of Capitalism'.

Society was reorganized by the barbarians on a rural instead of a city system, and the old juries, folkmoots, and other customs surviving from primitive communism were kept up. Feudalism, a chain of service made up of bonds of rights and duties, was imposed on this old system. No absolute ownership was recognized but in God. The king, as God's vice-regent, granted land on condition of service, and so down the scale. Religion was adapted to this system; Christianity, originally individual- istic, a personal mystic cult appropriate to late Roman society, now became a feudal church, believing in

an arbitrary irresponsible God of the universe, the proprietor of all things and persons, to be worshipped and not questioned; a being whose irresponsible authority is reflected in the world of men by certain other irresponsible governors whose authority is delegated to them by that supreme slave-holder and employer of labour in Heaven.[6]

Morris was certainly not a believer in a medieval golden age. He recognized that 'life was often rough and evil enough, beset by violence, superstition, ignorance, slavery; yet I cannot help thinking that sorely as folks needed a solace, they did not altogether lack one, and that solace was pleasure in their work'. There was no capitalism, no world market; production was 'for the supply of the neighbourhood, and only the surplus of it ever goes a dozen miles from the door of the worker'. Forestalling (buying in order to re-sell at a profit) and usury were illegal. Tenants were protected by customary laws, and landlords exacted from them not profit but limited duties of serfdom. Thus although—like their lords—they were subject to storm, plague, famine, and brigand-age, they could find satisfaction in their regular work.[7]

It was because craftsmen shared in this pleasure that the Middle Ages was the great period of popular art. They suffered neither the intellectual perfectionism nor the social slavery of the ancient world. They 'worked for no master save the public', for they sold their goods direct to the purchaser. In the towns the craftsmen formed guilds, 'what we should now call benefit societies', which helped those in financial difficulty and regulated entry into the craft. These workers' guilds challenged the patrician town corporations in the thirteenth century, and after a struggle secured recognition. With this new security the climax of medieval craftsmanship was reached. The treasured possessions of modern museums were 'the common household goods' of that time; while the hundreds of medieval churches, 'every one of which is a beautiful work of art', were built by 'country bumpkins'. They corresponded with 'ordinary little plain Nonconformist chapels' rather than a Victorian architect-designed Gothic church.[8]

Medieval craftsmen were all 'more or less artists' because 'they themselves were masters of their time, tools and materials'. They were taught their craft soundly as apprentices, and in this early stage of the guilds each apprentice became a master. There was little division of labour; 'the unit of labour was an intelligent man'. They

worked shorter hours than we do (even since the passing of the Factory Acts) and had more holidays. They worked deliberately and thoughtfully as all artists do; they worked in their own homes and had plenty of elbow room; the unspoiled country came up to their very doors . . . All their work depended on their own skill of hand and invention;

and above all, they were not pressed by continual hurry to turn out their work shabbily, but could afford to amuse themselves by giving it artistic finish.[9]

This great period of craftsmanship could be but a phase, for 'under all that rigidly ordered caste society of the fourteenth century, with its rough plenty, its sauntering life, its cool acceptance of rudeness and violence, there was going on a keen struggle of classes which carried with it the hope of progress of those days'. In the countryside the serfs were being freed, their duties commuted for rent, and some of them were drifting to the towns, where they became journeymen, the first 'free labourers'. This new journeyman class was at first protected by the guilds; their wages, hours and holidays were fixed, and very often a master was only allowed to employ a limited number of men. But these safeguards could not survive the rapid increase in migration, as landlords, seeing the money to be made from wool export, evicted tenants for sheep, using 'legal quibbling, direct cheating, downright violence' to create a landless labouring class which flooded into the towns. Thus the privileged guild craftsmen found themselves more and more an employing class. 'The huckstering landlord and the capitalist farmer drove the workman into the hands of the new manufacturing capitalist, and a middle-class of employers of labour was created.'[10]

By the sixteenth century, with the creation of an international market and a class of manufacturing employers, the first stage of capitalism had begun. The late medieval revolts of John Ball and the Anabaptists were 'the funeral torches of the Middle Ages'. The change was reflected both in art and in religion. Already by the fifteenth century English art had become 'rude, unfinished and barbarous'. On the Continent, where the divorce of the people from the land was less abrupt, the tradition of craftsmanship produced the 'blaze of glory' of the Renaissance, but it was stifled by the revival of intellectual perfectionism of the old classical kind, and by 1600 all but extinct. In religion the individualist ethic of early Christianity was revived, permeating Catholicism even where it was not supplanted by Protestantism. Property became absolute personal ownership, rather than a tenancy of God, and the workman free of servile duties—free to sell his labour.[11]

At this point the development of Britain and France, which were to be the key countries in the eighteenth and nineteenth centuries, diverged. In both countries centralizing monarchies had developed, but in England the monarchy and romantic aristocracy were defeated in the Civil War by the prosperous middle classes. Once a constitutional monarchy was established, and the middle classes were free to make their profits, Britain became

solid and settled; all the old elements of disturbance and aspiration hardened into constitutional bureaucracy; religion recognized as a State formality; . . . militant Puritanism buried deep under mountains of cool formality; . . . the nobility a mere titled upper order of the bourgeoisie . . . England is bourgeois and successful throughout its whole life; without aspirations, for its self-satisfaction is too complete for any, yet gathering force for development of a new kind,—as it were a nation taking breath for a new spring.[12]

In France, on the other hand, a centralized monarchy tried to create a state-run industrialism, in spite of the survival of medieval restriction and even serfdom. The nobility were reduced to vassal courtiers, 'with little influence in the countryside . . . mere absentee landlords of the worst type, endowed with privileges which could only be exercised at the cost of the starvation of the people and the exasperation of the Bourgeoisie, who furnished the funds for the Court glory'. The art of eighteenth-century France was 'the especial exponent . . . of the degradation which indicated the rottenness of society'. Molière, the one writer of genius, was driven to mere cynicism. 'The ladies and gentlemen of the period ignored the real peasants who were the miserable slaves of the French landlords, and invented in their dramas, poems, and pictures sham shepherds and peasants, who were bundles of conscious unreality, inane imitations of the later classics.' The visual arts were 'mere expensive and pretentious though carefully finished uphol-stery, mere adjuncts of pomp and state, the expression of the insolence of riches and the complacency of respectability'.

Absolutism was meanwhile being undermined by the growth of a respectable party of reform, of rational bourgeois humanitarianism, fed by the writings of Voltaire, Rousseau, and Diderot; a radical conservat-ism, but 'listened to and pondered by people who find that state of things unbearable'. Eventually discredited by military failure, entangled by corruption and bankruptcy, absolutism collapsed in the French Revolution.[13]

The revolution began and ended as a middle-class revolt. The first stage, up to the flight of the King, was overtly bourgeois; a constitutional monarchy, with the Church reduced to a salaried department, and feudal hindrances abolished. Disturbances like the rural 'Jacquerie' and the taking of the Bastille did not at first break this pattern. But with the threat of foreign armies, the shortage of food, and popular pressure, the bourgeois revolutionaries panicked, and started to quarrel. All that followed from the Terror to the fall of Robespierre was the work of a few revolutionists, each trying to keep level with the proletarian instinct, and each failing in turn. They had not the key to the great secret; they were still bourgeois, and still supposed that there must necessarily be a propertyless proletariat led by bourgeois, or at least served by them.

Undoubtedly the law of maximum prices and cumulative taxation of income helped the working classes, but they did not go to the root of the problem, which was capitalist exploitation. So with a series of quarrelling dictators killing each other, soon nobody was left

but a knot of self-seeking politicians of the usual type; they had only to keep matters going till they were ready for the dictator who could organize for his own purposes people and army, and who came in the shape of Napoleon. . . . It is commonly said that Napoleon crushed the Revolution, but what he really did was to put on it the final seal of law and order. The Revolution was set on foot by the middle-classes in their own interests; the sentence which Napoleon accepted as the expression of his claims, 'la carrière ouverte aux talents', is the motto of middle-class supremacy.

Although Napoleon was eventually defeated and the Bourbon monarchy restored, it was too weak to restore absolutism, and the middle class reasserted itself with the revolts of 1830 and 1848. The 1848 revolution had a popular element, but the democracy of Louis Napoleon was a façade of 'shameless corruption and repulsive vulgarity', of showy military enterprise and the rebuilding of Paris in the 'bread and pageants' tradition, allowing the country to get 'at last into full swing of the rule of successful stock-jobbery', as in Britain—but with 'more open blackguardism'.[14]

Meanwhile in Britain a period of industrial stress had occurred, caused by the evolution of capitalist manufacturing technique. The first stage had been simply the employment of journeymen craftsmen. This was followed by the transitional stage of organized 'division of labour', of work in specialized groups, so that the unit of labour became the group instead of the individual. Then, with the rapid development of machinery in the later eighteenth century, the workman was reduced to a machine operator. He could be forced to work for longer and longer hours, or replaced by equally overworked women and children who, because of their social dependence upon men, could be paid still less, and thus aid the capitalist in 'the general cheapening of labour'. This change, together with the geographical shift of industry towards the coal and water power of the north, caused a period of terrible distress and dislocation, with the 'half-blind instinct' of machine breakers, and the Chartist movement.[15]

Chartism was 'thoroughly a working-class movement', and although it failed because of its poor organization and its belief in political instead of economic solutions, Morris believed that it forced the capitalists to accept the Factory Acts, and the legalization of the trade unions. Chartism faded away with the general settling down of the economy after its earlier dislocation and the success of trade unions in improving the position of skilled workmen. Thereafter

the Liberal Party, a nondescript and flaccid creation of bourgeois supremacy, a party without principles or definition, but a thoroughly adequate expression of English middle-class hypocrisy, cowardice, and shortsightedness, engrossed the whole of the political progressive movement in England, and dragged the working-classes along with it, blind as they were to their own interests and the solidarity of labour.

Nevertheless, Chartism had not 'failed utterly: at least it kept alive the holy flame of discontent', and left a tradition of rudimentary socialism which continued to mature below the surface. For the modern socialist movement had now begun.[16]

Morris placed Robert Owen first among the early socialist thinkers. Owen's great New Lanark experiment, begun in 1800, was

briefly the conversion of a miserable, stupid, and vicious set of people into a happy, industrious, and orderly community, acting on the theory that man is the creature of his surroundings, and that by diligent attention to the development of his nature he can be brought to perfection. In this experiment he was entirely successful.

Through this practical example, and the co-operative experiments, labour value exchanges and communistic villages which he started less successfully later, Owen hoped to convert people to socialism. His mistake was not to realize the force of history; his 'total disregard of the political side of progress'.[17]

Historical understanding developed through the 'singular flashes of insight' of St Simon—that the French Revolution was a class struggle, and politics based on economics—and Fourier, who first saw the stages of historical growth. Proudhon produced the maxim, 'Property is Robbery', in 1839, and Louis Blanc, with his scheme of national workshops, the slogan, 'From each according to his capacity, to each according to his needs.'[18]

Ruskin also supported national workshops, but Morris did not regard Ruskin as 'a Socialist, that is not a *practical* one. He does not expect to see any general scheme even begun: he mingles with certain sound ideas which he seems to have acquired instinctively, a great deal of mere whims'. Nevertheless, Ruskin's 'Nature of Gothic' was 'one of the very few necessary and inevitable utterances of the century'; for although Robert Owen had shown 'how by companionship and good will labour might be made at least endurable', and Fourier had based his schemes on pleasurable inducements to labour, the key to the problem of work was discovered by Ruskin—'that art is the expression of man's pleasure in labour'. Pleasure and self-expression in labour thus early became a central doctrine for Morris, and was incorporated in his socialist criticism of capitalist society. Reading a speech made by an enlightened manufacturer to his workpeople, Morris was struck by a phrase:

I turned the intrusive sentence over again to my mind:
'No man would work unless he hoped by working to earn leisure': and I saw that this was another way of putting it: first, all the work of the world is done against the grain: second, what a man does in his 'leisure' is not work . . . I tried to think what would happen to me if I were forbidden my ordinary daily work; and I knew that I should die of despair and weariness . . . A poor bribe the hope of such leisure to supplement the other inducement to toil, which I take to be the fear of death by starvation.[19]

Apart from Ruskin, Morris did not attribute many of his socialist ideas to English writers. Certainly Kingsley and Carlyle had influenced him in early life—especially Carlyle's *Past and Present*, with his doctrines that 'All work is noble', and 'Cash-payment is not the sole nexus of man with man'; but Morris rejected Carlyle's ascetic puritanical doctrine of work as a means to self-redemption for Ruskin's positive view of work as central to self-fulfilment. And by the 1880s he had advanced far beyond these elementary criticisms of capitalism. The central figure in his socialist theory had become Karl Marx.

It should be said here that stories, such as those recorded by Bruce Glasier in his *William Morris and the Early Days of the Socialist Movement*, which portray Morris as hostile to Marx, are not seriously credible. It is true that he did not equate socialism with Marxism, particularly in terms of a doctrinaire acceptance of the labour theory of value which was then seen as Marx's keystone: 'socialism does not rest on Marxian theory; many complete socialists do not agree with him on this point.'[20] But he imbibed it with deep seriousness himself. Morris made two thorough readings of *Capital*, in French in 1883 and again in English in 1887, and made careful notes of it; he kept both editions in his library, well-thumbed. From this point onwards Marx's economics and doctrine of the class struggle appear in innumerable Morris lectures and letters; and there are many phrases in them derived from *Capital* as well as direct references to 'that great book'.

Nor was this the only source of his Marxism. He read Marx's *The*

Civil War in France. He was in intermittent contact with Engels, whose *Origin of the Family* clearly influenced Morris, and who sent him a copy of the *Condition of the Working Class in England in 1844* when it was translated in 1887—after which it was serialized in *Commonweal.* But equally remarkable was Morris's ability to absorb Marxist perceptions indirectly through his philosopher-friend Bax. Bax was a regular intimate of the Engels circle, and picked up impressions there of the contents of many of the unpublished writings of Marx which Engels was editing. Bax himself made surprisingly little use of such perceptions in his own individual work (in contrast to that written in co-operation with Marx); he seems essentially to have been a passive vehicle of ideas—both ways, for he also carried Morris's ideas to Engels. But Morris himself had an extraordinary ability to seize upon an idea and give it a place within his own. The 'spiral' dialectic of history we have already noticed. And there are other equally remarkable instances of parallels in phrasing between Morris's 1888 lecture on 'The Society of the Future' and Marx's 'Theses on Feuerbach', first published by Engels in German (which Morris could not read) in the same year with its statement of the social nature of human consciousness: 'if men taken individually are products of the conditions of their environment . . . it should be the business of man as a social animal, or, if you like, of society, to create the environment in which man is taken to be individually what he is. Man should and does create the conditions in which he lives; he is conscious of them and creates them with knowledge.' If Morris picked up some of these phrases this was because Marx was echoing what he already knew and had said himself in other words. It is an indication, not of a derivative Marxism, but of the closeness between the fundamental insight of two great critics of society and history.

The most direct fruits of Morris's study of Marx appear in the series of articles for *Commonweal*, 'Socialism from the Root Up', written with Bax in 1886–7, in which seven of the 25 articles are given to a summary of the economic theory of volume one of *Capital.* Undoubtedly Morris found these economic articles the most difficult in the series; with characteristic self-deprecation he recorded in his diary his visit 'to Bax at Croydon where we did our first article on Marx: or rather he did it: I don't think I should ever make an economist even of the most elementary kind: but I am glad of the opportunity this gives me of hammering some Marx into myself.' Nevertheless, the meetings continued regularly, with the result that the articles as finally presented were 'in the true sense of the word a *collaboration*, each sentence having been carefully considered by both authors in common'. Morris's mark in the style of writing and the illustrations chosen is obvious enough.[21]

The economic theory presented in these articles is worth repeating, because it shows Morris's understanding of Marxist economics—a direct and trenchant understanding. It followed the scheme of volume one of *Capital*, beginning with definitions.

Commodities were socially useful products of labour. By *value*, Marx always meant the amount of necessary social labour contained in a commodity, that is, the average labour time taken to produce it in a given society. *Use-value* was self-explanatory; and *exchange-value* meant the value of one commodity in relation to another.

Exchange of commodities begins with primitive barter. Then money, a universal expression of equivalent exchange value, takes the place of direct barter; the seller is given money, with which he buys another commodity. The first form of money was cattle, or in Scandinavia woollen cloth, but eventually gold was accepted, because it was portable, durable, and of stable value—'just as one speaks of indigo as a permanent dye, which it is relatively to other dyes, although none are absolutely permanent'. The primitive habit of hoarding gold, which is the germ of capital, then begins; and because hoarded money became a social power, in 'primitive social ethics, money was considered the embodiment of all evil'.[22]

The next stage in exchange was when the money-owner bought to re-sell at a profit, in order to get more money to buy a third commodity. The final stage, modern capitalistic exchange, began and ended with money, the only purpose of the exchange being to get more money. Thus in the first stage, the Homeric or medieval potter sold his pots and with the money bought meal, oil, wine, and flesh for his own consumption. Next the classical merchant shipped 'purple cloth from Sidon to Alexandria, sold his cloth there, and with money bought gum-Arabic (from the Soudan) and frankincense (from Arabia), which he sold at Athens, where again he shipped oil for another market. He always handled the actual goods he professed to trade in.' Medieval Venetian merchants were similar. In the final stage,

the modern man of Commerce necessarily begins his transaction with money. He buys, say, indigo, which he never sees, receives for it more money than he gave for it, and goes on steadily in this process . . . and all the goods in which he deals represent to him so much money: they are only present in his transactions nominally. Money is the be-all and end-all of his existence as a commercial man.

Capital arose from this circulation of commodities; but where did the increase in money come from?

It cannot have happened by the mere process of exchange: because that would mean that the whole capitalistic class was living by getting the better of the whole capitalistic class, which is impossible. The increase of money in the capitalistic process must come out of the labouring or productive class.

Ultimately the increase must come through purchasing a commodity which is *itself* a source of value and whose consumption *creates* value—that is, labour-power: a man with 'all that is in him as a wealth-producing machine'.[23]

In order to allow this purchase and use of labour-power, two conditions were necessary. The money owner must acquire the means of production and sufficient subsistence until his goods have been sold. The workman must be a 'free labourer'.

His labour-power must be bought and sold in the market on the same terms as any other commodity; there must be no interference with his selling it at the price which it will fetch, a high price when the competition among the capitalists is brisk, a low price when it is slack; and as he has no other commodity to sell except his labour-power, he is *compelled* to sell it—to be a 'free labourer'.

The cost of labour-power, like that of any other commodity, was the average social labour-time taken for its production—that is, the cost of the means of subsistence. Morris at first assumed that this meant that, although 'the standard of this subsistence varies somewhat: in times when commerce is brisk it will have a tendency to rise', the system prevented any general rise in working-class prosperity; for if the workers saved any earnings, rather than being able to use these savings, they would find their wages automatically lowered. Later, he defined wages as being 'just as little above mere subsistence (or starvation) wages as you will take without rebelling in some way'.[24]

The price of labour was thus fixed by market contract between the employer and workman. Morris quotes Marx:

He who was before the money-owner now strides in front as a capitalist: the possessor of labour-power follows as his labourer. The one with an air of importance, smirking, intent on business; the other timid and holding back, like one who is bringing his own hide to market, and has nothing to expect but—a hiding.

The essence of the contract was that the capitalist, who controlled the means of production, should own the product, rather than its immediate producer, the labourer; and that the labourer, while being hired for a whole day's work, should only be paid for his subsistence. Thus all his work after he had produced enough to pay for his subsistence was *surplus value*, appropriated by the capitalist.[25]

In this creation of surplus value, 'the tools, machinery, factories, means of exchange, &c., are only intermediate aids for putting the living machine into operation'. New inventions, and improved organization, could increase the rate of production of surplus value, but they would be useless without labour. Machinery and raw materials added their own cost—the amount of their value which they lost through wear and tear, or through total incorporation into the new product, or through disappearance—as 'the mordants used in dyeing cloth or yarn, or the gums, &c., used in textile printing'. These all had a constant value, which could be transferred to the new product, but could not be increased; they could only be aids to the increased value created by labour.[26]

This capitalist form of production was a historical development, not a natural state. The original accumulation of money, creating a class of money owners, was due to conquest, slavery, expropriation from the land, laws for forcing down wages, and plain robbery, rather than ancestral abstinence, which, in Marx's words, played in conventional economics 'about the same part as original sin in theology'.[27]

The money owner then became an employer, grouping workmen together in workshops to produce under his direction. This was the first stage of capitalism. At first these workshops were organized by simple co-operation, but then division of labour was introduced; either various crafts were combined under one roof (so that a coach manufacturer might bring together coach-builders, wheelwrights, upholsterers, and painters); or a formerly single craft was subdivided. Thus the workman could no longer produce anything on his own; he was a dependent member of a group, and the group was the unit of labour. Next machinery, worked by power, was introduced, so that the workman was 'no longer the principal factor in the work'; and finally, the whole factory was organized as a machine. 'The workman, once a handi-craftsman, having lost all control over the article he produced, next became a part of a human machine, and finally has become the servant and tender of a machine.' In this developed form of machine production, in Marx's words, 'we have in place of the isolated machine a mechanical monster whose body fills whole factories, and whose demon power, at first veiled under the slow and measured motion of his giant limbs, at last breaks out into the fast and furious whirl of his countless working organs'.[28]

248

Finally, Morris again quotes Marx, 'capitalistic production begets with the inexorability of a law of Nature its own negation'. The machine can work endlessly, driving the workman to the limits of endurance, forcing him to hate the machine. Productivity increases 'out of all proportion to the capacity of the capitalists to manage the market or deal with the labour supply; lack of employment is therefore becoming chronic, and discontent therewithal'. The same conflict between individual and social interests which caused the rise of capitalism will lead on to the extinction of the very capitalist property which it had produced and to the reassertion of common possession of the land and means of social production; a quicker process than the rise of capitalism, for in Marx's phrase, 'in the former case we had the expropriation of the mass of the people by a few usurpers; in the latter, we have the expropriation of a few usurpers by the mass of the people'. In short, to return to Morris, 'in the phrase "the class struggle" was involved not merely what was now called Socialism, but the whole of the progress of mankind from savagery to civilization'.[29]

Here was the force behind Morris's attacks on Victorian society. Armed with Marx's arguments, he challenged the basic assumptions of his middle-class contemporaries:

I hold that the condition of competition between man and man is bestial only, and that of association human. . . . A mask is worn by competitive commerce, with its respectable prim order, its talk of peace and the blessings of intercommunication of countries and the like; and all the while its whole energy, its whole organized precision is employed in one thing, the wrenching of the means of living from others.[30]

Nor did he accept the complacent belief that, whatever its faults, Victorian commerce had brought real prosperity. Even for the privileged, like himself, it was a system which stirred up demands which it could not fulfil. As he put it, prophetically: 'civilization has bred desires which she forbids us to satisfy, and so is not merely a niggard but a torturer too.' Or again, 'all civilization has cultivated our sensibility only to disappoint it'. For he could never forget 'the consciousness of the mass and suffering which lies below our lucky class, ugliness all about us, the world made for naught'. Had there been any real gains for that great majority? 'I tell you it is not wealth which our civilization has created, but riches, with its necessary companion poverty; for riches cannot exist without poverty, or in other words slavery. . . . What have you done with Lancashire? . . . Were not the brown moors and the meadows, the clear streams and the sunny skies, wealth?' Civilization 'has let one wrong and tyranny grow and swell into this, that a few have no work to do, and are therefore unhappy, the many have degrading work to do, and are therefore unhappy'—and their work alternating with inevitable unemployment and 'the danger of periodical semi-starvation'.[31]

The contrast ran through every aspect of civilized life: food, clothes, housing, education, even holidays.

If a professional man . . . does a little more than his due daily grind—dear me, the fuss his friends make of him! how they are always urging him not to overdo it, and to consider his precious health, and the necessity of rest and so forth! and you know the very same persons, if they found some artisan in their employment looking towards a holiday, how sourly they would treat his longings for *rest*, how they would call him (perhaps not to his face) sot and sluggard and the like.

There were, of course, individual employers on good terms with their men, 'and really unconscious of the war between them'; for 'the workman's real master is not his immediate employer but his *class*, which will not allow even the best intentioned employer to treat his men otherwise than as profit-grinding machines'.[32]

Similarly despite its superficial trappings, the whole legal and constitutional system was penetrated by the interests of industrial capitalism. The law itself provided moral backing to what would have once been seen as plain 'stealing'. And the monarchy, once the crown of feudal society, had become the symbol of the capitalist class. Morris had little patience with the nineteenth-century monarchy. At the time of the 1887 Jubilee, for example, he wrote in *Commonweal*:

Now that the monstrous stupidity is on us, . . . one's indignation swells pretty much to the bursting-point, and I really must take advantage of my position to relieve my feelings, even at the expense of being considered somewhat old-fashioned. And we must not after all forget what the hideous, revolting, and vulgar tomfoolery in question really means nowadays, or how truly its hideousness and vulgarity of upholstery symbolizes the innate spirit which has forced the skinny twaddle on a nation which is in the habit of boasting (how vainly!) of its practicality . . . [It represented commercial realities]—jobbery official and commercial, and its foundation the Privilege of Capital, set on a background of the due performance of the conventional domestic duties; in short, the representation of the anti-social spirit in its fulness is what is required of it.[33]

The pernicious spirit of capitalism was equally evident in the position of women and the character of the family in Victorian society. Morris's views on this are not always immediately obvious. Although very exceptional in his time for the complete absence of casual sexism in his writing, Morris followed, as we have seen, the convention of saying 'men' rather than 'persons' when he intended to mean both men and women. But there is no doubt that he felt strongly about the issue. He told Bernard Shaw, for example, that he 'did not consider a man a socialist at all who is not prepared to admit the equality of women'. An insistence on equality of condition between men and women under socialism occurs again and again in his writings. And he took evident trouble in working towards a convincing standpoint on the question. In his understanding of the social nature of female sexuality and personality he may have learned especially from his contact with Edward Carpenter. He also drew on his contact with the Engels circle, although possibly more through Eleanor Marx than Bax, who was undoubtedly a misogynist. Morris was clearly influenced both by Engels's *The Origin of the Family* and by Bebel's *Woman Under Socialism*—including his utopianism—making their ideas more widely available through Eleanor Marx's *Commonweal* articles. The key, as she put it, was to see that 'the woman question is part of the whole social question, that with the abolition of class-rule must come also the abolition of sex-rule, that the emancipation of man and of woman are equal necessities, that we cannot have the one without the other. Man and woman must both, in a word, become human beings.' Nor was Morris a passive recipient of this aspect of Marxist ideas. He rejected, for example, the scorn of housekeeping which Eleanor shared with other 'advanced women', arguing on the contrary that 'the secret of happiness *lies in taking a genuine interest in all the details of daily life . . .* ' And Morris himself had originally sketched out the especially cogent article of August 1885 which she wrote on the prostitution scandals revealed by the *Pall Mall Gazette*, supporting the raising of the age of consent but arguing that the root cause was women's economic dependence on men: 'so long, indeed, as we have two classes face to face, the one literally in a position to buy, and actually buying, the *bodies* of the other, so long will the crimes that necessarily result from such a system continue.' As Morris put it privately: 'nothing but the abolition of Capitalism can cure such evils: of course the article (Eleanor Marx) must take this line: I laid down the lines it must take.'

The Victorian middle-class home was based, in Morris's view, on a double hypocrisy. Its pretence of love and morality was a sham, for its true basis was 'a commercial agreement', economic support for the wife in return for her property and her body, both thenceforward the exclusive right of the male 'tiger' on the hearth. With poor chances for independent earning, middle-class women were almost forced into buying comfort (and a sexual relation) at the cost of freedom and full self-development—the husband, as Edward Carpenter wrote, 'shutting her more and more into the seclusion of the boudoir and the harem, or down to the drudgery of the hearth; confining her body, her mind; playing always upon her sex-nature, accentuating always that—as though she were indeed nought but sex; yet furious if her feelings were not always obedient to his desire . . . ' And how could they show real feeling, married in such a fashion, and often—in Morris's words— coming from a similar home where they had been 'brought up in affected ignorance of natural facts, reared in an atmosphere of mingled prudery and prurience'? But behind this lay a second hypocrisy—that of class inequality. Consequently the middle-class lady did not even carry out those tasks in the home which were left to her responsibility, but employed a 'poor drudge' from the working classes as a substitute. And Morris suffered from no illusion that the working-class woman gained much through her relative freedom to take paid work, for employers used the normal dependence of women on men to keep their wages still lower—indeed they took on women rather than men precisely to bring about 'the general cheapening of labour'. Thus while individually women, like coal pitbrow girls, gained by being permitted 'to work amidst filth for a small wage, it will be no boon to the working people in general . . . Capitalism *forces* (women) to accept such work now—at starvation wages; just as it forces males to accept work which is not fit for human beings.' The working-class woman had no choice but such work, or marriage—or prostitution. As Carpenter, following Morris, wrote, 'the "lady", the household drudge, and the prostitute, are the three main types of woman resulting in our modern civilisation from the process of the past—and it is hard to know which is the most wretched, which is the most wronged . . . '

Morris saw the denial of fulfilment and distortion to the personality of women as a fundamental deprivation for men too, whose sexuality and personality was consequently equally unbalanced. The journey of *The Water of the Wondrous Isles* is an exploration of sexuality, in which the warped, destructive extremes of pure femaleness (unrestrained consumption and sexuality in the Isle of Increase Unsought) and pure maleness (the barren sterility of the Isle of Nothing) must be passed before the couple reach true fulfilment, not in the selfish individualism of an idyll of romantic love, but as they reunite within their community of friends.

Because Morris believed the deprivations of both men and women to stem directly from the nature of the economic system, he could not see much hope in the pre-socialist middle-class feminist movement of the

1880s. They missed the root of the problem. 'A word may here be said to the "women's rights" group. They are far too apt to put women forward as *competitors* with men, and thereby injure the cause of emancipation of women which every socialist is bound to further . . . So long as men are slaves, women can be no better. Let women's rights societies adopt that motto—and act on it.' The need, in short, was for a socialist women's movement. It was not that the separate organization of women was irrelevant. Eleanor Marx, indeed, argued for a parallel campaign:

Women are the creatures of an organized tyranny of men, as the workers are the creatures of an organized tyranny of idlers . . . Their emancipation will come from themselves. Women will find allies in the better sort of men, as the labourers are finding allies among the philosophers, artists and poets. But the one has nothing to hope from man as a whole, and the other has nothing to hope from the middle class as a whole.

At the same time, since only socialist feminism challenged the economic basis of sex-rule, the dependence of women upon men could not be broken until both stood shoulder to shoulder to conquer the antisocial spirit of capitalism.[34]

The battle needed was a world-wide one, for already this antisocial spirit was international in its effects. This was why, at the height of the Irish Famine, when 'people were dying of starvation . . . butter, eggs and bacon were being transported to England to be sold at a profit there'. Further afield, the tyranny at home was paralleled by 'the disgraceful exploiting of savage tribes and barbarous peoples on whom we force at once our shoddy wares and our hypocrisy at cannon's mouth'. Wars were invariably at bottom market wars. 'For years past we English have been rather shy of them . . . and I will tell you why: It is because we have had the lion's share of the world market; we didn't want to fight for it as a nation, for we had got it; but now this is changing', forcing 'even the peaceable Gladstone' into bayonet wars.

Morris regarded the social effects of imperialism as an unqualified disaster:

No country is safe from its ravages; the traditions of a thousand years fall before it in a month; . . . the Indian or Javanese craftsman may no longer ply his craft leisurely, working a few hours a day, in producing a maze of strange beauty on a piece of cloth: a steam-engine is set a-going in Manchester, and that victory over Nature and a thousand stubborn difficulties is used for the base work of producing a sort of plaster of china-clay and shoddy, and the Asiatic worker, if he is not starved to death outright, as plentifully happens, is driven himself into a factory to lower the wages of his Manchester brother worker, and nothing of character is left him except, most like, an accumulation of fear and hatred of that to him most unaccountable evil, his English master. The South Sea Islander must leave his canoe-carving, his sweet rest, and his graceful dances, and become the slave of a slave: trousers, shoddy, rum, missionary, and fatal disease—he must swallow all this civilization in the lump.[35]

It was the loss of the elementary pleasure of creative work which angered Morris most in the spread of capitalism abroad. It was also one of his strongest personal complaints of its effects at home. He had

been gradually driven to the conclusion that art has been handcuffed by it, and will die out of civilization if the system lasts. That of itself does to me carry with it the condemnation of the whole system, and I admit has been the thing which has drawn my attention to the subject in general. . . . I love art, and I love history; but it is living art and living history that I love. If we have no hope for the future, I do not see how we can look back on the past with pleasure.[36]

Morris believed that the intellectual arts were sustained by the decorative arts, which in turn reflected the conditions of the craftsmen of each period. Since the rise of capitalism in the sixteenth century, 'art has been shut up in prison', so that by the nineteenth century 'whatever of art is left which is in any sense the result of continuous tradition is, and long has been, so degraded as to have lost any claim to be considered as art at all'. Social conditions had made real craftsmanship from the working class impossible. 'To expect enthusiasm for good workmanship from men who for two generations have been accustomed by the pressure of circumstances to work slovenly would be absurd; to expect consciousness of beauty from men who for ten generations have not been allowed to produce beauty, more absurd still.' So far from being simply unsophisticated, 'the ordinary man in the street' was 'steeped in the mere dregs of all the Arts that are current at the time he lives'; and all that remained of Victorian popular art was 'a ghastly pretence of ornament which is nothing but a commercial imposture, or at best but a foolish survival of a half-remembered habit'.[37]

Not only was craftsmanship almost extinct, but the terrible living and working conditions of the working classes had almost killed their aesthetic sensitivity. 'Nature, who will have us live at any cost, compels us to *get used* to our degradation at the expense of our losing our manhood, and producing children doomed to live less like men than ourselves. Men living amidst such ugliness cannot conceive of beauty, and, therefore, cannot express it.' It was natural enough for the working classes to think of art as being 'concerned only in making luxurious toys for rich and idle persons'; for even if the museums and art galleries were not 'shut in his face on the one day in the week' when he was free, 'think how it must be to a workman who has in him any artistic feeling, who, after spending an hour looking at beautiful works of art in a public place, has to go back again to his close wretched home, a den'. Morris could well understand that his *Commonweal* reader could not

imagine your daily life, still less your daily work, having anything to do with art: somebody else paints a picture which he hopes a rich man will buy . . . ; you look at it, . . . are sometimes perhaps a little amused by it, oftenest not, and go away quite forgetting what kind of thing it was, and by no means yearning to see another like it. Art, as you understand it, you feel you can do pretty well without: well so could I, although I am an artist.[38]

For the modern artist was isolated, not merely from the working classes, but from most of his middle-class public, who had been equally affected by the loss of creative forms of work.

Whatever hope we artists of these latter days have for the future rests on those who have to do with making things. People who have the unhappiness to live vague lives, and take their surroundings for granted, who look upon art as a kind of superstition of civilization, a sort of magic growth of certain morbid intellects: these can't help us.

Nor had Morris much patience with the 'mumbo-jumbo fetishism' and 'Art gammon and spinach' of the well-meaning art philanthropists who spoke of art with 'just the sort of tommy rot that curates talk about religion at mothers' meetings, and Oxford professors say about education at Cutler's Feasts'. 'Depend upon it, art, which is the very highest of realities, the explanation of the depth of them, can only be helped by people whose daily life consists in dealing with realities.' Among the middle class this meant only those 'of the professional classes who use their own hands and whose only master is the general public: that is, with the painters, etchers, machine inventors, experiment makers, or scientific men, and, above all, with the surgeons'.[39]

At the same time, because of the ugliness of the Victorian world, artists were either 'driven into seeking their materials in the imaginations of past ages', or into 'sentimentalizing and falsifying the life which goes on around them'. They were restricted by the degradation of craftsmanship to techniques such as painting and sculpture which they could execute themselves. They could not accept public tastes without descending to the level of the Royal Academy—'the worst collection of snobs, flunkeys, and self-seekers that the world has yet seen'. Inevitably they were forced to express themselves . . . in a language 'not understood of the people' nor is this their fault; if they were to try, as some think they should, to meet the public half-way, and work in such a manner as to satisfy only those prepossessions of men ignorant of art, they would be throwing away their special gifts . . . . : they have no choice save to do their own personal work without any hope of being understood as things now are; to stand apart as possessors of some sacred mystery, which, whatever happens, they must at least do their best to guard: and by this isolation their loss is great; great both to their own minds and to the work they produce.

The escapism of the romantic artist was 'quite plainly . . . a shortcoming', and his isolation, 'this lack of the general sympathy of simple people weighs very heavily on him, and makes his work feverish and dreamy, or crabbed and perverse'.[40]

For art, as for society as a whole, the only hope lay in social revolution.

The present was an irremediably 'shoddy age. Shoddy is king! From the statesman to the shoemaker, all is shoddy!' Morris predicted that as other ages were called

the ages of learning, of chivalry, of faith and so forth, so ours I think may be called the Age of makeshift. . . . We are too poor to have pleasant green fields and breezy moorland instead of these dreadful deserts that surround us here: too poor to have rational, properly planned cities, and beautiful houses fit for honest men to live in: . . . too poor to pull down our prisons and workhouses and build fair halls and public buildings on their sites for the pleasure of the citizens: too poor above all things to give opportunity to everyone to do the work which he can do best and therefore with pleasure in the doing of it.

Yet in daily life and daily work, in security and leisure, lay the only hope for a rebirth of art.

Shall man go on generation after generation gaining fresh command over the powers of nature, gaining more and more luxurious appliances for the comfort of the body, yet generation after generation losing some portion of his natural senses: that is, of his life and soul? . . . Consider what it means; loss of the sense of beauty. . . . Think of a race of men whose eyes are only of use to serve them to carry their food to their mouths without spilling it![41]

Morris was prepared to accept anything, even 'the seeming disappearance of what art is now left to us', to prevent that barren future. 'I am sure that that will be but a temporary loss, to be followed by a genuine new birth of art, which will be the spontaneous expression of the pleasure of life innate in the whole people.' If, in the process of change, present art must go, 'let it go. What business have we with art at all unless all can share it?'[42]

We have already seen how Morris expected this change through revolution, and how he worked for it. It is worth repeating his two basic assumptions about this revolution: first, that it could only come through the class war, which 'explains past history, and in the present gives us the only solid hope of the future . . .: revolution without the class struggle . . . is an absurdity and an impossibility'; and secondly, that revolution meant 'a change in the basis of society', which would not necessarily be 'accompanied by riot and all kinds of violence'. Morris refused to 'drop our purpose rather than carry it across this river of violence' but he hoped that the change would come easily: 'I will say once for all, what I have often wanted to say of late, . . . that the idea of taking any human life for any reason whatsoever is horrible and abhorrent to me.'[43]

So Morris, just as he saw the past as a social struggle, saw the present developing towards inevitable revolution, and that prospect was the basis of his hope. It made him look at the spread of the international socialist movement since the 1860s with optimism: the German party formed by Lassalle, which in spite of the banning of its meetings and press by the anti-socialist laws of 1878 had a following of 650,000; the French movement, which was recovering from the setback of the defeat of the Paris commune of 1870—a defeat which he saw as at the same time 'the day-dawn for us', a first 'heroic . . . attempt to establish society on the basis of the freedom of labour'; the 'extraordinary' growth of Dutch socialism since 1882; the vigorous movements in Belgium, supporting a daily paper, and Denmark, supporting two daily papers; the general sympathy with socialism in Austria; and the heroic struggle against absolutism in Russia. Even America was affected; with the influence of Henry George and militant trade unionism like the Knights of Labour, 'of late years there has been a remarkable development of the class-struggle there'. And in Britain, although socialism was poorly organized, its intellectual influence had spread rapidly; the trade unions showed signs of changing their position 'from being a mere appendage to capitalism to being organisations for a definite attack upon it'; and even the Irish diversion was 'at bottom a rebellion'.[44]

This confidence, as we have seen, rose and fell, but however slowly Morris thought that events were moving towards the revolution, it was always in terms of a struggle leading to an inevitable conclusion that he interpreted the past and present.

Here are two classes, face to face with each other. . . . No man can exist in society and be neutral, no-body can be a mere looker-on: one camp or another you have got to join: you must either be a reactionary and be crushed by the progress of the race, and help it that way: or you must join in the march of progress, trample down all opposition, and help it that way.[45]

257

13

THE SOCIALIST FUTURE

'Up at the League', *News from Nowhere* begins, 'there had been one night a brisk conversational discussion, as to what would happen on the Morrow of the Revolution, finally shading off into a vigorous statement by various friends of their views on the future of the fully-developed new society.' There was, as might have been expected, considerable disagreement. One of those present 'sat almost silent at the beginning of the discussion, but at last got drawn into it, and finished by roaring out very loud, and damning all the rest for fools'. How was it, then, that Morris saw the new society?[46]

Morris expected that the first stage after the revolution would be a transitional State Socialism. He regarded this as a disagreeable necessity, and did not elaborate its details. It was only certain that the state 'would hold all the means of production and distribution of wealth in its hands': credit, railways, mines, factories, shipping, land, and machinery. Once this was decided upon 'its execution will be easy, and the details of it will clear up one after the other'. The state might allow the use of these instruments of production for a rent, 'which rent would be used again only for the benefit of the whole community, and therefore would return to the worker in another form. It would also take on itself the organization of labour in detail, arranging the how, when, and where for the benefit of the public.' The state would pay wages and prices would be the cost of production.[47]

State Socialism could not, however, be the true society; the two words were contradictory—'it is the business of Socialism to destroy the State and put Free Society in its place.' Morris was particularly critical of socialists like the Fabians, who tended 'to over-estimate the importance of the *mechanism* of a system of society apart from the *end* towards which it may be used'. 'They can see nothing further than a crude and incomplete State Socialism, which very naturally repels many from socialism altogether.' Graham Wallas's definition of socialism in *Fabian Essays* was quite inadequate:

Socialism is emphatically not merely 'a system of property-holding', but a complete theory of human life, founded indeed on the visible necessities of animal life, but including a distinct system of religion, ethics, and conduct, which, if put into practice, will not indeed enable us to get rid of the tragedy of life, as Mr Wallas hints, but will enable us to meet it without fear and without shame.[48]

In his last years, as we have seen, Morris came to accept the usefulness of social reform before the revolution, but he continued to regard any half-way stage as a totally unsatisfactory goal.

The great mass of what most non-socialists at least consider at present to be Socialism, seems to me nothing more than a *machinery* of Socialism . . . ; [it] does not seem to me to be of its essence. Doubtless there is good in the schemes for substituting businesslike administration in the interests of the public for the old Whig muddle of *laissez faire* backed up by coercion and smoothed by abundant corruption, which, worked all of it in the interest of successful business men, was once thought such a wonderful invention, and which certainly was the very cement of society as it has existed since the death of feudalism. The London County Council, for instance, is not merely a more useful body for the administration of public business than the Metropolitan Board of Works was: it is instinct with a different spirit . . . and has already done something to raise the dignity of life in London amongst a certain part of the population, and down to certain classes. Again, who can quarrel with the attempts to relieve the sordidness of civilized town life by the public acquirement of parks and other open spaces, planting of trees, establishment of free libraries and the like? It is sensible and right for the public to push for the attainment of such gains. . . .

Nay, this Socialist machinery may be used much further: it may gain higher wages and shorter working-hours for the working-men themselves: industries may be worked by municipalities for the benefit both of producers and consumers. Working-people's houses may be improved, and their management taken out of the hands of commercial speculators. More time might be insisted on for the education of children; and so on, and so on. . . . But great as the gain would be, the ultimate good of it [would] depend on *how* such reforms were done—in what spirit; or rather what else was being done, while these were going on, which would make people long for equality of condition; which would give them faith in the possibility and workableness of Socialism. . . .[49]

Without this continual consciousness of its ultimate purpose, the movement might fail utterly:

For I want to know and ask you to consider, how far the betterment of the working people might go and yet stop at last without having made any progress on the *direct* road to Communism. Whether in short the tremendous organization of civilized commercial society is not playing the cat and mouse game with us Socialists. Whether the Society of Inequality might not accept the quasi-socialist machinery above mentioned, and work it for the purpose of upholding that society in a somewhat shorn condition, maybe, but a safe one . . . Instead of the useless classes being swept away by the useful, the useless classes gaining some of the usefulness of the workers, and *so* safeguarding their privilege: the workers better treated, better organized, helping to govern themselves, but with no more pretence to equality with the rich, nor any more hope for it than they have now.[50]

The force of this warning today is clear enough. But what alternative did Morris envisage? What was the ultimate society to which he was looking? Further than state socialism, Morris warned, 'all must be speculative'. But the speculation was nevertheless important. Morris's ideal society was inevitably constructed from the past. He recognized the danger of this himself. 'We cannot turn our people back into Catholic English peasants and Guild craftsmen, or into heathen Norse bonders, much as may be said for such conditions of life.' And *News from Nowhere*, with its timber houses and stone bridges, its handicrafts and gay costumes, does suffer from being superficially an attempt to do just that. Nevertheless, electricity is hidden behind the scenery, and the qualities which Morris picked out from the past do make a fundamentally new, and, one may think, wholesome basis for society.[51]

Well now, to begin with, I am bound to suppose that the realization of Socialism will tend to make men happy. What is it then that makes people happy? Free and full life and the consciousness of life. Or, if you will, the pleasurable exercise of our energies, and the enjoyment of the rest which that exercise or expenditure of energy makes necessary to us. . . . Therefore my ideal of the Society of the future is first of all the freedom and cultivation of the individual will, which civilization ignores.

Morris had no patience with Herbert Spencer's objection that socialism would kill individuality. 'Socialists no more than other people believe that persons are naturally equal.' Monotonous work and constant fear of hunger was already killing individuality 'among the millions of ordinary workers. . . . The mill-hand who is as much part of the machinery of the factory where he works as any cog-wheel or piece of shafting is, need not be very anxious about the loss of his "individuality" in a new state of things.'[52]

Nor would Morris accept Victorian middle-class life as the ideal future for all classes.

Is it conceivable . . . that the change for the present wage-earners will simply mean hoisting them up into the life of the present 'refined' middle classes, and that the latter will remain pretty much what they are now, minus their power of living on the labour of others? [Would, for example,] the family of the times when monopoly is dead be still as it is now in the middle classes, framed on the model of an affectionate and moral tiger to whom all is prey a few yards from the sanctity of the domestic hearth? Will the body of the woman we love be but an appendage to her property? . . . Shall we be ashamed of our love and our hunger and our mirth . . . ?[53]

The foundation of life in the new society would be 'a free and unfettered animal life for man first of all: I demand the utter extinction of all asceticism. If we feel the least degradation in being amorous, or merry, or hungry, or sleepy, we are so far bad animals, and therefore miserable men.' Good food, and good housing, were essential to bring physical health, to enable men to 'feel mere life a pleasure; to enjoy the moving one's limbs and exercising one's bodily powers; to play, as it were with sun and wind and rain; to rejoice in satisfying the due bodily appetites of a human animal'.[54]

This insistence on animal freedom did not mean that Morris believed in unfettered individualism in personal relationships. He believed, for example, that a new kind of sexual fulfilment would be possible not just from the breaking of the legal and economic fetters of the old society, but from the communal character of the new. 'We shall live among friends and neighbours with whom indeed our passions or folly may sometimes make us quarrel, but whose interests cannot really be dissociated from our own.'

In such an approach he differed from

our Anarchist-Communist friends. . . . For if freedom from authority means the assertion of the advisability or possibility of an individual man doing what he pleases always and under all circumstances, this is an absolute negation of society, and makes Communism as the highest expression of society impossible; and when you begin to qualify this assertion of the right to do as you please by adding 'as long as you don't interfere with other people's rights to do the same', the exercise of some kind of authority becomes necessary.

Pure anarchism would amount to 'unorganized monopoly, or the rule of the strongest individual'. On the other hand, with his yearning for freedom from conventional restraint, and his belief that the essential common good could prevail through reasoned self-interest with only minimal coercion, Morris closely understood the attractions of philosophical anarchism. He therefore, hoped to reduce all forms of authority, whether government, education, or systems of morality, to the minimum. The object of his society was to provide a framework for individual fulfilment rather than to organize all for the collective good.[55]

Under socialism Morris saw no need for a religious moral authority:

Real (I should call it ideal) Christianity has never existed at all. Christianity has developed in due historic sequence from the first, and has taken the various forms which social, political, and economic circumstances have forced on it; its last form moulded by the sordid commercialism of modern capitalism.

The ethic of socialism contained all that was valuable in Christianity, so that in the future society there would be no need for any separate religious ethic. Morris predicted a return to the social responsibility of primitive morality, widened beyond the immediate family group. He was not interested in any supernatural speculation. 'Religion to me means a habit of responsibility to something outside myself.' This responsibility did not need the authority of a God; he did not trouble much over the existence of God in these later years—'It's so unimportant, it seems to me.' He told Bruce Glaiser that

our beliefs, whatever they be, whether concerning God, or nature, or art, or happiness, are in the end only of account so far as they affect the right doings of our lives, so far, in fact, as they make ourselves and our fellows happy. And in actual fact I find the same amount of goodness and badness, happiness and misery among peoples of all creeds—Jew, Christian, and Gentile.[56]

Morris rejected any rigid rules in personal relationships. The existing marriage system, for example, he believed was as bad as any other form of property contract. It inevitably produced the demand for prostitution, just as poverty supplied the prostitutes. 'There is the closest of relations between the prostitution of the body in the streets and of the body in the workshops.' In the future marriage would be a voluntary agreement in which the couple would always remain free people. Marriage might be formalized, provided there was no 'artificial bolstering up of natural human relations' and 'no pretext of unity when the reality of it is gone'. There should be 'no unvarying conventional set of rules by which people are judged; no bed of Procrustes to stretch or cramp their minds and lives; no hypocritical excommunication which people are *forced* to pronounce'. There would be no such 'lunatic affairs' as divorce courts with the impossible task of 'enforcing a contract of passion'. Morris did not believe 'that we can get rid of all the trouble that besets the dealings between the sexes'. The problems of calf-love turning to early disillusionment, or the compulsion of unpredictable and too often unreasonable passions in later life, would always remain; 'but we are not so mad as to pile up degradation on that unhappiness by engaging in sordid squabbles about livelihood and position, and the power of tyrannising over children who have been the results of love or lust'.[57]

Some of the distress in sexual relations would be alleviated, Morris hoped, when work provided a second creative outlet: 'there are other pleasures besides love-making'. There would be more choice and variety, and also more sharing of work. All men and women would learn two or three crafts, as well as basic farming skills, and the domestic arts of cooking, sewing, and other housework. The latter would be greatly simplified when 'the chief meals could be eaten in common'— and Morris's plans for housing included communal laundries and kitchens, with 'the great hall for dining in, and for social gathering, being the chief feature of it'. In the new society 'men (and women too, of course) would do their own work and take their pleasure in their own persons, and not vicariously . . . The family of blood-relationship would melt into that of the community and of humanity.'

On the other hand, Morris did not expect a mere mechanical equality between the sexes. In the present situation child-bearing made women inferior to men, 'since a certain time of their lives they must be dependent on them'. But he disagreed strongly with those Victorian feminists who saw their solution in the repudiation of motherhood. On the contrary, once economic dependence was removed he believed that motherhood would be again as 'highly honoured' as it had been in the earliest human society. So would the domestic arts. Thus in *News from Nowhere* and the prose romances, some women choose to be warriors, others are masons leading a building team, and many join in fieldwork, while conversely a man like old Hammond is 'a pretty good cook himself'. Morris also makes the rare choice of giving the deepest insights of the book to a woman, Ellen. Nevertheless, most women freely choose fulfilment in motherhood and keeping a home. 'Perhaps you think housekeeping an unimportant occupation, not deserving of respect? . . . Don't you know that it is a great pleasure to a clever woman to manage a house skilfully . . . ?' Elsewhere Morris writes: 'Of course we must claim absolute equality of condition between women and men, as between other groups, but it would be poor economy setting women to do men's work.' In many men, such sentiments might be dismissed as hypocritical, but not so in Morris: for he did himself take a personal pleasure in 'the useful art of cooking a dinner', and he had dedicated the major part of his own professional life to improving the detailed setting of the home. It was part of his faith that in the future 'pottery, furniture and firegrates', dress, and cutlery, should all be both art *and* daily life. To Morris, as Mackail put it, 'the man lived in the house almost as the soul lived in the body.'[58]

For children, by contrast, he anticipated a more drastic break might be needed in order to free them from the authoritarian 'tyrannising' characteristic of Victorian parents. His own observation had led him to believe that natural parents were often the people least qualified to educate a child. Economic security would provide the basis for a new kind of childhood, drawing as much from the wider society as the home. 'We hold that children are *persons*, not *property*, and so have a right to claim all the advantages which the community provides for every citizen'. Even in the present, he doubted whether the parental home was of great educational value. 'Children bring each other up,' he often observed. When he was walking through the Glasgow slums

he remarked on the exceeding cleverness, and often ingenious wit, displayed by children when in play together, especially in the poorer districts where they were freer from the tutelage of grown-ups, and had developed clan or community traditions of their own. 'But the faculty soon withers,' he added; 'the poor things become dull and vacant-minded once they grow out of childhood and lose the sap of the common stem. The natural well-springs of their imagination become soiled and run dry.'

The essential accuracy of Morris's insight has been confirmed by recent studies of the language and lore of school children, and the measured decline in intelligence of the average school child as it progresses through school even today. He was right to be 'depressed by the mechanical drill' of Board Schools. And his solution, a completely informal and voluntary education, provides a striking anticipation of not just 'progressive' education but even the 'de-schooling' schemes of the mid-twentieth century—although he would not have expected more than very limited success from attempting either within the existing social system. He believed there would be no 'necessity for using compulsion towards rational education'. Education would be a continuous opportunity, always available, never imposed. If children did not want to learn any particular subject, they need not: it was 'no use forcing people's tastes'. If they were forced to learn mathematics they would only forget it.[59]

In any case the balance of education would be very much altered. Children would teach themselves to read from books at home, but they would not be taught to write until they were adolescent. Languages would be learnt verbally through exchanges with foreign children. Although one may agree with the emphasis which Morris wished to place on spoken language, his disregard of the need for practice in writing is revealing of himself. But he went further than this, suggesting that there would be less attention given generally to book-learning. The only essential education would in fact be in physical skills:

All people should learn how to swim, and to ride, and to sail a boat on sea or river; such things are not arts, they are merely bodily exercises, and should become habitual in the race; and also one or two elementary arts of life, as carpentry or smithying; and most should know how to shoe a horse and shear a

sheep and reap a field and plough it. . . . Then again there are things like
cooking and baking, sewing, and the like, which can be taught to every sensible
person in a few hours, and which everybody ought to have at his fingers' ends.

In the summer, children would be encouraged to camp out in the belts
of woodland surrounding the towns, increasing their self-sufficiency.
Morris believed that with the revival of the physical crafts interest in
literary culture would decline, and he did not regret this. For those who
wished to take their knowledge further, schools, libraries, and sufficient
leisure would provide the opportunity. It was Morris's belief that this
would bring, through *lifelong* education, a much wider literary culture.
For himself, the two things he would most want a future society to
produce were 'good houses and good books'. He believed that 'all men
should be educated, and have their due share in the stored-up
knowledge of the world, so vastly greater now . . . , but so much more
unequally shared'. And this was inconceivable while education was 'a
system of cram begun on us when we are four years old and left off
sharply when we are 18'.[60]

When Morris predicted that the twentieth century 'may be called the
Century of Education', it was certainly not in the conventional sense of
the words; yet some of his hopes were to be realized in the spread of a
new teaching which built on children's innate creativity. Among its
pioneers were two teachers, both shaped by the arts and crafts
movement, who became influential school inspectors between the wars.
Marion Richardson began as a Dudley art teacher to give children word-
pictures as a starting point rather than real objects to copy, and
discovered in their work 'an original and inner quality. It haunted me.'
She was confirmed in her belief that her children's painting had 'a vital
something' by comparing it with adult work at the first London Post-
Impressionist Exhibition. She recognized that she could 'fire and free'
this special quality in children's art, 'but I could not teach it; and my
whole purpose was now directed to this end, as I set out to learn with
and from the children'. Later especially encouraged by Roger Fry,
Marion Richardson developed children's art not only in painting, but in
producing painted furniture and block-printed fabrics for local homes,
and later still in calligraphy. Robin Tanner, combining teaching with his
own etching and printmaking, carried a similar approach into what he
called the 'golden age of primary education' in the 1950s. Yet there was
still a formidable resistance among teachers to his belief in children's
creative abilities, and he recounts how when he showed his children's
prints and paintings to one conference he was 'howled down by angry
teachers' who could not be convinced it was not his own adult work. Of

42. The rediscovery of creativity in ordinary children: encouraged by Robin Tanner, Wiltshire children paint a mural of 'Summer' to their own design, early 1930s.

Morris, Tanner wrote 'that giant of a man was my hero'. Here certainly in no small way was a recovery of 'the great neglected power of creation', as Ashbee put it, in which Morris so centrally believed.[61]

The diffusion of education through life was to be situated within the general return to a simpler life advocated by Morris. He wanted neither asceticism nor luxury. Luxury bred equal discontent with elementary pleasures.

Luxury rather builds clubs in Pall Mall, and upholsters them as though for delicate invalid ladies, for the behoof of big whiskered men, that they may lounge there amidst such preposterous effeminacy that the very plushed-breeched flunkies that wait upon the loungers are better men then they are. . . . Free men, I am sure, must lead simple lives and have simple pleasures: and if we shudder away from that necessity now, it is because we are not free men, and have in consequence wrapped up our lives in such a complexity of dependence that we have grown feeble and helpless. But again, what is simplicity?

Do you think by any chance that I mean a row of yellow-brick, blue-slated houses, or a phalangstere like an improved Peabody lodging-house; and the dinner-bell ringing one into a row of white basins of broth with a piece of bread cut nice and square by each, with boiler-made tea and ill-boiled rice-pudding to follow? No; that's the philanthropist's ideal, not mine; and here I only note it to repudiate it, and to say, Vicarious life once more, and therefore no pleasure.

No, I say; find out what you yourselves find pleasant, and do it. You won't be alone in your desires; you will get plenty to help you in carrying them out, and you will develop social life in developing your own special tendencies. . . . First you must be free; and next you must learn to take pleasure in all the details of life: which, indeed, will be necessary to you, because, since you are free, you will have to do your own work. That is in direct opposite to civilization, which says, Avoid trouble, which you can do by making other people live your life for you. I say, Socialists ought to say, Take trouble, and turn your trouble into pleasure: that I shall always hold is the key to a happy life.[62]

This making of work a central pleasure of life was fundamental to Morris's new society, and he predicted that the problem 'of fitting people's work to their capacities and not, as now, their capacities to their work, would be the most important reversal of the present system of labour'. Since there would be no compulsory allocation of work in his society, basic services would have to be made attractive, or they would stop. 'Vicarious servanting, sewer-emptying, butchering, letter-carrying, boot-blacking, hair-dressing, and the rest of it, will have to come to an end: we shall either make all these occupations agreeable to ourselves in some mood or to some minds, who will take to them voluntarily, or we shall have to let them lapse altogether.' One might think that some of these occupations, such as butcher's and barber's work, could have become satisfying skilled crafts when freed of their low nineteenth-century service status. But the principle is clear: work which was inessential and unpleasant would cease, while work which was essential and irremediably disagreeable must be shared; and 'as far as possible it should be done by machines'.

Morris certainly did not believe that all machinery should be abolished. 'We should be the masters of our machines and not their slaves, as we are now. It is not this or that tangible steel or brass machine which we want to get rid of, but the great intangible machine of commercial tyranny.' In the future people would do 'some things by machinery which are now done by hand, and other things by hand which are now done by machinery'. If an industry which had been mechanized could 'be carried on more pleasantly as regards the worker, and more effectually as regards the goods, by using hand-work rather than machinery, they will certainly get rid of their machinery'. But he foresaw a great role for labour-saving machinery, and hoped that through the simplification of life, the reduction of demand and the development of machinery, it would be possible 'to reduce the work of the world to a minimum . . . till at last pretty nearly everything that is necessary to men will be made by machines. I don't see why it should not be done. I myself have boundless faith in their capacity. I believe machines can do everything—except make works of art.' Morris recalled 'a passage from one of the ancient Sicilian poets rejoicing in the fashioning of a water-mill, and exulting in labour being set free from the toil of the hand-quern in consequence; and that surely would be a type of a man's natural hope when foreseeing the invention of labour-saving machinery'.[63]

The work which remained would give such satisfaction that 'after a little, people would rather be anxious to seek work than to avoid it; that our working hours would be rather merry parties. . . . than the grumpy weariness it mostly is now'. This does not mean that such work would be unalloyed pleasure, any more than sex under socialism. 'Whatever pleasure there is in some work, there is certainly some pain in all work': fear in starting, fear in changing, tiredness. 'But a man at work, making something which he feels will exist because he is working at it and wills it, is exercising the energies of his mind and soul as well as his body. Memory and imagination help him.' This combination of physical exercise with creativity was the key to satisfaction, to fulfilment in self-realization. 'If we work thus we shall be men, and our days will be happy and eventful.'[64]

Morris did not envisage, in the future society, an abolition of the division of labour. The solution he saw was in terms rather of variety of work.

Most people would carry on more than one occupation, and probably much of the best craftsmanship would be mere leisure activity. The most exhausting and rough types of work, such as coal-mining, would certainly only be part-time occupations. Some kinds of outdoor rough work, such as farm labour or building work, would probably seem generally attractive. 'Surely almost everyone would wish to take some share in field or garden work besides his indoor occupation, even if it were no more than helping to get in the harvest or save the hay; and such occasions would become really the joyous and triumphant festivals which the poets dreamed of them as being.'[65]

At the same time the conditions of factory work would be transformed. Morris described the conditions of industrial work as he imagined them in 'A Factory as it Might Be'. It would be a well-designed building, set in fine gardens. There would be no litter, no water-pollution, no fumes or smoke. It would be a social centre in its own right, with its restaurant, children's nursery and school, and concert hall, and would contain some first-rate paintings and sculpture.

It would combine work with technical and intellectual education, music, and drama. The work would have the attraction of being essential, and there would be no adulteration allowed in the product. Extensive machinery would be used, so that (with the reduction in demand) it would be possible to reduce hours of work to less than four a day, and this would not be all machine-tending:

The machine-tending ought not to require a very long apprenticeship, therefore in no case should any one person be set to run up and down after a machine through all his working hours everyday, even so shortened as we have seen; now the attractive work of our factory, that which it was pleasant in itself to do, would be of the nature of art; therefore all slavery of work ceases under such a system, for whatever is burdensome about the factory would be taken turn and turn about, and so distributed would cease to be a burden, would in fact be a kind of rest from the more exciting or artistic work.

People living under such conditions, Morris predicted,

having manual skill, technical and general education, and leisure to use these advantages, are quite sure to develop a love of art, that is to say, a sense of beauty and an interest in life, which, in the long run must stimulate them to the desire for artistic creation, the satisfaction of which is of all the pleasures the greatest.

Mankind would 'regain their eyesight, which they have at present lost to a great extent. . . . People have largely ceased to take in mental impressions through the eyes; whereas in past times the eyes were the great feeders of the fancy and imagination.' There would be a new, living school of art, which would be an essential part of people's lives; 'something which they can no more do without than water or lighting'.[66]

The simplification of demand and diversifying of work would be accompanied by a redistribution of the population. The great conurbations would be largely broken up and the villages and country towns repopulated. In *News from Nowhere* the people had flocked back to the countryside after the revolution and 'flung themselves upon the freed land like a wild beast upon his prey'. The result was a population spread over the whole country; all houses well set in gardens and near open spaces; communal buildings like public palaces of art enriching both town and village; and the countryside revitalized 'by the thought and briskness of town-bred folk'. Morris did not like the countryside as he knew it, with its poverty, its servile, worn people, its patched houses, and crumbling walls. He wanted

neither the towns to be appendages of the country, nor the country of the town; I want the town to be impregnated with the beauty of the country, and the country with the intelligence and vivid life of the town. I want every homestead to be clean, orderly, and tidy; a lovely house surrounded by acres and acres of garden. On the other hand, I want the town to be clean, orderly, and tidy; in short, a garden with beautiful houses in it.[67]

Morris believed that these changes could lead to a settled, completely decentralized life without any government in the modern sense. 'It will be necessary for the unit of administration to be small enough for every citizen to feel himself responsible for its details, and be interested in them; that individual men cannot shuffle off the business of life on to the shoulders of an abstraction called the State.' He envisaged a loose federalism. 'Nations, as political entities, would cease to exist; civilization would mean the federalization of a variety of communities great and small.' At one end would be the township and the local guild, which would carry on their administration by direct assembly. Decisions would be taken by majority, but after ample time for discussion and reconsideration if they were controversial, and it would be usual for the *status quo* to prevail where there was no clear majority. There is in Morris's vision of stable, well-integrated, dispersed communities a distinct mark of his exchanges with Kropotkin, whom he knew after 1886. And Morris expected—as most anarchists and many socialists in his time—that the abolition of property would remove the need for civil law, while crime would be reduced to occasional personal violence, which could be largely controlled by local public opinion.[68]

At the other end would be the central council of the socialist world, whose primary function would be to prevent any community from abandoning the fundamental principles of socialism: 'a safeguard against the heredity of bad habits.' This council would also collect and distribute information on the 'wants of populations and the possibilities of supplying them'. There would also be conferences of economic specialists. But Morris did not anticipate any need for continuous change and development once the legacy of capitalist poverty had been overcome in the transitional stage of state socialism. He seems to have believed that true communism would result in a static natural balance of supply and demand: 'in a society of inequality, a society in which there are very rich people and very poor ones, the standard of usefulness is utterly confused. . . . But in a society of equality the demand for an article *would* be a standard of its usefulness in one way or another.' In short, he expected that 'gradually all public business would be so much simplified that it would come to little more than a correspondence'.[69]

The essential condition of this new, simplified civilization would be equality, not equality of opportunity, or equality of desire, but equality of condition. 'Of course I admit that it is [no] more possible that men should be equal in capacity or desires or in temperament than that they should be equal in stature or weight: but in fact if there were not this inequality in this sense I doubt if we could have equality of condition.' This equality of condition, Morris believed, was possible because of the essential similarity of men's needs. What would be the purpose of giving a man a special reward for special work?

Give him more wealth? Nay, what for? What can he do with more than he can use? He cannot eat three dinners a day, or sleep in four beds. Give him domination over other men? Nay, if he be more excellent than they are in any art, he must *influence* them for his good and theirs if they are worth anything; but if you make him their arbitrary master, he will govern them, but he will not influence them; he and they will be enemies, and harm each other mutually. One reward you can give him, that is, opportunity for developing his special capacity; but that you will do for everybody, and not the excellent only.[70]

How will you sail a ship in a socialist condition? How? Why with a captain and mates and sailing-master and engineer (if it be a steamer) and A.B.s and stokers and so on and so on. Only there will be no 1st, 2nd and 3rd class among the passengers: the sailors and stokers will be well fed and lodged as the captain or passengers; and the captain and the stoker will have the same pay.[71]

Here, rather than in the medieval trimmings of *News from Nowhere*, is the heart of Morris's socialist society. He knew from his own experience that any worthwhile work well done was equal to any other. He had in turn thrown himself into poetry, architecture, stained glass, furnishing, pattern design, book design, dyeing, weaving, and political agitation: work of very dissimilar social standing, but all of undoubted value to himself. And as in these fields the zest and integrity of his example was more important than any detail of his work or theory, so it is not so much the details but the spirit of his Utopia which matters.

Certainly the gathering pace of change since his time has made Morris's ideal of stable communities seem an unlikely future. Much of its setting has been irreparably damaged too. The great elms at Kelmscott are all gone, felled from disease; at Godstow a roaring motor-route slices the Thames water-meadows, which to Morris were the most beautiful he knew anywhere. Yet at the same time the issues which he raised have become central to the very survival of human life on this planet. On the one hand a newer richer capitalism of the west throws crumbs from its table in hopelessly inadequate aid to the Third World which it has itself driven towards collapse; on the other the legacy of a suffocated state socialism has left formerly or still communist countries searching desperately to rediscover individual initiative. Our need has never been more urgent for a social economy which can halt the remorseless destruction of the natural world, defuse the constant threat of ultimate war, and divert the energies of men and women from the endless drive for competitive wealth towards other forms of creativity and fulfilment. Victorians could place themselves within the long perspective of history, past and future. Today time is running out.

Morris did not want to stand in the way of technical progress; indeed, he was relying on it for the fulfilment of his vision. On the other hand he denied that progress could only be achieved in an authoritarian and unequal society. Nor did he believe that progress was worthwhile unless it brought satisfaction in the nature of every day life, whether at home or in the workplace. The aim of progress should not be more leisure, more gadgets, with everyday work remaining equally monotonous: for leisure to those who did not find satisfaction in their daily work would always be empty. The aim should be varied, pleasant, and as far as possible creative work for all men and women, even if the only means was a simpler way of living. He was confident that with a lighter burden of work, a higher standard of food and housing, and a general opportunity for education, all human beings were capable of a far higher development of their physical health and intelligence: capable of a responsibility, creative imagination and sensitivity sufficient for full democracy and equality. This is why Morris is still relevant today: for we shall be satisfied by nothing less.

NOTES

For full titles see Bibliographical Notes

PREFACE

   1. Mackail, ii. 63; *New Review*, Jan. 1891; *Works*, xxiii. 210.

CHAPTER I

   1. *Daily Chronicle,* 23 Apr. 1895.
   2. *Works* i. 319; xvi. 68.
   3. *Works* xii, p. 259; Blunt, *My Diaries*, i. 283.
   4. *Letters* ii. 227.
   5. Mackail, i. 29.
   6. Burne-Jones, *Memorials*, i. 84.
   7. It was rediscovered after 1900—*Works*, xxi. p. xxx.
   8. *Letters* i. 20–2.
   9. Fitzgerald, *Burne-Jones*, 38.
 10. May Morris, i. 68.
 11. Mackail, i. 106.
 12. W. M. Rossetti (ed.), *Ruskin: Rossetti: Preraphaelitism*, London, 1899, 193.
 13. Mackail, i. 121.
 14. C. Y. Lang, *The Swinburne Letters*, New Haven, Conn., 1959, i. 17–18.
 15. *Magazine of Art*, 1904, 167.
 16. *Swinburne Letters* i. 18.
 17. *Letters* ii. 228.
 18. Rossetti (ed.), *Ruskin: Rossetti: Preraphaelitism*, 219.
 19. *Spectator*, 27 Feb. 1858.
 20. W. Minto (ed.), *Autobiographical Notes of the Life of William Scott,* London, 1892, 61.
 21. Mackail, i. 159.
 22. E. T. Cook and A. Wedderburn (eds.), *The Works of John Ruskin*, London, 1904, x, 193, 201.
 23. Mackail, i. 164.
 24. Taylor-Webb letters, Victoria and Albert Museum; W. B. Rossetti (ed.), *Rossetti Papers*, London, 1903, 347; Harvey and Press, 41.
 25. Taylor-Webb letters.
 26. *Blackwood's Magazine*, July 1869.
 27. *Nation*, 22 Aug. 1867; *Athenæum*, 15 June 1867.
 28. *Quarterly Review*, Jan 1872.
 29. Burne-Jones, *Memorials*, ii. 264–5.
 30. *Pall Mall Budget*, 11 Dec. 1869.
 31. *London Quarterly Review*, Jan. 1870.
 32. *Saturday Review*, 30 May 1868.
 33. *Temple Bar*, Nov. 1869.
 34. *Athenæum*, 17 Dec. 1870.
 35. Philip Henderson, *William Morris*, London, 1952, 22.
 36. Mackail, i. 310, 210.
 37. P. Lubbock (ed.), *The Letters of Henry James*, London, 1920, i. 16–19.
 38. May Morris, i. 539.

39. *Works* xxiv. 362–3.
40. *Letters* i. 172.
41. Ibid. 216.
42. *William Allingham: a Diary*, 162.
43. Rossetti to Jane Morris, 30 July 1869, British Museum.
44. Ibid. 31 Jan. 1870.
45. Ibid. 4 Feb. 1870.
46. Ibid. 1 July 1878.
47. Marsh, 89, 107.
48. British Library, Additional Manuscript, 45, 298.
49. Sparling, *Morris*, 100.
50. *Cambridge Review*, 26 Nov. 1896.
51. Ibid.
52. *Letters* i. 100.
53. Mackail i. 240; *Letters*, i. 146.
54. *Works* viii. 169, 53, 19–20.
55. *Letters* ii. 229.
56. Mackail i. 334–5.
57. *John Bull*, 31 Dec. 1870.
58. Mackail i. 295.
59. *Contemporary Review*, Mar. 1934.
60. *Letters* i. 126.
61. Ibid. 292.
62. *Letters* ii. 68, 70.
63. *Letters* i. 273, 275.
64. Ibid. 273.
65. Ibid. 417.
66. Ibid. 115.
67. Ibid. 394.
68. Shirley Nicholson, *A Victorian Household: Based on the Diaries of Marion Sambourne*, London, 1989, 154; Mackail, i. 231.
69. Mackail i. 239.
70. Glasier, *Morris*, 46.
71. *Letters* i. 203; *Works*, xvi. 287.
72. Mackail, i. 107.
73. Lethaby, *Webb*, 94.
74. *Letters* i. 218.
75. *Letters* i. 352.
76. Blunt, *My Diaries*, i. 283.
77. *Letters* ii. 14–15.
78. Ibid. 122.
79. May Morris, i. 201.
80. *Letters* ii. 173–4.
81. May Morris, ii. 404.
82. *Standard*, 5 Oct. 1896.
83. *Letters* ii, 397.
84. Ibid. 340.
85. Boos, *William Morris's Socialist Diary*.
86. May Morris, ii. 315.
87. Leatham, *Morris*, 98–9.
88. *Works* xvi. p. xvii.

89. *Letters* ii. 283–4.
90. Mackail, ii. 255.
91. Marsh, 171; Cockerell's diary, quoted in Peterson, *Ideal Book*, p. xi.
92. Faulkner, *Jane Morris to Blunt*, 30, 44, 31.
93. Ibid. 31–3, 53, 69.
94. Blunt, *My Diaries*, i. 296; *Journal of the William Morris Society*, 3 (1987), 27.
95. E. P. Thompson, 823.
96. *Works* xvi. 230.
97. Burne-Jones, *Memorials*, ii. 277.
98. Henderson, *Letters*, 385; Marshall, 305.
99. *Clarion*, 10 Oct. 1896.
100. *Saturday Review*, 10 Oct. 1896.

CHAPTER 2
1. *Works* xxii. 359, 365, 119–20.
2. Pevsner, *Pioneers*, 28, 39 ff.
3. Lethaby, *Webb*, 15.
4. Ibid. 24, 130.
5. *Works* i. 351.
6. Henderson, *Letters*, 323.
7. Ibid. 346.
8. May Morris, i. 277.
9. Ibid. 270–6; Le Mire, 85, 90.
10. *Works* xxii. 208.
11. *Letters* i. 486–7.
12. *Works* xxii. 315–18; Le Mire, 68–9.
13. *Works* xxii. 234, 322; xxiii. 147.
14. *Works* xxii. 328–9.
15. Ibid. 364.
16. Ibid. 329, 414; *Letters* ii. 839; Le Mire, 85.
17. *Works*, xxii. 315, 327; Le Mire, 80.
18. Warington Taylor to E. R. Robson, 28, Fitzwilliam Museum.
19. *Works* xxii. 329.
20. *Letters* ii, 623.
21. J. B. Glasier, *William Morris &c.*, London, 1921, 97.
22. Le Mire, 86; May Morris i. 283.
23. *Works* xxii. 429.
24. *Art Journal Easter Annual*, 1899, 1.
25. May Morris, i. 271; *Works* xxii. 92.
26. *Works* xxii. 392.
27. Lethaby, *Webb*, 119–20, 136.
28. G. G. Scott, *On the Conservation of Architectural Monuments and Remains*, London, 1864.
29. Henderson, *Letters*, 314.
30. May Morris, i. 123.
31. Ibid. 110, 154.
32. May Morris, i. 146.
33. *Works* xxii. 232.
34. *Works* xxii. 300.
35. S.P.A.B. report, 1892.
36. *Letters* i. 478.
37. *Letters* i. 362; May Morris, i. 123–4.
38. *Letters* ii. 79.
39. S.P.A.B. report, 1885.
40. *Letters* i. 376.

41. *Letters* ii, 438.
42. *Works* xxii. 170–3.
43. *Works* xxii. 72–3.
44. Le Mire, 51.
45. *Justice*, 19 July 1884; May Morris, ii. 127.
46. *Works* xxiii. 22.
47. *Justice*, 12 Apr. 1884.
48. *Works* xxiii. 209.
49. *Works* xxii. 114.
50. May Morris, ii. 474.
51. Naylor, *Bauhaus*, 9, 29.

CHAPTER 3

1. Aslin, *19th C. English Furniture*, 55.
2. Mackail, i. 113.
3. These tiles are not, as is generally thought, contemporary with the decoration, but were made for Bodley's fireplace in 1861. Only the coving was added in 1875. See *Ecclesiologist* 1864, 379; and R. Willis and J. W. Clark, *Architectural History of the University of Cambridge*, Cambridge, 1886, ii. 48. Nor is there any documentary evidence to support the attribution of these Cambridge stencil schemes to Morris, although they were carried out by the builder Leach with whom he frequently worked; they may have been designed directly by Scott or Bodley as architects (Duncan Robinson and Stephen Wildman, *Morris and Company in Cambridge*, Cambridge, 1980).
4. Burne-Jones, *Memorials*, i. 147.
5. *Works* xxii. 261–2.
6. *Ecclesiologist*, June 1854.
7. Gleeson White, *Studio*, Nov. 1897; *Art Journal*, May 1893.
8. *Works* xxii. 115.
9. Aslin, *19th C. English Furniture*, 58.
10. Crawford, *Ashbee*, 20, 28.
11. Halsey Ricardo in Gaunt and Clayton-Stamm, 17.
12. Leach, *Beyond East and West*, 66, 148–9.
13. Jewson, *By Chance I Did Rove*, 26–9; *Works*, xxii. 261–2.
14. F. M. Hueffer, *Ancient Lights*, London, 1911, lists the furniture designed for the firm by Brown, but without descriptions; 'Ford Madox Brown's Furniture', *Artist*, 1898, 44, and E. M. Tait, 'Madox Brown's Furniture Designs', *Furnisher*, 1900–1, 61, are the chief evidence. The stained glass panel by Brown of King Mark killing Tristram, at Bradford Art Gallery, designed in 1862, shows an extremely interesting settee of light green turned wood, which tends to support Tait's claims.
15. Walter Crane, *Daily News*, 20 Oct. 1896.
16. Edward Carpenter, *My Days and Dreams*, London, 1916, 217; W. B. Yeats, *Fortnightly Review*, Mar. 1903.
17. *Works* xxii. 48, 112–13.
18. Ibid. 77.

CHAPTERS 4 AND 5

1. *Works* xxii. 206–34.
2. *Works* xxiii. 150.
3. *Works* xxii. 180.
4. *Observer*, 6 Nov. 1949.

5. *Commonweal*, 6 Aug. 1887.
6. May Morris, ii. 134.
7. *Clarion*, 19 Nov. 1892, interview with Morris; part of the same statement is printed as a letter to Emma Lazarus, *Century Magazine*, July 1886.
8. *Works*, xxii. 169.
9. *Works*, xxii. 28.
10. *Works*, xxii. 177–9.
11. May Morris, i. 213–15.
12. Ibid. 251.
13. Ibid. 220.
14. *Works* xxii. 195.
15. Ibid. 107; Le Mire, 64.
16. *Works* xxii. 199.
17. Ibid. 200.
18. Ibid. 178, Warington Taylor to E. R. Robson, 3, Fitzwilliam Museum.
19. Annie Hall Thomas, *Maud Mohun*, 1872, quoted by Floud, *Penrose Annual*, 1960.
20. *Spectator*, 10 Aug. 1878.
21. Morris Dye Book, Victoria and Albert Museum, on loan from Mrs Dearle.
22. May Morris, i. 264.
23. *Letters* i. 345; Mackail, i. 316.
24. *Letters* i. 345–6.
25. Ibid. 266, 269.
26. Ibid. 272–3.
27. Ibid. 316.
28. Ibid. 313.
29. Ibid. 280.
30. Ibid. 334–5.
31. Ibid. 321, 337.
32. Ibid. 363.
33. Ibid. 337.
34. Ibid. 358.
35. Ibid. 364.
36. *Commonweal*, 6 Aug. 1887.
37. *Letters* i. 415.
38. Ibid. 365.
39. *Spectator*, 24 Nov. 1883.
40. May Morris; *Letters* i. 410.
41. Alan Johnson and Kevin Moore, *The Tapestry Makers: Life and Work at Lee's Tapestry Works, Birkenhead*, Docklands History Project, University of Liverpool, 1987, gives an exceptionally vivid account of conditions from workers' own memories; cf. Parry, *Textiles of The Arts and Crafts*, 133. The factory finally closed in 1970.
42. *Works* xxii. 194.
43. May Morris, i. 245.
44. Ibid.
45. Christopher Dresser, *Art of Decorative Design*, London, 1862, 143.
46. May Morris, i. 246.
47. *Works* xxii. 282.
48. Ibid. 192.
49. *Letters* i. 358.
50. May Morris, i. 249.

CHAPTER 6

1. Cartoons exist of all stages in the design. Although later cartoons only occasionally even suggest leading or tones, in the 1860s indications for colour, borders, patterns, lettering, and leading are frequent. They are not, however, always by the original artist. On one cartoon for Selsley, now at Birmingham, Rossetti scribbled to Morris, 'If you have to reduce it do it in general and then I'll draw it again. It strikes me now its done there's no space left for lead lines is there? Don't spoil this one as I'll make some use of it if you find it too big.' The cartoons must often have been worked up; and the meticulous scale drawings which exist for a few windows are presumably re-drawings by the firm's draughtsmen. Certainly Burne-Jones left the firm to produce 'prettified drawings' for clients from his designs. This limited responsibility of the original artist probably explains why Burne-Jones, as the continual scoffing in his account books with the firm suggests, regarded glass cartoons as something of a waste of his talent. In his list of works he notes only a few early and late windows made without Morris's help: for the rest 'many cartoons for windows, all these years, too many to number, and few of any importance'. (Burne-Jones papers, Fitzwilliam Museum.)

2. Fairfax Murray (1849–1919), an exceptionally able draughtsman who had started life in an engineer's office. He worked in Italy for Ruskin, who called him 'a heaven-born copyist', and his many copies of work by Rossetti and Burne-Jones are very difficult to distinguish from the originals. Became an Italian art expert, married an Italian and gradually drifted into the life of a dealer; important gifts to the Fitzwilliam Museum and Birmingham City Art Gallery.

3. Sewter, *Stained Glass*, 22.

4. *Art Journal*, Mar. 1905.

5. e.g. Dunton, Springthorpe, Yazor, and Ecclesfield in the gazetteer.

6. This window is attributed to Morris in *The Buildings of England, Somerset,* although the minute detail of parts of the drawing and the general use of mauve, dark gold, and various browns are unlike any Morris window. It is now known to have been designed by Burges and made by Saunders (J. M. Crook, *William Burges and the High Victorian Dream,* 1984, 225; Harrison, 55).

7. *Studio*, Feb. 1898, Jan. 1900.

CHAPTER 7

1. G. B. Hill (ed.), *Letters of Dante Gabriel Rossetti to Willaim Allingham,* London, 1897, 193; Dunlap, 142 and Plate 5.

2. *Studio* Winter Number 1896, 50.

3. Mackail, i. 116.

4. De Ricci and Wilson, *Census of Manuscripts*, 999, 1451, records the previous owner as Quaritch (1870) and Molini (1876), but others may be unrecorded.

5. Catalogue of Cockerell sale, Sotheby's, 10 Dec. 1956, quoted by Fairbank.

6. *Edward Johnston,* 97; Marion Richardson, *Art and the Child,* London, 1948, 55.

7. T. J. Cobden-Sanderson, *Journals,* London, 1926, 211–12; Callen, *Angel in the Studio,* 187–9.

8. Mackail, i. 189–90.

9. Franklin, *Printing and the Mind of Morris,* 16, 27.

10. 'Autobiographical Notes', William Morris Museum, Walthamstow (Lambourne, *Utopian Craftsmen,* 5).

11. May Morris, i. 311–12, 316.

12. Interviews, *Daily Chronicle,* 1893 and *Pall Mall Gazette,* 1891, reprinted in Peterson, *Ideal Book,* 92, 95.

13. *Saturday Review,* 26 Jan. 1889.

14. Mackail, ii. 215.
15. Cockerell, *Note*, i.
16. May Morris, i. 313.
17. Cockerell, *Note*, 3; May Morris, i. 252.
18. Sparling, *Morris*, 36.
19. May Morris, i. 317.
20. Blunt, *Cockerell*, 84; Susan Thompson, p. xiii.

CHAPTER 8

1. *Letters* i. 347.
2. A. Compton-Rickett, *William Morris: a Study in Personality*, London 1913, 33.
3. *Letters* ii, 589.
4. Ibid. 119.
5. Mackail, ii. 310.
6. E. P. Thompson, 878.
7. *Letters* ii, 517.
8. E. P. Thompson, 879.
9. *Letters* ii, 119; *Daily Chronicle*, 6 Oct. 1896.
10. Mackail, ii. 268.
11. *Letters* ii, 515.
12. Ibid. 517.
13. *Commonweal*, 18 Feb. 1888.
14. S. C. Cockerell, *A Note by William Morris &c.*, London, 1898, 28.
15. *Letters* ii, 755.
16. May Morris, i. 304–5.
17. *Commonweal*, 25 Aug. and 15 Dec. 1888.
18. *Works* xxii. pp. xvii–xxix.
19. E. P. Thompson, 881.
20. *Commonweal*, 22 June 1889.
21. *Works* xxii. 157.
22. *Letters* ii, 514–7; *Commonweal*, 12 June 1886.
23. E. P. Thompson, 878.

CHAPTER 9

1. *Letters* i. 419–20; ii. 215.
2. *Works* xxii, 26.
3. *Works* vii. 11–17.
4. W. B. Yeats, *Four Years*, Dundrum, 1921, 30.
5. W. B. Yeats, *Fortnightly Review*, Mar. 1903.
6. *Letters* ii, 836; Henderson, *Letters* 371.
7. *Athenæum,* 14 Sept. 1889; *Spectator*, 8 Feb. 1890.
8. *Speaker*, 10 Oct. 1896.
9. *Saturday Review*, 10 Oct. 1896.
10. Lucas, 278. The Ballantyne–Pan paperback editions of the prose romances were published in 1969–73.

CHAPTER 10

1. May Morris, i. 557.
2. *Works* vii. 436.

3. G. B. Hill (ed.), *Letters of Dante Gabriel Rossetti to William Allingham,* London, 1897, 201; *Athenæum,* 3 Apr. 1858; *Fortnightly Review,* 1 July 1867.

4. Mackail, i. 46.

5. *Works* i. 3–5.

6. Ibid. 80, 120.

7. Ibid. 107.

8. *Letters* i. 11.

10. *Works,* i. xxiii, 32.

11. Scott, *Primitiae,* 199–200.

12. *Works* i. 331–2.

13. Burne-Jones, *Memorials,* i. 297.

14. *Works* iii. 1; vi. 333.

15. *Works* iii. 3.

16. *Works* xxiii. 280.

17. Marshall, 75; Silver, 56; Hodgson, 62.

18. *Works* iii. 149.

19. Ibid. 11.

20. *Works* iv. 160.

21. Ibid. 85.

22. Ibid. 247.

23. *Works* vi. 65.

24. *Quarterly Review,* Jan. 1872; *Letters* i. 98 .

25. Ibid. i. 100.

26. *Works,* iii. 130.

27. C. Y. Lang, *The Swinburne Letters,* New Haven, Conn., 1959, ii. 68.

28. *Daily Chronicle,* 9 Oct. 1893; Mackail, i. 186.

29. *Letters* i. 155.

30. *Works* ix. 75.

31. Ibid. 5.

32. *Works* vi. 42.

33. *Works* vii. 286.

34. *Letters* i. 99.

35. Noyes, *Morris,* 118.

36. *Works* xii. 53.

37. May Morris, i. 475.

38. Hoare, *Morris and Yeats,* 68.

39. *Works* xii. 4.

40. *Works* xii. 202–5.

41. *Works* xii. 235.

42. *Athenæum,* 9 Dec. 1876.

43. May Morris, ii. p. xxxvii.

44. *Works* xxiv. 382–3.

45. *Works* xxiv. 369–70.

CHAPTER II

1. *Letters* i. 228.

2. Ibid. 28; Le Mire, 184–5.

3. *Letters* ii. 229.

4. *Letters* i. 331.

5. Henderson, *Letters,* 388–9; Mackail, i. 350.

6. May Morris, ii. 604.

7. *The Times*, 17 Jan. 1878.

8. *Letters* i. 435.

9. Ibid. 444, 450.

10. Ibid. 591.

11. J. L. Garvin and J. Amery, *The Life of Joseph Chamberlain,* London, 1932–51, i. 146.

12. C. D. H. Howard, *English Historical Review*, 1950.

13. A. L. Thorold, *The Life of Henry Labouchere,* London, 1913, 246.

14. Ibid. 250, 278.

15. Mackail, ii. 93.

16. *Letters* ii. 202.

17. Mackail, ii. 96.

18. *Letters* ii. 194.

19. Mackail, ii. 97; Meier, 305–314; *Works* xxiii. 278; Harvey and Press, 44.

20. *Works* xxiii. 162.

21. *Letters* ii. 200, 202, 222–3, 238; May Morris, ii 62.

22. *Letters* ii. 219; May Morris, ii. 152.

23. *Justice*, 9 Aug. 1884.

24. May Morris, ii. 590.

25. *Justice*, 12 July, 6 Sept. 1884.

26. *Letters* ii. 305, 341; *Works* xxiii. 208.

27. *Letters*, ii. 295.

28. *Letters* ii, 369.

29. Tom Mann, *Memoirs*, London, 1932, 57.

30. Hammersmith Socialist League minutes, 7 Jan. 1885.

31. Mann, *Memoirs*, 45–6.

32. Ibid. and *Commonweal*, July. Aug. and Sept. 1885.

33. Ibid. 1 May 1886 and Oct. 1885; Faulkner, *Jane Morris to Blunt*, 13.

34. *Commonweal*, July 1885.

35. Ibid. Jan. 1886; Kapp, ii. 91.

36. *Letters* ii. 255, 545, 547.

37. E. P. Thompson, 490; *Letters* ii, 438.

38. *Commonweal,* Mar. 1886.

39. Le Mire, 128; *Commonweal*, 26 Feb. 1887; Arnot (ed.), *Unpublished Letters*, 8.

40. E. P. Thompson, 578.

41. Mackail, ii. 193.

42. *Commonweal*, 19 Nov. 1887 and 28 Jan. 1888.

43. Kapp, ii. 230; *Letters* ii, 368.

44. *Commonweal*, 5 May 1888; Glasier, *Morris*, 202.

45. Mackail, ii. 238.

46. *Letters* ii, 791.

47. Henderson, *Letters*, 307.

48. *Commonweal*, 24 Aug. 1889.

49. Ibid. 3 May, 22 Mar., 7 June 1890.

50. Henderson, *Letters*, 349.

51. May Morris, ii. 350.

52. *Works* xxiii. 264–5, 267–9.

53. *Commonweal*, 25 Jan. 1890, 28 Sept. 1889.

54. *Letters* ii, 438.

55. *Justice*, 1 Mar. 1884.

56. *Works* xxiii. 213.

57. *Letters* ii, 646–8.
58. E. P. Thompson, 521–3.
59. J. Drinkwater, H. Jackson, and H. Laski, *Speeches in Commemoration of William Morris*, London, 1934.
60. Gould, *Early Green Politics*, 15.
61. Mackail, ii. 347.

CHAPTERS 12 AND 13

 1. E. P. Thompson, 836; postscript, 1977 edition, 784.
 2. Swenarton, *Artisans and Architects*, 67; Silver, *Romance*, 159.
 3. *Commonweal*, Apr. and May 1885; *Works* xxii. 4, xxiii. 203.
 4. *Commonweal*, 15 May 1886, 19 July 1890.
 5. *Commonweal*, 26 and 19 July 1890.
 6. *Commonweal*, 15 May 1886, 16 Aug. 1890;. E. P. Thompson, 830.
 7. *Works* xxii. 163; *Commonweal*, 9 Aug. 1890.
 8. *Works* xxii. 162–3, 304; *Commonweal*, 2 Aug. 1890.
 9. *Justice*, 15 Mar. 1884; *Works*, xxiii. 176, *Commonweal*, May 1885.
10. *Works* xxiii. 62; *Commonweal*, 9 Aug. 1890.
11. *Commonweal*, 29 May 1886, 9 Aug. 1890; *Works*, xxii. 160.
12. *Commonweal*, 5 and 12 June, 3 July 1886.
13. *Commonweal*, 3 July 1886.
14. *Commonweal*, 31 July, 11 Sept. 1886.
15. *Commonweal*, 14 Aug. 1886, 28 May 1887.
16. *Works* xxiii. 71–2; *Commonweal*, 28 Aug. 1886.
17. *Commonweal*, 30 Oct. 1886.
18. *Commonweal*, 30 Oct. 1886, 5 Feb. 1887.
19. *Letters* ii. 305; May Morris, i. 292–4; *Works*, xxii. 141–2.
20. *Letters* ii. 729.
21. E. P. Thompson, 891–8; Meier, 305ff., 347; British Museum Additional Manuscripts 45335.
22. *Commonweal*, 12 Mar. 1887.
23. *Commonweal*, 26 Mar., 30 Apr. 1887.
24. Ibid.; May Morris, ii. 160; *Commonweal*, 23 Feb. 1889.
25. *Commonweal*, 30 Apr. 1887.
26. *Commonweal*, 18 June 1887.
27. *Commonweal*, 6 Aug. 1887.
28. *Commonweal*, 23 July 1887.
29. *Commonweal*, 6 Aug. 1887; *Leeds Mercury*, Mar. 1890, quoted by E. P. Thompson, 633.
30. *Works* xxiii. 172, 186–7.
31. *Works* xxiii. 105, 158–9, 9; E. P. Thompson, 291–2.
32. *Works* xxiii. 240, 244.
33. Le Mire, 120; *Commonweal*, 25 June 1887.
34. British Museum Add. MSS. 50541(5); *Works*, xxiii. 94, and xvi. 56–9; *Letters* II, 443; *Commonweal*, July and Aug. 1885, 28 May 1887; Edward Carpenter, *Love's Coming of Age*, London, 1896, 36, 43; Edward and Eleanor Marx Aveling, *The Woman Question*, 1886.
35. *Works* xxiii. 6–9; Le Mire, 122; *Letters* ii. 340.
36. *Letters* ii. 202; *Works* xxii. 233.
37. *Works* xxii. 206–8; May Morris, i. 129, 307, ii. 392.
38. *Justice*, 15 Mar. 1884; *Commonweal*, Apr. 1885; May Morris, i. 383, 413, 408.
39. May Morris, i. 198, 152; Glasier, *Morris*, 89, 198.

40. *Commonweal*, Apr. 1885, 12 Apr. 1890; May Morris, ii. 388, 304; *Works*, xxii. 164.
41. *Clarion*, 19 Nov. 1892; May Morris, ii. 469, 478, 392.
42. *Letters* ii. 173; Henderson, *Letters*, 356.
43. *Commonweal*, 28 Sept. 1889; *Works* xxiii. 3; *Letters* ii, 307; E. P. Thompson, 684.
44. *Works* xxiii. 74; *Commonweal*, 17 Mar. 1888.
45. E. P. Thompson, 310.
46. *Works* xvi. 3.
47. *Works* xxiii. 232; *Letters* ii. 305.
48. *Commonweal*, 17 May and 25 Jan. 1890.
49. *Works* xxiii. 264–5.
50. *Works* xxiii. 267.
51. *Commonweal*, 18 May 1889; *Letters* ii. 306.
52. May Morris, ii. 456–7; Le Mire, 217; *Justice*, 26 Apr. 1884.
53. *Commonweal*, 18 Feb. 1888.
54. May Morris, ii. 457; *Works* xxiii. 17.
55. *Works* xxiii. 254; *Commonweal*, 18 May and 17 Aug. 1889.
56. *Commonweal*, 8 Mar. 1890; *Letters* ii, 777; Allingham, *A Diary*, 316; Glasier, *Morris*, 172.
57. E. P. Thompson, 817–19, *Works* xvi. 56–9.
58. *Works* xvi. 56–9; xxiii. 112, 199; *Letters* ii, 545; *Commonweal*, 28 May 1887; May Morris, ii. 128, 417, 462–8; Mackail, ii. 63.
59. *Works* vi. xiv; xvi. 30, 64; Glasier, *Morrris*, 108; May Morris, ii. 498; *Letters* ii, 545.
60. May Morris, ii. 462; *Works* xvi. 27–31; xxii. 63; *Commonweal*, 18 Feb. 1888; Le Mire, 156.
61. William Morris, *Some Thoughts on the Ornamental Manuscripts of the Middle Ages*, New York, 1934, 1; Marion Richardson, *Art and the Child*, London, 1948, 12–14; Robin Tanner, *Double Harness: an Autobiography*, London, 1987, 51, 100–1, 155; Crawford, *Ashbee*, 421.
62. May Morris, ii. 458–9.
63. *Commonweal*, June 1885; May Morris, ii. 460; *Works* xxii. 352, 166; xxiii. 24, 179; Le Mire, 155.
64. *Works* xxiii. 21, 99.
65. *Commonweal*, June 1885.
66. May Morris, ii. 130–9, 463; *Works* xxii. 422.
67. *Works* xvi. 71–2; Mackail, ii. 305–6.
68. *Commonweal*, 22 June 1889; *Letters*, 287.
69. *Letters* ii, 770–1; *Socialism, Its Growth and Outcome*, 291; *Works* xxiii. 272.
70. May Morris, ii. 199–200; *Works* xxiii. 234.
71. *Works* xxiii. 275.

BIBLIOGRAPHICAL NOTES

This is not intended to be a comprehensive Morris bibliography, but a summary of the main sources used in this book and the best directions for further reading. It is divided into chapters, but these separate lists need to be preceded by a few general sources.

First, the majority of Morris's writings are contained in *The Collected Works of William Morris*, 24 vols., London 1910–15, edited by May Morris (this is referred to as *Works*). Some important additional poetry and lectures were collected in May Morris, *William Morris, Artist, Writer, Socialist*, Oxford, 1936 (May Morris); in Florence Boos, *The Juvenilia of William Morris*, New York, 1983, and *William Morris's Socialist Diary*, London, 1985; and in E. D. Le Mire, *The Unpublished Lectures of William Morris*, Detroit, 1969. Morris's political articles in *Justice* (1884) and *Commonweal* (1885–90) have not been reprinted as a whole, although a revised edition of the series 'Socialism from the Root Up' was published as William Morris and E. B. Bax, *Socialism its Growth and Outcome*, London, 1893, and many of the others are extensively quoted in May Morris and in E. P. Thompson (see below). A complete and authoritative edition of Morris's poetry, edited by Florence Boos, is planned by the University of Virginia Press.

The complete correspondence of Morris is being edited by Norman Kelvin as *The Collected Letters of William Morris*, 3 vols., Princeton, NJ, 1984– . Volume 3 is yet to come, so for later years the principal source remains Philip Henderson (ed.), *The Letters of William Morris to his Family and Friends*, London, 1950 (Henderson, *Letters*). This must be supplemented by R. P. Arnot (ed.), *Unpublished Letters of William Morris*, Labour Monthly pamphlet, London, 1952; and the correspondence and quotations in E. P. Thompson and in Philip Henderson, *William Morris, His Life, Work and Friends*, London, 1967. The best selections of Morris's writing are G. D. H. Cole (ed.), *William Morris*, London, 1948 and Asa Briggs (ed.), *William Morris: Selected Writings and Designs* (Penguin Books), London, 1962.

The principal biography remains J. W. Mackail, *The Life of William Morris*, 2 vols., London, 1899 (Mackail). The outstanding subsequent biography is E. P. Thompson, *William Morris, Romantic to Revolutionary*, London, 1955 (and 1977) (E. P. Thompson), not only a definitive political study but an important reinterpretation of Morris's personal and literary life. Of more recent personal reassessments drawing on new material the best is Jack Lindsay, *William Morris, His Life and Work*, London, 1975. There has been no comparable assessment of Morris as an artist since Aymer Vallance, *William Morris, His Art, His Writing and his Public Life*, London, 1898 (Vallance), but a more up-to-date view is provided in Ray Watkinson, *William Morris as Designer* (Studio Vista), London, and a splendid visual survey in Gillian Naylor, *William Morris by Himself*, London, 1988. The best current brief introduction to Morris as a whole is Peter Stansky, *William Morris*, Oxford, 1983.

Regular bibliographies of writing on Morris are printed in the *Journal of the William Morris Society*. Two of the various 1984 exhibition catalogues deserve special mention: Joanna Banham and Jennifer Harris, *William Morris and the Middle Ages*, Manchester, 1984; and Sandy Nairne, *William Morris Today*, Institute of Contemporary Arts, London, 1984.

CHAPTER I

Principal sources are *Works*; *Letters*; May Morris; Mackail; E. P. Thompson; Lindsay. Few of the innumerable Morris biographies add much to these, except, among the earlier generation, H. B. Forman, *The Books of William Morris*, London, 1897; the contemporary notes of H. Allingham and D. Radford (ed.), *William Allingham: A Diary*, London, 1907, of A. M. W. Stirling (ed.), *The Richmond Papers*, London, 1926, of W. S. Blunt, *My Diaries*, i. London, 1919, of Viola Meynell (ed.), *Friends of a Lifetime: letters to Sir Sydney Cockerell*, London, 1940, and of the obituary by Theodore Watts-Dunton in the *Athenæum*, 10 October 1896; and the reminiscences of three socialists, J. Bruce Glasier, *William Morris and the Early Days of the Socialist Movement*, London, 1921; James Leatham, *William Morris, Master of Many Crafts*, Turriff, 1934; and H. H. Sparling, *The Kelmscott Press and William Morris, Master-craftsman*, London, 1924.

The most significant reinterpretations of Morris's life in recent years have been stimulated especially by the publication of the letters between Jane Morris and Rossetti and Blunt: John Bryson, *Dante Gabriel Rossetti and Jane Morris: their correspondence*, Oxford, 1976, and Peter Faulkner, *Jane Morris to Wilfrid Scawen Blunt*, London, 1981 (superseding his earlier summary, *William Scawen Blunt and the Morrises*, Exeter, 1981). Roderick Marshall, *William Morris and his Earthly Paradises*, Tisbury, 1979, is an imaginative interpretation of Morris's emotional life through his poetry, tinged with Indian mysticism. Much more solid reinterpretations are offered in recent work on Morris's relationship with women by Linda Richardson, 'William Morris and women: Experience and Representation', Oxford D. Phil. thesis, and Florence Boos, 'An (Almost-) Egalitarian Sage: William Morris's Later Writings and the "Woman Question" ', in T. Morgan (ed.), *Discourse, Gender and Power: Sage Writing and the Feminine*, New Brunswick, NJ—both forthcoming. Equally important is the outstanding Morris family biography, Jan Marsh, *Jane and May Morris: a Biographical Story 1839–1938*, London, 1986.

The re-evaluation of Morris as a designer was begun with the special contribution of Peter Floud (see Chapters 3 to 5), but his rediscovery as an entrepreneur belongs appropriately to the 1980s: Charles Harvey and Jon Press, 'William Morris and the Marketing of Art', *Business History*, 28 (1986), 36–54, and Press and Harvey, 'William Morris, Warington Taylor and the Firm, 1865–1875', *Journal of the William Morris Society*, 7 (1986), 41–4.

The most important biographies of Morris's friends are W. R. Lethaby, *Philip*

Webb and his Work, London, 1935; Georgiana Burne-Jones, *Memorials of Edward Burne-Jones*, London, 1904; Malcolm Bell, *Sir Edward Burne-Jones: a Record and Review*, London, 1898; Penelope Fitzgerald, *Edward Burne-Jones, a Biography*, London, 1975; H. C. Marillier, *Dante Gabriel Rossetti: an Illustrated Memorial of his Art and Life*, London, 1899; H. R. Angeli, *Dante Gabriel Rossetti, his Friends and his Enemies*, London, 1949; and O. Doughty, *A Victorian Romantic: Dante Gabriel Rossetti*, London, 1949. The group are delightfully depicted in H. M. Beerbohm, *Rossetti and his Circle*, London, 1922. See also Derek Hudson, *Munby, Man of Two Worlds*, London, 1972; Wilfrid Scawen Blunt, *Cockerell*, London, 1964; and for Fairfax Murray, W. S. Spanton, *An Art Student and his Teachers in the Sixties*, London, 1927. For a wider background to Morris's personality, see W. E. Houghton, *The Victorian Frame of Mind*, New Haven, Conn., 1957.

The unpublished sources used in this chapter include correspondence between Warington Taylor and Philip Webb at the Victoria and Albert Museum; and a letter from Miss Effie Morris on the Morris family and various papers relating to Frederick Leach at the William Morris Gallery.

CHAPTER 2

Principal sources are *Works*, xxii and xxiii; May Morris; Le Mire; *Letters*; W. R. Lethaby, *Philip Webb and his Work*, London, 1935; annual reports of the Society for the Protection of Ancient Buildings; N. Pevsner, 'Architecture and William Morris', *R.I.B.A. Journal*, March 1957, and *Pioneers of Modern Design*, revised edition, London, 1960; Paul Thompson, *William Butterfield*, London, 1971.

The best books on Victorian architecture generally are H. R. Hitchcock, *Architecture: Nineteenth and Twentieth Centuries*, London, 1958, and *Early Victorian Architecture in Britain*, London, 1954; H. S. Goodhart-Rendel, *English Architecture since the Regency*, London 1953; Peter Ferriday (ed.), *Victorian Architecture*, London, 1963; Basil Clarke, *Church Builders of the Nineteenth Century*, London, 1938; and J. M. Richards, *The Functional Tradition in Early Industrial Buildings*, London, 1958. On Ruskin and Morris: Michael Brooks, *John Ruskin and Victorian Architecture*, London, 1989, ch. xii. On Morris's subsequent influence on architecture, especially Mark Swenarton, *Artisans and Architects: the Ruskinian Tradition in Architectural Thought*, London, 1989; Godfrey Rubens, *William Richard Lethaby: His Life and Work, 1857–1931*, London, 1986; and Peter Davey, *Arts and Crafts Architecture: The Search for Earthly Paradise*, London, 1980.

CHAPTER 3

The best general books are E. Aslin, *Nineteenth Century English Furniture*, London, 1962; and R. W. Symonds and B. B. Whineray, *Victorian Furniture*, London, 1962. Other important contributions are in N. Pevsner, *Pioneers of*

Modern Design, revised edition, London 1960, and 'Art Furniture of the 1870s', *Architectural Review*, Jan. 1952; S. T. Madsen, *The Sources of Art Nouveau*, Oslo, 1956; E. Aslin, 'E. W. Godwin and the Japanese Taste', *Apollo*, Dec. 1962; Michael Archer, 'Pre-Raphaelite Painted Furniture', *Country Life*, 1 Apr. 1965; Charlotte Gere and Geoffrey Munn, *Artists' Jewellery: Pre-Raphaelite to Arts and Crafts*, London, 1989; and three articles by Peter Floud: 'Victorian Furniture', in L. G. G. Ramsey (ed.), *The Concise Encyclopaedia of Antiques*, iii. London, 1957; 'Furniture', in R. Edwards and L. G. G. Ramsey, *The Early Victorian Period*, London, 1958; and '1837–1910', *House and Garden*, Jan. 1953. An important new perspective is added by Anthea Callen, *Angel in the Studio: Women in the Arts and Crafts Movement 1870–1914*, London, 1979. Useful re-evaluations include Gillian Naylor, *The Arts and Crafts Movement: a Study of its Sources, Ideals and Influence on Design Theory*, London, 1971, and *The Bauhaus*, London, 1968; Lionel Lambourne, *Utopian Craftsmen: The Arts and Crafts Movement from the Cotswolds to Chicago*, London, 1980; Alan Crawford (ed.), *By Hammer and Hand: the Arts and Crafts Movement in Birmingham,* Birmingham Museums and Art Gallery, 1984; and Peter Stansky, *Redesigning the World*, Princeton, NJ, 1985.

The most important monographs on individual designers are W. R. Lethaby, *Philip Webb and His Work*, Oxford, 1935; W. R. Lethaby and others, *Ernest Gimson, his Life and Work*, Stratford-upon-Avon, 1924: Mary Comino, *Gimson and the Barnsleys*, London, 1980; Norman Jewson, *By Chance I Did Rove*, Cirencester, 1952; Alan Crawford, *C.R. Ashbee: Architect, Designer and Romantic Socialist*, New Haven, Conn., 1985; J. Mordaunt Crook, *William Burges and the High Victorian Dream*, London, 1984; Charles Handley-Read, 'Notes on William Burges's Painted Furniture', *Burlington Magazine*, Nov. 1963; 'Ford Madox Brown's Furniture', *Artist*, 1898, and E. M. Tait, 'Madox Brown's Furniture Designs', *Furnisher*, 1900–1; and Thomas Howarth, *Charles Rennie Mackintosh and the Modern Movement*, London, 1952. On potters, William Gaunt and M. D. E. Clayton-Stamm, *William de Morgan*, London, 1971; Bernard Leach, *A Potter's Book*, London, 1940, and *Beyond East and West: Memoirs, Portraits and Essays*, London, 1978; Michael Cardew, *Pioneer Potter*, London, 1988.

There are numerous general contemporary sources: C. L. Eastlake, *Hints on Household Tastes in Furniture*, London, 1868; Bruce Talbert, *Gothic Forms applied to Furniture, Metalwork, &c., for Interior Purposes*, London, 1867; E. W. Godwin, *Art Furniture*, London, 1877; R. W. Edis, *Decoration and Furniture of Town Houses*, London, 1881; W. Hamilton, *The Aesthetic Movement in England*, London, 1882; W. Crane, *William Morris to Whistler*, London, 1911; Ernest Willmott, *English House Design*, London, 1911; Reginald Blomfield, 'Furniture', *Magazine of Art*, Oct. 1896; and Aymer Vallance, *Artist*, 12 Oct. 1896 and 'British Decorative Art in 1899', *Studio*, 18, 1899–1900. There are collections of Morris and Company catalogues, which were not issued until after 1900, at the William Morris Gallery and the Victoria and Albert Museum.

Individual Morris schemes are described in the *Studio*, Sept. 1893 (Old Swan

House and Stanmore Hall), Nov. 1897 (1, Holland Park), Apr. 1898 (Buller's Wood), Oct. 1898 (1, Palace Green); and in *Country Life*, 15 Nov. 1904 (W. S. Blunt, Clouds), 7 May 1910 (Standen) and 16 June 1960 (Mark Girouard, Red House); and in Charles Mitchell, 'William Morris at St James's Palace', *Architectural Review*, Jan. 1947. The firm's later work is surveyed in Linda Parry, 'Morris and Company in the Twentieth Century', *Journal of the William Morris Society*, 6, (1985–6), 11–16.

Morris's theories are chiefly to be found in three lectures, *Works* xxii. 'The Lesser Arts of Life', 'The Beauty of Life', and 'Making the Best of it'.

The most important unpublished sources used are the drawings by George Wardle in the Print Room of the Victoria and Albert Museum, and the records of the decoration of the Green Dining Room at the Museum; the papers relating to Frederick Leach and photographs of Mrs Lousaka's house at the William Morris Gallery; the college records at Peterhouse, Cambridge, and the letters of Warington Taylor to E. R. Robson at the Fitzwilliam Museum. A superb collection of designs for the firm by Morris and others, formerly in the Dearle family, was recently rediscovered and is now held in the Helen and Sanford Berger Collection, Stanford University, California.

CHAPTERS 4 AND 5

The most thorough up-to-date reviews are provided by Linda Parry, *William Morris Textiles*, London, 1983, and *Textiles of the Arts and Crafts Movement*, London, 1988. The outstanding earlier contribution to the general study of Victorian pattern designs was made by Peter Floud, 'A calendar of English Furnishing Textiles 1775–1905', *Architectural Review*, Aug. 1956; 'Crafts then and now', *Studio*, Apr. 1953; '1837–1910', *House and Garden*, Jan. 1953; 'The Wallpaper Designs of C. F. A. Voysey', *Penrose Annual*, 1958; *English Chintz*, Victoria and Albert Museum Small Picture Book 22; 'English Chintz', *CIBA Review*, 1961/1; 'The English Contribution to the Early History of Indigo Printing', *Journal of the Society of Dyers and Colourists*, June 1960; and, with others, *Catalogue of an Exhibition of Victorian and Edwardian Decorative Arts*, Victoria and Albert Museum, 1955.

Other important sources are Barbara Morris, 'Textiles', in Ralph Edwards and L. G. G. Ramsey (ed.), *The Connoisseur Period Guide*, 1830–60, London, 1958; Charles Singer and others, *History of Technology*, London, 1954–8; C. M. Mellor and D. S. L. Cardwell, 'Dyes and Dyeing, 1775–1860', *British Journal for the History of Science*, June 1963; R. Haller and others, 'Indigo', *CIBA Review*, April 1951; Stuart Robinson, *A History of Printed Textiles*, London, 1969; Ray Watkinson, *William Morris as Designer*, London, 1967; Anthea Callen, *Angel in the Studio: Women in the Arts and Crafts Movement*, London, 1979; S. T. Madsen, *Art Nouveau*, London, 1967; N. Pevsner, *Pioneers of Modern Design*, revised edition, London, 1960; Alf Bøe, *From Gothic Revival to Functional Form*, Oslo, 1957; C. L. Eastlake, *Hints on Household Tastes in Furniture*, London, 1868; W.

Burges, *Art Applied to Industry*, Oxford, 1865; the *Studio* generally, but particularly *Studio Year Book*, 1906.

There are three notable monographs on particular techniques: Barbara Morris, *Victorian Embroidery*, London, 1962; Rozsika Parker, *The Subversive Stitch: Embroidery and the Making of the Feminine*, London, 1984; and C. E. C. Tattersall, *History of British Carpets*, Benfleet, 1934.

Morris's own views are principally in *Works*, xxii. ('The History of Pattern-designing', 'Some Hints on Pattern-designing', and 'Textile Fabrics'); May Morris, i. 'Technical Instruction' and 'Of Dyeing as an Art'; and *Letters*. Mackail, Vallance, and H. Marillier, *History of the Merton Abbey Tapestry Works*, London, 1927, have been largely succeeded by the more recent work of Barbara Morris, 'William Morris—a 20th Century View of his Woven Textiles', and 'William Morris—his Designs for Carpets and Tapestries', *Handweaver and Craftsman*, New York, Spring and Fall, 1961; and of Peter Floud, 'William Morris as an artist: a new View', and 'The Inconsistencies of William Morris', *Listener*, 7 and 14 Oct. 1954; 'Dating Morris Patterns', *Architectural Review*, July 1959. On the later work of the firm, Oliver Fairclough and Emmeline Leary, *Textiles by William Morris and Morris and Company, 1861–1940*, London, 1981. For future research, the Helen and Sanford Berger Collection constitutes an important new source.

CHAPTER 6

On stained glass generally, Herbert Read, *English Stained Glass*, London, 1926, is still a stimulating introduction. The technique is well described in Henry Holiday, *Stained Glass as an Art*, London, 1896; L. F. Day, *Windows*, London, 1897; and C. W. Whall, *Stained Glass Work*, London, 1905. On Victorian stained glass, see Martin Harrison, *Victorian Stained Glass*, London, 1980; A. C. Sewter, 'Victorian Stained Glass', *Apollo*, Dec. 1962; many useful mentions in John Betjeman's *Murray's Architectural Guides* and in N. Pevsner's *The Buildings of England*; the contemporary articles of T. F. Bumpus, *Architect*, 29 Sept. 1899 to 6 Dec. 1901; Henry Holiday, *Reminiscences of My Life*, London, 1914; and Margaret Starridi, *Master of Glass: Charles Eamer Kempe and the Work of his Firm in Stained Glass and Church Decoration*, London, 1988.

The definitive study of the firm's work is now A. C. Sewter, *The Stained Glass of William Morris and his Circle*, New Haven, Conn., 1974–5; see also his 'Notes on Morris & Co's domestic stained glass', *Journal of the William Morris Society*, Winter 1961; May Morris, i. 356–64; *Letters* i. 186; Mackail, ii. 41–2; and Vallance. The individual contributions of the partners are discussed in A. C. Sewter, 'William Morris's Designs for Stained Glass', *Architectural Review*, Mar. 1960; A. C. Sewter, 'D. G. Rossetti's Designs for Stained Glass', *Journal of the British Society of Master Glass-Painters*, 1960–1; W. R. Lethaby, *Philip Webb and his Work*, London, 1935; F. M. Hueffer, *Ford Madox Brown: a Record of his Life and Work*, London, 1896; and Martin Harrison and Bill Waters, *Burne-Jones*,

London, 1973. For North American work by the firm, see Marilyn Ibach, 'Morris and Company Stained Glass in North America', *Journal of Pre-Rephaelite Studies*, 5, (May 1985), 111–17.

In addition to cartoons, which are mentioned in the gazetteer, the chief manuscript sources are the notes by H. C. Marillier at the Birmingham City Art Gallery and by George Wardle at the British Museum; and the account books of Burne-Jones (at the Fitzwilliam Museum, Cambridge) and Webb (kindly shown to me by John Brandon-Jones). I owe a particular debt to the Whitefriars Stained Glass Studios, for showing me some of their Victorian cartoons and the modern stained glass technique, and to Charles Sewter, who supplied me with a then unpublished definitive list of all the important Morris glass in Great Britain, with the help of which I was able to see Morris windows in some 200 churches.

CHAPTER 7

For Morris's illuminations Joseph R. Dunlap, 'Morris and the Book Arts before the Kelmscott Press', *Victorian Poetry*, 13, 141–57, May Morris, i. 'The Illuminated Books of the Middle Ages', and Mackail. Victorian illumination must otherwise be studied through contemporary books such as W. and G. Audsley, *Guide to the Art of Illuminating and Missal Painting*, London, 1861; M. D. Wyatt, *The Art of Illuminating*, London, 1860; and the useful article by Margaret Armour, 'Beautiful Modern Manuscripts', *Studio*, Winter Number, 1896. Morris's manuscript collection can be traced through the catalogue of the sale at Sotheby's, 5 Dec. 1898; and S. de Ricci and W. J. Wilson, *Census of Mediaeval and Renaissance Manuscripts in the United States and Canada*, New York, 1935. For William Morris as a collector of manuscripts and early printed books, Paul Needham, Joseph Dunlap, and John Dreyfus, *William Morris and the Art of the Book*, London, 1976.

Morris's handwriting experiments are described in Alfred Fairbank, 'Morris and calligraphy', *Journal of the William Morris Society*, Winter 1961. His models can be studied in A. Fairbank and B. Wolpe, *Renaissance Handwriting*, London, 1960, and the modern revival of calligraphy in M. M. Bridges, *A New Handwriting for Teachers*, Oxford, 1899; Edward Johnston, *Writing, Illuminating and Lettering*, London, 1906; Priscilla Johnston, *Edward Johnston*, London, 1959; Peter Faulkner, *William Morris and Eric Gill*, London, 1975; and Marion Richardson, *Art and the Child*, London, 1948.

Morris manuscripts may be seen at the Bodleian Library, Oxford, the Victoria and Albert Museum, the British Museum, Birmingham City Art Gallery, and the Fitzwilliam Museum, Cambridge.

The background to Morris's printing is well covered by Ruari McLean, *Victorian Book Design*, London, 1963, and *Modern Book Design*, London, 1958. Morris's theories are brought together in William Peterson, *The Ideal Book: Essays and Lectures on the Arts of the Book*, Berkeley, Calif., 1982; and reevaluated by Colin Franklin, *Printing and the Mind of Morris*, Cambridge, 1986. His work is extensively discussed in Mackail; Vallance; H. H. Sparling, *The Kelmscott Press and William Morris, Master-craftsman*, London, 1924; S. C. Cockerell, *A Note by William Morris on his aims in founding the Kelmscott Press, together with a short description of the press by S. C. Cockerell*, London, 1898; Holbrook Jackson, *William Morris*, London, 1926; James Leatham, *William Morris, Master of Many Crafts*, Turriff, 1934; Thomas Balston, *Private Press Types*, Cambridge, 1951; and André Tschan, *William Morris*, Berne, 1962. Documentation is also provided by William Peterson, *A Bibliography of the Kelmscott Press*, Oxford, 1984. Peterson's *History of the Kelmscott Press* is forthcoming. His influence can be followed especially through Colin Franklin, *The Private Presses*, London, 1969; and Susan Otis Thompson, *American Book Design and William Morris*, New York, 1977.

CHAPTER 8

The chief sources are Mackail, i. 219–21, and ii. 340; *Letters*; and E. P. Thompson, 875–82. See also A. H. Warren, *English Poetic Theory, 1825–65*, Princeton, NJ, 1950.

CHAPTER 9

Morris's prose is published in *Works*, i, vii–viii, x, xiv–xxiii; May Morris; *Letters; Justice*, 1884, and *Commonweal*, 1885–90. In addition to Mackail, the most useful comments are J. N. Swannell, *William Morris and Old Norse Literature*, William Morris Society, London, 1961—for the translations; Jack Lindsay, *William Morris, Writer*, William Morris Society, London, 1961 and *William Morris, His Life and Work*, London, 1975; John Lucas, *Politics and Literature in the Nineteenth Century*, London, 1971; and for the prose romances Peter Faulkner, 'Morris and Yeats', *Journal of the William Morris Society*, Summer 1963; Carole Silver, *The Romance of William Morris*, Ohio, 1982; and Amanda Hodgson, *The Romances of William Morris*, Cambridge, 1987.

CHAPTER 10

Morris's poetry is published in *Works*, i–vii, ix–xiii, and xxiv; May Morris; and *Commonweal*.

Of the very large number of criticisms of Morris as a poet, the most valuable are Mackail; E. P. Thompson; Alfred Noyes, *William Morris*, London, 1908; Jack Lindsay, *William Morris, Writer*, William Morris Society, London, 1961 and *William Morris, His Life and Work*, London, 1975; John Lucas, *Politics and Literature in the Nineteenth Century*, London, 1971; B. I. Evans, *William Morris and his Poetry*, London, 1925; Geoffrey Tillotson, *Essays in Criticism and Research*, Cambridge, 1942; John Drinkwater, *William Morris: a Critical Study*, London,

1912; H. H. Sparling, *The Kelmscott Press and William Morris, Master-craftsman*, London, 1924; F. S. Ellis, 'The Life-Work of William Morris', *Journal of the Society of Arts*, 27 May 1898; William E. Fredeman (ed.), special issue devoted to Morris, *Victorian Poetry*, 13, Fall–Winter, 1975; Carole Silver, and Amanda Hodgson (see Chapter 9); Charlotte Oberg, *A Pagan Prophet: William Morris*, Charlottesville, Va., 1978; and with a psychoanalytic perspective, Frederick Kirchhoff, *William Morris*, London, 1979.

On Morris's early poetry, Florence Boos, *The Juvenilia of William Morris*, New York, 1983; Carole Silver (ed.), *The Golden Chain: Essays on Morris's Pre-Raphaelitism*, New York, 1982; and Florence Boos, 'Sexual polarisation in William Morris's *The Defence of Guenevere*', *Browning Institute Studies*, 13 (1985), 181–200.

For *The Defence of Guenevere*, W. Dixon Scott, 'The First Morris', in *Primitiae*, Liverpool, 1912, is also very important.

For the period of *The Earthly Paradise*, other useful criticisms are F. L. Lucas, *Ten Victorian Poets*, Cambridge, 1948; Graham Hough, *The Last Romantics*, London, 1949; W. Pater, *Appreciations*, London, 1889; George Saintsbury, *Corrected Impressions*, London, 1895; J. N. D. Bush, *Mythology and the Romantic Tradition in English Poetry*, Cambridge, Mass., 1937; and Blue Calhoun, *The Pastoral Vision of William Morris*, Athens, Ga., 1975. Florence Boos, *The Design of the Earthly Paradise*, is forthcoming.

For 'The Lovers of Gudrun' and *Sigurd the Volsung*, other important studies are D. M. Hoare, *The Works of Morris and Yeats in relation to Early Saga Literature*, Cambridge, 1937; J. N. Swannell, *William Morris and Old Norse Literature*, William Morris Society, London, 1961; E. Magnusson, in *Cambridge Review*, 26 Nov. 1896; H. Morley, in *Nineteenth Century*, Nov. 1877; G. T. McDowell 'The Treatment of the Volsunga Saga by William Morris', *Scandinavian Studies and Notes*, 7, 1921–3; and John Hollow (ed.), *The After-Summer Seed: Reconsiderations of Sigurd the Volsung*, New York, 1982.

CHAPTER 11

The principal political biography of Morris is now E. P. Thompson, which incorporates all that is useful in May Morris, ii., Mackail and J. B. Glasier, *William Morris and the Early days of the Socialist Movement*, London, 1921. Mackail and Glasier were in important respects seriously misleading, although much less distorted than, e.g. Lloyd Grey, and recently Willard Wolfe or le Bourgeois. In the revised edition (1977) E. P. Thompson thoroughly reviews subsequent political studies of Morris. For Morris's relationship with Eleanor Marx and Engels, see C. Tsuzuki, *The Life of Eleanor Marx*, Oxford, 1967; Yvonne Kapp, *Eleanor Marx*, ii. 1976; E. P. Thompson, *New Society*, 3 Mar. 1977, 455–8.

Morris's political writing is published in *Works*, xxii–xxiii; *Letters*; Le Mire; *Justice*, 1884; *Commonweal*, 1885–90; *Hammersmith Socialist Record*, 1891–3; and

Florence Boos, *William Morris's Socialist Diary*, London, 1985. Morris's relationship with feminism is discussed in Boos, 'An (Almost-) Egalitarian Sage', and Richardson, 'William Morris and Women' (see Chapter 1).

The minutes of the Hammersmith organizations are at the British Library; and other archives of the Socialist League and Morris's connections with the Engels circle at the International Institute of Social History, Amsterdam, the Bottigelli Collection, Paris, and the Institute of Marxism-Leninism, Moscow.

The best background studies of the Labour and socialist movement at this time are Henry Pelling, *The Origins of the Labour Party, 1880–1900*, London, 1954; Dona Torr, *Tom Mann and His Times*, London, 1956; C. Tsuzuki, *H. M. Hyndman and British Socialism*, Oxford, 1961; and A. M. MacBriar, *Fabian Socialism and English Politics, 1884–1918*, Cambridge, 1962. For the London background to Morris's work see my own *Socialists, Liberals and Labour*, London, 1967. Another dimension of Morris's subsequent political influence can be traced in Ian Brittain, *Fabianism and Culture: a study in British Socialism and the Arts, 1884–1918*, Cambridge, 1982.

The most useful introductions to the imperialist questions in which Morris was involved are A. P. Thornton, *The Imperial Idea and Its Enemies*, London, 1959, and R. Robinson and J. Gallagher, *Africa and the Victorians*, London, 1961; to the Eastern Question, R. W. Seton-Watson, *Britain in Europe*, Cambridge, 1937, and W. H. G. Armytage, *A. J. Mundella*, London, 1951.

CHAPTERS 12 AND 13

Morris's theoretical writings are published in *Works*, xxii–xxiii; May Morris; *Letters; Justice*, 1884; *Commonweal*, 1885–90; and *Socialism, its Growth and Outcome*. The interviews in *Clarion*, 19 Nov. 1892, and *Daily Chronicle*, 9 Oct. 1893, are also useful.

The best commentary on his political theory is E. P. Thompson; and more recently, Paul Meier, *La Pensée Utopiane de William Morris*, translated with the inapt title, *William Morris: the Marxist Dreamer*, Hassocks, 1978. Perry Anderson, *Arguments within English Marxism*, London, 1980, argues that Thompson underestimates Morris's originality (p. 157ff.).

The most useful commentaries on his theory of art are Peter Floud, 'Crafts Then and Now', *Studio*, Apr. 1953, and 'William Morris as an Artist: a New View', and 'The Inconsistencies of William Morris', *Listener*, 7 and 14 Oct. 1954; E. D. Le Mire, 'Morris's Reply to Whistler', *Journal of the William Morris Society*, Summer 1963; Alf Bøe, *From Gothic Revival to Functional Form*, Oslo, 1957; and N. Pevsner, *Pioneers of Modern Design*, rev. edn., London, 1960.

Morris's contribution to political thinking on the environment is re-evaluated in Peter C. Gould, *Early Green Politics: Back to Nature, Back to the Land, and Socialism in Britain, 1880–1900*, Brighton, 1988.

The collection on Morris as a utopian, Stephen Coleman and Paddy O'Sullivan, (eds.), *William Morris and News from Nowhere: a Vision for our Time*,

Bideford, 1990, includes O'Sullivan on Morris and ecology. My own 1990 Kelmscott Lecture, *Why William Morris Matters Today: Human Creativity and the Future World Environment*, will be published in 1991 by the William Morris Society.

A GAZETTEER

Outstanding **glass** at Winscombe (Saunders by Burges).

Cecil Higgins Museum, Bedford, has a collection of original Victorian **furniture** including a Burges room.

Important Morris **glass** at All Saints, Dedworth (1863–87); Cranbourne (c.1862); Tilehurst (1869); and Easthampstead (1876–1913). Also, at Fawley (1868, church by **Street**). Street's church at Boyne Hill, Maidenhead (1854) and his village schools at Eastbury (1851) and Brightwalton (1863, good glass, by Halliday, not Burne-Jones) are also worth seeing. The dining hall at Bradfield College has an outstanding Burne-Jones window made by Powell's (1857).

Tapestries in Eton College chapel. No good Morris **glass** but excellent work by other makers at Bletchley (Powell's, by Holiday, 1871), Haversham (east window, C. W. Whall, 1897), New Bradwell (proto-expressionist), Latimer (Powell's, 1873) and St Mary, Slough (at the town centre; west window, Wolmark, 1915). An outstanding Street church at Westcott (1867).

In Cambridge **decorative schemes** at Queens' College Hall (1875, with tiles), Peterhouse Hall and Combination Room (1868–74, with tiles and glass), Jesus College Chapel (1867–74, with glass) and All Saints' Church (1866, with glass). The Fitzwilliam Museum possesses many Morris **manuscripts**, one illuminated; Burne-Jones cartoons, account books and letters; Warington Taylor letters; and a sofa designed by Rossetti. Regent House has the great carpet from Clouds (1891). Outside Cambridge, Morris **glass** at Doddington; Stained Glass Museum at Ely cathedral.

Important Morris **glass** at St Philip, Alderley Edge (1874), Lower Marple (1869–73), Aldford (1878, in Grosvenor estate church of 1866 by John Douglas), and St Paul, Boughton, Chester (1881–1925, church with art nouveau decoration). Notable pictures and **cartoons** by Madox Brown, Rossetti, and Burne-Jones, at the Lady Lever Art Gallery, Port Sunlight.

CORNWALL

Important Morris **glass** at Ladock (1863–97) and St Michael Penkevil (1866). The Leach and Cardew **potteries** continue working in family hands at St Ives and Wenford Bridge, north of Bodmin.

CUMBRIA

Important Morris **glass** at Troutbeck (1873–98) and Staveley (1881–1907) and outstanding window at Brampton (1878–1920). Brampton church, Green Lanes House, Four Gables and cottages by Webb (1877), and the glass at Lanercost (1877), were all for George Howard of Naworth Castle.

DERBYSHIRE

Importand Morris **glass** at Darley Dale (1862); also Youlgreave (1878–94) and staircase glass at Thornbridge Hall College (1877).

DEVON

Important Morris **glass** at Tavistock (1876) and St John, Torquay (1865–90, a notable Street church). St Michael Pimlico, Torquay (1878, a fine church by Prichard) has been demolished and some of its glass transferred to Haddington in Scotland.

DORSET

At Cattistock, Morris **glass** (1882), with other glass, and stencil decorations by George Gilbert Scott (cf. Peterhouse); Pugin glass at Milton Abbey and Sherborne Abbey.

DURHAM

Important Morris **glass** at St Oswald, Durham (1866); outstanding Pugin glass at Ushaw College (from 1842); at Darlington good glass by Clayton and Bell and by Wailes.

ESSEX

Important Morris **glass** at Frinton-on-Sea (1862); also Aveley; outstanding glass by Burne-Jones made by Powell's at Waltham Abbey (1861).

GLOUCESTERSHIRE

The finest collection of early Morris **glass** anywhere at Selsley (1862, a splendid church by Bodley); another early window in Cirencester Agricultural College chapel (1865); **arts and crafts** churches at Kempley (1902, by Randall Wells) and Chalford. Ashbee and the Guild of Handicraft settled at Chipping Campden, where the arts and crafts east window of the parish church is by Henry Payne of Birmingham, c. 1920; Ashbee's own house was the Norman Chapel at Broad Campden; while Gimson and the Barnsleys moved to Sapperton, where Edward Barnsley built Upper Dorvil and Sydney Barnsley Beechanger (both 1902). At **Cheltenham Art Gallery** outstanding collection of their furniture and silver, other arts and crafts furniture, including work by Gordon Russell, and also the library of Emery Walker, and Morris's round table from Red Lion Square, rescued from the Kelmscott village hall. Fairford was one of Morris's favourite churches, not far from Kelmscott.

GREATER MANCHESTER

Good Morris **glass** at Albion Congregational Church, Ashton-under-Lyme (1893–6). At Manchester the Whitworth Art Gallery has a collection of glass (1860s onwards), **cartoons** and the Flora and Pomona **tapestries** and the City Art Gallery a major collection of pre-Raphaelite paintings.

HAMPSHIRE

Important Morris **glass** at Lyndhurst (1862–3, an outstanding church by William White, with a notable Clayton and Bell north transept window); and Bournemouth St Peter (1864, an important Street church—a small internal window in the south transept).

HEREFORDSHIRE AND WORCESTERSHIRE

Outstanding arts and crafts church at Brockhampton-by-Ross (Lethaby, 1901) with Morris **tapestries**; notable **glass** at Yazor (anonymous, 1866), Pudlestone (Hardman 1850–7, partly by Pugin), and Hereford cathedral (Hardman north transept, Charles Gibbs in Lady Chapel).

HERTFORDSHIRE

Important Morris **glass** at King's Walden (*c.*1869), Waterford (1875–1919), Furneux Pelham (*c.*1867–74) and Hatfield (1894).

HUMBERSIDE

Important Morris **glass** at Catton (1866, east of York); collection of **glass**, including Morris, at East Ravendale.

ISLE OF WIGHT

Important Morris **glass** at Gatcombe (1865–6).

KENT

Important Morris **glass** at Speldhurst (1873–1905) and Langton Green (*c.*1862–6); also Hildenborough (1876–81); Burne-Jones glass made by Powell's for King Street Congregational Church, Maidstone (1857) now in Chillington Art Gallery, Maidstone, and by Lavers and Barrand at Cobham (1863), a repeat of Topcliffe.

LANCASHIRE

Good Morris **glass** at Wigan (1868) and Lytham St Cuthbert (1875).

LEICESTERSHIRE

Good Morris **glass** at Sheepy Magna (1879); cottages by **Gimson** at Ulverscroft. Leicester Art Gallery has its collection of Gimson and Cotswold school furniture at Newarke Houses.

LONDON

Victoria and Albert Museum: the Victorian Primary Galleries include Morris furniture, candlesticks, table glass, tapestry tiles, and curtains, as well as work by his contemporaries—Burges, Norman Shaw, Godwin, Macmurdo, Lethaby, Voysey, Baillie Scott, Mackintosh; Morris glass (1862–90) is shown in the Bridge Corridor; the Green Dining Room, with decorations by the firm including windows (1866), contains important painted furniture and a carpet; the Department of Textiles has a large collection of Morris printed and woven textiles, several embroideries and carpets, and the Forest and Orchard tapestries; the Department of Circulation has Morris wallpapers, printed and woven textiles, sample books, paintings and furniture; the Department of Ceramics has de Morgan and Martin pottery; the Print Room has a large collection of Morris cartoons, Kelmscott Press proofs, and the George Wardle drawings; the Library has various papers and the illuminated Book of Verses (1870).

William Morris Gallery, Walthamstow: large collection of Morris wallpapers, printed and woven textiles; some furniture, tiles, carpets, and rugs; the Woodpecker tapestry and the Rounton Grange embroideries; personal relics; a large collection of cartoons, manuscripts, papers and cuttings relating to Morris, and a comprehensive library including a set of Kelmscott Press books; pottery by de Morgan and the Martin brothers; nineteenth-century paintings.

British Library: largest single collection existing of Morris literary manuscripts, correspondence, and other papers.

The National Portrait Gallery has the portrait of Morris by G. F. Watts and the **Tate Gallery** 'La Belle Iseult' by Morris and 'April Love' by Arthur Hughes, bought by Morris in 1856.

At Whitelands College, Wandsworth, the chapel (1930, by Giles Gilbert Scott) retains earlier good Morris **glass** (1876–93) along with rare electric light fittings and a reredos by Kate Faulkner, and correspondence with Morris and Company. Other notable Morris glass is at Kentish Town parish church (1863), All Saints, Lower Common, Putney (1876–1913), Holy Trinity, Sloane Square (1890, a fine church by Sedding with other windows by Richmond and Whall), St Peter, Vere Street (1881–92) and Christchurch, Waterfall Road, Southgate (1862–1913); outstanding glass by Holiday at St Mary Magdalene, Woodchester Street, Paddington (1868, a splendid Street church); St Luke, Caversham Square, Kentish Town (1868); Westminster Abbey (1868, nave south aisle; third from west); and Southwark cathedral (1893, west); also by Clayton and Bell and by Powell's at St James the Less, Thorndike Street, Pimlico (1858–65, a notable Street church). **Old Battersea House** (De Morgan Foundation), contains an outstanding collection of de Morgan pottery, paintings, and some Morris furniture; de Morgan tiles *in situ* may be seen at The Richmond Fellowship, 8 Addison Road, Kensington. **Red House**, Red House Lane, Bexleyheath, may be visited by written appointment with Mr and Mrs Edward Hollamby; the Webb house (1859) remains unaltered and still contains some of its original furniture. Houses by Webb at 19 Lincoln's Inn Fields (1868), 1 Palace Green (1868), 35 Glebe Place (1869) and 91–101 Worship Street (1861–3). At Beddington there is an organ case decorated by Morris (1869). **Kelmscott House**, 26 Upper Mall, Hammersmith, may be visited; it is now a William Morris Centre and headquarters of the William Morris Society. The homes of Emery Walker, T. J. Cobden-Sanderson, and the Doves Press are close by. **Linley Sambourne House**, 18 Stafford Terrace, Kensington, open to the public weekly by the Victorian Society, includes original Morris papers as part of an interior furnished in an eclectic taste in 1874.

MERSEYSIDE

The finest collection anywhere of later Morris **glass** at All Hallows Allerton (1875–86); other good Morris glass in Liverpool and St John Tue Brook (1868, notable Bodley church), St Stephen Gateacre (1883), Knotty Ash (1872–90), Halewood (1874–92), and Ullet Road Chapel (1903–14)

NORFOLK

Notable Morris **glass** at Sculthorpe (1865–6) and Antingham (1865); also outstanding glass at Thursford (Albert Moore, 1862), and Dunton (Heaton, Butler and Bayne, 1863).

NORTHAMPTONSHIRE

Outstanding collection of Morris **glass** at Middleton Cheney (1863–93); good Morris glass at Guilsborough (1875–1909) and Peterborough cathedral (*c.*1862, south transept).

NORTHUMBERLAND

Important Morris **glass** at Haltwhistle (1872).

NOTTINGHAMSHIRE

Notable Morris **glass** at Coddington (1865–81, and decorations), Whatton (1878), and High Pavement Chapel, Nottingham (1904–7, a violent church by Stuart Colman); also fine glass by Heaton Butler in St Mary, Nottingham (south transept).

OXFORDSHIRE

Kelmscott Manor, which contains many relics of Morris, hangings, embroideries, carpets, furniture, and paintings by Rossetti, has been thoroughly restored and reopened to visitors. The village includes cottages by Webb and Gimson, and Morris and Janey are buried in the churchyard. Nearby churches which Morris admired include Langford, Broadwell, Little Faringdon, Black Bourton, and Bampton. (See also under Wiltshire and Gloucestershire.) Morris **glass**, also close to Kelmscott, at Eaton Hastings (1874–1934) and Buscot (1892–1922). Buscot House (National Trust) has a collection of Rossetti and Burne-Jones paintings; the fourteenth-century barn at Great Coxwell (National Trust) is also nearby. **Street** began his architectural career at Wantage, and his vicarage (1850) and convent (1854) there, his church at East Hanney (1855), and school at Denchworth (1851) are worth seeing.

Important Morris **glass** at Bloxham (1869–1921) and Bicester (1866). In Oxford, Burne-Jones cartoons at the Ashmolean Museum; Morris **papers** and **illustrated manuscripts** in the Bodleian Library; the Star of Bethlehem **tapestry** and Morris **hangings** in Exeter College Chapel; and important **glass** in the Cathedral (1872–8, and the Latin Chapel Burne-Jones window made by Powell's in 1857), St Edmund Hall Chapel (1864–5) and Manchester College Chapel (1895–9).

SHROPSHIRE

Outstanding Morris **glass** at Meole Brace (1870–1); also Calverhall (1875).

SOMERSET

Good Morris **glass** at Over Stowey (1873–1922) and a notable late window at Langport (1899). **Decorations** at Hornblottom, designed by T. G. Jackson (1872–4), worth comparison with Morris. The Holburne Museum at Bath has a collection of arts and crafts **furniture** and **pottery**.

STAFFORDSHIRE

Important Morris **glass** at Onecote (1863 – transferred from the vicarage), Amington (1864), Cheddleton (1864), Brown Edge (1872–4), Madeley (c. 1873), Tamworth (1873–1904) and Leigh (1874–1913); important glass by Pugin at St Giles, Cheadle (from 1841), and by Clayton and Bell at Denstone (1861, church by Street).

SUFFOLK

Important Morris **glass** at Hopton (1881–1903, a violent church by S. S. Teulon); also by Holiday at Lackford (1871).

SURREY

Important Morris **glass** at Banstead (1863); important glass by Powell's at Ockham (1875). Benfleet Hall, Fairmile, Cobham, was built by Webb immediately after Red House (1860). Arts and Crafts church by Sidney Barnsley at Lower Kingswood (1890).

SUSSEX

Outstanding Morris **glass** at Rotherfield (1878) and St Michael, Brighton (1862, a vigorous church by Bodley, with additions by Burges, 1881, containing equally good glass by Lonsdale); Morris glass also at St Leonards-on-Sea Greek Orthodox (1881) and (from 1893) at Rottingdean, where Burne-Jones's house faces the Green. Painted tile reredos at Findon (1867). **Standen**, East Grinstead, by Webb (1892), retains its original Morris wallpapers, is owned by the National Trust and open weekly.

TYNE AND WEAR

Morris **tapestry** and **carpet**, Gimson lectern and altar cross, at Roker (1906, outstanding church by E. S. Prior); important Morris **glass** at Christchurch, Sunderland (1862–5) and at Sacred Heart, Gosforth (1875); notable Pugin glass in Newcastle R.C. cathedral (from 1844).

Important Morris **glass** at Bishop's Tachbrook (*c.*1863) and St Nicholas Beaudesert, Henley-in-Arden (1868, just east of the main street); also in the chapel of Heycester's Hospital, Warmick (1866).

WEST MIDLANDS

Birmingham Art Gallery has the most important collection of Burne-Jones cartoons and other glass cartoons, notes, and photographs of Morris glass by H. C. Marillier, Morris textile designs, the Holy Grail tapestries, an illuminated manuscript and a major collection of pre- Raphaelite paintings and drawings; important **glass** in Birmingham at the Cathedral (1885–97) and St Mary, Acocks Green (1895, a vigorous church by J. C. Bland).

    Wightwick Manor, Wolverhampton (National Trust) has a collection of Morris wallpapers, Morris hangings, an outstanding embroidery, de Morgan pottery, a Voysey chair, a Bodley settle, Kempe glass, and a collection of paintings, by Burne-Jones and other artists of the period.

WILTSHIRE

Notable Morris **glass** at Rodbourne (1862–3), Sopworth (1870), and Salisbury cathedral (1879); other important glass by Clayton and Bell (Salisbury cathedral), and Powell's (Mere, Beechingstoke, Codford St Peter, and Salisbury cathedral). Inglesham church, near Kelmscott, was repaired with the help of Morris in 1888–9.

WORCESTERSHIRE

Good Morris **glass** at Rochford (1865) and Ribbesford (1875). Madresfield Court chapel has notably complete arts and crafts decoration of 1902 by Birmingham artists and Ashbee's guild.

YORKSHIRE

Outstanding collection of early Morris **glass** at St Martin, Scarborough (1861–73, church by Bodley); important glass also at Nun Monkton (1873), Knaresborough (1873), Pool-in-Wharfedale (1866), Tadcaster (1879), Welton (1877–98); Brighouse St Martin (1874–97); Leeds, St Saviour (1870–8, although the Pugin glass of *c.*1845 is finer), and St Peter, Bramley (1875–82); and Bradford cathedral (1864), Art Gallery (from 1862), Farnham (1876), and St James, Thornton (1876, a bold church by Healey). Burne-Jones glass for Lavers and Barraud (*c.*1860) at Topcliffe. Other important glass by Clayton and Bell at

Howsham (church by Street, 1859), by Saunders at Skelton and Studley Royal (both churches by William Burges, 1871) and by their pupil William Dixon at Ecclesfield (south transept).

Smeaton Manor is one of Webb's best later houses (1877). Cottages at Baldersby, and schools and parsonages at Cowick, Hensall and Pollington (1854) by Butterfield anticipate Webb's Red House style.

The **Ruskin Museum** at Norfolk St, Sheffield, houses the collection Ruskin made for the St George's Guild, visited by Morris when he came to speak for the Sheffield Socialist Society in February 1886. The Guild's St George's Farm at Totley and Edward Carpenter's smallholding at Millthorpe, where Morris stayed in 1885, are on the south-west edge of Sheffield.

WALES

Important Morris **glass** in Glamorganshire at Llandaff cathedral (1866–74), Baglan (1880, a good church by Prichard), Coity (1863), and St John Baptist, Cardiff (1869, in town centre); elsewhere at Forden, (1873) and Llanllwchaiarn (c. 1870), Montgomeryshire, St Florence, Pembrokeshire (1873), Newton Nottage, Glamorgan (1877), and Hawarden, Flintshire (1897). The firm's window of Christ and The Boy Scout at Roch, Pembrokeshire (1917), represents their post-Morris nadir.

SCOTLAND

Important Morris **glass** at Greenock Old West Kirk (1868), Paisley Abbey (1874–9), Haddington St Mary (1878–95, including some transferred from Torquay), Dundee Council Chambers (1889), and King's College Chapel, Aberdeen (1897–8); other good glass at Dalkeith Roman Catholic church (1868), Gordon Chapel, Fochabers (1877–1919), Monifieth (1876) and Broughty Ferry St Stephen (1884), Kirkcaldy old church (1886) and St Brycedale (1889–92), and Glasgow University Bute Hall (1893–1900). An exceptionally good late window of 1899 at Bothwell.

CHANNEL ISLANDS

Important **glass** mainly by Morris himself at St Stephen, Guernsey (1864–70, church by Bodley).

THE NETHERLANDS

The archives of the Socialist League and other Morris **papers** are held at the International Institute of Social History, Amsterdam.

INDIA

Important Morris **glass** at Calcutta Cathedral (1874).

AUSTRALASIA

Important Morris **glass** at Norfolk Island (1876–9); other Morris glass at Newcastle cathedral (1906).

NORTH AMERICA

Outstanding Morris **glass** at Trinity Church, Boston (1883–7) and at Trinity Church, Saugerties-on-Hudson (1874); other glass at Our Saviour, Monmouth St, Boston, Massachusetts (1883); St Peter's, Albany (1881) and Incarnation, Madison Avenue, New York (1885); Presbyterian Church of St Andrew and St Paul (1885–1903) and Christ Church Cathedral (1902–11), Montreal; and Second Presbyterian Church, Chicago (c.1902). An unrivalled set of Morris **cartoons and designs** is held in the Helen and Sanford Berger Collection, Stanford University, Palo Alto, California. Important collections of Morris literary **manuscripts** at the Henry Huntingdon Library, San Marino, Duke University, North Carolina, the University of Texas at Austin, the Houghton Library at Harvard, and the University of British Columbia, Vancouver. The Pierpoint Morgan Library, New York, holds over 200 medieval manuscripts and early printed books from William Morris's own library at Kelmscott House, bought in 1902. The Delaware Art Museum at Wilmington holds the only significant contemporary collection of pre-Raphaelite paintings, made by the industrialist Samuel Bancroft, including Rossetti's 'Found' (1859) and 'Water Willow' (1871) of Janey at Kelmscott; also Ashbee silverware. Many examples of Morris printed books, de Morgan pottery, and no doubt furniture, textiles and papers, exist in other private and public collections, for which a full list is wanted.

THE WILLIAM MORRIS SOCIETY

The Society was formed in 1955 to deepen understanding and stimulate a wider appreciation of Morris, his friends and their work. The Society organizes exhibitions, visits, and lectures, which it publishes, together with the *Journal of the William Morris Society*. It encourages the continued manufacture of Morris textile and wallpaper designs, and re-publications of his works, and tries to maintain contact between those who are interested in all aspects of the work of William Morris. The society's headquarters is now Kelmscott House, Hammersmith, Morris's London home from 1878 onwards, through the years of socialism, the later romances, and the Kelmscott Press.

There is already a small collection of material relating to Morris and work by the firm, and the hope is to assemble in the long run the full resources through documents and reproductions needed to study his work. The aim is not to create a museum but an active centre, adding also to the practical classes and production in printing which is already taking place. Inquiries are welcome at the William Morris Society, Kelmscott House, 26 Upper Mall, Hammersmith, London W6 9TA: tel. 081–741–3735.

THE SOCIETY FOR THE PROTECTION OF ANCIENT BUILDINGS

The society was founded by William Morris in 1877 and carries on its work, more than ever important today: further information from the Secretary, 37 Spital St, London E1.

THE VICTORIAN SOCIETY

The society was formed as an offshoot of the above in 1958. Its objectives are both to protect and to study the best Victorian and Edwardian architecture, craftwork and design: further information from the Secretary, 1 Priory Gardens, Bedford Park, London W4 1TT.

WILLIAM MORRIS SOCIETY IN THE UNITED STATES

Inquiries to Mark Samuels Lasner, Apartment 101, 1870 Wyoming Avenue, N. W., Washington, D.C. 20009.

INDEX